Given to me
by Mark Webb
3-28-70
Ace

BENEDICT ARNOLD'S NAVY

BENEDICT ARNOLD'S NAVY

*The Ragtag Fleet that Lost the
Battle of Lake Champlain but
Won the American Revolution*

James L. Nelson

Camden, Maine • New York • Chicago • San Francisco • Lisbon
London • Madrid • Mexico City • Milan • New Delhi • San Juan
Seoul • Singapore • Sydney • Toronto

The **McGraw·Hill** Companies

2 3 4 5 6 7 8 9 DOC DOC 9 8 7 6
© 2006 James L. Nelson

Library of Congress Cataloging-in-Publication Data
Nelson, James L
  Benedict Arnold's navy : the ragtag fleet that lost the Battle of Lake Champlain but
won the American Revolution / James L. Nelson.
     p. cm.
  Includes bibliographical references and index.
  ISBN 0–07–146806–4 (hardcover : alk. paper)
1. Valcour Island, Battle of, N.Y., 1776. 2. Arnold, Benedict, 1741–1801. 3. United
States—History—Revolution, 1775–1783—Naval operations. 4. United States—
History—Revolution, 1775–1783—Campaigns. 5. New York (State)—History—
Revolution, 1775–1783—Naval operations. 6. New York (State)—History—Revolution,
1775–1783—Campaigns. 7. Champlain, Lake, Region—History, Naval—18th century.
8. Champlain, Lake, Region—History, Military—18th century. 9. United States.
Continental Navy—History. I. Title.
  E241.V14N45 2006
  973.3'5—DC22   2006006491

Questions regarding the content of this book should be addressed to
International Marine/McGraw-Hill
P.O. Box 220
Camden, ME 04843
www.internationalmarine.com

Questions regarding the ordering of this book should be addressed to
The McGraw-Hill Companies
Customer Service Department
P.O. Box 547
Blacklick, OH 43004
Retail customers: 1–800–262–4729
Bookstores: 1–800–722–4726

Maps on pages ix-x by International Mapping

That the Americans were strong enough to impose the capitulation of Saratoga was due to the invaluable year of delay secured to them in 1776 by their little navy on Lake Champlain, created by the indomitable energy, and handled with the indomitable courage of the traitor, Benedict Arnold.

ALFRED T. MAHAN
The Influence of Sea Power upon History, 1660–1783

For my darling Lisa. . . . click

Contents

Photos and illustrations may be found following page 155

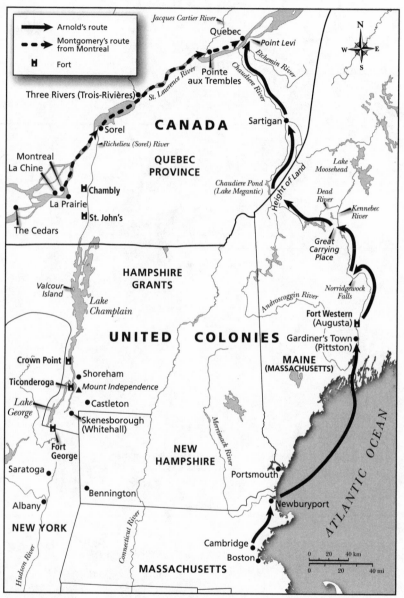

THE ASSAULT ON QUEBEC: 1775

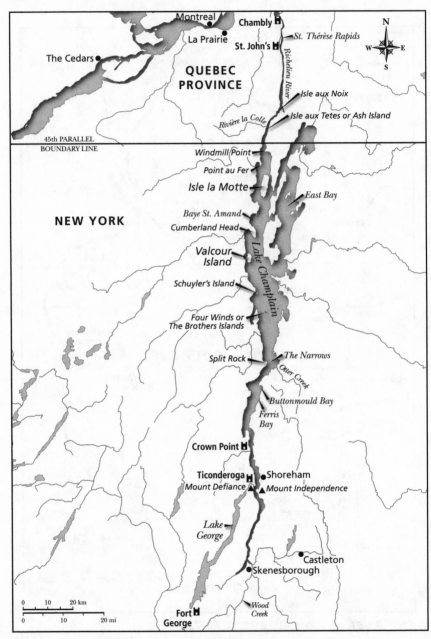

LAKE CHAMPLAIN AND LAKE GEORGE: 1776

PROLOGUE: *October 11, 1776*

THE WIND is from the north, and the schooner *Royal Savage*, tucked in behind Valcour Island, tugs at the end of her anchor cable. The flagship of the American fleet on Lake Champlain, she is one of fifteen small vessels anchored in a line between the island and the western shore of the lake.

Benedict Arnold stands on the quarterdeck, a boat cloak all but covering the blue-and-buff regimental coat he wears underneath. Of middling height, stout and muscular, his dark hair bound in a queue, Arnold is very much a man in command.

Arnold is an officer in the United States Army, a brigadier general. He is now also commodore of the Lake Champlain fleet, a grand-sounding title for the commander of this odd assortment of vessels.

The wind is brisk, kicking up a short chop on the open waters of Lake Champlain and setting the tail of Arnold's cloak slapping against his legs. The early morning sun is low in the southeast, its light hard and sharp, leaving the eastern shore of the lake in shadow and the long line of the Green Mountains beyond etched sharply against the pale blue sky.

The western shore of Valcour Island is also in shadow, but on the New York side of the lake the sunlight falls on the late autumn foliage, the yellows of the birch and beech and the reds of the maple alight in a blaze of color. Great tracts of virgin forest, spruce and fir, stretch west toward the Adirondack Mountains, which just this morning the men woke to find capped with the winter's first snow.

But Arnold is not looking at the scenery. The fleet has not shifted anchor in two and a half weeks, and there is nothing onshore that he has not seen already. Rather, his attention is fixed on the guard boat that he sent onto the open lake just two hours ago, and that is now tacking against the north wind, beating back to rejoin the fleet.

Arnold looks out over the vessels under his command, a mix of galleys and gondolas, a schooner, and a sloop. The vessels are not nearly
as well armed, well manned, or numerous as he had hoped they would
be, but there is nothing more he can do. Shifting his gaze southward
over the schooner's rail, Arnold can see miles up the lake, toward Fort
Ticonderoga and Mount Independence. There the outnumbered and
poorly equipped Northern Army of the United States is dug in, waiting for the British hammerblow from the north.

Most of the American soldiers around Lake Champlain consider
theirs to be a powerful naval force, superior to the British fleet just
completed at the north end of the lake. As a former ship's captain,
Benedict Arnold has a better understanding of such things than do
the landsmen who make up the Northern Army, and he is not so
sanguine.

The enemy's fleet, Arnold knows, will be formidable. It has behind
it the full resources of the British navy, whereas Arnold himself has
spent the past months begging for the most basic supplies: gunpowder, shot, sailcloth, and rope to fit out the vessels he has. The British
fleet will be manned by picked sailors from the men-of-war on the St.
Lawrence River. They are perhaps the finest seamen in the world. As
to the "sailors" in his own fleet, Arnold wrote days ago that "few of
them were ever wet with salt water."

But Arnold has shaped them through training and discipline, and
he has reason to hope that they will give a good accounting of themselves. Now, under his exacting and critical gaze, the men go about
their morning routines, stowing away what bedding they have, clearing the decks for the day's work.

The vessels, particularly the gondolas, which are little more than
big, open boats, offer little in the way of shelter. Discomfort has turned
to suffering in the increasingly bitter weather and the violent autumn
storms that lash the fleet. The men have lived for months aboard these
vessels, with their clothes in rags and with no coats, gloves, or socks to
defend against the cold. Seeking shelter ashore is far too dangerous.
The woods are filled with British troops and their Indian allies—
knowledge gained the hard way, at the cost of men's lives.

As the guard boat closes with the anchored fleet, a flash and a puff of gray smoke shoot from the muzzle of the swivel gun on its bow, followed a second or two later by the flat report of the gun. It is the pre-arranged alarm signal and can mean only one thing. Today is the day. The British fleet is underway.

A long and brutal eighteen months of fighting have carried Arnold to this place. A year ago on this very day, he and his men were deep into their march to Quebec, struggling to drag bateaux and supplies over the Great Carrying Place in the wilderness of northern Maine. Since then, he has seen heady winter days, when the conquest of Canada seemed within the grasp of the United Colonies, and then a nightmare spring, when his sick, starving, utterly defeated men were driven from Canada by the redcoats and Hessian mercenaries, as if the entire Northern Army of the United Colonies was no more than a poorly trained local militia.

That army has seen a long procession of general officers during the Canadian campaign—Philip Schuyler, Richard Montgomery, David Wooster, John Thomas, Arthur St. Clair, John Sullivan, and now Horatio Gates—but no other general has served as long or been as deeply involved in the fighting as Arnold. Other officers have taken time to travel to Philadelphia and woo members of the Continental Congress, but Arnold has not left the front lines for a year and a half.

In truth, in October 1776, there are not many officers anywhere in the Continental army who have seen as much hard campaigning as Benedict Arnold.

The guard boat comes about on its final tack and stands in for the *Royal Savage*, drawing alongside the flagship. The officer in the stern-sheets shouts up to the quarterdeck the news that Arnold is expecting. For days a south wind has held the British fleet at bay, but now, with the wind out of the north, six sail of the enemy have been seen weathering Cumberland Head and standing southward up the lake.

Arnold issues orders for his fleet to make ready for the fight. He dispatches scouts to the north end of Valcour Island to keep an eye on the approaching enemy. He passes the word for his senior officers—Brigadier General David Waterbury, second in command, and Colonel

Edward Wigglesworth, third—to repair aboard the *Royal Savage* for a council of war.

In an instant the quiet anchorage at Valcour Island becomes a whirl of sound and activity. The gondolas are cleared for action: the awnings that offer some shelter to the men aboard are rolled back, the powder cartridges are passed along to the gunners and rammed down the barrels of the 9- and 12-pounder cannon, buckets of water are set out, and lengths of slow match are wound around linstocks and lit, ready to set off the fine priming powder in the guns' touchholes.

On board the galleys, sand is spread on the decks for greater traction, rammers, worms, and sponges are laid along, and muskets are charged and primed. The 18-, 12-, and 9-pounder guns on the broadsides are hauled inboard for loading, their wooden wheels screeching under the weight of the gun barrels. The rudimentary officers' quarters under each quarterdeck are broken down and stowed away to make room for working the guns, the only thing that will matter this day.

On board the sloop *Enterprise*, which will serve as a hospital ship, Dr. Stephen McCrea ties on his apron, clears a space, and lays out his scalpels and forceps, his probes, retractors, amputation knives, and bone saws. His work will take place in the dimly lit 'tween decks, on a moving platform, with British round shot pounding the ship.

On the quarterdeck of the *Savage*, Arnold confers with Waterbury and Wigglesworth on how the enemy should be met. Arnold has long planned for this moment, positioning his fleet so that the British will have to make a difficult upwind approach under American gunfire.

Waterbury, however, does not agree with Arnold's battle plan and says so. The second in command fears being trapped in Valcour Bay, and wants instead to sally forth and meet the British on open water. Arnold listens to Waterbury's objections, then overrules him. The commodore does not lack confidence in his own decisions.

Arnold orders the *Royal Savage* and the galleys *Congress*, *Washington*, and *Trumbull* to get under way, to show themselves to the enemy. There is a chance that the British will sail right past Valcour Island and never see the American fleet there, and Arnold does not want that to happen. He does not want to chase the British fleet up the lake; he wants them to come and fight on his terms.

He orders Wigglesworth to take one of the yawlboats and beat up to the north end of Valcour Island to augment the shore lookout observing the enemy's advance. It is nine-thirty in the morning.

Arnold himself leaves the *Royal Savage*, transferring his flag to the galley *Congress*. *Savage* is the roomiest ship in the fleet, the most comfortable for living aboard and conducting the business of commodore, but she is not the best fighting vessel. *Congress* boasts far more firepower than the schooner's unimpressive six 6-pounder guns. *Royal Savage* has already proven herself to be a poor sailer, whereas *Congress*, with her lateen rig and ability to move under oar, is far more maneuverable.

Still, Arnold intends to return to *Royal Savage* after the battle. He leaves all his personal effects, including his papers, in the schooner's great cabin.

The men on board the galleys and the schooner heave at handspikes thrust into anchor windlasses, and, with a steady click, click, click of the pawls, the dripping anchor cables are hove in and snaked down into the holds below. Soon the four vessels are under way, sailing a beam reach around the southern end of Valcour Island.

As the island slides past their larboard sides, the northern end of the lake opens up to them, and Arnold catches his first sight of the British fleet about eight miles to windward. There is a sense of culmination in this moment, as if the curtain is opening on the final act of the past half year's drama. This will be the climactic scene, his fleet contending with the British for mastery of Lake Champlain.

But Arnold knows, as does Guy Carleton, the governor of Quebec and commander of the British forces, that there is far more at stake than possession of a single lake in the barely settled north woods. Champlain leads to Lake George, and from the south end of Lake George, an easy march would take an invading British army to the Hudson River and Albany. From Albany the Hudson runs straight and deep all the way south to New York City and the Atlantic Ocean.

Even now, a combined force of British and Hessian troops, thirty thousand strong, the largest army ever assembled on North American soil, holds the southern end of the Hudson River at New York City. Arnold knows that more than a month ago a major battle was fought on Long Island. He knows that Washington's army has suffered a defeat, although the details have still not reached this northern outpost. Four days ago, Arnold wrote, "the Affair of long Island, seems, still in Obscurity—I am Very Anxious for Our Army, & Friends."

The details might remain vague, but the danger is clear. A British army invading south from Canada could link up with a British army marching north from New York. Meeting at Albany, they would cut the country (just this year dubbed the United States) in two.

In fact, that invasion, spearheaded by the British fleet to the north and a naval expedition up the Hudson from New York, has already begun. Benedict Arnold understands that holding Lake Champlain is crucial to holding America together, that the outcome of this day's fight could well determine the outcome of the entire war for American Independence.

General Gates's orders to Arnold are not about defending one lake. Rather, Gates has called on Arnold for the "judicious Defense of the Northern Entrance into this side of the Continent. . . . I doubt not you will secure it from further Invasion."

Chafing at the infighting and ineptitude that he has witnessed in the army and in the Continental Congress, Arnold has had reason at times to wonder about the dedication of his countrymen to the cause he has so wholly embraced. Just days ago he wrote to Gates, "Is It possible my Country Men can be, callous to their wrongs, or hesitate one moment, between Slavery, or Death . . . ?"

The man who will be infamous for betraying his country is at this moment as dedicated to the cause of independence as any man who will ever wear the Continental uniform.

The northerly wind makes *Congress* heel to starboard as she stands across the lake, taking the chop on her larboard quarter. Arnold positions himself at the weather rail of the quarterdeck. He looks north, facing into the breeze. The sails of an enemy fleet more powerful than his own are spread over the northern horizon. The British are running down on them, cleared for action, guns loaded and ready to run out, their well-trained and disciplined crews standing ready at quarters.

It will not be long now. Within hours, Arnold knows, he will once again be fighting for his life, for his men, for the liberty of the country he loves.

1775

CHAPTER *I The War Begins*

IN THE SPRING of 1775, the storm that had been gathering for a decade broke at last.

On the night of April 18, British troops marched from their Boston garrison to seize colonial munitions in the nearby town of Concord. The next morning they were met on Lexington Green by a small band of American militia, the "minutemen," citizen-soldiers turned out by the alarm raised by the British regulars' approach. There, in the early morning hours, the first shots of the American Revolution were fired. By the time the British troops moved on, ten Americans were wounded and eight lay dead.

Word of the fighting swept ahead of the marching troops. Seemingly out of nowhere, an American army numbering in the thousands materialized, as every militia unit within a half day's march raced to join the action.

By day's end, the one-sided showdown on Lexington Green had become the bloody, running battle of Lexington and Concord. Colonial militia chased General Thomas Gage's British forces back to Boston, leaving 250 redcoats and 95 Americans killed and wounded along the way.

It was not the first time that colonial militia had mobilized for an alarm, but it was the first time that a genuine battle had ensued. American militia continued to pour into the countryside around Boston even after the remnants of Gage's column had returned to the safety of the city. After previous alarms, the militias had dispersed once the danger had passed, but this time the American citizen-soldiers did not go home. Rather, they stayed in the field and put the city of Boston under siege.

The suddenness of this change was reflected in the words of a young British naval officer in Boston who wrote, "In the course of two days, from a plentiful town, we are reduced to the disagreeable necessity of living on salt provisions, and we are fairly blocked up in Boston."

Almost spontaneously, the smoldering hostilities between the Americans and the British government in London had turned violent, and the American colonies were at war.

The year before, Gage had attempted to prevent the increasingly radical Massachusetts legislature from meeting. A number of delegates had met anyway and formed themselves into the Massachusetts First Provincial Congress, which, in utter defiance of the Crown, assumed governmental responsibility over the colony.

Members of the Provincial Congress were selected to form a Committee of Safety, which would oversee the militia and other matters of public concern. Following the Battle of Lexington and Concord, the Committee of Safety sent a circular letter throughout New England, calling for men to augment the militia units surrounding Boston. In short order a colonial army of thousands was mustered, the biggest army ever assembled in New England. Events began to spin out of control.

Those early days of what would become the American Revolution were an enormously confusing time. An army had come together and fought the British with no forethought, no flag or uniform, and under no unifying authority beyond the Massachusetts Committee of Safety. It was unclear who, if anyone, was in charge.

Though colonists had begun referring to themselves as Americans during the French and Indian War two decades before, the colonies themselves remained at most a loose federation, united only in their disaffection toward England's policies, and not even uniformly in that. The First Continental Congress was the only body that represented all thirteen colonies, and it had adjourned more than five months earlier, after agreeing to a boycott on trade with England and petitioning King George to redress colonial grievances. The delegates had not created anything that could be considered a federal government, and had certainly not authorized open rebellion.

The Second Continental Congress was not yet in session, and would not be for another month. The highest authorities who might speak for the rebels were the individual colonial governments, and they were making little effort to work in concert, save for their ongoing support for the beleaguered city of Boston.

Indeed, soon after the Battle of Lexington and Concord, the colonies of Massachusetts, Connecticut, and New York nearly came to loggerheads as they raced off in separate directions. On May 5, members of the New York Assembly, acting on their own accord, sent a letter to General Gage in Boston with a request that Gage "immediately order a cessation of further hostilities, until His Majesty can be apprised of the situation of the American Colonies."

The New Yorkers were still under the impression, shared by many Americans, that King George III would put a stop to Gage's aggression if his Majesty only understood the truth. On the same day the letter to Gage was written, two members of the New York Assembly sailed for England to explain that truth to the king.

Three days before that, and to the horror of the Massachusetts Provincial Congress, the Connecticut Assembly dispatched two ambassadors to meet with General Gage regarding the current crisis. The Massachusetts Provincial Congress managed to head off the emissaries, informing them that "Any proposals . . . made separately by a single Colony, may produce most tremendous events with regard to America." The issues were ironed out before any real animosity developed among the colonies, but the incident served to illustrate the free-for-all nature of the opening days of the Revolution.

And into these confused and violent affairs marched Captain Benedict Arnold.

Native Son

Benedict Arnold V, of New Haven, Connecticut, was descended from a long and distinguished line of Arnolds in America. The first American Arnold, William, arrived with his family in Massachusetts Bay fifteen years after the Pilgrims, part of the Puritan exodus from England. He soon left Massachusetts, following Roger Williams to Rhode Island. There Arnold and his son, the first Benedict, purchased nearly ten thousand acres of land, establishing themselves as one of the wealthiest families in the colony. By the mid-1600s, the first Benedict Arnold had succeeded Roger Williams as governor of Rhode Island. Rather than adhere to the practice of primogeniture, Benedict Arnold I divided his property among his heirs, and his son, Benedict Arnold II, did the same. Benedict Arnold III inherited only a tiny fraction of the original Arnold holding.

By the time Benedict Arnold IV, the father of Revolutionary War Benedict Arnold was born, the family fortune was greatly diminished, and the remaining property too small to be further divided. Instead, the great-grandson of the governor of Rhode Island was given an apprenticeship to a cooper and forced to make barrels for a living.

But Arnold's father was more ambitious than that. He left Rhode Island for Norwich, Connecticut, a thriving and growing town on the Thames River. There he made a good marriage to the widow of a prosperous merchant for whom he had worked, gaining not only a wife of good lineage but the merchant's business as well, which Arnold made even more prosperous. When Benedict Arnold was born, his father was a civic leader in Norwich, and the Arnold name was on its way back up among the leading families in New England.

That trajectory did not last. By the time Benedict Arnold was a young teenager, his father had started drinking hard, driven to it perhaps by the deaths of four of his six children. The fortune and the social standing of the Arnold family fell precipitously, and young Benedict's boarding-school education, which he had begun receiving in preparation for college, came to an end as the family's money ran out. Rather than an educated young gentleman, Arnold became an apothecary's apprentice, and that only through the influence of his mother's relatives.

Arnold's father cost the family not only its fortune but its reputation; his heavy drinking made him an outcast and an embarrassment. Benedict was well aware of the cloud of shame that now hung over his family, and he grew determined to dispel it and return the name Arnold (which meant, originally, "honor") to its rightful place.

That drive made Arnold extremely jealous of his reputation. At a time when honor was far more than a vague notion—when, indeed, men willingly fought to the death for it—Arnold would stand out for his prickly response to any slight.

In his early twenties, Arnold moved to New Haven. There, with the help of his mother's family, with whom he had apprenticed, he set up as an apothecary and merchant. Hardworking, smart, and ambitious, Arnold thrived in business. Though early historians, particularly those of the Revolutionary War generation, have suggested that Arnold was common, vulgar, and depraved, he was in fact none of those things. Rather, he was a successful, athletic, handsome young man who enjoyed and was enjoyed by the young women of New Haven.

By the mid-1760s, Arnold was a shipowner as well, as his father had once been. The elder Arnold had sailed as captain of the merchant vessels he owned, and may well have taken his son with him on some of those voyages. Benedict Arnold, like his father, went to sea, making trading voyages in his own merchant vessels to the West Indies and Canada. His specialty was horses, which he exported to the Caribbean and to Canadian cities. After the start of the war, that trade would earn him the derisive sobriquet of "horse trader" or "horse jockey" among the British, who did not care to credit any American with being a soldier or a gentleman.

Arnold spent considerable time in the West Indies, and it was there that he fought a duel with another ship captain over a perceived slight. The duel ended after the first exchange of shots with the captain apologizing, Arnold having sworn to kill him with a second shot.

In Arnold's numerous voyages to Canadian ports, including Quebec and Montreal, he made contacts that would serve him well during his later fighting there. His seagoing experience would make him the army officer most qualified to take charge of the waterborne defenses of Lake Champlain.

Through industry, frugality, and adroit business practices, all part of his Puritan New England heritage, Arnold became one of the wealthiest men in New Haven. Being thus nouveau riche gave him little standing among New Haven's old guard, but it increased his stature among the working people, those men and women who would form the bedrock of the Revolution. In 1765—the same year the British Parliament passed the Stamp Act, the first major attempt to levy internal taxes on the colonies—Arnold joined the New Haven lodge of the Freemasons. His membership in that fraternal organization gave him important social connections and, in years to come, fellowship with many of the Revolution's leading lights, including George Washington and Benjamin Franklin.

In 1764, Arnold married Peggy Mansfield. Little is known about Peggy, though her family was an old and distinguished one in New Haven, which no doubt appealed to Arnold. Theirs appears to have been a happy and loving marriage. By 1772, the couple had three sons—Benedict, Richard, and Henry.

In the years leading up to the Revolution, Arnold spent most of his time at sea and did not participate much in pre-war protests, but his sympathies were clearly with the Sons of Liberty: Samuel Adams, John Hancock, Virginia's Patrick Henry, and their ilk. Arnold was in the West Indies in 1770 when he heard the news of the Boston Massacre. In a letter written to a friend about that incident, he revealed his political leanings, as well as his penchant for unequivocal action. "Good God!" Arnold wrote, "are the Americans all asleep, and tamely yielding up their liberties, or are they all turned philosophers, that they do not take immediate vengeance on such miscreants?"

As importers of taxable goods, American sailors and shipowners were on the front lines of tariff issues, and they were predisposed by perspective and circumstance to side with the Revolutionaries. Like virtually all colonial ship captains, Arnold was a part-time smuggler. Britain's import and export duties were not just an abstract notion to him, they were a part of his professional life, and he resented them.

Benedict Arnold was thirty-four years old when fighting broke out in Massachusetts in the spring of 1775. He was of average height for his day, around five feet five inches tall, though his stocky build made him appear shorter. He was athletic and strong; his hair and his complexion were dark, his eyes light. He had a prominent, hawklike nose. A soldier who fought with him at Saratoga would describe him as "dark-skinned, with black hair, and middling height; there wasn't any waste timber in him; he was our fighting general, and a bloody fellow he was." Arnold was disciplined and businesslike, no Puritan by any means, despite a Puritan heritage and upbringing, but not much given to frivolity either, and not one to suffer fools or incompetents. It was his sense for discipline and order that would make him an ideal soldier, if not always an ideal American soldier.

Baron Frederick von Steuben famously compared Prussian, Austrian, or French soldiers with the Americans he commanded, saying, "You say to your soldier, 'Do this,' and he doeth it, but I am obliged to say 'This is the reason why you ought to do that,' and he does it."

Arnold would have flourished in command of a European army, where the rights and concerns of the rank and file mattered not a whit. His rigid personality would become a hindrance commanding an army of republicans, who were jealous of the liberty, equality, and independence for which they were fighting. Still, for the first five years of the Revolution, Benedict Arnold would be the very image of the American citizen-soldier: brave, dedicated, and selfless, with a genius for military matters that came not from formal training, which he did not have, but from native ability.

The Road to War

Arnold's entrée into military service came in December 1774. On the twenty-seventh of that month, sixty-five men gathered at Beers' Tavern in New Haven for the first meeting of the Second Company Governor's Foot Guard, which had been organized that autumn largely through Arnold's efforts. Like all New England militia units, the Governor's Foot Guard elected their officers. It was a measure of the esteem in which he was held that Arnold was elected captain, the chief officer of the Second Company.

In April 1775, when word reached New Haven of the fighting at Lexington and Concord, the Second Company of Guards mustered fifty-eight men. In their elegant scarlet regimental coats with buff facings and silver buttons, their waistcoats and breeches of white linen, they made a stirring martial sight, but they had few guns and little powder or ammunition.

The Second Company voted to join the militias massing around Boston. The selectmen of New Haven, however, representing the city's old guard, had different ideas, and decided that the Governor's Foot

Guard should stay home. What's more, the selectmen held the keys to the local magazine, New Haven's storehouse of arms and ammunition. Without guns and powder, the Second Company was little more than a bunch of men in fancy uniforms.

But Arnold was not disposed to let the selectmen stop him. Followed by a large mob of New Havenites, he marched his troops off to Beers' Tavern, where the selectmen were meeting. Positioning his men outside, Arnold sent one of his officers in to demand the keys to the magazine.

David Wooster, a prominent citizen and a man with whom Arnold would later tangle in Canada, stepped out of the tavern to assure Arnold that he, Arnold, had no authority to demand the keys or to march off to Boston.

Arnold reportedly told Wooster, "None but Almighty God shall prevent my marching." He gave Wooster five minutes to produce the keys, after which he said that his men would break into the storehouse. Arnold was not bluffing, and the New Haven leaders knew it. They gave in to his demands, and, soon after, the smartly equipped and fully armed militia marched out of New Haven, north toward Massachusetts.

Many of the leaders of the Revolution understood how ill-prepared the colonists were for the war that was coming. "We have not men fit for the times," John Adams had confided in his diary in 1774. "We are deficient in genius, education, in travel, fortune—everything." Accepting command of the American army on June 16, 1775, George Washington would tell the Second Continental Congress, "I beg it may be remembered by every gentleman in the room that I this day declare with utmost sincerity, I do not think myself equal to the command I [am] honored with." Leading his men toward Boston, Arnold seems not to have been tortured by any such self-doubts. He had his weaknesses, but a lack of confidence was not among them.

As he led his men up the dusty post road, Arnold may have thought he was simply marching to Cambridge. In fact, he was taking the first steps on the road that would lead to Lake Champlain, to the winding path from Ticonderoga to Canada, to Valcour Island, and ultimately to Saratoga. He was marching to a destiny that he would never have chosen or even imagined.

CHAPTER **2** *The Road to Ticonderoga*

THE MEN OF THE Second Company Governor's Foot Guard, with Benedict Arnold at their head, were eager to join the fighting around Boston, 140 miles away. Shouldering their firelocks, they marched along the road north out of New Haven to where it met the Connecticut River in Wethersfield, just south of Hartford.

From there the men continued north along the west bank of the river to Springfield, Massachusetts. After crossing the river by ferry, they tramped east on the post road for the final half of the trek to Cambridge. Their journey took them through farmland and small towns, along roads dotted by wayside taverns. As the men traveled north, the oak, chestnut, and hickory of southern New England mingled with white pine and hemlock in denser forests.

Along the way, Arnold happened to meet up with Colonel Samuel Holden Parsons, who was on his way back to Hartford from Cambridge to recruit more men. Parsons, having been with the army around Boston, was "concerned for . . . the want of heavy cannon." Before they parted company, Arnold, who had traveled in Canada, mentioned Fort Ticonderoga on Lake Champlain, giving Parsons an account of the old fort's condition and the number of cannon to be found there.

Arnold and his men arrived in Cambridge on April 29, just ten days after the Battle of Lexington and Concord. The journey could not have been completed any faster. But Arnold's thoughts were now on Ticonderoga, and his entrepreneurial spirit, which had taken him from poor apprentice to wealthy merchant, began to infuse his thinking about military affairs.

The next day Arnold approached the Massachusetts Committee of Safety, which included Joseph Warren and John Hancock. The committee was mainly responsible for overseeing the Massachusetts militia, but Arnold wanted to broaden the men's horizons. He wanted to tell them about Fort Ticonderoga.

The fort stood near the southern end of Lake Champlain in the colony of New York, just north of the outlet from Lake George. The most powerful defensive point in the region, it had been the site of a number of bloody struggles. Construction was begun by the French in 1755, at the outbreak of the French and Indian War. Its builders named it Fort Carillon, something of a mispronunciation of the name of a local fur trader, Philippe de Carrion du Fresnoy, who had established a trading post there in the previous century.

Fort Carillon was a massive and imposing fortification when it was completed around 1758, a wood, earth, and masonry structure with heavy guns thrusting out in every direction. Two major battles were fought there during the French and Indian War, first in 1758, when the British under General James Abercromby failed to dislodge the French, and again the following year when the French abandoned the fort in the face of General Jeffrey Amherst's overwhelming force. The British renamed the fort Ticonderoga, and it would remain in their hands for the next sixteen years.

About seventeen miles north of Ticonderoga stood the other major fortification on Champlain, Crown Point, at the tip of a peninsula overlooking a narrow constriction of the lake. Until 1755, Crown Point had marked the southernmost French incursion into British America. The original fortification, built by the French in 1731, had been called Fort Frederic, and it was the strongest point on the lake until Fort Carillon was constructed. Like Ticonderoga, Crown Point had been taken and garrisoned by the British during the French and Indian War.

Still nearly wilderness by the time of the Revolution, interrupted only by a few small and scattered settlements, the southern end of Lake Champlain would have been an odd place for two major fortifications were it not far more than just a lake in the woods. It was, instead, a major link in a water route that was of vital strategic importance in any conflict in the New World.

A glance at the map of the eastern part of North America reveals an interesting quirk of geography—a nearly unbroken, almost perfectly north-south chain of rivers and lakes from the Atlantic Ocean off New York City right up to the St. Lawrence River, which in turn leads to the major centers of population, trade, and power in eastern Canada and the Great Lakes.

The southern end of that route, well traveled at the time of the American Revolution, began with the Hudson River, stretching north from New York City to within eight miles of Lake George. That eight-mile overland stretch to the head of the lake was the only real break in the entire water route. At the bottom, or northern, end of Lake George, the water "contract[ed] itself in breadth to the size of an inconsiderable river," then emptied into Lake Champlain just south of Fort Ticonderoga. Just before disgorging into Lake Champlain, the river tumbled over a series of falls impassable by boat. The route around those falls—called, appropriately enough, the Carrying Place—was about two miles in length.

About a hundred miles down the lake from Ticonderoga, just north of 45° north latitude, the border between America and Canada, Lake Champlain tapered abruptly into a river. In colonial times there was little agreement as to the name of the river. A Revolutionary War–era map refers to it as "River Chambly, called also River Richelieu and River Sorel." A British officer in 1776 referred to it as "River Richelieu tho it is more commonly called the River Sorel." Today it is indisputably known as the Richelieu, though Sorel seems to have been the name most commonly used in the latter 1700s.

The Richelieu River in its turn ran north and emptied into the St. Lawrence between Montreal and Quebec, providing access to the Great Lakes and the Atlantic Ocean. The entire drainage from the head of Lake George to the St. Lawrence was thus south to north, so that to travel south on Lake Champlain or Lake George was to travel "up" the lake.

The strategic value of that waterway had been recognized for as long as there had been fighting in the Champlain valley. The chain of rivers and lakes allowed rapid movement of troops and *materiel* through otherwise impenetrable wilderness. Such ease of movement made possible an invasion of America through the back door of Canada, or, vice versa, an invasion of Canada from New York. An army holding undisputed possession of the entire watercourse could prevent any sizable enemy force from crossing from one side to the other, thus effectively cutting off New England from the rest of the colonies.

Such an attack up Lake Champlain to the Hudson would be suggested by nearly every British general officer in America, including Thomas Gage, William Howe, and James Murray, who had commanded in Canada during the French and Indian War. John Burgoyne, the British general who would finally get the opportunity to put this theory to practice, had long advocated a move south through the rivers and lakes as the most efficient strategy for winning the Revolution. He would write,

> I have always thought Hudson's River the most proper part of the whole continent for opening vigorous operations. Because the course of the river, so beneficial for conveying all the bulky necessaries of an army, is precisely the route that an army ought to take for the great purpose of cutting the communications between the Southern and Northern Provinces, giving confidence to the Indians, and securing a junction with the Canadian forces.

Fort Ticonderoga and Crown Point were built not to defend a patch of wilderness but to defend a vital link between Canada and the American colonies.

But few people in America were yet thinking in those terms. They were thinking rather of the one thing that Ticonderoga still had in abundance—big cannons, and plenty of them.

The Secret Mission

In a report to Joseph Warren and the Massachusetts Committee of Safety, Benedict Arnold gave what would turn out to be a highly accurate account of the situation at Ticonderoga. The fort was "in a ruinous condition," he noted, but it did boast "eighty pieces of heavy cannon, twenty brass guns, from four to eighteen pounders," as well as mortars, small arms, stores, and a sloop "of seventy or eighty tons." Ticonderoga, Arnold assured them, "could not hold out an hour against a vigorous onset."

Arnold, who had probably never been to Ticonderoga, must have gained this intelligence while visiting Montreal during his merchant days, and he was right about the state of the works. By 1775 the fort was a near wreck, "composed of decaying Wood and Earth . . . ," one British officer wrote. Since the end of the French and Indian War in 1763, all of Canada and the American colonies had been in British hands, and there had no longer been any great need to defend the water passage from the St. Lawrence to the Hudson. Fort Ticonderoga became little more than a wilderness way station, and soon it began to fall apart.

Arnold's evident efforts to acquaint himself with the situation at Ticonderoga would suggest that he had been thinking about military strategy long before the fighting at Lexington and Concord. Now he needed only the means and authority to act on the plans he had been considering.

The Massachusetts Committee of Safety decided to give him what he wanted. On May 3, 1775, they issued orders to Arnold that read, "Confiding in your judgment, fidelity and valor, we . . . appoint you Colonel and Commander-in-Chief . . . to march on the Fort at Ticonderoga."

Arnold was granted a "body of men, not exceeding four hundred." The catch was, he would have to recruit them himself from western Massachusetts, New York, and the area called the Hampshire Grants, now Vermont.

The committee did give Arnold one hundred pounds in cash and two hundred pounds of gunpowder as well as flints, musket balls, and ten horses. His orders—written, ironically, by Benjamin Church, a leader among the Massachusetts patriots but also a British spy and one of the Revolution's first traitors—were to take Ticonderoga and send back to Massachusetts whatever Arnold considered "serviceable to the Army here." But the committee, too, was starting to think in wider terms.

Rather than simply ordering Arnold to plunder the fort and return, they instructed him to leave at Ticonderoga "what may be necessary to secure that post, with a sufficient garrison." Joseph Warren and other committee members were already considering a larger sphere of conflict.

No one seems to have considered what authority the Massachusetts Committee of Safety had to order any of this. Ticonderoga was in New York, not Massachusetts, and the tiny garrison there posed no threat to Boston. The Massachusetts Committee was certainly aware that it was, in essence, ordering the invasion of New York. On May 3, the day that Arnold's orders were issued, Warren wrote to the New York Committee explaining that his committee was considering a proposal to capture Ticonderoga, but that "we would not, even upon this emergency, infringe upon the rights of our sister Colony." Warren asked that the New York legislators "give such orders as are agreeable to you." Then the committee dispatched Arnold to Ticonderoga before that letter could possibly have reached New York.

While all the fighting to that date, including the bloody battle in Lexington and Concord, could be construed as defensive from the Americans' point of view, this was clearly an offensive move—an unprovoked attack on a British fort. Though the action would have far-reaching implications for all the colonies, it was ordered by a small group of Massachusetts men at the urging of a Connecticut militia officer. Such was the confused nature of events in the spring of 1775.

Benedict Arnold, now a colonel in the service of Massachusetts, set out at once to round up his troops.

Connecticut Joins the Fray

As with any plan that turns out well, there would soon be plenty of people claiming credit for the idea of capturing Ticonderoga. Samuel Parsons would write, "'tis matter of diversion to me to see the various competitors for the honor of concerting and carrying this matter into execution." Attempts at self-promotion aside, it was true that a number of people had been considering the move since the beginning of 1775.

After talking with Arnold, Colonel Samuel Holden Parsons traveled on to Hartford. Like Arnold, he continued to mull the idea of taking Ticonderoga. On April 28, the day before Arnold arrived in Cambridge, Parsons convened a small group of Hartford's leading citizens, among them Christopher Leffingwell and Silas Deane, who had been part of the Connecticut delegation to the First Continental Congress. The committee agreed that the capture of Ticonderoga was a goal worth pursuing, and it dispatched Captain Noah Phelps and Mr. Bernard Romans that same day to organize troops in Massachusetts and the Hampshire Grants for a move on the fort.

Earlier, Leffingwell had been talking with Edward Mott, a captain in Parsons's regiment, about the siege of Boston and what might be done to bolster the American troops there. Mott, too, had suggested an attack on Ticonderoga. When the ad hoc Hartford committee called on Captain Mott to solicit his opinion, Mott told them much the same thing that Arnold had told Parsons: Ticonderoga "might be taken by surprise by a few men if properly conducted."

The Hartford group was sold. On the same day they heard the proposal from Parsons, and two days before Arnold gave his report to the Massachusetts Committee of Safety, the Hartford committee asked Mott to join with Phelps and Romans and "search into the situation of said Garrison & if [Mott] thought proper, to take possession of the same."

Mott agreed. He rounded up five men in Hartford to join him, and on April 29 they gathered up their muskets and cartridge boxes, then mounted horses and headed north, a day behind Phelps and Romans. Parsons's Hartford committee issued Mott three hundred pounds from Connecticut's treasury, a more generous grant than the one to Arnold from the Massachusetts Committee. What they could not offer, however, was even the veneer of authority that the Massachusetts Committee of Safety conferred on Arnold.

The Massachusetts Committee of Safety was a legitimate government body, at least in the eyes of Americans, even if it did not have explicit authority to send troops into New York to capture British forts. The Connecticut effort was entirely the work of a few citizens. Though it would later be suggested that Connecticut's governor and Council of Safety had initiated the plan, and that John Adams and John Hancock were present at the inception, the fact is that the entire enterprise was set in motion by five men acting on their own, with no legal authority. Colonel Parsons would later make a point of stating that the five men "procured the money, men &c. and sent out on this expedition without any consultation with the Assembly or others."

In 1775, western Connecticut and Massachusetts were on the edge of the wilderness. Traveling to Salisbury, in the northwest corner of Connecticut, Mott and his band rode over rough dirt roads cut through virgin forest, moving from one small township to the next where people wrested an uncertain living from timber and livestock. The concerns of Boston and Hartford may have seemed far removed from those places, but the spirit of rebellion was evident and growing.

In Salisbury, Captain Mott recruited another sixteen men but decided to add no more for the time being, because "we meant to keep our business a secret and ride through the country unarmed till we came to the new Settlements on the Grants." In fact, the Hartford group of five had instructed Mott not to raise any men at all before reaching the Hampshire Grants, in case the British should be alarmed by reports of armed men riding toward Ticonderoga.

On May 1, Mott's party reached the town of Pittsfield, in the Berkshire Hills at the western end of Massachusetts. Not long before, several Pittsfield Tories had been forced into hiding by an increasingly militant patriot faction. There, Mott and his men encountered Colonel James Easton, who commanded a local militia regiment, and a young attorney named John Brown. Brown, as it happened, had been sent earlier in the year by the Boston Committee of Correspondence on a secret mission to Montreal to gather intelligence and to try to convince the Canadian people to support the American cause.

During that mission, Brown had received intelligence regarding Ticonderoga, and upon returning to Massachusetts had been one of the first to suggest that the fort should be seized immediately if war with England were to break out. Brown, like Parsons and Arnold and so many others, understood the lesson of the French and Indian War, in which control of Lake Champlain had been so hotly disputed. Even before most Americans were thinking in terms of a genuine, protracted war, these men were eager to realize the strategic advantage of taking and holding the lake.

On learning of Brown's previous mission, Mott confided in him and Easton. The Pittsfield men agreed to join Mott, but warned him (incorrectly, as it turned out) that in the Hampshire Grants, "the people were generally poor, it would be difficult to get a sufficient number of men there." Easton offered to raise troops from his own regiment, and soon an additional thirty-nine men had been added to Mott's forces.

The next day, part of the company continued on to Williamstown, in the northwest corner of Massachusetts. Despite their attempts at secrecy, however, these armed men on horseback attracted attention. Settlers, fully aware of the fighting a hundred miles east around Boston, took the men for a band of Loyalists, and the alarm spread. The Williamstown militia snatched up muskets and powder and turned out "20 or thirty People Arm'd . . . ," ready to do battle with Mott's recruits.

Happily, the misunderstanding was straightened out before any musket balls flew. The people of Williamstown helped Mott's men gather provisions "Such as Bisket & Pork," and a number of townspeople agreed to join the expedition.

Mott had not yet assembled enough men to take Ticonderoga, but he was not concerned. He knew just where to find the men for this enterprise, and soon his band was riding north again, to Bennington, in the Hampshire Grants, the seat of the Green Mountain Boys.

The Green Mountain Boys

In the early spring of 1775, when John Brown had suggested to the Boston Committee of Correspondence that Ticonderoga should be taken, he added, "The people on New Hampshire Grants have engaged to do this business, and in my opinion they are the most proper persons for this job."

By "the people on New Hampshire Grants," Brown meant the Green Mountain Boys, a quasi-legal militia formed in 1770, not by any government body but by a gathering of settlers, with "Colonel" Ethan Allen at its head.

Allen was an enigmatic man, big and blustering, a sometimes violent demagogue and iconoclast who was, at the same time, a master of self-promotion and the author of a number of books and pamphlets. The first edition of his *Reason the Only Oracle of Man*, written in 1784, would be burned up along with the printer's shop in an apparent act of arson prompted by the book's deist ideas and its vicious attack on the Bible.

The Green Mountain Boys, whom Allen led, had been organized for protection not from the British but from the colony of New York, in the wake of a New York court decision rejecting the claims of Hampshire Grants settlers to land they were already farming. The disagreement had become so heated that the New York government had put a hundred pound bounty on Allen's head.

As hostilities with Britain escalated, the Green Mountain Boys saw the American struggle with England as a larger version of their own struggle with New York, and, rebels themselves, they naturally sided with the patriots. Allen had been eager to grab Ticonderoga since the beginning of the year but had lacked any authority or justification for doing so. Soon both would come from an unexpected quarter.

Among Mott's troops were Levi and Herman Allen, younger brothers of Ethan. Herman was sent ahead to Bennington to alert Colonel Allen about the call to arms, so that by the time Mott arrived, the Green Mountain Boys, more experienced in fighting than most legitimate American militia units, were ready to go.

Meanwhile, off in the Massachusetts countryside, Benedict Arnold was recruiting men for the very same mission.

CHAPTER *3* *A Gathering of Strength*

ARRIVING IN BENNINGTON, Mott and his men gathered at Stephen Fay's famous tavern, birthplace of the Green Mountain Boys five years before and still their unofficial headquarters. Fay's, a square, unpainted building, would later be known as the Catamount Tavern after the stuffed mountain lion that the Boys mounted on the tavern sign.

Fay's was a raucous place, the social epicenter of a small frontier town and the far-flung farms of the region. It was frequented by the kind of rough frontier men—such as the Green Mountain Boys—who had the strength and courage to carve a life from the forests of the Hampshire Grants. The same qualities that made them successful settlers made them good fighting men as well, but their stubborn independence and unwillingness to yield to authority did not necessarily make them good soldiers. Soldiering called for discipline and order.

Mott's men met a few of the Green Mountain Boys in Fay's big room and celebrated with riotous enthusiasm, making plans and passing the "flowing bowl." It was not a sophisticated crowd. At one point the men amused themselves by spying on a newlywed couple in bed, "very Loving which Serv'd for a great Merryment for the Company."

The men whom Mott had sent ahead were also there, save for Noah Phelps and another who had gone off to reconnoiter Ticonderoga, and Jeremiah Halsey and John Stephens, who had gone to Albany to gauge local New York attitudes about the capture of Ticonderoga.

Soon Ethan Allen blew into the tavern with more than a hundred of his Green Mountain Boys, ready for action. Among them was the huge woodsman Seth Warner.

A longtime cohort of Allen's, Warner, like Allen, had earned the distinction of having a bounty placed on his head by the colony of New York. Ethan Allen, the vocal self-promoter, would establish his name for history despite his rapid flameout and near nonparticipation in the Revolution. Warner, by contrast, was a quiet and unassuming man, and though he would go on to achieve a formidable record fighting the British, his name would always be much less famous than Allen's.

The men at Fay's Tavern called a council of war, with James Easton as chairman. There were now present around seventy men from Massachusetts and 140 Green Mountain Boys. The council decided to send troops to cover the roads leading to the places that the rebels hoped to capture: Fort Edward, on Lake George; Skenesborough (now Whitehall), at the southern tip of Lake Champlain; and Ticonderoga and Crown Point.

Incredibly, the British still had no word of the gathering threat, and, by stopping anyone from approaching or leaving the British posts, Mott and company hoped to keep it that way. (Allen would later take full credit for securing the roads. Although in his correspondence Allen was good about giving credit to anyone but Benedict Arnold, his later autobiography, *A Narrative of the Captivity of Col. Ethan Allen*, would leave the impression that almost no one besides himself did anything of note.)

Soon after, Halsey and Stephens returned from Albany and reported "the People Unanimously Disposd in Favour of Liberty." Philip Schuyler, a prominent local who would soon be in military command of the entire northern theater, offered forty barrels of provisions from his own stores.

That night, Bernard Romans, who had been sent north with Phelps ahead of Mott by the Hartford committee, and who had joined Mott on the road, left the group. "[W]e were all glad," Mott reported, "as he had been a trouble to us, all the time he was with us." The man who was "a trouble" to Mott and his crew would later be regarded by Benedict Arnold as "a very spirited, Judicious Gentleman, who has the Service of his Country much at Heart."

The men spent three nights at Fay's Tavern before continuing on. As they rode north, a heavy spring rain began to fall, leaving already bad roads thick with mud. Epaphras Bull, who had joined Mott's band in Massachusetts, wrote, "Got Well Soak'd," with words capitalized for emphasis. They traveled in small groups, perhaps to attract less notice, with orders to meet up again at Castleton, fifty miles north of Bennington and twenty-five miles by road from the lakeshore opposite Ticonderoga.

By Sunday, May 7, most of Mott's men had assembled at Castleton. Another committee was formed, this time with Mott as chairman, to decide how to proceed and who should lead the expedition. The first decision was to send part of their forces under the command of Captain Herrick to the town of Skenesborough at the very head of Lake Champlain, to "Secure young Major Schene."

"Young Major Schene" was Andrew Skene. His father, the ardent Loyalist Philip Skene, was a fifty-two-year-old Scotsman with an impressive military career in service to the Crown that included fighting in the Spanish Main and at the bloody battle of Culloden, where the British crushed the Stewart faction under Bonny Prince Charlie. Philip Skene had been wounded during Abercromby's unsuccessful attack on Ticonderoga in 1758, but he recovered to participate in General Jeffrey Amherst's capture of the fort the next year. Amherst had left Skene in charge of Ticonderoga while he pressed his campaign against the French.

Sometime during his military service on Champlain, Skene conceived the idea of establishing a great estate on the shores of the lake. In 1764 he petitioned for and was granted a royal patent to twenty-nine thousand acres at the southern end of Champlain, where he established the township of Skenesborough. By 1775, Skenesborough boasted a post office, sawmills, an ironworks, a general store, and a small sloop; it was, in effect, a colonial-era planned community in that barely settled region of New York, the personal fiefdom of Philip Skene.

While Mott and his committee were expanding their mandate to include taking Skenesborough, Philip Skene was in England, a fact known to the committee. As it happened, he sailed for America several weeks later aboard the ship *Prosperity*, having apparently assured the British ministry that he would be able to bribe the entire Continental

Congress to give up its resistance to royal authority. A few days before arriving in Philadelphia, the *Prosperity* spoke another vessel that informed them of the Battle of Lexington and Concord. Skene and the few British officers on board attempted to gain control of the *Prosperity* and sail her to British-held Boston, but they were "overpowered by the Captain and crew," placed in confinement, and, upon arriving in Philadelphia, were charged with mutiny. Skene would later be exchanged to join General Burgoyne at Saratoga, where Skene's blundering and miscalculations would help Burgoyne achieve his stunning defeat.

But all that was in the future as the committee continued to make its plans. After taking Skenesborough, Herrick and his men were to send boats from there up to Shoreham, on the Hampshire Grants side of Lake Champlain, across from Ticonderoga. Meanwhile, Captain Asa Douglas was to proceed to Crown Point, north of Ticonderoga, where his brother-in-law lived. There, Douglas was to hire more boats from the British garrison, which would have been a neat bit of irony had it worked. The attack on Ticonderoga would take place in less than three days, on the morning of Wednesday, May 10.

There remained only to decide who would lead the military operation against Ticonderoga. Mott would later inform the Massachusetts Provincial Congress that the leaders were chosen according to the number of men they had raised—Colonel Ethan Allen as first in command, followed by James Easton and Seth Warner.

But this was most likely a rationale created after the fact. By insisting that command had been awarded on the basis of the number of men raised, Mott could offer a logical reason for his subsequent opposition to granting Benedict Arnold a leadership role. Certainly there never was any real question of who would lead; this was primarily an operation of the Green Mountain Boys, and the Green Mountain Boys would be led by Ethan Allen alone.

With the plan set, Captain Herrick and his men marched off to Skenesborough, twelve miles away. Ethan Allen left the main body of men and proceeded to Shoreham to meet with other prospective recruits. As far as Allen and his men knew, the garrison at Ticonderoga was still in the dark about the impending attack. A mere nine days after the Hartford committee's first meeting to discuss Ticonderoga, everything seemed ready.

Then Benedict Arnold arrived.

"The People Will Be a Little Averse . . . "

Since receiving his commission from the Massachusetts Committee of Safety on May 3, Benedict Arnold had been riding the length of Massachusetts, drumming up troops.

Travel was no easy matter along the rough roads, especially in the sparsely settled country west of Springfield. Mud, rain, and the difficulty of recruiting a small army slowed his progress, but still Arnold moved with impressive speed.

With him were the few captains he had brought from Cambridge, including Eleazer Oswald, a distiller and fellow New Haven man who would be with Arnold through much of the next few years' fighting.

Arnold's recruitment efforts had been meeting with some success. He sent out circular letters that were to be passed from town to town, urging the "Gentlemen," the towns' leading citizens, to "send forward as many men to join the army here as you can." The letters offered wages of forty shillings per month and assured their readers that Arnold had provisions enough for five hundred men, though the Committee of Safety had authorized him to raise no more than four hundred. By May 8 he had raised about 150 men but they were not ready to move immediately, as were the Green Mountain Boys.

Arnold arrived in Williamstown, where Mott's men had been greeted by an armed citizenry, soon after the Connecticut group had moved on. It was there, most likely, that Arnold got wind of the Connecticut-sponsored effort to take Fort Ticonderoga and realized that he was out of time. If he hoped to participate in the attack, he could not wait for his own recruits to gather. Commission in hand, Arnold leaped on his horse and rode hard for Castleton.

Reaching Castleton shortly after Ethan Allen had left for Shoreham, Arnold tracked down the Connecticut men and presented a startled Edward Mott and his committee of war with the commission from the Massachusetts Committee of Safety. Mott later told the Massachusetts Provincial Congress (perhaps disingenuously) that his committee was "extremely rejoiced to see that you fully agreed with us . . ." on the need to take Ticonderoga.

Benedict Arnold was not a subtle man, nor was he an astute political operative, qualities that would have served him well in the republican army of what would soon be declared the United Colonies. Someone with more tact and sensitivity might have worked the crowd into some sort of mutual understanding, but Arnold, with his characteristic bluntness and certitude, insisted that he alone should have command of the troops gathering to attack Ticonderoga, because he was the only one with a valid commission.

Mott reported that the committee was "shockingly surprised when Colonel Arnold presumed to contend for the Command of those forces that we had raised." Mott told Arnold that they "could not surrender the command to him" because the men had joined under the condition that "they should be commanded by their own officers."

But Arnold had a point about his commission, and Mott and the others realized that he could not be dismissed out of hand. "How the matter will be Transacted when we all meet I Cant Say," wrote Bull, who was part of Mott's committee, "but believe the People will be a Little Averse to his taking the Command."

It was an understatement. The Green Mountain Boys were furious at the prospect of this blustering stranger taking charge, and they would not have it. But although Mott's committee might have been formed to give a legal veneer to the proceedings, Allen was the one who really had authority over the men, and Arnold was at least astute enough to realize that. The next morning he left for Shoreham to find Allen.

Neither the Green Mountain Boys nor Easton's men liked the looks of this. "When Col. Arnold went after Col. Allen," Mott wrote, "the whole party followed him, for fear he should prevail on Col. Allen to resign the command."

With Arnold racing after Allen, and most of the troops racing after Arnold, Mott and a few others were left to bring up the packhorses. As a result, Mott would miss the attack on Ticonderoga.

Arnold arrived at Shoreham with the Green Mountain Boys close behind, and there Arnold confronted Ethan Allen. It must have made for a startling contrast. The stocky Arnold, though not short by the standards of the day, would have looked like a bantam cock beside the tall, lean men from the Hampshire Grants. Arnold wore the bright scarlet regimental coat of the Governor's Foot Guard. The Green Mountain Boys wore rough homespun linen clothing, fringed hunting frocks, and mud-splattered gaiters, with long knives or tomahawks thrust in their belts. Their only bits of "uniform" were the fir sprigs they wore in their hats.

Arnold showed Allen his commission and demanded that he be allowed to lead the attack. The Boys were adamant that Arnold should have no command. They "were for clubbing their fire-locks and marching home."

It's not clear why Allen did not dismiss Arnold out of hand. Allen had nearly two hundred armed men behind him, whereas Arnold had nothing but a piece of paper and his own chutzpah to back him up. Perhaps Allen saw the potential value of having another officer to blame if things went badly. Almost certainly he saw that Arnold's commission would give the enterprise a greater legitimacy, and he may have figured that it was better to have Arnold at his side rather than running around causing trouble elsewhere.

Whatever his reasons, Ethan Allen agreed to "issue further orders jointly" with Arnold, or, as Epaphras Bull put it, Arnold would "take the Left hand of Coll. Allen." Allen assured the Green Mountain Boys that if Arnold had command of them, they would have the same pay they were promised under Allen's command. But the men said "they would damn their pay" and would not be commanded by Arnold.

Eventually, however, Allen convinced the Boys to accept the decision. It was, after all, a concession in name only, because no one intended to listen to Arnold anyway. Arnold's take on the negotiations was that they agreed to a joint command "until [Arnold] could raise a sufficient number of men to relieve [Allen's] people."

About that time, Noah Phelps, who had been sent by Parsons's committee from Hartford with the now-departed Bernard Romans, returned from reconnoitering Ticonderoga. Dressing himself to look like a settler, he had entered the fort ostensibly in search of a barber to shave him. Security at Ticonderoga was clearly not all it could have been; Phelps was able to wander around inside the fort, asking questions in feigned ignorance. He now confirmed how poorly garrisoned Ticonderoga was. Allen's men considered Phelps's report "favorable news."

With the issue of command settled and with confirmation that Ticonderoga was still unaware of the danger, everything was in place for the attack. About eleven-thirty on the night of May 9, Ethan Allen, with Benedict Arnold at his side, headed out. Behind the co-commanders marched the combined forces of the Green Mountain Boys and the troops recruited from Connecticut and Massachusetts.

In the cool air of the early spring night, they quickly covered the half mile from Shoreham to Hand's Cove, on the edge of Lake Champlain. The moon was just a few days from full, providing light enough for the men to move down a backcountry road that was probably more like a trail.

At Hand's Cove they expected to meet the boats sent by Herrick from Skenesborough and Douglas from Crown Point, which would allow the troops to cross the lake en masse. Instead, they found only a single bateau drawn up on the shore, left there by some local. Huddled on the dark shoreline, the men waited quietly, hoping that the boats would show up, but none did.

Finally, with the night advancing, they could wait no longer. Allen, Arnold, and about forty of the Green Mountain Boys piled into the single bateau and rowed out across the dark water. After crossing the mile or so of open water unseen, they landed about a half mile south of Ticonderoga. They climbed ashore and hunkered down and the bateau was sent back for another load.

While the first group had been crossing the lake, the men still on the eastern shore found another small boat. When the first boat returned, they prepared to cross the lake again with two more boatloads of men to join Arnold and Allen on the western shore. Before they could, a storm blew up, with strong, gusting winds and driving rain. There was nothing the men could do but wait miserably on the eastern shore of the lake for the squall to pass. When at last it did, they clambered into the found boat and the bateau and crossed to the western shore, bringing the total number of troops on the Ticonderoga side to around eighty. Another ninety or so men were left on the eastern shore, unable to find room in the two crowded boats.

It was then about four o'clock in the morning, and the sun would soon be rising. Benedict Arnold would later recall that some of the men were in favor of postponing the attack until the rest of the men could be ferried over. In a letter most likely written by Arnold under the pseudonym Veritas, Arnold claimed to have told the men that "he would enter [Ticonderoga] alone, if no man had the courage enough to follow him."

In Ethan Allen's recollection, it was he, Allen, who "harangued the officers and men" to spur them on. Allen's speech, as he reproduced it in his autobiography, was long-winded and preposterous, saying in part, "we must this morning either quit our pretensions to valor or possess ourselves of this fortress in a few minutes; and, inasmuch as it is a desperate attempt, which none but the bravest of men dare undertake, I do not urge it on any contrary to his will."

Another in the party recalled Allen whispering, "Let's go," which is probably closer to the truth. Whatever was said, just before sunrise on the morning of May 10, 1775, the joint command of Ethan Allen and Benedict Arnold advanced toward Fort Ticonderoga. The fighting in the northern theater of the American Revolution was about to begin.

CHAPTER *4 The Taking of Ticonderoga*

IT WAS JUST AFTER four in the morning when the combined forces of the Green Mountain Boys and the Connecticut and western Massachusetts recruits moved on Fort Ticonderoga. The men were formed up in three ranks, muskets ready. At their head marched Ethan Allen and Benedict Arnold. It took only a few minutes to close the distance to the outer wall.

Ticonderoga's main gate was closed with a heavy, iron-bound oak door, but in that door was a smaller door, called a wicket gate, just big enough to accommodate one man at a time, and that entrance stood open. Guarding the wicket gate was a single, none-too-alert sentry. Allen and Arnold approached to within ten yards before the sentry noticed them. Panicked, he tried to fire on the strangers, but the powder in his musket was damp. When the flintlock made only an impotent snapping sound, the sentry turned and fled into the fort, allowing the Americans to stream through the open wicket gate.

One can well imagine Benedict Arnold and Ethan Allen each sprinting hard to be the first through the gate. Which one it was will never be known. Arnold claimed he was "the first person that entered the fort, and Colonel Allen about five yards behind." Allen, as a rule, does not mention Arnold at all, save for one letter to the Committee of the City of Albany in which—quite likely in an effort to attach himself to Arnold's Massachusetts commission and thereby enhance his standing in a colony that considered him an outlaw—he states that "Colonel Arnold entered the fortress with me side by side."

Behind the officers, the men poured in through the wicket gate, shouting "No quarter!" and giving the Indian war whoop that the Green Mountain Boys had adopted. Only a few sentries were awake, and those were caught completely by surprise. As Allen's men wrestled with one of them, the soldier lunged out with his bayonet, slightly wounding one of Allen's officers. Allen, sword drawn, was ready to kill the man, but instead he "altered the design and fury of the blow" and struck him with the flat of the blade on the side of his head, wounding him slightly.

While the Americans rampaged over the fort, Ethan Allen demanded that the wounded sentry tell him where the commanding officer could be found. The sentry pointed to a set of stairs in the front of one of the barracks, and Allen, with Benedict Arnold still doggedly at his side, went to demand the first British capitulation of the war.

Lieutenant Feltham and Captain Delaplace

Ticonderoga was garrisoned by troops of the 26th Regiment of Foot, based in Canada. At the time of the attack there were forty-five officers and men on hand, with at least five of the men considered "old worn out & unserviceable." A number of the garrison's soldiers had their families with them, and there were almost as many women and children at the fort as there were rank-and-file troops fit for duty.

The fort's commander, Captain William Delaplace, had his wife and two children with him. For some time, Delaplace had been concerned about Ticonderoga's vulnerability and its attractiveness as a target. In February 1775, he had written General Thomas Gage in Boston to alert the commander in chief of the British troops in the colonies of two possible instances of American intelligence gathering. Gage dismissed Delaplace's concerns, saying that the men whom Delaplace had seen were just more of the "Numbers of Armed Vagabonds" in the region. Gage was probably right. American interest in Ticonderoga had been growing in various quarters, but it would not be organized for another two months or more. Still, Gage wrote Delaplace that those concerns should "put you on your Guard."

They did. Delaplace next wrote to Guy Carleton, governor of Quebec, for reinforcements, and Carleton ordered "a subaltern and 20 men to be sent in two or three separate parties . . . ," hardly an overwhelming force. Had Carleton been less stingy with his men, it might have changed the course of the Revolution. But in the spring of 1775, Carleton had just enough troops to protect Quebec and Montreal.

The first reinforcements left Canada for Ticonderoga around April 12. A few days later a second party, ten men under the command of Lieutenant Jocelyn Feltham, followed them. Feltham had been a commissioned officer since 1766 and had already spent time in the Lake Champlain region. He had been second in command at Crown Point when the barracks caught fire in 1773, which led to the British all but abandoning the fort. Feltham had met John Brown during Brown's intelligence gathering trip to Canada.

Feltham's party arrived at Ticonderoga around April 29. The lieutenant's orders were to turn the men over to Delaplace and a Lieutenant Wadman, who had likewise been ordered to the fort. But because Wadman had not yet arrived, Feltham's orders were to wait at Ticonderoga until he did. As a result, Feltham would come in for more excitement than he might have expected in that crumbling wilderness outpost.

News traveled slowly to the far-flung settlements on Lake Champlain. In the early morning hours of May 10, 1775, with armed American militia gathering in the darkness a mile away, the people at Fort Ticonderoga still did not know about the fighting in Lexington and Concord and the outbreak of war. Governor Guy Carleton in Quebec would not learn about "the rebels having commenced hostilities in . . . Massachusetts . . ." until May 19, exactly a month after the event.

On May 20, Carleton would learn about the capture of Fort Ticonderoga.

Lieutenant Jocelyn Feltham had not been lodging at Fort Ticonderoga. Thinking that Wadman might arrive with family in tow, Feltham had "left the only tolerable rooms there" for his replacement. But a few nights before the attack, he had become ill and decided to avail himself of the empty rooms. He was fast asleep in the officers' quarters when he found himself startled awake by the sound of "numbers of shrieks, & the words no quarter, no quarter."

Feltham leaped out of bed. He could tell by the noise that an "arm'd rabble" was inside the fort. The door to his room and the back door of Delaplace's both opened onto the same wing of the fort. Still in his nightshirt, Feltham raced to Delaplace's door and knocked, hoping to receive orders from the commanding officer, or to wake him if he was still asleep. There was no reply. The door was locked.

Feltham returned to his room long enough to pull on his waistcoat and coat. He considered rallying the garrison himself, but it was clear that he would never make it, because "there were a number of rioters on the bastions" just outside the door to his room.

Once again he left his room and tried to raise Delaplace. This time the "rioters" saw him and gave chase, but Feltham managed to get into Delaplace's rooms ahead of them. Delaplace was awake now, and the two men conferred. Feltham offered to force his way to the barracks and rally the men of the 26th to the fort's defense.

Another door from Delaplace's rooms opened onto a set of stairs that led down to the fort's grounds, and Feltham thought perhaps he could get to the troops that way. He was wrong. "[O]n opening this door," he recalled, "the bottom of the stairs was filld with the rioters & many were forcing their way up." Leading the rush were Ethan Allen and Benedict Arnold.

"In the Name of the Great Jehovah . . ."

Ethan Allen charged up the stairs, sword drawn. Seeing a pants-less officer whom he took to be Delaplace, he demanded surrender. In Allen's own account of the meeting, preserved in the legend that Allen himself created,

> . . . the Captain came immediately to the door, with his breeches in his hand, when I ordered him to deliver me the fort instantly:
>
> He asked me by what authority I demanded it.
>
> I answered him, "In the name of the great Jehovah, and the Continental Congress."

Presumably the great Jehovah was aware of Allen's activities, but the Continental Congress would have been surprised to learn of their part in the affair. They were not even in session. The Second Continental

Congress would meet for the first time a few hours after Ethan Allen claimed to have uttered those words.

In truth, it is unlikely that Allen ever said any such thing. Great orations appear in Allen's autobiography even as other participants, such as Benedict Arnold and John Brown, disappear. But until the early twentieth century, Allen's was the only detailed account of the taking of Ticonderoga, a fact that helped sustain the myth that Allen created. In 1928, however, a report written by Lieutenant Jocelyn Feltham was discovered among the papers of Thomas Gage. Feltham, a more disinterested observer than either Allen or Arnold, gives a different view of the action.

The officer "with his breeches in his hand" whom Allen saw was not Delaplace but Feltham, who was stepping out of Delaplace's rooms in the forlorn hope of reaching the fort's troops. Instead, he walked right into a rush of Allen's men. The Americans had broken open the doors of the rooms that usually housed the junior officers, and, finding them empty, were making for Delaplace's quarters.

Feltham tried to address the "rioters" but could not make himself heard. He signaled for them to stop mounting the stairs; incredibly, they did, and "proclaim'd silence among themselves."

The lieutenant began to address the Americans "in a stile not agreeable to them," most likely in the officious tones of a British army officer. He demanded to know on what authority they had invaded one of His Majesty's forts and who were their leaders. Feltham was stalling for time, thinking that the fort's garrison would rally and counterattack at any moment, "expecting to amuse [the Americans] till our people fired."

The Americans were not amused. Allen, sword in hand, and Arnold beside him, stepped forward. They supplied Feltham with their names and told him they had a joint command, Arnold explaining that his instructions were from the Massachusetts Committee of Safety and Allen that his were from the colony of Connecticut. Arnold would later show Feltham the commission given him by the Committee of Safety.

Allen, still thinking that Feltham was the commanding officer, held his sword over the lieutenant's head while his men aimed their muskets at the officer. According to Feltham, Allen said, "he must have immediate possession of the fort and all the effects of George the third."

The difference between Ethan Allen, the brawling backwoodsman, and Benedict Arnold, with his strict, prickly sense of military discipline and protocol, became clear during this encounter. According to Feltham, Allen swore that if the fort were not surrendered, or if any of the British troops fired, "neither man woman or child should be left alive in the fort." Allen, by his own account, offered to "sacrifice the whole garrison."

Arnold took a more moderate tone, demanding surrender "in a genteel manner." But of course Feltham could not surrender the fort, because he was not the commanding officer. When the Green Mountain Boys and Brown and Easton's Massachusetts men realized this, they were ready to break in Delaplace's door, but Benedict Arnold prevented them from doing so.

Soon Captain Delaplace, now fully dressed, appeared on the landing. Benedict Arnold asked Delaplace "to deliver up his arms, and he might expect to be treated like a gentleman." Delaplace clearly had no choice, and he surrendered Fort Ticonderoga.

Feltham was placed under guard in Delaplace's room, and Delaplace was escorted down the stairs and onto the parade ground, presumably to order his men to surrender. In any event, the rank and file were not much inclined to fight. A number of the soldiers were apparently taken while still in bed after the attackers beat down the doors of the barracks. Soon the entire garrison was paraded without arms before the victorious Americans.

With Fort Ticonderoga in American hands, the question became what to do next. Beyond a vague idea that cannon should be sent to Boston, neither the Massachusetts Committee nor the Connecticut group had given any firm orders concerning what steps should be taken after the fort was captured.

For the Green Mountain Boys, though, the next step was obvious. It was time to celebrate.

CHAPTER **5** *To the Victors*

BEFORE THE CELEBRATIONS could begin in earnest, a few things required attention, foremost among them making certain that Ticonderoga was secure. For the next few weeks, the specter of the British retaking the fort would haunt Ticonderoga's new masters, though in fact, given Carleton's less than aggressive nature and dearth of troops, their position was not as precarious as they thought.

The British troops were mustered without arms on the parade ground, their muskets locked in a single room with a heavy guard. Soon afterward, and with exquisitely bad timing, the unfortunate Lieutenant Wadman, for whom Lieutenant Feltham had been waiting twelve days, arrived on the scene and was made prisoner.

Around ninety of Allen and Arnold's men were still waiting on the other side of the lake, and they were transported to Ticonderoga as quickly as possible. Captain Seth Warner was one of the men who had missed the action. Once Warner arrived at the fort, the huge woodsman was dispatched with forty-five men to capture Crown Point, but that order was then "Countermanded till the Arrival of more men . . . ," and Warner was called back before he had gotten far.

By noon all of the men who had gathered at Shoreham had crossed the lake to the fort, and the pillaging began. Feltham reported that the men came "to join in the plunder which was most rigidly perform'd as to liquors, provisions, &c whether belonging to his majesty or private property." Ethan Allen would later write that the "conquerors . . . tossed about the flowing bowl."

Arnold the disciplinarian was aghast at the behavior of the Green Mountain Boys. On the march to Cambridge with the Governor's Foot Guard, Arnold and all of his officers and men had signed articles agreeing to "conduct themselves decently and inoffensively," promising to avoid "Drunkenness, gaming, profanity and every vice." Such was Arnold's vision of military conduct. It was not a vision shared by the Green Mountain Boys.

Express couriers were sent out from Ticonderoga to Massachusetts and Connecticut with word of the capture. Arnold sent word to the Massachusetts Congress, explaining, "There is here at present near one hundred men who are in the greatest confusion and anarchy; destroying and plundering private property, committing every act of enormity and paying no attention to the public service. . . . Colonel Allen is the proper person to head his wild people but entirely unacquainted with military service."

Once again, Arnold tried to assert his authority as the only "legally authorized" commander at Ticonderoga, attempting to "forbid the soldiers plundering and destroying private property." Once again, the Green Mountain Boys would have none of it. According to Mott, who had missed the capture but arrived at Ticonderoga later that morning, the troops "declared they would go right home, for they would not be commanded by Arnold." (Arnold reported, "The soldiers threatening to leave the garrison on the least affront.")

Arnold still believed that he and Allen were issuing orders jointly, but he would soon be disabused of that notion. There ensued "a great quarrel with Col. Arnold, who should command the Fort . . . ," according to Elisha Phelps, Noah's brother. Stubborn as he was, Arnold displayed great physical courage while insisting on his right to issue orders. The furious Green Mountain Boys threatened his life, but still the Massachusetts colonel insisted that the command was rightfully his.

The question of legal command was settled, after a fashion, when Edward Mott reconstituted the council of war that had been formed in Castleton. The council gave Colonel Ethan Allen written orders, saying, "Whereas, agreeable to the power and authority to us given by the Colony of Connecticut [which was dubious at best] we have appointed you to take the command of a party of men, and reduce and take possession of the Garrison at Ticonderoga." Allen was ordered to "keep the command and possession of the same" until he received further orders from the colony of Connecticut or the Continental

Congress, the first time the notion of congressional control had been introduced.

Questionable though the committee's authority to issue such an order was, it was enough for the men at Ticonderoga. Now, even the pretense of authority that Arnold had enjoyed was gone. "The power is now taken out of my hands and I am not consulted, nor have I a voice in any matter," Arnold wrote to the men who had sent him to Ticonderoga. "There is not the least regularity among the troops, but everything is governed by whim and caprice."

Though they had dismissed Arnold, Mott's council did seem to recognize that the Massachusetts Committee of Safety exercised some authority over events at Ticonderoga. They wrote to the committee explaining Connecticut's part in the taking of Ticonderoga, and complaining that Arnold, though "not having enlisted one Man," still "refuses to give up his Command, which causes much Difficulty."

Despite the "Difficulty," further steps were taken to shore up the Americans' hold on Lake Champlain. Seth Warner and his men once again set out for Crown Point by boat, but headwinds forced them back to Ticonderoga. A day or so later they managed to reach Crown Point, where the garrison of one sergeant, eight privates, and ten women and children surrendered without a fight. One of the privates deserted to the Americans, and the rest were removed as prisoners of war to Ticonderoga.

The garrison of the 26th Regiment of Foot, after surrendering Ticonderoga, would not spend another night at that post. The day of the fort's capture, Allen appointed Epaphras Bull to escort the rank-and-file soldiers to Hartford. That evening the prisoners, save for the fort's baker, John McDonald, and another private who joined the American cause, were marched three miles to the landing at the foot of Lake George. Though Feltham requested that he accompany the men, no officers were allowed to go, presumably to deprive the enlisted men of leadership.

John Brown also left Ticonderoga at that time (Bull noted in his journal that "Esqr. Brown is Determin'd to go with me"). Brown understood that the one who reported the news of the capture to the Continental Congress would glean for himself a good part of the glory.

The officers—Delaplace with his wife and children, Feltham, and the unfortunate Wadman—were sent to Skenesborough, which had been captured by Captain Herrick and the men sent from Castleton and was now under the control of Elisha Phelps. There they joined Andrew Philip Skene, his two sisters, and his aunt, who had also been taken prisoner, along with a Mr. Brook, a Skene family employee, who was considered by Elisha Phelps to be "a bigger enemy to his country [America] than Major Skene."

From Skenesborough Delaplace, Feltham, and Wadman were sent to Hartford, where they repeatedly requested that the government of Connecticut define their status. Soon after, the Skene family was released and allowed to return to Skenesborough or to Quebec, but the officers would remain prisoners of war for the next year at least.

Mission Creep

The original instructions from the Hartford committee and the Massachusetts Committee of Safety had involved no more than capturing Ticonderoga and sending the fort's cannons to Cambridge. Even before the fort was taken, the mission had been expanded by its participants to include capturing Skenesborough. Now, with Ticonderoga, Crown Point, and Skenesborough in American hands, patriot ambitions spread rapidly in every direction.

When Epaphras Bull arrived with his prisoners at the head of Lake George, he found that the fort there, Fort George, had been taken by Bernard Romans (whom Mott had earlier described as "a trouble to us"). The entire water route from Crown Point south to New York City was now in colonial hands, and the Americans were beginning to look north.

It was broadly understood that future possession of Crown Point and Ticonderoga depended upon controlling Lake Champlain; if the lake could be used by the enemy to transport troops, the fortifications would not stand. The most powerful force on the lake at that time was a British sloop mounting six guns, which Benedict Arnold had mistakenly believed would be found at Ticonderoga. In fact, the sloop sailed out of St. John's on the Richelieu River, where a small British garrison manned an old French fortification. American attention soon turned in that direction.

On the day after Ticonderoga was taken, Mott's council of war mentioned in its letter to the Massachusetts Committee that they were "still raising supplies for the purpose of . . . taking the Armed Sloop." Ethan Allen also had his sights set on the sloop.

Benedict Arnold, stripped of any authority, spent the next four days after the capture of Ticonderoga "As a private Person, often Insulted by him [Allen] and his Officers." The Green Mountain Boys continued to tear the place apart in their extended drunken celebration, and they were not happy to have the somber Arnold stomping about and interfering with their fun. Not only did they threaten Arnold's life, they actually shot at him (but missed) on two occasions, suggesting that their drunkenness might have done him some good.

Nevertheless Arnold, naturally stubborn and certain that he was in the right, refused to yield. Although he felt that it was his "duty to remain here against all opposition until I have further orders . . . ," he did request that the government in Massachusetts replace him so that "a proper person might be appointed in my room." It was a request that Arnold would make often during his military career. He could not tolerate the idea of command without the certain knowledge of his superiors' confidence in him.

Arnold did not waste his time as a "private Person," however. He made as careful an inspection as he could, finding that the fort was indeed "in a most ruinous condition and not worth repairing." So bad was its condition that Arnold could not count all the cannon, because "many of them are buried in the ruins." More big guns were at the edge of the lake, but with the lake level high from spring runoff, the cannons were under water.

The chaos at Ticonderoga prevented Arnold from a more detailed inventory, beyond observing that "there are many cannon, shells, Mortars &C which may be very serviceable in our Army in Cambridge." As for transporting the guns to Cambridge, Arnold had neither the means nor the men, and Allen seemed to have forgotten about that part of the mission altogether.

Like others, Arnold was thinking about the sloop that was cruising the lake somewhere to the north of them. Initially he was helpless to do anything about it, but as the days passed the balance of power began to shift. Fifty of the men whom Arnold had recruited in Massachusetts arrived at the fort, led by Arnold's militia captains, Eleazer Oswald and Jonathan Brown (not to be confused with Pittsfield attorney John Brown). Arnold sent them to Skenesborough to take possession of the schooner that had belonged to Philip Skene but was now in American hands.

By May 14, the schooner, rechristened *Liberty*, arrived at Ticonderoga with Oswald, Brown, and Arnold's men on board. Another fifty or so of Arnold's recruits arrived at the same time, making about a hundred troops who recognized him as their commander. Arnold and Bernard Romans established contact and began making arrangements to transport serviceable cannon to Albany.

Further, the Green Mountain Boys started to melt away. They had not signed up for a long-term enlistment, and with the fun over and spring planting to be done, they began to return to their farms. Soon Arnold could report, "Allen's party is decreasing & the Dispute between us subsiding."

"Masters of the Lake"

The first use the Americans made of Fort Ticonderoga's ordnance was to arm the schooner *Liberty* with "4 Carriage & 6 Swivil guns" in preparation for taking the sloop. Ethan Allen, who was no sailor, wrote to Governor Trumbull in Connecticut that he expected it to take ten days for the schooner to be "rigged maned and armed" so that he—Allen—could "make an Attack on the armed Sloop of George the Third." Meanwhile, Arnold, who was a sailor, wrote to the Massachusetts Committee of Safety that he intended "setting out in her [the *Liberty*] directly . . . to take Possession of the Sloop."

In this matter Arnold prevailed, an indication of the extent to which, four days after being sidelined, he had superseded Allen as military commander at Ticonderoga. On May 15, the day after the *Liberty* arrived at Ticonderoga, she was under way again with Arnold, Oswald, and thirty men aboard and a bateau in company. Headwinds prevented them from getting any farther than Crown Point, about eighteen miles down the lake from Ticonderoga, where they anchored for the night.

The next day the winds continued northerly, but Arnold was too impatient to wait. He left the schooner under the command of Captain Sloan, with Oswald in command of the troops, and set out in the boats with around twenty men, intending, if need be, to row the 110 miles to St. John's.

The *Liberty* soon got under way as well, beating north against the wind. Around noon the crew spied a boat bound up the lake, and sent off the *Liberty*'s coxswain to bring it in. The boat, it turned out, was the post boat from Montreal bound for points south. On board was an ensign of the 26th Regiment of Foot named Moland, with correspondence from Guy Carleton destined for General Gage in Boston.

The letters turned out to be of great interest to the Americans. In particular, an official list of troops, known as a *return*, written from Montreal revealed that there were only 717 British troops in Canada, of the 7th and 26th regiments, seventy of whom, unbeknown to Carleton, the Americans had already captured. Now the patriot forces knew just how weakly defended Canada was.

About a month later, Ensign Moland would join Lieutenant Feltham as a prisoner of war in Hartford.

Liberty anchored for the night at Split Rock, less than twenty-five miles north of Crown Point. The next day, May 17, the wind came around from the south, blowing "a fair gale," and *Liberty* ran down the lake, overhauling Arnold's boat. Arnold and his men came back aboard the schooner, and it continued north, towing the bateau astern. By eight that evening the men were within thirty miles of St. John's when the wind died, and *Liberty* again came to anchor.

But Arnold was not about to wait. He and Oswald and thirty-five men armed and manned the bateau and the *Liberty*'s boat and rowed through the night, arriving at St. John's at sunrise, around six in the morning. They slipped into a small creek, then sent one man ahead to determine whether the garrison was alert to their coming. Tormented by "numberless swarms of gnats and muskitoes," Arnold and his men sat crammed together in their boats, swatting miserably at the remorseless bugs and awaiting word from their scout.

Finally returning, the scout reported that the garrison had received word of the taking of Ticonderoga and Crown Point but was unaware of the armed men just half a mile away. "We directly pushed for the shore," Oswald wrote, "and landed at about sixty rods distant from the barracks."

The garrison, consisting of a sergeant and twelve men, was not taken completely by surprise; they were under arms when the Americans landed. But seeing such an overwhelming force (almost three to one) "marching up in their faces," they dropped their muskets and fled to their barracks, then gave themselves up.

The sloop, the *Betsey*, "of about 70 ton with 2 brass 6 pounders & 7 men," was anchored in the river. It, too, was taken with no resistance.

The Americans' hold on St. John's was precarious. The captain of the garrison, on hearing of the trouble at Ticonderoga, had opted to personally race off to Montreal to gather troops to retake the fort, and was "hourly expected with a large Detachment." There was also a garrison at Chambly, twelve miles down the Richelieu River from St. John's, which consisted of a captain and forty men, and they, too, were reportedly on their way to St. John's. Arnold later wrote, "it seemed to be a mere interposition of Providence that we arrived in so fortunate an Hour."

Arnold decided not to press his luck. The Americans loaded on board the sloop those stores that they thought worth taking, including fourteen stand of arms, along with their fourteen prisoners. There were nine large bateaux at the place, and four of these, along with their own boats, were taken in tow. The five others, "being Out of repair," were destroyed.

While at St. John's, Arnold was approached by a man named Moses Hazen, who had his home nearby. Though Arnold did not know it, Hazen was a former British army officer. Always eager to demonstrate his legitimacy, Arnold explained to Hazen that he was operating under a commission from Massachusetts and told him about the taking of Ticonderoga and Crown Point, the first Hazen had heard of it. It was a brief, chance meeting, but in the years to follow, the lives and careers of Hazen and Arnold would become intricately entwined.

Two hours after the taking of St. John's, a "fine gale arose from the north!" as Oswald enthusiastically reported. Providence did indeed seem to be smiling upon Arnold and his men. The sloop's British crew had nearly finished preparing the vessel to get under way, so the Americans needed only to weigh anchor and set sail and they were off, running up the river before a northerly wind.

Arnold set a course for Fort Ticonderoga, and around noon was surprised to encounter Ethan Allen and about ninety of his "Mad Fellows" (Arnold's description) crowded into four bateaux. They had left Crown Point soon after Arnold and rowed north, intent on joining the attack on St. John's. The mission was apparently not well thought out. Allen's men were "in a starving Condition" for want of provisions. Despite his earlier treatment at the hands of the Green Mountain Boys, Arnold supplied them with food.

The two colonels discussed Allen's plans. It was his intention to take and hold St. John's, a plan he may have come up with on the spur of the moment as the only way of outdoing Arnold, who had already taken St. John's once. To Arnold it appeared "a wild, impracticable Scheme," given the reinforcements on the march from Chambly and Montreal. What's more, it was pointless, because the Americans were now "Masters of the Lake."

Allen would not be persuaded, and after leaving Arnold he continued north. Landing about a mile upriver from St. John's, he sent scouts ahead to assess the situation. They returned with reports of a large contingent of British troops moving down from Montreal. Allen's men, too exhausted to consider fighting a superior British force, crossed the river and camped for the night on the eastern shore.

That night Allen penned a wildly optimistic letter to the "Mer-chants that are friendly to the cause of liberty in Montreal." In that correspondence he asked that they forward five hundred pounds' worth of "provisions, ammunition and spirituous liquors" to St. John's for the use of his troops, which he called "the advanced guard of the Army." The tone of the letter suggested that Allen considered St. John's as good as captured.

The next morning the Green Mountain Boys were roused from their slumber by "a discharge of Grape shot from six field pieces & a discharg of Small Arms from about 200 Regulars." The British rein-forcements had arrived to drive the Americans away. Allen described the sound of the guns as "Music . . . both terrible and Delightful," but it signaled the end of the Green Mountain Boys' attempt on St. John's. The men tumbled into their bateaux and rowed off, leaving three be-hind in their haste.

After leaving Ethan Allen, Arnold sailed his small fleet up the lake to Fort Ticonderoga, where he set about repairing the two vessels and improving their armament. He was, at that moment, in command of the only naval force on Lake Champlain, and the undisputed master of the lake.

CHAPTER *6 The Northern Theater*

WITH TICONDEROGA secured, word of the capture went out to the colonial committees involved. Because most of the men initially at the fort were Ethan Allen's, and because Allen was far more adept at self-promotion than was Benedict Arnold, it was Allen's version of the story that reached the committees first.

To be sure, Ethan Allen had no guarantee that the story would be told the way he wanted. James Easton was sent to carry word of the action to Cambridge. Easton's version, reported in the *Oracle of Liberty*, read, "The commanding Officer soon came forth; Col. Easton clapped him upon the Shoulder, told him he was his Prisoner, and demanded, IN THE NAME OF AMERICA, an instant Surrender of the Fort." This is the only account to claim that it was Easton who captured Delaplace; apparently Easton had sense enough not to promote this version too widely.

The Veritas letter, published more than a month later and believed to have been written by Arnold, was largely a refutation of Easton's account. According to Arnold, Easton was "the last man that entered the fort, and that not till the soldiers and their arms were secured, he having concealed himself in an old barrack near the redoubt, under the pretense of wiping and drying his gun."

That might have been excessively harsh. Arnold and Easton had become bitter enemies during the contentious wrangling over command before and after the attack on Ticonderoga. They would come to blows a month later.

As it happened, Captain Delaplace also saw Easton's report, and he weighed in, saying, "I cannot . . . do less than contradict the many particulars therein contained, knowing them to be totally void of truth." Perhaps, Delaplace suggested, Easton had assumed that a prisoner of war such as himself would never see the account. Delaplace went on to write, "I solemnly declare I never saw Colonel Easton at the time the fort was surprised."

Those denials, of course, came some time after Easton reported to the Massachusetts Congress. On May 17, in a letter to the Connecticut Assembly, the Massachusetts Provincial Congress recorded that they had

> received authentick intelligence that the Fort at Ticonderoga is surrendered into the hands of Colonel Ethan Allen . . . occasioned by the intrepid valour of a number of men under the command of the said Colonel Allen, Colonel Easton . . . and others . . .

Nowhere in the account of the fort's capture did the Massachusetts Congress mention the man they themselves had sent, Benedict Arnold.

Massachusetts had good reason to disavow any role in the fort's capture, however. Already coping with the burden of a siege army outside Boston, they did not care to take custody of Ticonderoga and assume the concomitant cost of the garrison's maintenance as well. In the same report, the Massachusetts Congress resolved that "The Colony of Connecticut are hereby desired to give directions relative to the garrisoning and maintaining" of Ticonderoga, "until the advice of the Continental Congress can be had at that behalf."

What Massachusetts wanted from the deal was cannons. Having received reports from Allen's men of Benedict Arnold's disruptive behavior, the Massachusetts Provincial Congress requested of Connecticut that Arnold be appointed to transport guns to Cambridge as "a means of settling any disputes which may have arisen between him and some other officers."

On May 15, word of the fort's capture reached the New York Committee in New York City. Ticonderoga was within their borders, but they wanted nothing to do with it. The committee wrote to the Continental Congress to say that as "we do not conceive ourselves authorized to give any opinions on a matter of such importance, we have thought it proper to refer it to the Congress."

As the colonies continued to pass responsibility for Ticonderoga back and forth, they were really just marking time, waiting for the newly assembled Second Continental Congress to take over. On May

18, the situation officially came to the Congress's attention with a report from John Brown detailing the capture of Ticonderoga and the larger situation in Canada. When he was done, Brown withdrew and the Congress took up the matter.

The Second Continental Congress had been in session for just eight days, and the colonies were exploding around them. Through no action of their own, the delegates found themselves confronted with a shooting war in Massachusetts and an American army seemingly sprung from the earth. The new Congress represented a group of colonies that had no unified plan or vision, and now American forces had captured three of King George's forts and had staged a military incursion into Canada to attack and plunder St. John's. Many in Congress still hoped for a peaceful reconciliation with Great Britain—a reconciliation that seemed more improbable with each fresh report.

The Continental Congress was hardly ready to take bold action. Rather than issue orders themselves, they decided to "earnestly recommend" that the colony of New York "cause the said cannon and military stores, to be removed from Ticonderoga to the south end of Lake George." They suggested that New York call on New Hampshire, Connecticut, and Massachusetts for men to guard the ordnance, and added that an exact inventory of the guns and stores should be taken "in order that they may be safely returned when the restoration of the former harmony between Great Britain and these colonies so ardently wished for by the latter shall render it prudent."

Congress had managed to come up with a plan on which Arnold and Allen could agree, and both agreed that it was a bad one. As it happened, both men were at Crown Point when the news arrived, and they detailed their objections in separate letters.

Benedict Arnold wrote to the Massachusetts Committee of Safety that he "was equally surprised and alarmed . . . that the Continental Congress had recommended the removing of all the cannon, stores, &C at Ticonderoga, to Fort George, and evacuating Ticonderoga entirely." Ticonderoga, he argued, was the "only key of this country," and giving it up would leave the "very extensive frontiers open to the ravages of the enemy" and expose to danger the five hundred families that lived north of the fort. On the same day, May 29, Arnold wrote to the Continental Congress, introducing himself as "commanding officer" of Ticonderoga and expressing the same sentiments, albeit in less emphatic language.

Ethan Allen likewise pointed out to the Congress that the settlements would be ruined by such a move, because those inhabitants, the Green Mountain Boys, had helped with the capture of the forts and "have incensed Governor Carleton and all the ministerial party in Canada against them." Unlike Arnold, Allen went on to urge an invasion of Canada, believing that this would rally the many Canadians who were friendly to the American cause. Giving himself credit for Arnold's work, he wrote, "Provided I had but five hundred men with me at St. Johns, when we took the King's sloop, I would have advanced to Montreal." But in this notion, Allen was too far ahead of the Continental Congress. The politicians in Philadelphia who were looking to see the British guns "safely returned" to their owners and harmony with England restored were in no mood to invade Canada.

The New Hampshire Assembly, with settlements along the Connecticut River that would be left vulnerable by a retreat from Ticonderoga, also expressed its concerns to Congress. The order to abandon Ticonderoga, they wrote, "has very much dampened the expectation of the people of this Colony . . . ," leaving the settlements vulnerable to "Canadians and savages . . . to ravage."

The Massachusetts Congress also felt that "maintaining a post at Ticonderoga, or Crown Point, is of the utmost importance." In a long letter to Governor Trumbull of Connecticut, the Massachusetts Congress expressed its amazement that the Continental Congress could even think of abandoning the posts. Granting the benefit of the doubt, Massachusetts professed certainty that the Continental Congress, "upon better information, and knowledge more just . . . will be fully convinced of the great impolicy of abandoning Lake Champlain."

New York, meanwhile, willfully or otherwise, failed to understand what the Continental Congress was suggesting. Writing to his brother, Governor Trumbull of Connecticut said, "I am glad to find, per our letters from New York, that their Congress do not construe the resolution of Grand Congress to intend an evacuation of Ticonderoga and Crown Point, but only a removal of such artillery, stores, &C. to Fort George and keep possession above."

In fact, New York was misconstruing the intent of Congress, which really did mean for the posts to be abandoned. But soon enough the delegates to Congress would change their minds.

The Army of the United Colonies

Throughout the month of May, the Continental Congress continued to organize and define its role with respect to the colonial governments. This process prompted a reexamination of Congress's plans for Ticonderoga, as did the pointed criticism engendered by the initial idea of removing the guns and abandoning the post.

Then, on May 31, Congress received a letter that Benedict Arnold had written eight days earlier—the first correspondence that Arnold had sent to the Congress. A man named Butterfield, one of the men whom Ethan Allen's party had abandoned when they fled St. John's, had managed to escape and make his way back to Crown Point, arriving on May 23. He reported to Arnold that there were "about 400 Regulars at St Johns . . . making all possible Preparation to Cross the Lake and Retake Crown Point and Ticonderoga."

Arnold immediately began organizing the defense of the posts under his command. He sent word to Skenesborough and Fort George ordering the men there to muster at Crown Point, and he alerted the Massachusetts Committee of Safety and the Continental Congress of the danger.

That same evening a man named Adams arrived with further intelligence from St. John's. According to Adams, there had been only 120 regulars at St. John's when Ethan Allen was fired on, and those troops had since left for Chambly. Arnold accepted this intelligence (which was in fact closer to the truth) and countermanded his order for the troops to muster at Crown Point.

But the threat, real or otherwise, of British regulars sweeping down from Canada was enough to persuade Congress that the posts on Lake

Champlain should not be abandoned. Despite the involvement of several colonies in the taking of Ticonderoga, Connecticut had become the de facto leader, and the Congress was happy for it to continue as such. After considering Arnold's letter of May 23, the Congress resolved that

> the Governor of Connecticut be requested immediately to send a strong re-enforcement to the garrisons of Crown Point and Ticonderoga; and that so many of the Cannons and other Stores be retained as may be necessary for the immediate defense of those posts.

Having agreed to retain the posts, however, the Congress wanted to curb any further enthusiasm. Because congressional actions had "nothing more in view than the defense of these Colonies," Congress resolved that "no expedition or incursion ought to be undertaken . . . against or into Canada." It further ordered that resolve to be "immediately transmitted to the Commander of the Forces at Ticonderoga." That was Arnold, but the Congress did not name him specifically, because it did not at that time know who was in charge. (Arnold's letter of May 29, in which he objected to the plan to abandon Ticonderoga and introduced himself as "commanding officer" there, had not yet arrived.) For good measure, the resolve was translated into French and sent on to Quebec.

As May turned to June, the military issues before the Continental Congress became too pressing to ignore. The army that had first assembled for the fight at Lexington and Concord had not dispersed. Rather, it continued to grow, and now held the British army under siege in Boston. Civilian leaders in Massachusetts were not comfortable hosting an army—even an American army—without government backing. "[W]e tremble," they wrote, "at having an army (although consisting of our countrymen) established here, without a civil power to provide for and control them."

The application from Massachusetts ended by requesting that the Continental Congress take over administration of the army. "As the army now collecting from different Colonies," they pointed out, "is for the general defense of the rights of America, we would beg leave to suggest to your consideration the propriety of your taking the regulation and general direction of it."

Even before receiving that request from Massachusetts, the Continental Congress was starting to take ownership of the men mustered outside Boston—and, by extension, the garrisons on Lake Champlain. On the same day that a committee was appointed to consider the Massachusetts letter, another was appointed "for the purpose of borrowing the sum of Six Thousand Pounds . . ." and to "apply the said sum of money to the purchase of Gunpowder for the use of the Continental Army."

Having accepted the idea of a "Continental Army," Congress quickly sketched the organizational details, setting the pay of officers and privates and creating a fill-in-the-blank enlistment form. A committee that included delegates George Washington and Philip Schuyler was formed to draft "Rules and regulations for the government of the Army." On June 14 they resolved to raise six companies of riflemen from Pennsylvania, Maryland, and Virginia to be sent to "join the army near Boston."

The next day, Congress made what would prove to be one of the most important decisions of the war. It resolved that "a General be appointed to command all the Continental Forces raised, or to be raised, for the defense of American liberty," then it "proceeded to the choice of General, when George Washington, Esquire, was unanimously elected." Five days later he was ordered "to the Colony of Massachusetts-Bay, to take charge of the Army of the United Colonies."

Less than two months after the spontaneous outbreak of war, the Continental Congress had taken charge of the mixed bag of militia gathered around Boston and designated it a national army. The remote outposts on Lake Champlain—Ticonderoga and Crown Point—captured on dubious authority and almost on a whim, were now considered the United Colonies' chief defense against an invasion from Canada.

CHAPTER *7* *A Change in Command*

FAR FROM THE wrangling and machinations in colonial capitals and Philadelphia, Benedict Arnold oversaw his uncertain command on Lake Champlain. Ethan Allen was still there with a handful of Green Mountain Boys, though by May 23 Arnold could report that "Col Allens men are in General gone home." Allen continued to race around the Champlain area, making grandiose plans and firing off letters, but two weeks after the taking of Ticonderoga his authority had been eclipsed by Arnold's.

Arnold approached his new command with the energy and dedication that would mark his military career on both sides of the conflict. His first priority was getting the schooner *Liberty* and the sloop *Betsey*, now renamed *Enterprise* into the best condition possible for their new role as American men-of-war. "All hands," he wrote in his memorandum book, "Employed in fixing the Sloop Schooner & putting them in the best posture of Defense." The *Enterprise* was fitted out with six carriage guns and twelve swivels, the *Liberty* with four carriage guns and eight swivels.

Arnold personally visited local sawmills to see about acquiring sawn planks for gun carriages and for rebuilding the forts' ruined barracks. He supervised the transport of extra cannon across Lake George to Fort George. He set men to work digging out guns that were buried in the rubble of the old forts, as well as "Near One Ton of Lead & Iron Ball."

As a mariner, Arnold fully appreciated the importance of naval superiority on Lake Champlain. He understood that one could not put a soldier on board a ship and call him a sailor, that real sailors were needed for the vessels. He wrote repeatedly to the colonial governments for "Gunners and Seamen to man the two Vessels, being in Great want of them at Present."

Arnold was not alone in this plea. The Continental navy would forever suffer from a shortage of experienced sailors. In every port, privateers were fitted out by wealthy owners who could offer better pay, easier discipline, less danger (privateers did not make a habit of fighting men-of-war), and the chance for a larger share in a valuable prize. The following year, Congress would try to slow the rush of sailors shipping aboard privateers by including in its instructions to privateer captains that "One Third, at the least, of your whole Company shall be Landsmen," but that did little to solve the sailor deficit.

It was even harder to entice men to serve on Lake Champlain, a wilderness outpost far from the pleasures of a seaport town, and with no chance at all of prize money. Arnold was forced to take command of the *Enterprise* personally, a distraction from his other duties. During his entire career on Lake Champlain, Arnold would feel the want of real sailors and complain bitterly about it.

Some sailors did come, in small numbers, and he set them to work "making Sails & fixing Battoes." But two small vessels and a few bateaux were not enough to maintain control over the lakes and transport troops and supplies where needed, so Arnold's thoughts turned to expanding the fleet. He sent out requests for ship carpenters, caulkers, rope of various diameters, duck canvas, sail needles and palms, and all the materiel and manpower needed to build a freshwater fleet.

Soldiers continued to arrive as well, sent by colonial governments, until Arnold's troops numbered several hundred. He organized provisions and work parties, kept close track of the barrels of pork and flour consumed, sent out scouts, and continued to update the various congresses and committees that had an interest in Ticonderoga. Troops that were not on work details, called "fatigue duty," were kept busy at military drills.

Though Arnold continued to "hope some Gentleman Will soon be appointed in my Room here who is better able to serve the Public . . . ," he must have felt a certain sense of pride and accomplishment in all he achieved in just a few weeks and with such meager resources. He had no reason to suspect that the rug was about to be pulled out from under his feet.

The Command of Fort Ti

Arnold's letter of May 29 to the Continental Congress, in which he had warned of the dangers of abandoning the fort, had also included a report of what had transpired on Lake Champlain since his arrival two and a half weeks earlier. Writing as "commanding officer here," he mentioned to the Congress that he had come to understand that "the Committee of Safety of the Massachusetts-Bay have not informed you of my appointment or instructions from them."

A more astute political operative would have sensed danger in the fact that the Continental Congress did not even know who he was. Arnold may have had a genius for soldiering and an ego that left him ever alert to insults, but he was politically naive and had little appreciation for the games required for advancement.

This, perhaps, was in part a result of his time at sea. Men accustomed to the clear-cut hierarchy of a blue-water ship are often less adept at navigating social and political shoals on shore. In particular, those who have enjoyed the absolute authority of a ship's captain—especially those who, like Arnold, have also been part owners of the vessels they commanded—have rarely grasped the importance of self-aggrandizement or currying favor for getting ahead on land.

Whereas the likes of James Easton or John Brown might run off to deliver reports to colonial assemblies or the Congress, thus making themselves known as men-on-the-scene, Arnold, to his own detriment, preferred to remain on the front lines and attend to military matters. On the very day he was relieved of command, a day when he was attending to business at Crown Point with "Carpenters Employed as Usual, People on Duty & Sealing Guns," Ethan Allen and Seth Warner were appearing before the Continental Congress, in part to advance their own causes. Arnold's preference for fighting over schmoozing would forever be a handicap to his career, and would play a big part in his eventual fall from grace.

Events in the spring of 1775 outpaced not only Benedict Arnold's political acumen but the speed of communications in the colonies as well. Arnold's letter of May 29 to Congress was moot before it was written. On May 27, responding to Massachusetts' request that Connecticut assume responsibility for the northern garrisons, Governor Trumbull wrote the Massachusetts Congress to say that he would be sending a thousand men to Ticonderoga. Trumbull's next task was to appoint a commander for those men, and there is no evidence to suggest that he considered Arnold.

Arnold probably thought that his solid work in organizing defenses and establishing naval superiority on the lake would guarantee his position should he wish to keep it. In fact, he had worked himself into perfect expendability. He was a Connecticut man who had talked the Committee of Safety in Massachusetts into his commission and orders. A stranger to Massachusetts, he had no one there to advocate for him, particularly when the Bay Colony was trying to distance itself from Ticonderoga.

Arnold's natural base of support should have been Connecticut, but Edward Mott's faction was the favored Connecticut party, and Arnold had managed to alienate most of them along with their hangers-on, proficient self-promoters such as Easton and Brown.

On May 29, the day Arnold wrote to the Continental Congress that he was the commanding officer at Ticonderoga, Trumbull picked as commander Benjamin Hinman, a fifty-five-year-old colonel with Connecticut's 13th Regiment of Horse who had solid political connections. Hinman had already served as an officer at Crown Point during the French and Indian War. Now he would be heading there again.

As Connecticut was making arrangements to get its troops to Ticonderoga, Massachusetts was taking steps to get its men out. The Massachusetts Provincial Congress created yet another committee to determine how its Committee of Safety had managed to give Arnold a commission and send him to Ticonderoga in the first place. The Committee of Safety wrote to Arnold informing him that "the Congress have taken up this matter" of Ticonderoga, and Arnold was now to report to Congress.

At the same time, the Massachusetts Provincial Congress dispatched Colonel Joseph Henshaw to Connecticut to see whether that colony would be taking over the northern posts. Henshaw was instructed, after having found out what Connecticut planned, to ride to

Ticonderoga and there meet with Arnold. If Connecticut was not sending troops, Henshaw was to tell Arnold to carry on until receipt of further orders. If Connecticut was sending men, Henshaw was to inform Arnold that it was the Massachusetts Congress's desire that he "return and Render Accounts of his expenses in that Expedition in order that he may be honorably discharged." But if Henshaw found that the General Assembly of Connecticut had made no decision at all, he was to prod them into one, then report back to Massachusetts.

Henshaw left Watertown, Massachusetts, on Sunday, May 28, and arrived in Hartford three days later. There he met with the governor and Connecticut's Council of Safety, nine men who functioned much as the Massachusetts Committee of Safety did, though the Connecticut Council was entirely subordinate to the governor. Henshaw was informed that Colonel Hinman would be marching to Ticonderoga with a thousand men, along with "artificers, and five hundred pounds of powder, provisions, &C," and that Albany was raising four companies as well. Henshaw also learned that Massachusetts was expected to keep its troops there to cooperate with those of the other colonies.

That same day, May 31, Arnold's May 23 letter warning of a possible attack by the British at St. John's reached the Continental Congress, which immediately resolved to ask Governor Trumbull to send reinforcements to the garrisons at the northern posts. In a letter dispatched to Hartford that afternoon, Congress added that Trumbull should "appoint a person in whom he can confide to command the Forces at Crown Point and Ticonderoga." Trumbull's June 9 reply to John Hancock, president of the Continental Congress, reported that, "by a wonderful coincidence of counsels," Congress's request had been "nearly complied with before the receipt of it."

Meanwhile, having learned Connecticut's intentions, Henshaw decided to forgo traveling on to Ticonderoga and instead return to Massachusetts to see what further action the Provincial Congress might wish to take. Before leaving Hartford, he wrote a note to Arnold informing him that Hinman would be taking command of Ticonderoga, and he was to "continue with Col. Allen to put the place in the best posture for defense."

Henshaw did not specify that Arnold was to be a subordinate of Hinman. Indeed, there seemed to have been little discussion of what Arnold's role would be. Trumbull certainly was aware of the part that Arnold was playing and gave him more apparent respect than Massachusetts did. At one point Trumbull sent off two hundred pounds cash and four hundred pounds of gunpowder "in consequence of our last letters from Colonel Arnold." In writing to the Massachusetts Congress, Trumbull did not say that Hinman would be in overall command of the region, only that he would "take command of our Troops on those stations."

Thus Arnold received no indication that Hinman would supersede him. Because Arnold had made his base at Crown Point, he believed that a new command at Ticonderoga would not alter his own command status. He continued to write to Governor Trumbull with reports from Crown Point, and Trumbull continued to respond as if nothing had changed.

The Provincial Congress of Massachusetts did not help matters. When it learned from Henshaw that Connecticut expected the Congress to maintain its regiment on Lake Champlain, which meant that it still needed Arnold, it finally found some good words for its Connecticut-born colonel. Writing to Arnold on June 1, the Massachusetts Congress assured him that it had "the greatest confidence in your fidelity, knowledge, courage and good conduct," and asked that he "dismiss the thoughts of quitting your important command at Ticonderoga, Crown Point, Lake Champlain, &C." It went on to say that Arnold should continue his command "over the forces raised by this Colony" until New York or Connecticut should take over.

In that same letter, it informed Arnold that a thousand men were marching from Connecticut to "re-enforce the Army now at Crown Point, Ticonderoga, &C." The Congress gave no hint that the commander of those forces was to be Arnold's superior. The Congress also saved itself some money by giving Arnold permission to spend 160 pounds that he had found aboard the British sloop, specie that Arnold had not touched because he considered it the property of the sloop's former captain.

Arnold didn't realize that Massachusetts was no longer exercising control over the northern posts, and it was only reasonable that he should interpret those words to mean that he was still in overall command.

"He would not be second . . ."

By the middle of June, the frontier outposts of Ticonderoga and Crown Point were bustling. An account of stores received at Albany and sent on to Fort George and points north included hundreds of barrels of pork, flour, peas, and rice. The report stated that "twenty wagons are constantly employed" moving stores from Albany to Fort George, with ten to twelve more to be added.

Hinman's men were filtering into Ticonderoga, and by June 15 they were mostly there. Arnold, meanwhile, had carried on relentlessly. Earlier in the month he had sailed his squadron north to within twenty miles of St. John's. There he sent out sixty men in three bateaux to "Get all possible Intelligence," while the men who remained behind got to work "Baking Bread getting Timber for Oars." After the scouts discovered the number of regulars at St. John's— around four hundred—and were driven off by musket fire, the squadron returned up the lake.

Arriving at Crown Point on June 10, Arnold encountered a problem that he might have thought he was done with. Ethan Allen, James Easton, Samuel Elmore, and others were at the fort and had, Arnold wrote, "Called a Counsell of their Officers & others not Belonging to My Regt," apparently in the hope of once again taking command. Arnold sent ashore a note assuring Allen and the others that he would not "Suffer, any Illegal Councells Meetings, &C as they Tended to raise a mutiny."

Allen backed down for the same reason that Arnold had once yielded to him—he did not have the men to enforce his command. The next morning, Arnold, not taking any chances, doubled the guard "to prevent any Mutiny or Disorder." Allen and his cohorts made ready to abandon Crown Point to Arnold, but in a last act of defiance they attempted to leave "without showing their Pass."

Allen's boat was brought to and the men came ashore. Arnold, while speaking privately to Elmore, was interrupted by James Easton, who insulted him. For Arnold it was the last straw. He knew that Easton had been defaming him behind his back, and now the man had the temerity to insult him in front of another officer. Arnold "took the Liberty of Breaking his head," then insisted that Easton draw his sword and settle the matter honorably. Easton refused, though he had "a hanger on his side & Cases of Loaded Pistols in his Pocket."

Because Easton would not fight like a gentleman, Arnold "kicked him very heartily" to "the great satisfaction of a number of gentlemen present." It must have been enormously satisfying to Benedict Arnold, and perhaps the memory still gave him some comfort when, a week and a half later, Easton got the last laugh.

This period marked the high point of Arnold's command on Lake Champlain, though, in reality, he was not in command at all and simply did not yet know it. He was feeling confident enough on June 13 to draft a long letter to the Continental Congress outlining intelligence he had received from Montreal that the region's Indian tribes had agreed not to help the British troops. He went on to point out how few troops Carleton had, just 550 effectives spread out over more than half a dozen posts. "If the honorable Congress should think proper to take possession of Montreal and Quebec," he wrote, "I am positive two thousand men might easily effect it."

Arnold proposed a detailed plan for the invasion. Realizing that it would be necessary to "give satisfaction to the different Colonies," he suggested that the invading army be made up of forces from New York and Connecticut as well as his own five hundred men. Aware by then of Hinman's being ordered to Ticonderoga, Arnold suggested that "say one thousand men" from Hinman's regiment be added to the invasion force, which would have left Hinman to defend Ticonderoga single-handedly. Arnold also specified that the army should include "no Green Mountain Boys."

After laying out the plan, Arnold (like Allen before him) suggested that "if no other person appears who will undertake to carry the plan into execution, I will undertake it . . . without loss of time."

On June 17, Arnold got his first hint of trouble. While the men at Crown Point were busy "Getting Timber Fixing Barracks, Making Oars, & Digging," Colonel Hinman arrived from Ticonderoga to inform Arnold that he, Hinman, was now in command of Crown Point. But Hinman had no written orders stating that specifically, and Arnold refused to give up command. Happily, Benjamin Hinman was not as volatile or prickly as Arnold, or the meeting might have become an ugly confrontation. Instead, Hinman returned to Ticonderoga, and Arnold continued on.

Worse was coming. The Massachusetts Congress, upon hearing that Hinman had been sent to Ticonderoga, became concerned that Arnold might still consider himself in command. On June 14 the Congress appointed a three-man committee to proceed to Crown Point and Ticonderoga with a wide mandate, "fully empowered to do every thing on behalf of this Colony for the effectual securing and maintaining these posts." Primarily, they were to determine "in what manner the said Colonel Arnold has executed his said commission and instructions."

It could only appear supremely insulting to Arnold that the Massachusetts Congress should, at that late date and after all that he had done, decide it was time to become "fully acquainted with the spirit, capacity, and conduct of the said Arnold." No politically connected Massachusetts native would have been subjected to such an interrogation, but Arnold was not that. Massachusetts wanted him subservient to Hinman or gone.

On Friday, June 23, the committee of three arrived at Crown Point, finding "the said Arnold claiming the command of said sloop and a schooner," it reported to the Massachusetts Congress, "and also all the posts and fortresses at the south end of Lake Champlain and Lake George." The committee informed Arnold of its mission, and Arnold, incredulous, asked to see a copy of the men's orders, which they provided. Arnold was stunned by what he read. The Massachusetts Congress, which just days before had begged him not to resign his command, now told him that he could continue on "under the command of such chief officer as is or shall be appointed by the Governor of Connecticut . . . ," but only if this committee, which knew nothing about him or the situation on the ground there, found his performance satisfactory. To add to the insult, Hinman's commission was of a more recent date than Arnold's, making Hinman technically junior.

Arnold was understandably furious. He "seemed greatly disconcerted . . . ," the delegation reported, "and declared he would not be second in command to any person whomsoever." With that, Arnold went off to consider his next move.

Calculated or not, the orders of the Massachusetts Congress were perfectly tailored to enrage Arnold. There was nothing more odious to him than occupying a position for which he was not considered competent. In a scathing letter to the committee, Arnold wrote that "it appears to me very extraordinary that the Congress should first appoint an officer and afterwards, when he has executed his commission, to appoint a Committee to examine if he was fit for his post."

The committee's instructions led Arnold to believe that the fitness of the men who served under him would also be judged, and those found unfit would be dismissed, "lose their former time and service, and [be] reduced to the distress of begging their bread until they can get home to their friends." Arnold, who cared very much for the men under his command, considered this intolerable.

To top it all, the Massachusetts Congress had not sent him the money they had promised to discharge the debts he had accrued to maintain his troops. This left him a choice of leaving Crown Point with money still owed—a "dishonor" by his lights—or discharging those debts with his own money, though he had already advanced for the cause a hundred pounds from his personal funds.

Benedict Arnold did not have to think long about his course of action. On June 24 he submitted to the committee a letter resigning his commission, "not being Able to hold it any longer with honor." He wrote to Captain Herrick, commanding Arnold's men at Ticonderoga, that he should give up the command to Hinman, and told his men at Crown Point that they were disbanded.

With Arnold's resignation, another officer was needed to command the Massachusetts troops, so the committee chose the man who had made himself so conspicuous to the Massachusetts Congress and who was still hanging around Ticonderoga—James Easton. That done, the committee climbed into a boat and left Crown Point.

Arnold's concern that his men would not be paid the money owed them soon spread among the men themselves. Arnold wrote in his memorandum book that he "Applied to the Committee of the Mass. Bay for Cash to Pay of the Regiment, which they Refused." The men were not happy, and "some of them became dissatisfied and mutinous," the committee reported.

At noon, Arnold went on board the *Enterprise* to eat dinner. While he dined in the great cabin, a band of armed men formerly under his command stormed aboard and confined him below, while others took a boat and went after the committee. Arnold complained to the men "of the Insult Offered me . . . ," but the men assured him that they bore him "no Personal Ill will, but were Determined to stop the Committee & oblige them to Pay of the Regiment."

That they managed to do. The committee delivered to Easton 280 pounds for paying the men who had engaged under him, and the "mutiny" dissolved.

The quick resolution of the issue—and the fact that Arnold was a victim of the uprising, not an instigator—did not stop his detractors from using it against him. Edward Mott, who was at Ticonderoga at the time, later wrote to Trumbull accusing Arnold of having led the mutiny, and even charging him with firing swivel guns at the committee and threatening to deliver the sloop and the schooner to the regulars at St. John's.

Stripped of his command and without a commission, Arnold spent a few days at Crown Point settling his affairs and perhaps hoping for good news from some quarter. None came, and on July 4, 1775, Benedict Arnold left the Lake Champlain region. It would be nearly a year before he returned to engage once again in a lopsided fight for control of the lake, but by then the advantage would be entirely on the side of the British.

CHAPTER *8 Command of the Northern Department*

FOUR DAYS after appointing George Washington commander in chief of the Continental army, the Congress chose Philip Schuyler, Esquire, as one of the army's four major generals. The other three were Artemas Ward, Charles Lee, and Israel Putnam.

At the time, Schuyler was serving in the Congress as one of the delegates from New York. He was forty-one years old, born and raised in Albany, fourth-generation New York Dutch aristocracy. His father had died when he was eight, and ten years later, when Philip had come into his majority, he had waived his right to primogeniture so that his two brothers and sister might have a share of the large Schuyler estate.

While in his early twenties, Schuyler had served with distinction as captain of a company of colonial troops during the French and Indian War. Early in the war he had seen action at Crown Point and Lake George, and later served as a deputy commissary under General Bradstreet. Much of his later business dealings involved selling supplies to the army.

When the Continental Congress asked the New York Provincial Assembly to nominate a major general, the Assembly was unanimous in its choice of Schuyler. Listing such requirements as "courage, prudence, readiness in expedients," the Congress went on to assert that a general should have "an extensive acquaintance with the sciences, particularly the various branches of mathematical knowledge." To the Congress, Schuyler was the very model of a modern major general.

Soon after accepting his commission, Schuyler began advising the Continental Congress on the best ways to organize procurement and distribution of supplies. "On this head I can speak with confidence," he wrote, "because I have had long experience."

Rich, handsome, well liked, well respected, and notoriously gracious, father of two lovely daughters, Schuyler had it all, save for good health. As a young man he had been chronically ill, suffering apparently from a type of rheumatism, and age had not improved things. On hearing of Schuyler's appointment, a friend wrote to tell him that his country placed "the greatest Confidence" in his abilities, then went on to say, "I wish I could say so much for your Constitution, and that it may be equal to the arduous Task you have to engage in is my sincere prayer." Health issues would plague Schuyler all his life and seriously curtail his military service.

Schuyler was no fire-breathing radical in the mold of John or Samuel Adams. His patriotism was subdued enough that he was accused by some (behind his back) of being a closet Tory. But he was certainly not that, and indeed he might have seemed like a radical when set against the politically conservative leaders of the colony of New York.

Vast Confusion

On June 23, Philip Schuyler rode out of Philadelphia in the company of Washington, Charles Lee, and Thomas Mifflin. They arrived in New York City on the same day that New York's Loyalist royal governor, William Tryon, returned from England, creating an awkward social dilemma for New York's elite, who felt obligated to call on both parties.

The next day Washington gave Schuyler his orders. "You are to take upon you command of all the Troops destined for the New York Department," he wrote, "and see that the orders of the Continental Congress are carried into execution." This, at last, would settle the confused question of command on the lakes. Schuyler was also to "keep a watchful eye on Governor Tryon . . ." and prevent him from doing anything harmful to the American cause, even if that meant arresting him.

Washington left New York for Cambridge the next day, while Schuyler remained in the city, organizing supplies to be sent north. Even before he arrived at the lakes, Schuyler understood that boatbuilding would be a priority. In a request to the New York Provincial

Congress for supplies, he included "1 ton of oakum: 30 barrels of pitch . . . 10 bolts of sailcloth: 1500 oars."

Schuyler was met in New York by two regiments from Connecticut, one commanded by Colonel David Waterbury, the other by Brigadier General David Wooster. Wooster, the man who had tried to refuse Benedict Arnold the keys to the New Haven armory, was a crotchety sixty-five-year-old New Haven merchant, a sometime ally and sometime adversary of Arnold.

On June 27 the Continental Congress issued more specific orders for Schuyler. He was "to repair, as soon as conveniently he can, to the posts of Ticonderoga and Crown Point, to examine into the state thereof, and of the Troops now stationed there . . . into the state also of the Sloop and other navigation on the Lakes." Not yet aware that the Massachusetts Committee had cut Benedict Arnold off at the knees, Congress also told Schuyler he was to "confer with Colonel Hinman and Colonel Arnold."

Schuyler departed New York by boat. When he arrived in Albany on July 9, he was greeted in a manner befitting a hometown hero. Albany's political and civic leaders met him at the dock, and he was escorted by the City Troops of Horse to city hall, where he heard a speech congratulating him on his appointment. This being Albany, however—not Boston—the speech placed even greater emphasis on decrying the need to take up arms against Britain.

The newly minted major general replied in kind, promising to "most cheerfully return my sword to the scabbard . . . whenever my constituents shall direct, or whenever a happy reconciliation with the Parent State shall take place." Then the assembled crowd retired to a local tavern called, ironically, the King's Arms.

It would be some time before Schuyler sheathed his sword. In Albany he began getting a sense for what he was up against. He wrote to the Continental Congress:

> The unhappy controversy which has subsisted between the officers at Ticonderoga, relative to the command, has, I am informed, thrown everything into vast confusion. Troops have been dismissed, others refuse to serve, if this or that man commands. The sloop is without ei-

ther captain or pilot, both of which are dismissed or come away; I shall hurry up there much sooner than the necessary preparations here would otherwise permit, that I may attempt to introduce some kind of order and discipline.

The situation with supplies, he found, was no better. A return from Hinman informed him that there were only 41 barrels of flour among the three forts, though 477 barrels had been sent, amounting to "about ninety-five thousand, four hundred rations." The same return indicated that the troops had apparently consumed a startling sixty-five thousand rations of pork. Schuyler concluded that "a very considerable waste or embezzlement has taken place."

Colonel Benjamin Hinman was in over his head. In fact, he had received no orders other than to reinforce the garrison. In a postscript to his letter to Schuyler, he wrote, "I await, Sir, with impatience for your arrival, as I find myself very unable to steer in this stormy situation." Among Hinman's pressing concerns were "a constant cry for rum, and want of molasses for beer."

While still at Albany, Schuyler received an unexpected guest, Benedict Arnold, who had just given up the command at Crown Point and was on his way home to New Haven. The two men had never met and had little in common, but they got on well, helped no doubt by Schuyler's courteous manner and a mutual interest in the Champlain region. Schuyler certainly knew something of Arnold; as a Continental congressman, he had no doubt followed Arnold's activities closely. Now, as general of the Northern Department, Schuyler was eager to hear about the tactical situation at Ticonderoga, and Arnold was happy to discuss it.

Schuyler helped to assuage Arnold's hurt ego by assuring him that the Continental Congress was pleased with the manner in which he had conducted himself on Lake Champlain. Schuyler was impressed enough by Arnold that he even offered to use his considerable influence to help Arnold procure "an agreeable post in the army."

At Schuyler's request, Arnold drafted a report on the state of the forts for the Congress. Not surprisingly, given his recent ouster from command, Arnold's report was fairly pessimistic, complaining, among other things, of a "great want of discipline and regularity among the troops." Arnold added, "On the other hand, the enemy at St. Johns [is] indefatigable in fortifying, and collecting timber (supposed) for building a vessel."

Schuyler, like Arnold, appreciated the importance of naval superiority on the lake, and felt that the lack of a captain for the sloop was a particularly serious shortcoming. He wrote to the New York Congress to send up "a person fit to confer such an important command upon."

"Not one earthly thing has been done . . ."

Schuyler finally reached Ticonderoga on July 18, and he was not impressed. Arriving at the north end of Lake George around ten o'clock that night, he found a single sentinel on duty at the small blockhouse at the head of the Carrying Place. The sentry, upon being informed that the major general was in the boat, hurried off to wake the three-man guard, but he had no luck. Schuyler, walking unchallenged into the stockade, came upon another guard "in the soundest sleep."

"With a pen-knife only I could have cut off both guards, and then have set fire to the blockhouse . . . ," Schuyler informed Washington.

The only improvements to the works, Schuyler found, had been made by Arnold, and that work had stopped when Arnold left. "At Crown Point an intrenchment was begun to shelter the troops, before my arrival," Schuyler wrote to Congress, "but nothing has been done at this place [Ticonderoga] and we are in a perfectly defenseless state."

Illness, too, was starting to appear. The men had no tents and were crowded together, wrote Schuyler, "in vile barracks, which, with the natural inattention of the soldiery to cleanliness, has already been productive of disease, and numbers are rendered daily unfit for duty."

A Canadian who arrived from the north confirmed Arnold's intelligence that the British at St. John's were preparing timber for building a vessel. Schuyler was eager to stop them "by going to St. John's with a respectable body . . . to prevent the regular Troops from getting a naval strength."

Unfortunately, Schuyler found that "not one earthly thing has been done here to enable me to move hence." Even if the troops had been well armed and equipped, which they were not, there were no boats to transport them down the lake, and none of the boatbuilding supplies that Schuyler had ordered—oakum, pitch, nails, and sundry other necessities—had arrived. With nothing else for his carpenters to do, Schuyler set them to repairing the local sawmills and "procuring timber and planks for the boats" against the day when they would have the means to turn the planks into bateaux.

Knowing that his former neighbor Philip Skene had established a number of facilities at Skenesborough, Schuyler dispatched men to determine what state they were in. "I arrived the 22 and find the Saw mill Repaired in part and expect to get it fit to Run this week," Paul Yeats reported. Skene's ironworks as well were found nearly operational.

Schuyler had almost three thousand men under his command, including Wooster's and Waterbury's regiments, which Congress had ordered to remain outside New York City for the time being. Congress ordered that "a body of troops, not exceeding five thousand, be kept up in the New York Department." That number of men, equipped and trained, would be some time in coming, but Schuyler was eager to move on St. John's with the troops he had on hand.

He correctly viewed the St. John's fortification, situated above the falls of the Richelieu River, as the most logical staging area for a British push up the lake. Scouts on board the schooner *Liberty*, sent down the lake, discovered that the garrison had only about 450 regulars, but they were fortifying and preparing to mount cannon. The longer they had to dig in, the harder they would be to dislodge.

Schuyler bought or leased every boat available, but that amounted to transport for only about five hundred men. By late July he was still "chagrined that I have not yet any of the stores here (nor do I learn that they are arrived at Albany) for building craft to carry me across this lake."

Boatbuilding would occupy much of Schuyler's attention for the next year and more. It commenced during the last week of July 1775 with construction of a large open boat called a gondola, not unlike the ones that would be built the following year. On July 31, Schuyler wrote to Congress that "I have a boat on stocks, sixty feet in length, which I hope to finish this day week. I suppose she will carry between two and three hundred men. Another of the same size is to be put up today, so that I hope soon to have vessels enough to move on."

If New York was not forthcoming with boatbuilding supplies, the Provincial Congress did at least send a captain for the sloop *Enterprise*—Captain James Smith, who took command on August 1. On August 2 the commodore (as he referred to himself) declared the vessel "to be of very little use to the service," because in her "present state, the vessel might be easily taken by four batteaus, with one swivel gun and ten men armed in each."

It is hard to imagine what Smith thought might be done to make the sloop safer from such an attack—a difficult thing for any small vessel to defend against—but he apparently did suggest some alterations to Schuyler. But all of Schuyler's carpenters were building boats, and he did not want to pull them from that work, so the *Enterprise* went unaltered.

At the same time, Schuyler received more detailed intelligence regarding St. John's from a Canadian, John Duguid, who had been employed as a cooper at the garrison and "thought it his duty" to report what he'd seen. Duguid described in detail the two fortifications there, one nearly complete, and further informed Schuyler that the British were building not one but two vessels, both about fifty-five feet long on the keel, "to mount sixteen or eighteen guns each, the most of them twelve pounders."

Duguid reported that the frames of the vessels had been built at Chambly, below the falls of the Richelieu, and transported to St. John's on a convoy of thirty to forty wagons. He speculated that the ships, which were under construction in the space between the two fortifications, were well along toward completion, and "when the vessels are finished, they propose to bring them upon the lake."

The only good news in Duguid's report was that the British had only "two small batteaus at St. John's, about ten at Chambly." The regulars would not be coming in force to Ticonderoga anytime soon. But if the British finished their vessels and got them up to Champlain, they would once again be masters of the lake just three months after the Americans had wrested that title from them.

Schuyler was determined not to let that happen, and there were two things he could do to stop it. One was to meet naval strength with strength, but to do that he would need real shipwrights, not the house carpenters he had building boats. "If Congress should think it necessary to build vessels of equal or superior strength to those building at St. John's," he wrote, "a number of good ship-carpenters should be immediately sent up."

That, however, was not an immediate solution, not with the great head start that the British already enjoyed. There was only one practical way to secure the lake—an invasion of Canada and the capture of St. John's.

CHAPTER *9 North to Quebec*

WHILE AT ALBANY meeting with Schuyler, Benedict Arnold received tragic personal news. On June 19, a day that he had been organizing his troops at Crown Point, Arnold's wife, Peggy, had died. She was just thirty years old.

Though it is unclear why she died, Peggy's health had always been frail. That there is no surviving correspondence to shed light on her illness is hardly surprising; during his trading voyages, Arnold had complained often of his wife's failure to write. It is likely that he'd had no inkling that she was sick. To add to the tragedy, three days later Peggy's father, who had been recovering from an illness, died as well.

Leaving Albany, Arnold hurried to New Haven and the family that was waiting there—his three sons, ages seven, six, and three. Arriving home, he found that his sister, Hannah, had taken over the care of the boys. Together, the little Arnold family visited the graves of Peggy and her father. Arnold's grief, he wrote to Silas Deane, would have been intolerable "were it not buried in the public calamity."

Through most of his marriage, Arnold had spent little time at home, a source of friction with his wife. Peggy's death did not change Arnold's ambitious nature, and the call to action was pulling him back to the fight. Arnold loved his boys—often during his voyaging he had written of his longing to return to them—but in truth he was too rest-less to sit idly at home, and that native restlessness was only exacer-bated by his grief. "[A]n idle life under my present circumstances," he wrote, "would be but a lingering death." After three weeks with his boys, Arnold bade them farewell, left them in the care of Hannah, and once more rode off toward the sound of the guns.

By the first of August, Arnold was in Watertown, Massachusetts, lis-tening not to guns but to bureaucrats picking apart his expense accounts. He appeared before the Massachusetts Provincial Congress to "render his account of the disposition of the money, ammunition and other things" that Massachusetts had provided him, as well as "the debts he has contracted on behalf of this Colony." The haggling went on for nearly three weeks, with the Provincial Congress arguing each claim and making such helpful suggestions as telling him to "produce a receipt from Colonel Easton, of the delivery of said Oxen, Horses, Cows, &C.," if he wished to be compensated for their cost.

In the end the Provincial Congress reimbursed Arnold a little more than 195 pounds, less than half of what he claimed. Six months later, after Arnold had made himself a national hero, the Continental Congress would award him an additional 245 pounds for his Ticonderoga expenses, but for the time being he could do no more than accept Massachusetts's niggling compensation.

Arguing with small-minded politicians, however, was not Arnold's idea of fighting, and he continued to pursue the other kind, in which he excelled. Being close to Cambridge and the headquarters of the army's new commander in chief, Arnold took the opportunity to present himself to George Washington.

Like Schuyler, Washington was a former member of the Continental Congress. He was aware of Arnold's record, and he received Arnold warmly. With the Continental Congress having come around to the idea of a Canadian invasion, Washington—ever mindful that military command in the United Colonies should remain subservient to civil authority—was now thinking along those lines as well. Indeed, earlier in the month Schuyler had written to Washington asking if the rumors he had heard were true, that such an invasion had already been launched. Washington assured him that "no troops have been detached from Boston to Canada." But it would not be long.

In his letter of June 13 to the Continental Congress, Arnold had already drawn up and forwarded plans for an invasion by way of St. John's and Montreal. He and Washington no doubt discussed the idea of a second attack up the Kennebec and Dead rivers of Maine, then down the Chaudiere River in Canada to Quebec. It was an idea that had been floating around for some time, and one that captured Washington's imagination and interest.

Canada was a plum that appeared increasingly ripe for the plucking. If Canada were to join the American resistance, it would open a second front and deprive the British of friendly or neutral ports on the western side of the Atlantic in which to stage troops and harbor and repair ships.

Most of America's military and political leaders felt that Canada could be taken easily, because the Canadians would rise up to join Americans in throwing off the British yoke. This line of thinking was just as optimistic as the persistent British belief that a fifth column of Loyalists would rise up to join the fight against the rebels, and it was just as wrong.

Right or wrong, however, such thinking led immediately to a consideration of the best way to invade Canada. The traditional routes to Quebec were down Lake Champlain from the south or up the St. Lawrence River from the east, but no army could hope to move undetected along those water routes. The route through Maine was the one approach by which a surprise attack could be made on the interior of Canada, a way to sneak unseen through Quebec's back door.

The prospect of mounting an attack was attractive to Washington, who was starting to chafe at the inactivity of siege warfare. His first proposal for a frontal assault on Boston had already been rejected by his officers, and he was eager to take some bold action, even vicariously. Not yet two months into his command, he could see the effect of inactivity on his army. At the end of the year, many of his troops' enlistments would expire, and without some fresh development to interrupt the monotony of the siege and reignite their fervor, they were all too likely to melt back into the countryside from which they had emerged.

Then, too, as a veteran of the French and Indian War, Washington had a strong appreciation for the strategic importance of Canada. He would later write to Arnold, "I need not mention to you the great importance of this place [Quebec], & the consequent possession of all Canada in the Scale of American affairs . . . to whomsoever It belongs, in there [sic] favour probably, will the Ballance turn."

By August 20, Washington had made up his mind. He sent an express rider hurrying off to Schuyler "to communicate . . . a plan of an expedition which has engrossed my thoughts for several days: It is to penetrate into Canada by way of Kennebeck River and so to Quebec." Washington told Schuyler he could spare a thousand to twelve hundred men for the expedition.

The expedition through the Maine wilderness would be effective only if Schuyler could launch a simultaneous invasion down Lake Champlain and the Richelieu River to attack Montreal. Washington envisioned a two-pronged invasion, forcing the British to divide their forces or abandon one of the cities. "Carleton . . . ," Washington proposed to Schuyler, "must either break up and follow this party to Quebeck by which he will leave you free passage, or he must suffer that important place to fall into our hands."

With summer drawing to an end, Washington was eager to move ahead before the end of the campaign season, but he needed to know Schuyler's intentions. "Not a moment's time is to be lost in preparation for this enterprise," he told Schuyler, and asked the New Yorker to send back word of his plans with the express rider who had delivered his letter.

Schuyler was already making preparations to move on Canada, and he welcomed Washington's participation. The tired express rider was sent thundering back with a letter assuring Washington that Schuyler was aware of "the necessity of penetrating into Canada without delay." Schuyler went on to say, "your Excellency will easily conceive that I felt happy to learn your intentions, and only wished that the thought had struck you sooner."

One of the American Revolution's most extraordinary feats of endurance, courage, perseverance, and leadership was about to get under way.

The Path through the Woods

Soon after Washington heard from Schuyler, the "Detachment from the Continental Army against Quebeck" was organized. A great many men, weary of the seemingly unending siege and eager for action, stepped forward to volunteer. Of those, nearly eight hundred were selected. The troops were divided into two battalions, the First Battalion, under Lieutenant Colonel Roger Enos, and the Second Battalion, under Lieutenant Colonel Christopher Greene. Greene was a cousin of thirty-three-year-old Brigadier General Nathanael Greene, of Rhode Island, one of Washington's most trusted officers and a man who, like Arnold, had almost no prior military experience.

Under each of the two lieutenant colonels was a major, and each battalion was further divided into five companies, each led by a captain.

Also joining the expedition were about three hundred riflemen from Pennsylvania and Virginia. Their leader was the imposing Daniel Morgan, who would become one of the outstanding officers of the Revolution and whose accomplishments, like Arnold's, would be largely overlooked by Congress.

The riflemen were a different breed from the merchants, sailors, tradesmen, and farmers who made up most of the Continental army from New England. Well acquainted with woodcraft and Native American hunting and fighting techniques, they were less settled even than the Green Mountain Boys. They carried long rifles, tomahawks, and long "scalping knives" and dressed in fringed hunting shirts and Indian-style leggings. They were skilled and intrepid fighting men, though their disdain for authority ("rude and hardy . . . unused to the discipline of a camp . . . ," Private John Henry called them) made them problematic soldiers. Still, their wilderness experience was very much what Arnold needed.

Arnold's planned route to Quebec through northern Maine was based on copies he possessed of the map and journal of the capable and adventurous Captain John Montresor. Montresor had first come to North America during the French and Indian War as an ensign under the command of General Edward Braddock, under whom George Washington had also served. The young ensign saw fighting at Quebec and many of the other major actions of that conflict.

In 1760, Montresor, by then an experienced wilderness scout, led a party south from Quebec, arriving in late February in Topsham,

Maine, along the route that Arnold now proposed. The party nearly died. By the end of their journey they were reduced to eating their shoes, bullet pouches, belts, and a few raw woodpeckers.

That experience might have served as a warning to Arnold, who was preparing to march just as the cold weather was approaching, but unfortunately Montresor did not write about it. Instead, his journal covered a second trip, one made during the more agreeable months of June and July. Basing his march on that information, Arnold underestimated the real difficulties he would face heading into the northern Maine woods so late in the season. Most of the route would be traveled by boat, which Arnold and Washington thought would be no great hardship. According to Washington, "the Land Carriage by the Rout proposed is too inconsiderable to make an Objection."

While Arnold was conferring with Washington, Montresor, it happened, was just a few miles away, serving as an engineer for General William Howe in Boston. The following year he would be named chief engineer of the British forces in America. It would be Montresor who brought word under flag of truce to the Americans concerning the hanging of the spy Nathan Hale, and who reported Hale's last words, "I only regret that I have but one life to lose for my country."

Montresor had served with the British army in North America for twenty-two years. No British officer knew America better than he did. Montresor would have been a major general in the Continental army, but due to his lack of wealth and pedigree he never rose above captain in His Majesty's forces.

Fort Western

By the second week in September, the troops began assembling in Cambridge, from whence they would march north to Newburyport, a coastal town about thirty-five miles away near the New Hampshire border. On September 11 the battalions received their orders and headed off "by different detached parties for the more convenient marching and lodging." The lodging was not always top-notch. The expedition's surgeon, sharp-humored twenty-two-year-old Dr. Isaac Senter, noted that "the fleas and other Tory insects not a little free with our property, we thought best to decamp very early this morn."

Washington had already given Arnold informal orders, but on September 14 he sent Arnold, now commissioned a colonel in the Continental army, official notice that he was to lead his detachment of the army through the Maine wilderness to Quebec's back door. "You are intrusted with a command of the utmost consequence to the interest and liberties of America," Washington wrote to Arnold before launching into the specifics.

Washington, like the Continental Congress, was aware that invading a country without annoying its inhabitants would require a tricky balancing act. Indeed, Washington understood that a Canadian campaign "must fail of Success" if the Canadians would not "cooperate or at least willingly acquiesce." He knew that few Canadians could be enticed to join the colonies to their south if they viewed the Americans as hostile conquerors. He told Arnold that he and his men should "consider yourselves as marching, not through an enemies' Country, but that of our friends and brethren." The bulk of Washington's letter exhorted Arnold to be careful that no insult be directed to the Canadians.

Along with that notice, Washington issued final instructions for Arnold's march that contained more of the same. Recalling, perhaps, the confusion at Ticonderoga, he also told Arnold that if he were to meet up with Schuyler, as intended, he was to be Schuyler's subordinate and not to consider himself "upon a separate & independent Command."

Arnold, attending to last-minute details, did not leave Cambridge until the morning of September 15 but managed to reach Newburyport the same evening, even after stopping in Salem to eat and to procure two hundred pounds of ginger and teamsters to haul 270 blankets. The last of the troops reached Newburyport by Saturday, September 16. That night, in accordance with Washington's orders, Arnold sent out three boats to make certain that no British men-of-war were lurking along their intended sailing route. One boat was dispatched to the Isles of Shoals, just off the Maine–New Hampshire border; one to the mouth of the Kennebec River—the expedition's immediate destination—and one to scout inshore along the coast.

The next day being Sunday, the men attended church according to their denominations. Simeon Thayer, a captain in Greene's battalion, wrote that the officers "paraded our men, and went to meeting under arms." Presumably it was not a Quaker meeting.

That night Arnold began loading the men on board the transports—eleven sloops and schooners—but headwinds prevented them from leaving port. With about a hundred troops on each of the vessels, described by one soldier as "dirty coasters and fish boats," quarters were tight. That, and the temptations of Newburyport, including the "many pretty girls" reportedly on shore, left the men eager to get back to dry land. "[F]inding it difficult to keep the men on board," Thayer wrote, "we were obliged to keep a guard over them."

On Monday, one of the boats that Arnold had sent out returned to report no enemy vessels between Newburyport and the mouth of the Kennebec, but the wind still held them in harbor. Finally, on Tuesday, September 19, the wind swung around from a favorable quarter and the little fleet got under way. For most of the day they enjoyed good weather, but as evening came on it began to rain, and the rising wind kicked up a heavy swell, which (according to Senter) "occasioned most of the troops to disgorge themselves of their luxuries so plentifully laid in ere we embarked."

That night the vessels hove to off the Maine coast, and the next morning proceeded with the weather still "very thick and foggy, attended with rain." Around nine in the morning they arrived at the mouth of the Kennebec, save for a few of the vessels that had become separated from the fleet. Once in the river, they anchored and sent ashore for fresh provisions, because, as Arnold reported, "many of the people were extremely seasick."

For the next few days the fleet worked its way up the Kennebec River, hampered by headwinds and groundings. Two vessels that had missed the mouth of the river came instead by the Sheepscot River, from which an upriver waterway led to the Kennebec, and they rejoined the fleet on September 21. By Friday, the twenty-second, the transports had arrived at Gardiner's Town (today Pittston, Maine), about thirty miles upriver from the coast.

While still in Cambridge, Washington and Arnold had met with Reuben Colburn, who had traveled there from Maine, and contracted with him to build "Two hundred light Battoes Capable of Carrying Six or Seven Men each." Colburn was given about three weeks to complete the job, an extremely short time for so big a task. He returned to Gardiner's Town, gathered up anyone he could find with boatbuilding experience, and set to work.

Colburn was further hampered by a lack of seasoned wood. All the dried wood he had laid in had already been used in the season's construction, so he was forced to use freshly cut green wood, which would invariably shrink, twist, and crack as it dried.

Not surprisingly, the results of Colburn's efforts where not what Arnold had hoped for. On inspection, Arnold found the bateaux "smaller than the directions given, and very badly built." Arnold ordered twenty more bateaux to make up for the boats' small size.

Colburn, however, would not be washing his hands of the problem once Arnold was on his way. His contract called for him to "Engage a Company of Twenty Men" to travel with Arnold, serve as guides, and maintain the bateaux. Reuben Colburn would travel all the way to Canada with Arnold, patching up the battered boats as he went.

Colburn was also ordered to "bespeak all The Pork, and Flour" he could find on the Lower Kennebec to supply the expedition. Along with the bateaux, these supplies were still accumulating at Gardiner's Town for transporting upriver.

Anxious to push on, Arnold sent the bulk of his forces ahead while a number of men under Lieutenant Colonel Enos stayed behind to ferry the bateaux and supplies upriver when ready. The main body continued aboard the transports to the head of navigation, then disembarked and walked the remaining five miles to Fort Western, in what is modern-day Augusta.

The easy part of the expedition was over.

CHAPTER *10* *Invading Canada*

THE COMMANDER of British forces in Canada, the man whom Arnold and Schuyler would be fighting, was Major General Guy Carleton, the fifty-one-year-old governor of Quebec Province. Carleton, from County Down in Ireland, was of Scots-Irish ancestry, the third son in a family of minor landowners. He had begun his military career as an ensign in the 25th Regiment of Foot, and soon enjoyed a certain degree of patronage in Parliament along with the friendship of James Wolfe, who would go on to be one of the leaders of the British army during the French and Indian War.

Advancement in the British army usually involved purchasing successively higher commissions, which Carleton was able to do. When James Wolfe, by then General Wolfe, was appointed to lead British forces against the French at Quebec, he tapped Carleton to be quartermaster general. King George II refused the appointment, angry that Carleton had spoken ill of Hanoverian troops, but Wolfe was so insistent that Carleton accompany him to Quebec that the king eventually relented.

Carleton was with Wolfe in September 1759 when Wolfe staged his bold attack on Quebec across the Plains of Abraham. The British won a major victory when the French under General Louis Joseph, Marquis de Montcalm (who the year before had successfully defended Ticonderoga) sallied forth from the city and fought on the open ground. Wolfe was killed, as was Montcalm. Carleton received a slight wound but a major boost to his reputation.

(Another officer who greatly enhanced his reputation at Quebec was William Howe, then a young lieutenant colonel, who led a detachment of light infantry up the cliffs to spearhead the attack. In October 1775, Howe became Thomas Gage's replacement as commander in chief of the British troops in America.)

That battle delivered Quebec to the British, and the end of the French and Indian War delivered all of Canada. Carleton became lieutenant governor of Quebec in 1766, and governor a year later.

In 1770 Carleton returned to England, where he married Lady Maria Howard, the daughter of Lord Howard, the second Earl of Effingham and a close friend of Carleton. The match gave Carleton entrée into the upper echelon of British government and the ranks of the aristocracy. He also managed a promotion to major general.

During the next four years, Carleton campaigned for Parliament to pass the Quebec Act. Among other things, the act gave religious freedom to the many French Catholics in the province, who did not particularly care to be ruled by the Protestant British, despite what most British officials thought.

Although the Quebec Act was welcomed by French Canadians, particularly the elites, who found their former power renewed, it was decried by Americans, because it also stopped any western expansion of the lower colonies and it legalized Catholicism. A decade and a half before the First Amendment codified religious tolerance, Americans in general and New Englanders in particular were not much interested in pluralism, especially not when it extended to popery.

The Quebec Act was considered one of the "Intolerable Acts" by American revolutionaries and, along with taxation without representation and myriad other infringements, another reason for war with England. Not surprisingly, however, the American fear and loathing of Catholicism would become one of the great obstacles in the Continental Congress's efforts to convince French Canadians to throw in with them.

In the fall of 1774, Carleton returned to the Province of Quebec to resume his duties as governor. He was a good governor, astute, creative, and determined. He was a solid military commander as well, but cautious, a trait that would lead to more than one missed opportunity, allowing the Americans to live and fight again.

By the spring of 1775, half a year after Carleton's return, the ordered world of British North America seemed to be falling apart. On May 19, Carleton received word from General Thomas Gage about the fighting at Lexington and Concord. The next day, Moses Hazen, who had met Arnold during Arnold's brief capture of St. John's, arrived at Quebec to inform Carleton about the raid on the St. John's garrison and the taking of Ticonderoga. Carleton later wrote to the Earl of Dartmouth, who was then the American secretary—the minister in charge of overseeing British interests in North America—that the attack was carried out by "one Benedict Arnold, said to be a native of Connecticut and a horse jockey."

Later that evening another express arrived with news of Ethan Allen's attack and how it had been driven off by a column of regulars under the command of Major Charles Preston, marching from Montreal. Carleton immediately ordered "the little force" under his command, about four hundred men in the 7th Regiment of Foot, also known as the Royal Fusiliers, and about three hundred men in the 26th Regiment of Foot, "to assemble at or near St. John's." He called on local leaders to rally the people to defend Canada. In response, the locals spoke effusively and did nothing.

By the end of June, Carleton had about five hundred troops at Chambly and St. John's, which virtually stripped other Canadian posts of men. The previous year, with tensions mounting in Massachusetts, Carleton had sent two of his four regiments to reinforce Gage in Boston, confident that, if need be, his loss would be made up by Canadian militia.

Now he was beginning to appreciate his miscalculation. Canadian towns, like their American counterparts, were expected to maintain citizen militias. They did, in theory, but French Canadians who, only a dozen years earlier, had become unwilling subjects of King George were not exactly rallying to the Union Jack. Carleton declared martial law and ordered the militia enrolled, and he himself took post at Montreal to be closer to the fighting.

He also wrote to the Earl of Dartmouth requesting ten thousand men with artillery and engineers, as well as a naval contingent. Such a force, he wrote, "might have a great influence over the whole continent and very effectively second those of General Gage." Even before the shooting had begun in earnest, Carleton was thinking of cutting the colonies in two down the Champlain corridor to the Hudson.

Appreciating, as Schuyler did, the importance of naval superiority on Lake Champlain, Carleton "sent down to Quebeck for all the ship-carpenters that could be got . . . ," and ordered them to St. John's to start building ships. Thus the great race for naval control of Lake Champlain, which would end at Valcour Island in October 1776, made its halting start in the summer of 1775.

But Carleton could not march to Albany or even take back the lake with five hundred men. His immediate strategy was to reinforce and strengthen St. John's and Chambly to stop the rebels from descending the Richelieu River, and to build vessels for the defense of the lake. For the time being, there was nothing more he could do except plead with London and wait for the rebels to come.

"The gentleman and the soldier . . ."

Like Washington, Major General Philip Schuyler was eager to invade Canada. Indeed, Schuyler had, if anything, greater motivation for such a move. Whereas Quebec posed no imminent danger to Washington's army outside Boston, Schuyler correctly saw the garrison at St. John's, and even more so the British naval construction going on there, as an immediate threat. Crown Point and Fort Ticonderoga had long been considered the strategic epicenter of the region, and no one had any doubts that the British would want them back.

Congress was fully behind the invasion plan by September 1775. Indeed, as early as June 27 the delegates had resolved that Schuyler should take possession of St. John's, Montreal, and "other parts of the country" if Schuyler "finds it practicable, and that it will not be disagreeable to the Canadians."

The intelligence that Schuyler was receiving from St. John's grew increasingly alarming. In late August, John Brown, who had returned to Ticonderoga with Ethan Allen, scouted the north end of the lake aboard the *Enterprise*. He reported the vessels being built at St. John's to be "very forward . . . their hulls seem to be finished, being blacked up to their gunwales . . . they will be ready to sail in one week, or ten days." He correctly surmised that if the vessels made it onto Lake Champlain, then "the [American] expedition is up for this year."

So it was with a sense of relief that Schuyler read of Washington's plans for an invasion and his commander in chief's hope that they might launch simultaneous attacks northward. The reports that Schuyler had received, he wrote to Washington, left "not a trace of doubt in my mind as to the propriety of going into Canada; and to do so it has been my determination."

By the end of August, while Washington and Arnold were preparing for the march to Quebec, Schuyler was back in Albany preparing to launch his attack on St. John's. A large part of the planning and organization fell to his second in command, Brigadier General Richard Montgomery.

Montgomery was thirty-nine years old, described as "well-limbed, tall and handsome, though his face was much pock-marked" with smallpox scars, and a man who had already achieved impressive credentials. A native of Ireland and a graduate of Trinity College in Dublin, he had served as an officer with the 17th Regiment of Foot in Canada during the French and Indian War. He had been with Wolfe during the siege of Louisburg and with Amherst when the British captured Ticonderoga and Crown Point, the glory days for those fortifications.

In 1772, Montgomery sold his commission and emigrated to the colony of New York, where he purchased a farm of no great size near New York City. Like Guy Carleton and George Washington, Montgomery married into influence, in his case a union with Janet Livingston, daughter of Robert Livingston. Montgomery's new father-in-law was one of the most powerful and influential men in New York by dint of the Livingston family's wealth and many generations of prominence in the colony, and Montgomery's social status rose by association. He served as a delegate in New York's first Provincial Congress. On June 22, 1775, when the Continental Congress was choosing the army's eight brigadier generals, Richard Montgomery was number two.

He was a good choice, well connected and intelligent, a former British army regular and a natural leader. Schuyler would come to see him as "endowed with shining abilities." George Morison, a soldier in Arnold's regiment, thought Montgomery was "born to command. His easy and affable condescension . . . creates love and esteem; and exhibits him the gentleman and the soldier."

The Invasion of Canada

Montgomery was organizing the troops at Ticonderoga when he read the intelligence regarding the British vessels at St. John's. He knew there was no time to delay. On August 25 he sent an express to Schuyler in Albany telling the major general that he was "resolved to proceed with what force he could carry."

Thanks to Schuyler's boatbuilding efforts, the Americans finally had the means to get down the lake. The two flat-bottomed gunboats that Schuyler had ordered had been launched and christened the *Schuyler* and the *Hancock*. They were sixty feet long and able to carry some 250 men and five 12-pounders each, but a lack of gun carriages meant that only one gun was actually mounted. Between these and other boats at their disposal, the Americans could move thirteen hundred men, and provisions enough to feed them for twenty days.

The garrison at St. John's, by comparison, consisted of twenty-eight officers and 425 men of the 26th Regiment, along with seventy-five "Carpenters Sailors and Canadians" and about seventy women and children. The British would be outnumbered nearly three to one, but they had had months to fortify, and they knew their business.

On the evening of August 28, about twelve hundred men under Montgomery's command boarded the watercraft at Ticonderoga and headed north down Lake Champlain. Sailing through the night, they arrived the next day at Crown Point, where they stayed until the thirty-first before continuing north, leaving behind a number of men too sick to go on.

Schuyler was then in Albany at a conference with representatives of the Six Nations, a confederacy of Indian tribes consisting of the Cayuga, Mohawk, Oneida, Onondaga, Seneca, and Tuscarora. The American commissioners hoped to convince the tribes to fight for the American cause or at least remain neutral. The Indians were more interested in neutrality, claiming in a joint statement that "we bear an equal proportion of love to you, and the others over the great waters, in the present dispute, and we shall remain at peace and smoke our pipes."

On hearing from Montgomery that he was launching the attack on St. John's, Schuyler gave orders for the rest of the troops in the area as well as artillery to be brought up in support. Then he himself hurried north to catch up with his army, despite being "much indisposed with a bilious fever." Schuyler's chronic ill health was becoming more of a problem as he made his way to Ticonderoga.

On September 2, Montgomery's troops arrived at Isle la Motte, which sits like a loose cork in a bottleneck where Lake Champlain narrows into the Richelieu River, about ten miles south of the border with Canada. Rain and high winds detained the troops there, allowing the ailing Schuyler to catch up with them on September 4.

That same day, with Schuyler now in command, the army moved on, covering twenty-five miles to the swampy Isle aux Noix, fifteen miles upriver from St. John's. There Schuyler drew up a declaration, to be circulated among the inhabitants of the region, stating that "the Grand Congress have ordered an Army into Canada to expel from thence, if possible, those British Troops, which, now acting under the orders of a despotick Ministry, would wish to enslave their countrymen." He assured the Canadians that the invasion was ordered "in the fullest confidence that it would be perfectly agreeable to you."

The declaration was the kind of high rhetorical nonsense that Americans were forever directing at the citizens of Canada in hopes of inspiring an American-style zeal for liberty, a thing the Canadians never quite embraced. Like the Indians, Canadians preferred to watch from the sidelines and lend lukewarm support to whichever side seemed to be winning, or at least doling out the most specie.

On September 6 the army was under way again. Leaving all their provisions, save four days' worth, as well as more sick men at Isle aux Noix, they boarded their boats and headed downriver on their final push for St. John's. Schuyler still hoped, as American leaders always did, that Canadians would rise up and join them.

By two in the afternoon the transports were just a couple of miles above the fortifications. The British opened up on them with cannon, but the range was too great. The Americans would be most vulnerable when they were landing, and Schuyler guessed that the British troops would sally out to hit them then. To counter such an attack, Schuyler and a small contingent went on ahead to stage a feigned landing within a mile and a half of the fort.

British artillery blasted away, tearing up the water with round shot and grape; as Schuyler put it, the Americans were "Saluted with a warm cannonade." Then Schuyler wheeled his boats around and retreated, landing his entire force unopposed a half mile farther up the river.

Once the army had gained the swampy shore, they formed and began to advance on St. John's, intending to reconnoiter the defenses. Part of Colonel Waterbury's regiment swept forward, working around the left wing of the fort. A deep, muddy brook blocked their path, and the Americans slogged through it and clambered up the other bank. Suddenly the woods exploded with small arms fire. Waterbury's men had stumbled right into an ambush set up by a division of Canadians and Indians hidden in the thick forest.

Five Americans were shot dead in the first volley, with eight privates and three officers wounded. The American line wheeled left and attacked. For half an hour the two sides kept up a heavy fire, until at last the advancing Americans sent the defenders racing back to the fort, keeping up a rearguard action as they did.

It was too late in the day for further action. The Americans retreated to the edge of the river and threw up a small breastwork, "within Reach of the Enemys Shells, which in the Evening began to come plentifully into the Camp." Finding that sleep was difficult with mortar shells whistling into camp and exploding in showers of jagged iron, Schuyler and Montgomery marched the men three quarters of a mile farther south and threw up a new breastwork, clear of enemy artillery.

That night a local man, whose name Schuyler would not commit to paper, came into the camp with intelligence regarding the situation at St. John's. He informed Schuyler that the schooner was launched and had one mast stepped and the second ready to go, and that the ship would be ready to sail in just a few days. He told the major general that there was a considerable body of regulars and Indians at St. John's and that the fortifications were nearly complete, strong and bristling with cannon.

Schuyler's dream of a fifth column of Canadians was quashed when the informer told him that "he does not believe our Army will be joined by one Canadian. That they wish to be neuter on the occasion; but if we should penetrate into Canada, it would not displease them, provided their persons and properties were safe, and we paid them in gold and silver for what we had." It was a tellingly accurate assessment of the Canadian attitude in general.

The next morning Schuyler called his field officers together for a council of war, sharing the intelligence he had received the night before. The officers agreed that it was "indispensably necessary" to prevent the schooner from getting into Lake Champlain. Because the regulars at St. John's had considerable artillery and the Americans had none, there was not much the Americans could do about the schooner while they were camped outside the British fortifications.

The best course, it was decided, was to return to Isle aux Noix, build a proper fortification there, put a boom across the narrow channel, and "make such Preparations there as may effectually prevent the Enemys naval force from entering the lake." With that resolved, the Americans got back into their boats and returned upriver.

The Reinvasion of Canada

Landing again at Isle aux Noix, Schuyler gave orders to begin fortifying the island and constructing a boom. The troops were joined by three hundred Connecticut soldiers and four hundred from New York, bringing the force to about seventeen hundred. A smattering of artillery had arrived as well, and more was on its way aboard the *Enterprise.*

On September 9, Schuyler received a letter from James Livingston, a Canadian serving with the American army and a distant relative of Montgomery's wife. Livingston suggested that the garrison at St. John's might be taken after all, and that the Canadians would in fact

be disposed to join the Americans. Schuyler was still waiting for his artillery to come up, but on the tenth he sent five hundred men back to
St. John's to maintain the siege. The next day, however, the men were
back at Isle aux Noix, having been driven off by the regulars.

Sickness spread among the soldiers camped on the marshy island.
By September 12, Schuyler reported "upwards of six hundred sick."
Schuyler himself was among them, too sick even to get out of bed, laid
low by the ailments that had plagued him most of his life.

Despite the setbacks, Schuyler and Montgomery were ready to try
again, but now it was the weather that stopped them. A heavy late summer rain fell in sheets, lashing Isle aux Noix and churning up the
river. There was no chance of managing the boats in such a downpour.
As the army huddled under what meager shelter they could find and
waited for the weather to clear, Ethan Allen arrived at camp, eager to
participate in taking Canada. This time he came alone.

Earlier in the year, Allen and Seth Warner had convinced the Continental Congress to establish a genuine Green Mountain Regiment,
to legitimize the ad hoc force they had assembled over the previous
five years. Congress had agreed, and the officers of the new regiment
were elected by a committee chosen from various towns in the Hampshire Grants.

Twenty-three officers were elected. Command of the regiment went
to Seth Warner, but Ethan Allen, who had alienated many of the Green
Mountain Boys with his constant bragging after the capture of Ticonderoga and his foolish attempt on St. John's, was left out in the cold.

Now he was looking for a new opportunity. "I always dreaded his
impatience of subordination," Schuyler wrote of Allen, "and it was not
until after a solemn promise, made me in the presence of several officers, that he would demean himself properly, that I would permit him
to attend the Army." Having promised to behave himself, Allen
headed north to recruit an army of Canadians, and Schuyler's army
waited to board their boats for St. John's.

When they finally did, they left without Schuyler. The major general, debilitated with illness, knew that he would be of little use. On
September 16 he "was put into a covered boat" and taken up the lake

to Ticonderoga. On his way up the lake, he met Seth Warner and 170 Green Mountain Boys bound down to join Montgomery, "the first that have appeared of that boasted corps."

Soon Schuyler was back at Ticonderoga. Though he would continue to serve for the next year and more as commanding officer of the Northern Department, he would never again travel north of Crown Point. Most of his active duty would be spent at Albany.

The Second Reinvasion

"Lords Day, September 17," Benjamin Trumbull, a Connecticut chaplain, private soldier, and orderly, wrote in his journal, "The Army embarked a Third Time for St John's."

Benedict Arnold and his men were still in Newburyport, waiting for a favorable wind to take them to Maine, when Montgomery launched his final attack on St. John's. His original force, as well as the disparate troops that had since joined him, including Warner and his Green Mountain Boys, were loaded aboard the sundry watercraft. Montgomery's flotilla included the bateaux, the two big gondolas *Schuyler* and *Hancock*, the sloop *Enterprise*, and the schooner *Liberty*. It was the most powerful naval force the lake had seen since the end of the French and Indian War.

Before leaving for Ticonderoga, Schuyler had conferred with Montgomery on the plan of attack. Their greatest concern was that the British schooner, with the sixteen 12-pounders she was supposed to mount, would get among the bateaux and tear them apart before the troops could reach the shore. To counter that, the two American sailing vessels and the gondolas, along with ten bateaux filled with picked men, would take station in the river between the schooner and the landing place above the fort. If the schooner made an appearance, they would engage her while the rest of the troops swarmed ashore.

Once the men were ashore, they were to surround St. John's, cutting off communication with the garrisons at Chambly and Montreal. Then they would begin erecting batteries and digging approaches, the traditional tactics of siege warfare.

The landing went pretty much as planned. Shots were fired from British boats, and the fire was returned, with casualties on the British side but none among the Americans. Soon Montgomery's men were huddled behind the breastworks they had built during the first invasion. A regiment under Colonel Timothy Bedel was sent to the lower breastworks, the ones from which the men had earlier been driven out, to serve as an advance guard.

The next day the Americans heard gunfire from north of the fort. John Brown, whom Montgomery had sent from Isle aux Noix a few days before with a small detachment, had taken position in the breastworks north of St. John's. Now three to four hundred regulars sallied forth from the fortification to drive them off. Bedel's regiment, with Montgomery in the lead, hurried off to Brown's aide.

By the time they arrived, the regulars had driven Brown and his men out of the breastworks and had taken the ground. At the sight of the relief column, however, the British fired a few rounds from their field-pieces and retreated into the fort before Montgomery could engage.

It was the last real action they would have. On that same day, the dreary work of siege warfare began.

CHAPTER *11 Into the Wilderness*

AFTER THEIR ARRIVAL at Fort Western, in Maine, around September 24, Arnold and his men spent the next few days organizing for their march north while supplies and bateaux were ferried up from Gardiner's Town. The early autumn weather, "rainy and cold," was already hinting at how brutal it could become. Some of the men had no tents, and the dilapidated fort offered little shelter.

Before the main body started north, Arnold dispatched Lieutenant Archibald Steele and six men in two birch bark canoes to Chaudiere Pond, also called Lake Megantic (the name by which it is now known), the headwaters of the Chaudiere River, some hundred miles northwest as the crow flew but double that or more by twisting waterways. There Steele was to gather any intelligence he could get from the Indians.

Arnold sent another group in the same direction to survey the route to the Dead River, which emptied into the Kennebec some eighty miles upriver from Fort Western.

Arnold's plan was to "divide the detachment, for the conveniency of passing the carrying places." He split his army into four divisions to be sent out at staggered intervals, rightly envisioning chaos at the portage bottlenecks if all thousand or so men tried to pass at the same time. The first division would carry minimum provisions as they hacked a road through the wilderness. The last division, headed by Lieutenant Colonel Enos, in command of the First Battalion, would carry the bulk of the supplies over trails ostensibly prepared for them.

On Monday September 25, one week after Montgomery had begun the siege of St. John's, Arnold sent off the first division, which consisted of the three companies of riflemen under Daniel Morgan. It had been Arnold's intention to send Colonel Greene first, with one company of riflemen and two of "Musketeers," but the captains of the rifle companies objected, saying they would be commanded only by

93

Morgan or Arnold himself. It was the legendary independence of the riflemen, who would not be ordered around like common soldiers.

Morgan told Arnold that that arrangement was Washington's intention, though Washington had never suggested any such thing to Arnold. Rather than precipitate a confrontation at the very start of the expedition, Arnold let the riflemen go.

Morgan's men headed off in the evening hours, while the rest of the men continued to prepare, though they were "very nigh in readiness to march," as Senter reported. Arnold was taking advantage of the riflemen's wilderness experience, sending them ahead to "clear the roads over the carrying places." In particular they were to clear a portage along the Great Carrying Place, a stretch of wild country, interrupted by a few ponds and lakes, over which the bateaux would have to be dragged to meet up with the Dead River, which would lead to a portage to Lake Megantic. Their route was literally an uphill climb as they worked their way up to the height of land, the high country that divided the Dead River from Lake Megantic, and sent the water of the Dead River running south, while Lake Megantic drained into the Chaudiere River, which in turn emptied into the Saint Lawrence near Quebec.

The next day, a week after leaving Newburyport, the second division took to their bateaux and headed upriver, carrying with them provisions for forty-five days, the same as Morgan's men. The third division left the following day.

On Thursday, September 28, Arnold sent out most of the fourth division. Lieutenant Colonel Enos was still in Gardiner's Town, seeing that the last of the bateaux and supplies were sent upriver. Arnold ordered him to send along any men still left behind, and to send the sick back to Newburyport aboard the schooner *Broad Bay*, which had carried Arnold and others to Fort Western. Enos was to "bring up the rear, and order on all stragglers . . . and hurry on as fast as possible without fatiguing the men too much." He was also ordered to bring "all the carpenters of Captain Colburn's Company," the twenty men contracted, along with Colburn himself, to accompany the expedition as scouts and maintain the boats.

Arnold did not leave Fort Western until most of the others had gone ahead. Rather than travel by bateau with one of the divisions, he took to a birch bark canoe, which allowed him the speed and mobility to keep track of the entire column. His old friend Eleazer Oswald accompanied him, serving as secretary, pro tem.

The troops heading upriver in their loaded bateaux found the going easy at first, but soon the river grew shallow and rocky and the current correspondingly swift. Caleb Haskell, in Captain Samuel Ward's company of Greene's battalion, noted, "We begin to see that we have a scene of trouble to go through in this river, the water is swift and the shoal full of rocks, ripples and falls, which oblige us to wade a great part of the way."

Each division covered around four miles on the first day, some men going by bateau, some marching along the shore. They camped by the river. The third division "encamped at night by the edge of a cornfield and fared very sumptuously."

Arnold, by contrast, moved quickly, leaving Fort Western at noon and stopping at Vassalboro, eight miles upriver, to exchange his canoe, which had proved "very leaky." He covered another six miles before stopping for the night.

Eighteen miles above Fort Western, in what is today Winslow, Maine, stood Fort Halifax, which was in even worse repair than Fort Western, consisting of "old block houses and a stoccade in ruinous state." There, too, was the first carrying place, "97 rods," or a little more than five hundred yards of relatively easy portage. Benedict Arnold arrived there on the last day of September to find Henry Dearborn and William Goodrich's companies, part of the third division, hauling their boats and supplies overland around the falls of the river.

That afternoon Arnold had dinner with a man named Crosier, whom he hired, with his team, to transport the column's baggage five miles over land. Later, Arnold pushed on to camp in the woods with Return Jonathan Meigs, the major who commanded the third division.

As September turned to October and the column advanced farther north, away from the moderating influence of the sea and into higher altitudes, the weather became increasingly bitter. "Last night, our clothes being wet," Thayer wrote in his journal, "were frozen a pane of glass thick, which proved very disagreeable, being obliged to lie in them." Other troubles began to appear. The Kennebec River north of Fort Halifax grew increasingly shallow and swift, forcing the men "to get out and wade, pulling the boats after us."

Within days of departing Fort Western, the bateaux began to suffer from their poor construction. "[M]any of the bateaux," wrote rifle-man George Morison, "were so badly constructed that whether in or out of them we were wet . . . in several of them our provision and camp equipage were much injured." Dr. Senter was forced to spend four dollars to purchase a non-Colburn-built bateau, writing that otherwise he could "not proceed by water without destroying my medicine, stores, &C."

The second carrying place at Skowhegan proved quite a bit more difficult than the first, "a ragged rock, near on 100 feet in height and almost perpendicular," over which they had to haul baggage and bateaux. The mostly fine weather they had enjoyed through the end of September came to an end, and a bitterly cold October rain began to pour down, adding to the men's growing discomfort.

"We have but a melancholy prospect before us . . ."

In the first week of October the column reached Norridgewock as the bateaux continued to fall apart. "By this time," Senter wrote, "our bat-teaux were nothing but wrecks, some stove to pieces, &C."

They had not yet even arrived at the difficult part of the march, and already the water pouring into the boats was ruining foodstuffs. The casks that held bread and peas were not waterproof, and invading mois-ture swelled the contents and burst the casks, spoiling the food just as the column was leaving behind the last settlements where more could be obtained. The carpenters who had come with Colburn were put to work fixing the bateaux, but at that point, far from a boatyard and sawn and seasoned lumber, there was only so much that could be done.

Norridgewock was the northernmost point of civilization, such as it was, and the men spent several days there hauling their equipment over the mile-and-a-quarter portage around the falls, though happily they had two ox-drawn sleds "employed in carrying the batteaux, provisions, camp equipage, &C." Passing through the village on October 2, Arnold wrote, "here we leave the English settlements, no inhabitants being above the falls."

Just past the Norridgewock portage, Arnold caught up with Daniel Morgan and the head of the column. The riflemen, moving fast, proceeded on to the Great Carrying Place, while Arnold remained behind to see the rest of troops past the falls. For six days the column struggled around the portage, hauling boats and supplies, repairing bateaux, and inspecting food and discarding what had spoiled.

By October 8 the entire column, including Enos's rear division, had carried around the Norridgewock Falls, but a torrential downpour kept them in camp for the day. It being a Sunday, some of the exhausted men saw the rain as the work of God. "Providence . . . sent us a day of rest . . . ," one wrote. The following morning the last of the men took to the river above the falls and pushed on.

By the time Enos's rear division was passing the Norridgewock Falls, the second division was meeting up with the riflemen at the Great Carrying Place, about thirty-five miles upriver. Just to get there they had had to portage around another set of falls, through water that was starting to freeze over, fighting powerful currents. Arnold, who tended to downplay any difficulty in his reports, called the river "very rapid indeed."

The Great Carrying Place consisted of three ponds connected by four portages that led from the Kennebec River to the Dead River, about twelve and a half miles in total. Morgan's men had made some progress in cutting a path, but now more men were set to it, some men "employed in cutting and clearing a road, and others in carrying." The recent rains had left the ground soft and muddy, "much of the way knee deep in mud and water." It had taken the riflemen three days to portage just five miles to the first pond. "[W]e had not even the shape of a road," rifleman George Morison wrote, "but as we forced it."

Soon most of the column was strung out along the Great Carrying Place, moving boats and gear over wild, broken country. The men discarded anything that was not absolutely necessary. The salt pork was removed from its barrels and strung on poles for easier carrying, the barrels left behind.

The men's health began to deteriorate. Despite the numerous ponds and streams they encountered, the water "was of the worse quality . . . quite yellow," according to Dr. Senter, who wrote that many of the men "were in a sad plight with the diarrhoea." Heavy work and a diet of salt pork left the men parched, but no sooner did they drink the water "than it was puked up by many of the poor fellows."

If there was one bit of solace, it was the good fishing found in the ponds, enough to make a modern angler green with envy at the abundance of fish and lack of catch limits. The men were able to hook trout averaging a half pound apiece, "nothing being more common," Arnold reported, "than a man's taking 8 or 10 Doz in one hours time."

It was not possible for the struggling men to carry the sick along with them. Arnold ordered Meigs to construct a log house on the second portage where the sick could be left behind, which Senter called "Arnold's Hospital" and Private Abner Stocking called "Fort Meigs." Arnold also ordered another log house built at the head of the Great Carrying Place to house sick men and stores.

For days the column struggled over the Great Carrying Place, dragging bateaux through mud up to their knees, stumbling over fallen trees and trails "choked with Roots" too numerous for the ax-men to clear away. One man was killed when the rising wind brought a tree down on top of him. Arnold considered it "remarkable" that no one had drowned. Despite the extraordinary hardships, morale remained high.

On October 13 snow began to mix with the rain that had plagued the troops on and off. From near sea level at Fort Western, the column had climbed to more than a thousand feet of elevation, and that with the advancing season made for increasingly tough conditions.

That day Arnold, who was near the head of the column on the Dead River, composed a letter to a friend in Quebec, John Dyer Mercier, whom he knew from his merchant days. He asked Mercier for intelligence as to troop strength in that city. In the letter, Arnold claimed to have two thousand men, more than double his actual number. The exaggeration was most likely meant to bolster confidence among his friends in Canada and to frighten his enemies if the letter should fall into their hands.

The letter, sent off in the care of two Indians who had been traveling with the column, arrived safely in Quebec but did not reach Mercier. Instead it fell into the hands of Lieutenant Governor Hector Cramahé, who, forewarned, began to prepare his city for Arnold's attack.

Arnold also wrote to Schuyler to make certain that the general knew of his expedition and asking for any "intelligence or advice you can communicate . . . as this detachment was intended to co-operate with your Army." That letter most likely went with some of the sick who were being sent back to Cambridge.

By October 17, Colonel Greene's division, now the head of the column, was struggling up the Dead River, but their food was running out. With the terrible difficulty of moving stores through wilderness country, the head of the column had marched beyond their supplies. Arnold wrote to Enos at the rear of the column that there was only one barrel of flour and ten barrels of pork for the division, which must have numbered around four hundred men. Arnold ordered thirty-one men out of each company to go back, rendezvous with Enos, and bring up supplies. The rest he set to work rolling gunpowder and musket balls into paper cartridges in anticipation of the attack on Quebec.

On October 20, with the food situation growing more critical, the men at the head of the column slaughtered an ox they had with some difficulty been driving along with them. The pound of fresh meat per man "was a very agreeable repast." The troops "had been principally upon salt [pork] for twelve days, and that scanty."

By the next day the last of the column was over the Great Carrying Place and into the Dead River, which Private Stocking found "so remarkably still and dead, that it is difficult to determine which way it runs." This, at least, allowed the men to take to their oars and row upstream, though the ease of rowing on still water was broken by the need to haul bateaux and gear around impassable sections of river, often several times a day.

As if muddy, broken ground, heavy gear, and near starvation were not enough, even heavier rains set in around October 19 and continued unabated for days. "[A] Prodigious fall of rain for 2 days past," Arnold wrote in his journal on the twenty-first, "has raised the River upwards of three feet."

That night as the men slept, the runoff from the storm made the river rise quickly. At four o'clock in the morning Arnold and the men in his camp "were waked by the freshet which came rushing on us like a torrent." They grabbed what gear they could and dragged it to higher ground, though a barrel of flour and a barrel of gunpowder, which they could ill afford to lose, were swept away.

Dawn brought a heartbreaking scene to the suffering troops. The Dead River had risen eight to ten feet in the night and flooded all the land around. It was now nearly impossible to determine the river's course, and the current was flowing so fast that, as Dr. Senter recorded, "we could only advance by one lying on the bow of the boat, pulling with his hands by the small bushes, while others proceeded upon the bank, holding on by the painter."

Until that point the column had been split between men marching along the shore and men in the bateaux, but for those near the middle and end of the column, marching on the flooded shore was no longer an option. Unfortunately, there were also now fewer boats. "The number of bateaux were now much decreased," Senter wrote. "Some stove to pieces against the banks, while others became so excessive leaky as obliged us to condemn them." Benedict Arnold, generally so upbeat, wrote in his journal, "our Provisions almost exhausted, & the incessant rains for three days has prevented our gaining anything considerable, so that we have but a melancholy prospect before us." Then he added, "but in general in high spirits."

Still worse was yet to come.

"To go through or die"

In some places it was still possible for the men to march along the riverbank, but the flooded land made navigating difficult. On the day after the flood, a group of men marching ashore took the wrong route. The men in bateaux had to catch up with them, "inform them of their mistake, & direct their march."

As they continued north, the men found the river "narrow and excessive rapid." Only with great difficulty could they make headway. The men at the front of the column had been on half rations for some time, and starvation was starting to seem like a real possibility. Then, in the racing water, seven bateaux overturned, and "much of the flour, ammunition and a number of guns were lost," wrote Morison, "besides a large sum of money destine to pay off the men. This was a cruel misfortune and was sensibly felt by all." Incredibly, no one drowned in the accident, though now the prospect of starving to death was even more real.

Realizing that it was time to regroup, Arnold "ordered a counsell of warr summoned of such officers as were Present." Many of the troops were too sick or weak to continue on. It was agreed "to send back immediately the disabled and the sick, with provisions sufficient to carry them to the first inhabitants on the Kennebec River," Stocking wrote. As a result, twenty-six men from that division were sent back, along with orders for the other divisions to send their sick and infirm back with three days' rations, enough to get them to Enos's division at the rear of the column.

Arnold ordered Enos, who still had the bulk of the supplies, to provide the sick with provisions enough to get them to Norridgewock. He was then to "proceed with as many of the best men of your division as you can furnish with 15 day's provision." The rest, sick or well, were to be sent back.

It was clear that the column needed food, and quickly. Arnold dispatched Captain Oliver Hanchet with fifty men to push on quickly to the French town of Sartigan (now St. Georges) in Canada to secure provisions from the inhabitants and bring them back to the starving men. That night, along with the usual rain, it snowed, and the men woke to find it two inches thick on the ground.

Dr. Senter was near the rear of the column, somewhere ahead of Colonel Enos's division. On October 24 the bateaux "loaded with invalids, and lamentable stories of the inaccessibleness of the river,"

passed him on their way back to Norridgewock. One of the sick told
Senter that "the army were all returning," save for Arnold and a few others, and urged the doctor to turn back, but Senter would not be moved.

He may have wondered whether he had made the right decision.
Shortly after talking to the invalids, Senter came across the wreckage
of the bateaux that had overturned in the stream. Two miles farther
along, he ran into Lieutenant Colonel Greene's division. They had
stopped and were waiting for Enos to catch up, hoping that Enos's division would have supplies. Greene's men had nothing to eat "except a
few candles, which were used for supper and breakfast the next morning, by boiling them in water gruel, &c."

"Every prospect of distress," Senter wrote, "now came thundering
on with a two fold rapidity." Greene, like Arnold, saw that it was time
to make a decision. He sent an express upriver to Arnold to inform
the commander of the state of his men, and he sent an express downriver to Enos, the column's other lieutenant colonel, requesting that
Enos and his fellow officers hurry up to Greene's camp "to attend in
consultation."

In the late morning, Enos joined a council of war with Greene and
his officers and a number of the malcontents from the fourth division,
many of whom had refused to leave Cambridge until they were given a
month's pay in advance. "Here sat a number of grimacers," the obser-
vant Senter wrote, "melancholy aspects who had been preaching to
their men the doctrine of impenetrability and non-perseverance. Col.
Enos in the chair."

The question before the council was whether some of the rear division should turn back, as Arnold had ordered, or if they all should
turn back. "The party against going," Senter wrote, "urging the impos-
sibility, averring the whole provisions, when averaged, would not support the army five days." Finally, the matter was put to a vote, and a majority of officers were in favor of pressing on, while sending a part of
the company back, per Arnold's orders. Enos voted in favor of pushing on to Canada, but, according to Senter, "had undoubtedly pre-
arranged to the contrary, as every action demonstrated."

Following the meeting with Greene's men, Enos and his officers held another meeting among themselves, and the outcome was more to their liking. It was decided that they would "not rush into such imminent danger" but instead turn back.

The men who advocated going on were not pleased by this decision, but there was little they could do. They requested that Enos's men divide the supplies, with a majority going to those who were continuing on to Canada and were much farther from resupply than those going back. Enos's men would not consent, and, in fact, said they would not give up any of their supplies. "To compel them to a just division," wrote Senter, "we were not in a situation, being the weakest party." Finally, Enos's men agreed "with ye utmost reluctance," according to Thayer, to give up four barrels of flour and two of pork.

The next day Thayer and a volunteer took a boat back to Enos's rear division to get the promised supplies. Though Enos's men were "overflowing in abundance of all sorts," they refused to give up even the supplies promised. In the end, Thayer went away with only two barrels of flour, "cursing the ill-heart'd minds of the timorous party."

Enos and his men, along with the sick and the shirkers, turned back and eventually reached Cambridge little worse for their adventures. Washington, horrified at what Enos had done, ordered him arrested and tried. On the very day that Arnold was sending an advance guard to meet Montgomery outside Quebec, the court of inquiry met, and though the judges found Enos's conduct was "of not as heinous a nature as first supposed," they recommended a court-martial.

A number of eyewitnesses to Enos's conduct testified at the court-martial, but of course they were the very officers who had returned to Cambridge with him. Had the likes of Senter or Thayer been present, things might have been different, but those men were fighting in Canada. Enos was acquitted with honor, though rightly condemned in public opinion. Shortly after, he resigned from the army.

Meanwhile, the men in Greene's division, abandoned by Enos, resolved "to go through or die." They jettisoned everything that was not entirely necessary and pressed on.

News of Enos's defection with most of the reserve stores moved up the marching column and brought with it shock and grief. Stocking recalled that the news "excited in us much manly resentment."

Thayer was as concerned about the loss of troop strength as he was about the supplies, noting that, "We were Small, indeed, to think of entering such a place as Quebec." Reflecting the general attitude toward those who turned back, Thayer wrote, "our men made a General Prayer, that Colo: Enos and all his men, might die by the way, or meet with some disaster, Equal to the Cowardly dastardly and unfriendly Spirit they discover'd."

But Thayer, in an Olympian effort to find a silver lining, realized that now the rest of them had great motivation to continue on. "But being now almost out of Provisions we were sure to die if we attempted to return Back. — and We Could be in no Worse Situation if we proceeded on our rout."

Through all this, Arnold continued to exert remarkable strength and leadership. After expressing his dismay at Enos's desertion, Stocking wrote, "Our bold though unexperienced general discovered such firmness and zeal as inspired us with resolution. The hardships and fatigues he encountered, he accounted as nothing in comparison with the salvation of his country."

Arnold, Stocking, Thayer, Senter, and the rest stumbled on through the wilderness, north to Quebec, now with the very real possibility of starvation along the way, and an unknown enemy waiting at the end.

CHAPTER *12* Montreal

SOME TWO HUNDRED miles due west from where Arnold and his men were plunging into the wilderness, Brigadier General Richard Montgomery's troops, surrounding the fortifications at St. John's, used shovels, picks, and axes to improve their breastworks and make them ready for artillery.

The siege was a misery as soon as it began. A camp was set up about a mile and a quarter from the British fort in a low, swampy area, "so that the Tents and all the Streets between them were wet and miry, so that in the wet and rainy Seasons the mud and Water was near over Shoe." The Americans' armed vessels were anchored about 150 yards upriver from the encampment, in a line across the Richelieu, keeping a wary eye on the British ships.

As the American army settled in, Montgomery sent Major John Brown with fifty men to La Prairie, across the St. Lawrence from Montreal. The road from St. John's to La Prairie was a rough, pitted, bone-jarring stretch of packed dirt and mud, but it would have been sufficient for the British to move supplies from Montreal to the besieged garrison. It was Brown's job to stop that from happening. A few days later, Seth Warner and his Green Mountain Boys were sent to reinforce Brown's detachment.

As the British, holed up in the fort, began feeling the noose tighten, they blazed away with artillery, concentrating on the growing American earthworks, keeping up "a warm fire on them . . . but did little Damage," one American wrote. Finally, on September 25, Montgomery's batteries to the south were complete enough for the Americans to mount guns on them, and soon they were returning the British gunfire. Trumbull reported, "A very hot fire continued on both Sides till night."

If the gunfire was hot, the weather was decidedly not. The same rainy weather that would plague Arnold on his march to Quebec swept first through the Champlain valley. Morale was dampened along with everything else. "This is as Dark a Season as ever the Troops saw during the whole Siege of St. John's," Trumbull wrote. "The Weather was exceeding discouraging, the ground on which the Army were encamped exceeding mudy and Wet."

Montgomery complained to Schuyler that the sick men he sent to Ticonderoga to convalesce never seemed to make it back to St. John's. Schuyler replied that the "greater part of them are so adverse to going back that they pretend sickness and skulk about."

The Fall of Ethan Allen

On September 28, Arnold had sent his last division off from Fort Western on a march that would make his reputation as a bold and courageous leader. That same day, word arrived at St. John's of Ethan Allen's latest endeavor, a debacle that would seal his reputation as a reckless and foolish grandstander.

Allen had gone to Canada to recruit Canadians to the American cause. Meeting with little luck in that pursuit, he set his sights on a more ambitious goal. At La Prairie he conferred with John Brown, his former associate in the capture of Ticonderoga, and the two men hatched a scheme to cooperate in taking Montreal. Had things gone as planned, they might well have succeeded.

On the morning of September 25, Allen led a mixed force of about 110 Americans and Canadians (English and French) north of the city. There they took cover and waited, straining to hear the three shouted huzzahs from south of Montreal that would signal that Brown had crossed the river from La Prairie to launch his attack.

Hours passed, and anxiety mounted, but the huzzahs never came. Allen would later write that the idea for taking Montreal had been Brown's, but why in the end Brown did not join the attack would remain unclear. Whatever the reason, Brown's failure left Allen in a fix—he could neither attack for want of troops nor effectively retreat.

Montreal was a city on an island, and Allen could not hope to cross back over the river in broad daylight.

Guy Carleton was still in Montreal, having remained there to direct military operations in that part of Quebec Province. Hearing that Allen's men were on the outskirts of the city, he set about organizing his forces for the city's defense. The Canadians in the city had not heretofore shown much interest in taking up arms against Americans, but the threat of immediate attack aroused their martial spirit. About three hundred men, of whom only fifty or so were British regulars and officers, armed themselves, sallied forth from Montreal, and hit Allen's little force head on.

It was not much of a fight. Allen's Canadian troops caved and fled, leaving a small core of men to battle overwhelming odds. They fought hard, dropping back and firing from what cover they could find, while Carleton's troops kept up a furious musket fire. Finally the American troops were surrounded and forced to surrender, Ethan Allen among them. For all the shooting, only two men, both British, were killed, and a little more than a dozen wounded. Allen would afterward remark, "I never saw so much shooting result in so little damage."

Soon after, Allen was clapped in irons in the hold of a naval schooner, and later transferred to a ship bound for England. The bright spark that was Allen's Revolutionary career, a spark ignited five months earlier at Fort Ticonderoga, was extinguished.

No one on the American side was happy about this news, but concern over Allen's fate was the least of it. "I have to lament Mr. Allen's imprudence and ambition," Montgomery wrote to Schuyler. Allen's actions would hardly inspire the kind of confidence and trust the Americans had been hoping to instill in their Canadian brethren.

Mud and Mire

As September turned to October, the siege of St. John's dragged on, with little action beyond a desultory shelling between besiegers and besieged.

Schuyler maintained command at Ticonderoga, although, because he was forwarding men on to Montgomery as soon as they arrived, he had only about sixty effectives in the garrison. Schuyler's problems with provisioning were surpassed only by his problems with discipline and his officers' "scandalous want of subordination and inattention to my orders." He assured Washington that "if Job had been a general in my situation, his memory had not been so famous for patience."

Among the problems vexing Schuyler was what to do regarding a naval force on Lake Champlain. He believed (incorrectly, as it turned out) that an American victory at St. John's would obviate the need for American men-of-war on the lake. He informed the Continental Congress that if they wanted ships, the best he could do was to cut timber and prepare roads in preparation for construction in April, as "Winter is so severe in this Latitude that no Building can be carried on."

By the second week in October, Richard Montgomery was ready to turn up the heat on the British garrison. The siege was proving brutally hard on his men. "Our People have lived in mud and mire most of the Time since they began the Siege," Trumbull wrote. The weather was cold and unsettled, and the men, already miserable, were soaked again and again by driving rain.

Earlier in the month a group of Canadians, fighting on the American side under Major James Livingston, had begun work on a battery on the east side of the river, across from the British fort's north redoubt. Twice the British left the confines of their fort and crossed the river to drive them off, neither time with any success. The Canadians, however, were less of a threat than the British might have imagined, and, more than a week after starting, the battery was still not done. The Canadians, Montgomery observed, "don't love work."

Montgomery's plan was to build another battery on the west side of the fort. It was an idea he had been considering for some time. To that end he had ordered a road cut to the location. Fascines, tightly bound bundles of sticks used to build the sides of earthworks, were fashioned. But Montgomery's troops were becoming even more impatient than Montgomery, and were eager to get home before winter set in. Major Brown, back from La Prairie, alerted Montgomery to the grumbling, and assured him that if some steps to end the siege were not taken in the next few days, there would be a mutiny.

On October 11, Montgomery called a council of war. All the field officers gathered in his tent to hear his proposal for a battery to the west, which they all unanimously rejected. The officers felt, as apparently did the men, that a battery on the east side of the river, opposite the fort, expanding on the effort begun by Livingston's Canadians, "would make a greater impression" on the British garrison.

Montgomery was in a bind. He was certain he was right, but he also comprehended his own "unstable authority over troops of different Colonies, the insufficience of military law, and my own want of power to enforce it."

Though his men were ostensibly part of the Continental army, in truth the army of 1775 was still more a gaggle of militia than a unified force. Worse, they were, in Montgomery's words, "troops who carry the spirit of freedom into the field, and think for themselves." Such free thinking among liberty-minded American soldiers would anger and baffle officers throughout the war, from Washington to Arnold, from John Paul Jones to Baron Frederick von Steuben, many of whom would echo Montgomery's words.

Montgomery had no choice but to acquiesce. In disgust he wrote to Schuyler, "I cannot help observing of how little purpose I am here." He added, "I would not stay an hour at the head of troops whose operations I cannot direct" had he not been afraid that his leaving would cause a stampede of men behind him. Certain that St. John's would not be taken, he suggested that Schuyler prepare Ticonderoga for Carleton's attack the following spring, a move no one doubted that Carleton would make.

Construction of the new battery on the east side of the river began that day. At three in the afternoon, two hundred men of Colonel James Clinton's regiment crossed the river, rowing through a hail of grapeshot from the fort that thankfully failed to hit anyone. The next day they began "cutting and carrying fascines & stakes." As soon as night fell the men worked furiously to erect the battery, finishing it before dawn. A line of trees between the new battery and the riverbank was left standing to hide the new construction from the British.

Among the men working on the battery was yet another Livingston, twenty-seven-year-old Major Henry Livingston, of the 3rd New York

Continental Line, whose great-aunt was Janet Livingston, Richard Montgomery's wife. "The Enemy probably never knew any thing we were abt," Livingston wrote, "altho they were not more than 450 yards off."

The following day the men wrestled two 12-pounders, each weighing more than one and a half tons, along a road "excessively wet & rooty" and mounted them in the battery. That night they cut down the foliage between the battery and the river, opening up a field of fire on the fort.

The next day the new battery and all the others ringing St. John's opened up on the fort. The British replied in kind, concentrating on the new battery on the east side of the river, pounding it with round shot, then switching to exploding shells when the round shot proved ineffective.

The British schooner, "a very handsome, elegant vessel," according to Livingston, with guns mounted and boarding nets rigged, was right in the line of fire. So too was the second vessel, launched some time after the Americans had arrived at Isle aux Noix. She was supposed to be a sloop, but, for lack of rigging, was serving as a row galley.

The British warped the vessels in close to shore, the best they could do, but it could not save them from the American guns. On the first day the new battery opened up, the schooner was sunk. "We shot so many Balls thro her," Livingston wrote, "that next morning she lay careen'd so low that the water ran into her port holes." A few days later the American battery fired red-hot shot into the schooner in an attempt to burn her. Happily, that ill-conceived plan failed when the shot passed clean through the hull.

That vessel, the most powerful on the lake, was no longer a threat to the Americans. But having sunk in shallow water, she could still be raised, and could still do good service for whoever owned her.

Domino Effect

While Montgomery and his army were trading shots with the holdouts at St. John's, Major John Brown, with his fifty Americans, and Major

James Livingston, a Canadian who had managed to recruit about three hundred fellow Canadians, were opening another front. The garrison at Chambly was situated about fifteen miles down the Richelieu River from St. John's, almost due east of Montreal, and Brown and Livingston set about building a battery with which to pound the small fort into submission.

On the night of October 15, a bateau manned by Canadians and carrying a 9-pounder for the Chambly battery, ran past St. John's and down the rapids in the Richelieu River. Unfortunately, Montgomery had failed to alert Colonel Bedel, stationed a mile and a half downriver, that the bateau was coming. Bedel's men fired on the boat until the bateau's crew members were able to inform them that they were all on the same side. Luckily, no one was hurt.

The next night a second cannon was run past the St. John's garrison. The garrison at Chambly, consisting of eight officers, about eighty soldiers, and about a hundred women and children, was not interested in a long siege, nor were the unimpressive masonry walls of Fort Chambly able to withstand much of a pounding from the American battery. On October 18 the Chambly garrison surrendered.

Major Stopford, of the Royal Fusiliers, commanding at Chambly, proposed that the "garrison, officers, and men not to be made prisoners, but to march unmolested . . . drums beating, colours flying . . . by the shortest road to Montreal." Major Brown did not agree, and suggested it would be better were "the garrison, officers, and men to surrender themselves prisoners of war." Because Major Brown was the one with artillery, his suggestion was adopted.

The capture of Chambly yielded a trove of supplies desperately needed by the men at St. John's. Along with barrel upon barrel of flour, rice, peas, and pork, Chambly held 124 barrels of gunpowder, more than sixty-five hundred musket cartridges, and 150 French muskets.

The capture of Chambly gave a big boost to morale at St. John's. The formerly gloomy Montgomery wrote Schuyler that "The troops are in high spirits," and, thanks to the captured gunpowder, "unless some unlucky accident befalls us, we shall accomplish our business here." The one thing they did not find at Chambly was rum. "Let us have rum, my dear General," Montgomery added, "else we shall never be able to get though our business."

While the fighting went on at Chambly and St. John's, American forces across the river from Montreal continued to watch the city for activity. "Well and hearty," wrote John Fassett, a captain in Warner's regiment, "but nothing to do."

On October 26, Governor Guy Carleton, still in Montreal, sent a fleet of bateaux probing along the American defenses on the south side of the St. Lawrence River. The Americans followed the bateaux's progress along the river, exchanging brisk fire with them, musket balls flying "thick as hailstones." As evening fell, the British retreated to Montreal.

Four days later, Carleton made one final push to break out and relieve St. John's. With thirty-four boats loaded with regulars, he crossed the St. Lawrence and attempted a landing at Longueuil, directly across the river. There to greet the governor were Seth Warner and his Green Mountain Boys, along with the 2nd Regiment of Yorkers, about 350 men in all, and a 4-pounder that Warner had just received the evening before.

Lining the riverbank, the Americans poured small arms fire into the regulars as they waded ashore. For hours the two sides exchanged fire. The Americans, finding cover behind dunes and pine trees, kept the British pinned on the shore. Finally, as daylight began to fade, the Americans brought up their 4-pounder and turned it on the regulars. That was enough for the British, who had thought that the Americans did not have artillery. They scrambled back into the bateaux and returned, defeated, to Montreal. "This," Montgomery wrote to Schuyler, "I believe, is his [Carleton's] last effort." He was right.

The Second Taking of St. John's

Upon receiving word of the surrender of Chambly, Montgomery had sent a note under flag of truce to Major Charles Preston, the commanding officer of the men of the 26th Regiment at St. John's, requesting that he allow the Americans' boats to pass downriver to collect the prisoners at Chambly and their baggage. "Their number of women," Montgomery wrote, "and quantity of baggage is astonishing." Preston agreed to the brief cease-fire. When it was over, the terrific artillery duel resumed, both sides flailing away with round and grapeshot.

Word of Carleton's defeat at the hands of the Green Mountain Boys reached Montgomery on October 30, along with a few British prisoners from that action. Montgomery knew that it was all but over for the British in Canada, and he was sure that Preston would agree. He sent one of the prisoners into the fort at St. John's to inform Preston of this latest development.

Preston replied that the prisoner was "frequently subject to fits of insanity," and was not to be believed. True or not, however, Preston understood the futility of holding out much longer. He told Montgomery that if the garrison was not relieved in four days, he would surrender.

Montgomery then sent another prisoner into the fort, a Mr. Depane from Montreal, who apparently enjoyed greater mental stability than the first man, to reiterate the story of Carleton's defeat. Unwilling to wait any longer, Montgomery informed Preston that the "advanced season of the year will not admit of your proposal," and if they did not surrender on that day, "the garrison shall be prisoners of war, without the honors of war, and I cannot ensure the officers their baggage."

That did it. On November 2, after forty-five days of siege, St. John's surrendered. The garrison was allowed to "march out with the honors of war," the articles stated, "due to their fortitude and perseverance." They were to remain prisoners of war in America until they were exchanged or until the "unhappy differences shall be compromised."

St. John's was even more of a bonanza than Chambly. Although the stores were meager—the garrison had been on half rations for some time—the Americans found a significant number of heavy guns. And, more importantly, there was the schooner, which the Americans found was named *Royal Savage*. The other vessel, nearly complete but for her masts and rigging, would become the schooner *Revenge*. Those ships, frantically built by the British in their attempt to regain control of Lake Champlain, would now help further cement American domination there.

On to Montreal

As soon as St. John's capitulated, Montgomery sent a body of men north by the road to La Prairie to reinforce the troops outside Montreal. Colonel Bedel, echoing the old pirates' mantra, wrote, "In about four days we shall have either a wooden leg or a gold chain at Montreal."

It was clear enough, however, that taking Montreal would not result in many wooden legs. Major Brown wrote to Montgomery on November 7 that the local merchants had held a council and requested that Carleton give them an idea of what the fate of the city would be. Carleton had reportedly told them "he should quit the Town in a day or two, and they might take care of themselves."

In the days following the surrender of St. John's, Montgomery continued to forward men to Montreal, among them David Wooster's regiment, which the Continental Congress had earlier ordered north from its encampment near New York City. Wooster was already causing problems, superseding Schuyler and acting beyond his authority. Schuyler, in fact, had been wary of sending Wooster to St. John's, concerned "that he might create Difficulties, If he should join the Army under General Montgomery." In the end, Schuyler had no choice, because Wooster's men, in the spirit of local militia, would not march without Wooster at their head.

Moving the army north toward Montreal was slow going. The weather grew increasingly bitter, snow mixing with rain and covering the ground. The troops, poorly dressed, poorly equipped, half soaked, and half frozen, trudged along the broken road, heavy muskets resting on shoulders, cartridge boxes, haversacks, and canteens hanging at their sides. Teams of oxen and horses were hitched to the heavy artillery taken at St. John's, with gangs of men heaving and pushing the wooden carriages through ruts and mud. Local teamsters, working for hard cash, drove wagons groaning under the extraordinary loads of supplies and equipment needed to maintain even a small army in the field.

In those harsh conditions, the men and tools of siege warfare slogged their way from St. John's to Montreal.

As Montgomery made preparations for moving on Montreal, several matters concerned him, chief among them that he had not yet heard from Benedict Arnold despite having dispatched two letters to him. With the success of his venture so nearly complete, Montgomery needed only for Arnold to succeed as well, and all of Quebec Province—nearly all of Canada—would effectively be theirs.

Other concerns were money and manpower. Despite their recent success, things were not going entirely well for the American forces in the north. American paper money was useless in Canada, and it was getting harder and harder to acquire provisions and supplies from a population that wanted hard currency. Many of the troops' enlistments were due to expire, and they had no desire to remain any longer. Schuyler wrote to the Continental Congress, "few of the troops to the northward would re-engage. . . . They have such an intemperate desire to return home, that nothing can equal it." Congress could not have been surprised; they were hearing the same message from General Washington in Cambridge.

Montgomery managed to convince a significant portion of his men to remain until April, but, in fact, he and Schuyler were also eager to abandon their military careers. Montgomery asked Schuyler if his, Schuyler's, health would not permit him to winter in Montreal, where he could take over the command of the army. "I am weary of power," Montgomery wrote, "and totally want that patience and temper requisite to such a command."

Schuyler was also ready to be done, and informed Congress that he felt exactly as Montgomery did, as would "every man of sentiment, who is drove to the necessity of wheedling, coaxing, and even lying . . . in order to carry on the service." In the end, though, and for very different reasons, neither man would soon be returning to civilian life.

By November 12, a good part of the Northern Army had crossed the St. Lawrence and was employed setting up batteries in the suburbs of Montreal. Montgomery wrote to the citizens of Montreal requesting that they take "such measures as will prevent the necessity of opening my batteries upon the Town." He pointed out that "many innocent people must suffer" from shelling and any concomitant fires at that time of the year. He urged the people to appeal to Governor Carleton to offer no resistance, but in fact Carleton had fled the city the day before.

The inhabitants of Montreal were in perfect agreement with Montgomery, and, because the governor was gone, there was no need to ask his opinion. A hastily formed council drew up articles of capitulation, promising, in essence, that it would not resist the Americans if the Americans did not interfere in any way with commerce, religious practice, travel, or anything else.

The American general replied that, because Montreal had "neither ammunition, artillery, troops nor provisions," the ad hoc council was really not in a position to claim "title to a capitulation." Nonetheless, the American brigadier general agreed to nearly all the council's demands. On November 13, Montgomery and his army entered Montreal without resistance.

The plan for a two-pronged attack on Canada had, so far, worked almost perfectly. All of Quebec Province seemed to lie at the Americans' feet. But the question remained—where was Benedict Arnold?

CHAPTER *13* *The March to Quebec*

AT THE END of October, while the siege of St. John's was nearing its triumphant conclusion and the suffering of the American troops encircling the fort was on the verge of being mitigated, Arnold and his men were still deep in the wilderness. They were in much worse shape than Montgomery's men, suffering through the same abysmal weather but with the added difficulty of having to transport boats and supplies through wild, broken country. And their situation would only get worse. As bad as things might have been for Montgomery's troops, Arnold's would gladly have traded their lot for the simple boredom and discomfort of siege warfare.

Around the time that Carleton was sending his regulars across the St. Lawrence in an attempt to drive off Seth Warner and the Green Mountain Boys, Arnold dispatched Captain Oliver Hanchet and his men to press on quickly to Sartigan to procure supplies for the men dying along the trail. Arnold himself followed Hanchet's detachment with another column of about seventy men. The weather was increasingly fierce—"Snowed and blowed very hard," Arnold wrote.

On October 27, Arnold's column reached the head of the Dead River and the chain of ponds and portages leading to Lake Megantic and the Chaudiere River. This was the height of land, which Morison deemed "The Terrible Carrying Place." Incredibly, the suffering and hardship of Arnold's men was about to get worse.

A thick snow that had fallen some days before still covered the ground. Dragging bateaux and supplies over barely existent trails, the men could not distinguish solid footing from icy bog. They were constantly breaking through thin ice, plunging knee or even waist deep into freezing water, then marching on with shoes and pants frozen solid in the cold air.

The "dismal portage" was more than two miles long, "plentiful strewn with old dead logs, and with every thing that could render it impassable." The boats were dragged uphill over "a considerable ridge covered with fallen trees, stones and brush," this labor performed by men who, in some cases, had eaten no more than a pint of flour per day for two weeks.

Once over the carrying place, Arnold's party put into a narrow stream that carried them north to Lake Megantic. Happy as they must have been to be rowing rather than dragging their bateaux, the going was not easy, the stream twisting in every direction and clogged with "Loggs, &c. which we were obliged to cut away."

On that stream, Arnold met Lieutenants Steele and Church coming back from a scouting mission to the French inhabitants at Sartigan. They reported that the locals were "rejoiced" to hear that the Americans were coming and "will gladly supply us with provisions." These were words to fill Arnold's heart with joy, as was the additional intelligence that Carleton was at Montreal and there were few troops at Quebec.

At four that afternoon, Arnold and his detachment left the stream and rowed into the open water of Lake Megantic. They covered about three miles, then camped at a "considerable wigwam" they found on the shore. Around sunset they spied Hanchet and his men, who had become lost, on shore a few miles away. Arnold sent the bateaux to fetch them.

That evening, Arnold took time to compose a number of letters to his officers and to Washington and sent them back down the line. A letter was dispatched to the officers in each division, telling them of the good news that Steele and Church had delivered, with instructions that all the men should be informed. Not realizing that Enos had already abandoned him, Arnold sent word that the lieutenant colonel should choose an officer who was too sick to go on to carry his correspondence back to Cambridge. He closed with "I hope soon to see you in Quebec."

Having crossed the "considerable ridge," Arnold and his men found themselves "Bidding adieu to the Southern Waters." They had crossed the head of drainage for streams flowing south to the Atlantic. Lake Megantic and the Chaudiere River, like Lake Champlain and the Richelieu, flowed north toward the St. Lawrence. Though the Chaudiere River was "very Rapid, full of Rocks and Dangerous," at least the current from that point on was with them, and carried them along "at the rate of eight or ten miles an hour."

Arnold again pushed on ahead of the troops, now with just fifteen men in company, including the redoubtable Eleazer Oswald. That day three of their bateaux were swept up in the river's dangerous current, driven on the rocks and wrecked. With most of their remaining provisions lost, Arnold pressed on with just six men in the two remaining bateaux. They covered forty miles the second day, with the Chaudiere River becoming wider and less treacherous, despite their having to portage around numerous rapids.

On October 30—the day that Sir Guy Carleton staged his last attempt to break out of Montreal—Arnold's band covered another twenty or so miles down the Chaudiere, finally reaching the first house on the river, the very feather edge of French Canadian civilization. Having emerged at last from the wilderness, Arnold now had to ensure that the hundreds of men strung out behind him made it through as well.

"A transition from death to life"

Arnold's message of October 27 concerning the French inhabitants' approbation of the American invasion greatly improved morale as it moved down the column. On the day it arrived at Senter's division, the men had gathered up rawhides intended for making moccasins, chopped them up, boiled them, and drunk the juice. Arnold's note was read "to the unspeakable joy of the whole camp." Now, with some hope of relief, the officers ordered the men to move on as quickly as possible. Too weak and unwilling to struggle with their burden any longer, the men abandoned their bateaux at the height of land, and the column advanced on foot.

The joy the men felt, however, was premature. Arnold had not yet procured and forwarded supplies; he was only reporting what Steele had told him concerning the people's willingness to help. The column still faced days of tramping through a snowy wilderness with little or no food. Some, thinking relief was at hand, ate the last of their provisions, only to die of starvation when fresh supplies failed to reach them in time. Many of the companies became lost in the swamps despite Arnold's careful directions. In many cases the loss of time proved fatal.

On October 31, Daniel Morgan's bateaux were wrecked in a waterfall, the men "losing everything except their lives," save for one man who drowned—incredibly, the first drowning of the expedition. Others were now dying from hunger, exhaustion, and exposure. "Instead of the diarrhoea, which tried our men most shockingly in the former part of the march, the reverse was now the complaint . . . ," Senter wrote. Constipation was hardly a surprise, given their diet, which now consisted of cakes made from flour and water, as well as "shaving soap, pomatum [a kind of lotion for the skin], and even the lip salve, leather of their shoes, cartridge boxes, &c," none of which tended to promote intestinal health.

Some of the men were still appreciative of what they had. Morison wrote in his journal, "No one can imagine who hath not experienced it, the sweetness of a roasted shot-pouch to the famished appetite."

By the first of November the column was strung out in a long, disorganized line along the trail. There was no longer any unit cohesion, and "the orders were for every man to do for himself," Thayer wrote, "as well as he could." Senter and the others recognized the need for this brutal order. "Life depended upon a vigorous push for the inhabitants, and that did not admit of any stay for any person." Many of the men were now barefoot, their shoes either worn away or having been eaten.

In his journal, Henry Dearborn reported that, "This day Capt Goodrich's Company Kill'd my Dog, and another dog, and Eat them." Other witnesses reported that virtually no part of the dogs that could be considered edible were left unconsumed. It is indicative of just how extraordinary and repulsive the idea of eating dog was to Americans that nearly every man who kept a journal mentioned this incident, and that the dogs survived as long as they did before being eaten.

Finally, on November 2, those troops who were still marching were delivered from their suffering. Thayer wrote that he "discovered . . . some men and horses and cattle making toward us, at which sight Capt. Topham and myself shed tears of joy, in our happy delivery from the Grasping hand of Death. The Drover was sent toward us by Col. Arnold, in order to kill them [the cattle] for our support."

Immediately upon arriving at Sartigan, Arnold had arranged for provisions to be sent upriver for the relief of the column, with drovers herding cattle along the riverbank and men dispatched by canoes to carry food. In a letter to his officers, he urged those who still had provisions "to let this pass on for the rear; and those who want will take sparingly as possible, that the whole may meet with relief."

The joy felt by the men at the arrival of food on the hoof was universal and overwhelming. "This sudden change was like a transition from death to life," Morison wrote. Senter reported that "Exclamations of Joy. –Echoes of gladness resounded from front to rear."

The drovers slaughtered and roasted the animals wherever they met knots of men, then carried meat up the trail to others who had not yet arrived. Many of the soldiers could not wait for the meat to be cooked. "I got a little piece of the flesh," Stocking wrote, "which I eat raw . . . and thought I feasted sumptuously."

Arnold's column was six weeks out of Newburyport and had been more than a month in the wilderness. From Fort Western they had traversed 180 miles of wild country. Now, just a little more than sixty miles more would put them on Point Levi, across the river from Quebec.

Point Levi

Arnold's remaining force numbered around six hundred, sickness, death, and Enos's desertion having cut the number of effectives almost in half. They were battered, worn down, and deprived of much of the gear with which they had set out, but they were alive, and the supplies passing back down the line were likely to keep them that way. The French Canadians and Indians they met treated them kindly, and cheerfully sold them food and alcohol at exorbitant prices.

The column was still spread out over twenty miles or so of trail. "Our army was in a very scattered condition," Senter wrote, and "expresses were sent to hurry them on as fast as possible."

On November 5, Arnold received bad news via a messenger from Quebec. A second letter he had written to a friend in Quebec, this time from Sartigan, had been intercepted by the British. In the letter, Arnold had written that he led "a large detachment from the American Army." He had asked for intelligence regarding British troop strength, and added, "I hope to see you in Quebec in a few days."

Arnold did not know that his first letter had ended up in the hands of Lieutenant Governor Hector Cramahé, but now he understood that the British were alerted to his coming, and surprise—the American's best weapon—was lost. His only hope now was that the British would not have the time or troops to reinforce the city before he and his men arrived.

The army pushed on, the going still hard through mud and blizzards of snow. Private James Melvin of Dearborn's company wrote of "very bad traveling, as it was all the way to Quebec. Twelve miles was through the woods, in the night, mid leg in mud and snow." Senter, who had rented a horse, claimed that the mud was up to the horse's belly. But they were well fed now, and most had shelter for sleeping, so their present circumstances could not compare with the nightmare in the wilderness.

On Wednesday, November 8, while Montgomery's men were marching from St. John's to demand the surrender of Montreal, Arnold and most of his men arrived at Point Levi. "We were filled with joy at this event," wrote Morison, "when we saw ourselves at the end of our destination." But they still had to cross the river to Quebec before they could even begin the genuinely difficult part of their mission, the reason they had come so far, the capture of the city itself.

Quebec City

The exhausted, cold, bedraggled men who stood on the edge of the St. Lawrence River and looked across that water toward Quebec City could not have felt overly sanguine about their chances of taking that place. It was for good reason that the city was called "The Gibraltar of America."

Quebec City sat astride a point of land at the confluence of the St. Lawrence and St. Charles rivers. On its St. Lawrence side, the city perched atop a two-hundred-foot cliff that tumbled almost straight down into the river. This was known as the Upper Town. A great cluster of buildings sat on that high ground, and rising above their roofs were the tall spires of the city's many churches. Sprawling along the riverfront at the foot of the cliffs, pressed between the Upper Town to the west and the water to the south and east, was the Lower Town, part of which was taken up by the Cul de Sac, Quebec's sheltered harbor.

The Lower Town and the suburbs that surrounded Quebec City to the north had grown up outside the walls, and were unprotected and vulnerable to attack. But a garrison drawn up behind the high stone walls on the cliff top would be brutally difficult to dislodge.

Samuel de Champlain had recognized the strategic advantages of those cliffs looming over a narrow section of the river when he founded Quebec City in 1608. Now the poorly equipped men of Arnold's column, with no guns more powerful than their muskets, must have wondered how they would ever take such a formidable citadel.

At Point Levi, a letter from Richard Montgomery managed to catch up with Arnold. Arnold wrote back, congratulating Montgomery on his recent victories and admitting that he had arrived at Quebec much later than he had expected, explaining that "I was not then apprised or even apprehensive of one half of the difficulties we had to encounter."

Arnold already believed that the British knew he was coming, and what he found at Point Levi confirmed it. Every boat on the Americans' side of the river had been removed or destroyed to prevent his men from crossing. Happily, they had at their disposal some twenty birch bark canoes that had been brought by forty "savages" who had joined Arnold's forces.

The Americans had more than just the river to contend with, however, in their crossing to Quebec City. Two British men-of-war were anchored between them and their landing place on the Quebec side. One was the frigate *Lizard*. The other was the sloop-of-war *Hunter*, a vessel smaller than a sixth-rate frigate, rigged like a ship and commanded by a master and commander rather than a post captain.

Although the garrison at Quebec was aware of the presence of the Americans, the ships apparently were not. The day after Arnold's arrival, the *Hunter* sent a boat, commanded by a midshipman named MacKenzie, the captain's younger brother, to Point Levi to retrieve some oars that had been made at the mill there.

As the boat crew clambered ashore, the Americans fired on them, sending them rushing back to their boat, so panicked that they left the midshipman behind. MacKenzie, who was no more than fifteen, leaped into the river and tried to swim away, but he was caught and dragged back to land. The *Hunter* blasted away with grape- and round shot, to no effect. Midshipman MacKenzie became a prisoner of war, and was apparently well liked and well treated by Arnold's men.

The other thing holding Arnold's men on the south shore was the wind, which continued to blow fiercely for days, too strong to risk crossing the water in canoes. Preparing for an attack on the city, and understanding how dangerous idleness was to morale, Arnold set the men to building scaling ladders, much as he had had them making musket cartridges on the Dead River. He also continued to accumulate canoes, until he had gathered up about thirty-five.

On the night of November 12 Arnold held a council of war to decide whether or not they should attack Quebec once they crossed the St. Lawrence. Their situation did not look promising. The American column was at half its original strength, battered from its march through the wilderness and lacking much of its equipment. The British were aware of the men's presence and had taken steps to strengthen the garrison. The day before the meeting, a deserter from Quebec named Halstead had informed the Americans that a column of the Royal Highland Emigrants had just recently arrived to reinforce the city.

Indeed, ever since reaching Point Levi, Arnold had been thinking that the opportunity to take Quebec might well have passed. Writing to Montgomery, he had stated that "if any opportunity offers of attacking

Quebec with success," he would try, but if not he would join Montgomery at Montreal. But Arnold was a fire breather and still eager for
an all-out assault, as were his more aggressive officers, in particular
Daniel Morgan and Christopher Greene. The others disagreed, and a
majority of officers at the council of war voted to delay any attack, "to
the great mortification of the opposite party."

If they were not going to attack, they could at least lay siege to the
city or join Montgomery, and prevent any additional reinforcements
from reaching the garrison at Quebec City, but all those things required gaining the other side of the St. Lawrence.

By the night of November 13, the wind had subsided enough for canoes to venture onto the river. Around nine o'clock the men and
boats began to assemble, and soon the lead division was under way,
with Halstead as pilot. A detachment of about fifty men was left behind under the command of Captain Oliver Hanchet, who resented
the assignment.

Through the dark night, the canoes nearly silent, the Americans
passed undiscovered right between the two men-of-war. Even the men
in the guard boats that were rowing patrol around the ships failed to
see them. The canoes landed at Wolfe's Cove, named for General
James Wolfe, who had landed there on his successful though fatal attack on Quebec in 1759.

For hours the canoes crossed and recrossed the river, until around
four in the morning all five hundred or so of Arnold's men, save for
Hanchet's company, were outside Quebec.

It was not until the crossing was complete that a barge from the
Lizard closed with the shore. Arnold hailed the barge crew and ordered
them to land, which, not surprisingly, they declined to do. The Americans fired into them and "perceived by ye screaming and dismal lamen-
tations of the crew that there were some of them kill'd or wounded."
Arnold later reported that "we fired on the frigate's barge and killed
three men . . . ," though how he came about that number is unclear.

Arnold's column would have been in a good position for a surprise
attack, but the firing on the barge "prevented our surprising the town,"

as Arnold wrote to Montgomery. And of course the council of war had already decided not to attack, a fact which Arnold did not include in his letter. Perhaps he did not want to admit to Montgomery that his officers had declined to take the bold action; writing to Schuyler some time later, Arnold again failed to mention that fact.

Or perhaps Arnold simply did not want to admit that fact to any British officer who might intercept the letter. "I have been so unfortunate in my former letters," he wrote, "I don't choose to commit every intelligence to writing."

CHAPTER *14* *Quebec Besieged*

THE CAPITAL CITY of Quebec, outside of which Arnold and his men stood, was as well prepared for their arrival as it could be, which is to say, not well prepared at all.

At the onset of trouble, Carleton had tried to rally Canadians to the British cause. Indeed, the British government from the king on down seemed to take it for granted that thousands of Canadian militia—who, in the case of Quebec Province, would be primarily French Canadians—were to be had for the asking. The American Secretary, William Legge, the Earl of Dartmouth, had written to Carleton in July saying, "The King relies upon the Loyalty and Fidelity of his Canadian subjects for their assistance to suppress the Rebellion," and if Carleton were to "see no objection," he was to "take the proper steps for raising a Body of 3,000 Canadians." Before those orders were sent, Dartmouth upped that number to six thousand.

That the king and the secretary for North America could even ask such a thing showed a serious lack of understanding of their Canadian subjects. Carleton tried to raise Canadian militia, but he met with virtually no luck. Hector Cramahé, the lieutenant governor of Quebec, assured Lord Dartmouth, "No means have been left untried to bring the Canadian peasantry to a sense of their duty and engage them to take up arms in defense of the province, but all to no purpose." Many French Canadians considered the rebellion a fight between Englishmen and none of their concern.

While Carleton was still in Montreal, Cramahé was left to see to the defenses of Quebec. His entire force consisted of twenty men of the Royal Fusiliers, the militia, composed of residents of the city, and eighty men under Lieutenant Colonel Allan Maclean, who had only recently arrived at Quebec.

Maclean, a Scotsman and a veteran of the British army, had earlier in the year enlisted a force of fellow Scots who, like himself, were former soldiers who had emigrated to the colonies. These tough, experienced troops became the Royal Highland Emigrants. Seventy of them augmented the garrison at St. John's.

As impregnable as Quebec could be, it, like Ticonderoga and Crown Point, had fallen into disrepair, with no cannon mounted and gaping holes in the walls. The soldiers and militia had worked furiously to repair the breaches and strengthen the other defenses as they waited for the enemy to come.

The one advantage the British enjoyed was a strong naval presence. In July, Carleton had written to Admiral Samuel Graves in Boston asking for shipwrights and two sloops of war. Graves could not supply the former, but the latter he could. The brig-of-war *Gaspee* was already at Carleton's disposal at Montreal, and in late September Graves ordered the sloop-of-war *Hunter,* of ten guns and eighty men, to sail for Canada. On October 12, *Hunter* "came too with the Best Bower in 18 fathom water off the Town of Quebec."

The following month, on November 5, the frigate *Lizard*, with twenty guns and 130 men on board, arrived at the city from England. The Earl of Dartmouth had arranged for the *Lizard* to escort the store ship *Jacob* to Quebec, carrying arms, equipment, and uniforms for the initial three thousand Canadian militia he had ordered Carleton to raise.

Four days later the *Jacob* arrived, the two ships having lost each other in a Gulf of St. Lawrence fogbank. John Hamilton, captain of the *Lizard*, agreed to Carleton's request that he stay to aid in the defense of Quebec.

With a near universal lack of cooperation from the Canadians, many of whom were leaning toward the victorious Americans, all that Carleton had to defend Quebec Province were the seven hundred or so British troops under his overall command. One hundred had been lost at Chambly. On November 4 he learned that four hundred more had been made prisoners of war at St. John's.

Carleton blamed the loss of St. John's and Chambly in part on the lack of shipwrights who might have constructed a fleet to defend the lake, an accusation that was probably valid. Considering how apprehensive the Americans were about even one partially finished schooner, a naval force might have made a big difference, perhaps even halting any American effort. Carleton assumed there was an abundance of qualified men in the maritime provinces of Canada, but he received only a few from Halifax, and they did not arrive until a month after Montgomery had surrounded St. John's.

The loss of the garrison was also brought on, Carleton felt, by "the corruption, and I may add by the stupid baseness, of the Canadian peasantry," who failed to rally to their new government.

With St. John's gone, Carleton knew that Montreal would not stand long, and that the people of the town would make no effort to defend it. Lieutenant Colonel Maclean, whom Carleton had sent up the Richelieu with a combined force of Fusiliers, Highlanders, and Canadian militia, had been abandoned by the militia and forced to take refuge with his men on a few ships anchored in the St. Lawrence.

And now there was a new threat. "Accounts say B. Arnold is on the Chaudière with twelve or fifteen hundred men," Carleton wrote to Dartmouth. Carleton did not hold out great hopes for Quebec. Still, with the Americans closing in from two sides, it was clear to everyone that the only option left to the British troops was to secure themselves for the winter in the walled city and hope for reinforcements in spring. As 1775 drew to a close, victory was on the side of the Americans, and the outlook for the British army in Canada was bleak.

Retreat to Quebec

Guy Carleton had the brig *Gaspee*, two armed vessels, and eight merchantmen waiting at Montreal to carry his garrison downriver to Quebec. Once news of the capitulation of St. John's reached him, he was ready to go, but an adverse wind kept the ships at anchor. Meanwhile, the passage downriver looked more and more precarious as American forces pushed into Canada. "The rebels are now upon the north shore of the St. Lawrence," Cramahé reported to Dartmouth from Quebec, and "have cut off the communication by land with Montreal." The river was the only route to Quebec open to Carleton, but the Americans were closing that as well, bringing up heavy guns and erecting batteries on shore and afloat that commanded the St. Lawrence below Montreal.

Finally, on November 11, the wind swung around, and Carleton marched his garrison, about ninety men in all, down to the waiting ships. For Carleton it was not a moment too soon, because Montgomery's troops were already stationing themselves on the outskirts of the city. An hour before sunset, the eleven-ship convoy weighed anchor and stood down the river for Quebec.

They did not get far. The next day one of the armed vessels ran aground, and considerable time was wasted getting her off. Then, as the convoy neared the mouth of the Richelieu River, the wind died, then came up again from the east, and once again the fleet was stuck at anchor.

With the ships wind-bound, American batteries began to open up on them. From Montreal, Montgomery hurried guns downriver to cut off the British retreat. A note demanding surrender was sent out under flag of truce.

The same day that Carleton found himself stuck under American guns on the St. Lawrence River, Maclean and what was left of the Fusiliers and the Royal Highland Emigrants, about two hundred men, slipped into Quebec. They were one day ahead of Arnold's reaching the city.

On November 15, after enduring three days as targets, Carleton's fleet shifted anchor several times to get out from under the American batteries, but to no avail. The captains of the merchant vessels, particularly those carrying gunpowder, were increasingly restive.

Surrender or disaster, one or the other, was just a matter of time, and Carleton knew it. On the night of November 16, he "with great difficulty procured the master of one of the vessels" to take him in a whaleboat and row silently past the American batteries. Farther down the river they met up with the merchant vessel *Fell*, bound for Quebec, and Carleton took passage with her.

"Had I been ten days sooner . . ."

Arnold's officers had voted not to attack Quebec, but Arnold hoped that the garrison in Quebec would come out and attack him. Friends in Quebec kept Arnold informed of what was happening behind the walls. The day his troops crossed the river, Arnold wrote to Montgomery that he thought Maclean would come out and fight, and that the Americans were "Prepared and anxious to see him."

If the view of Quebec from Point Levi was of an impregnable castle on a cliff, the view from the land west of Quebec was a little more encouraging. From where Arnold's men stood on the Plains of Abraham, they looked over a few miles of open country, rolling, snow-covered fields broken by a smattering of trees and farmhouses. At the far end of that open country stood the fortifications that enclosed Quebec City, a series of formidable stone walls and bastions that ran right across the point of land on which the city was located, from Cape Diamond in the south right up to the cliffs above the St. Charles River to the north. There were six main gates in the wall, each of them shut tight.

A few suburbs made up mostly of wood frame houses had grown up outside the walls. The most substantial of these was the suburb of St. Roch, just beyond the northwest corner of the city's wall.

Arnold posted sentries along the approaches to the city gates and in the suburbs, cutting off Quebec's communications with the outside world. On the morning of November 14, a handful of British soldiers slipped out and captured one of the sentries. As they raced with their captive back to the safety of the walled city, they were pursued by American troops, but managed to get through the gate ahead of them.

Thinking that this, perhaps, was the beginning of an all-out attack, Arnold "rallied the main body," according to Meigs, and marched them to within fifty yards of the city walls. There the Americans gave the British "three huzzahs, and marched our men fairly in their view."

But the British knew better than to come out and risk losing a battle when they were safe behind Quebec's walls. That was, after all, how the French had lost Quebec in the first place. The British "answer'd them with three cheers of defiance, & saluted them with a few cannon loaded with grape & cannister shot." Finally the Americans returned to their camp. When Arnold sent an officer under flag of truce to negotiate for the sentry's release, he too was fired on, "contrary to humanity and the laws of nations."

For the next few days, Arnold continued to probe the walls of Quebec. He reported to Washington, "We marched up several times near the walls, in hopes of drawing them out but to no effect."

On November 18, having been told by a deserter from the city that the defenders might attack the following day, Arnold ordered a complete inventory of the men's arms and ammunition. What he found was not encouraging. Many of the cartridges that appeared serviceable were in fact ruined, so that there was no more than five rounds per man, "and near one hundred guns unfit for service. Add to this," he wrote to Montgomery, "many of the men invalids, and almost naked and wanting every thing to make them comfortable," including shoes.

This news changed Arnold's strategic thinking. If the march through the Maine woods had not been so brutal, things might have been different. "Had I been ten days sooner," Arnold wrote to Washington, "Quebec must have inevitably fallen into our hands." That was probably truer than even Arnold realized. The return of Colonel Allan Maclean and his men on November 12 had done much to augment the force behind the walls and to bolster the resolve of Hector Cramahé, who was not a particularly strong or courageous leader.

Now the Americans were in no condition to storm the reinforced garrison at Quebec. Exactly two months after boarding the transports at Newburyport, Arnold was forced to do the one thing he hated most. He retreated.

AT THREE in the morning on November 19, the main body of Arnold's forces, about 550 effectives, moved out, leaving behind a small detachment to keep an eye on Quebec City. That night the men arrived at Pointe aux Trembles, now known as Neuville, about twenty miles upriver from Quebec. As they marched along the St. Lawrence, they were passed by a vessel downbound from Montreal.

That vessel was the *Fell*, on which Carleton had taken passage. But even if the Americans had known that, they had no artillery to prevent a ship from sailing past them on the river. The *Fell* stood on downriver, past Wolfe's Cove and Cape Diamond, then rounded up in the Cul de Sac and dropped anchor under the guns of Quebec City. Governor Carleton had returned.

That same day, the fleet of vessels that Carleton had left under the guns of the American batteries on the St. Lawrence River surrendered to Montgomery's troops. Along with the ships and their crews were the soldiers who had left Montreal with Carleton.

Arnold set about getting his "little corps," as he described them to General Montgomery, back into condition to fight. He procured leather and set the men to making moccasins. He wrote to Montgomery with a list of clothing "absolutely necessary for a winter's campaign," which included six hundred stockings, five hundred yards of wool for breeches, and a thousand yards of flannel or baize for shirts.

Arnold also sent an officer to meet with merchants whom Arnold knew in Montreal to buy clothes for the men. Arnold, who would after his treason be lambasted for his avarice, instructed the merchants that if the officer did not have "cash sufficient for his purpose, any articles you are kind enough to furnish him with, you will please to place to my account, which I will see duly paid"—and this after he had been so badly used by the Massachusetts Provincial Congress for doing the same thing at Ticonderoga.

Having realized that his depleted force was too small to take the city alone, Arnold now awaited "with great anxiety the arrival of Gen. Montgomery," figuring that together they would "knock up a dust with the garrison at Quebec." Arnold estimated that the effort would require at least two thousand men.

Through the rest of November, Arnold and his men remained at Pointe aux Trembles. "Preparations is making," Meigs wrote, "and things seem ripening fast for the assault on the works of Quebec."

As late as November 13, Montgomery had received no word from Arnold. But in a letter intercepted when the Americans took Montreal, he learned that Arnold and his men had made it through the wilderness and were now outside Quebec. Finally, with lines of communication more secure, the two officers were able to correspond. Montgomery needed two weeks to organize things in Montreal before leaving David Wooster in command there and heading off to join Arnold.

Finally, on December 1, "to the great joy" of Arnold's men, General Montgomery arrived with three armed schooners, part of Carleton's little fleet captured near the mouth of the Richelieu. Aboard the vessels were soldiers, artillery, ammunition, and, most welcome of all, clothes, which the men "stood in much need of . . . ," wrote Morison, "inasmuch that many of us were partly naked by the time we reached the frontier." The clothes were for the most part captured British uniforms. Before the attack on Quebec, the men would be ordered to wear hemlock sprigs in their hats to distinguish themselves from the enemy.

Montgomery brought 300 New Yorkers "equipped for a winter campaign," as well as 160 of John Brown's men. He also brought with him the confidence acquired from his recent string of successes. "The garrison consists of Maclean's banditti," he wrote to Schuyler. "I propose amusing Mr. Carleton with a formal attack, erecting batteries, etc." His self-assurance and military bearing impressed and encouraged the troops.

Arnold's men were turned out for Montgomery's inspection. Standing in line for review, Arnold's veterans were hardly the picture of crisp, disciplined soldiery. They were gaunt and emaciated, with torn breeches and stockings hanging in rags, tattered coats made from blankets or the well-worn fringed hunting frocks of the riflemen, bits of cloth wrapped around their heads to defend against the biting cold, and battered hats pushed down over those. But Montgomery saw beyond that. "The General complimented us on our appearance," Meigs wrote. Indeed, Montgomery saw something special in Arnold's hard-bitten men who had already endured so much for the cause, their ragged appearance notwithstanding. Writing to Schuyler, Montgomery observed:

> I find Colonel Arnold's corps an exceedingly fine one, inured to fatigue, and well accustom to cannon shot, (at Cambridge). There is a style of discipline among them, much superior to what I have been used to see this campaign. He himself is active, intelligent and enterprising.

The two senior officers, aggressive fighting men both, wasted no time preparing to attack Quebec. The day after Montgomery's arrival, in a driving rain, Arnold ordered a division of men to begin transporting artillery and supplies downriver. Oliver Hanchet was selected to lead the detachment, but he refused, "alleging that the Danger of such an undertaking was too imminent." Arnold was furious at this reaction from an officer he had once trusted, and threatened to have Hanchet arrested. Arnold called next on Captains Topham and Thayer. The officers flipped a coin for the privilege of undertaking the mission, and Thayer won.

The following day, as Thayer and his men loaded guns and stores in the bateaux, the rest of the army decamped and marched back to Quebec, where they resumed the siege. It was snowing hard that evening as Thayer got under way, the men having to "cut through the ice for 1/4 mile." They rowed eighteen miles through the dark, with the night "so cold that we strove with the utmost Eagerness to Row, in order to keep ourselves from being frozen."

The bateaux became separated in the blinding snow, and Thayer ordered muskets fired so they could find one another. Finally, as they closed with their landing place, the boats went aground, heavy laden with guns and a coating of ice. The men, "being very impatient and not willing to remain there long," jumped into water up to their armpits, waded to land, and found horses to drag the boats ashore.

General Montgomery had already put considerable thought into the taking of Quebec, understanding that "til Quebeck is taken, Canada is unconquered." There were only three ways it might be done. The city could be invested, or surrounded by the army, with all communication cut off until the inhabitants were starved into submission, but Montgomery did not have men enough to do that. They could lay siege to the city, dig trenches, and begin a systematic bombardment, but it was not possible to dig trenches in the frozen ground, nor could the troops have lived in them in that bitter cold, and "the lightness" of the American artillery would do little against Quebec's massive walls.

That left a frontal assault as the only real option.

There were advantages to storming the bastions. The sheer size of Quebec's fortifications did not allow Carleton's small force to cover all parts of the walls. The attackers could strike anytime, so the "Carletonians," as Senter called them, would have to be always on watch. Montgomery hoped that this need for constant vigilance would wear down the defenders and "breed discontents that may compel Carleton to capitulate."

Arraying the men around the city, Arnold ordered Hanchet's company and two others to take a forward position, stationing themselves at one of the farmhouses that dotted the countryside just outside the city walls. Again Hanchet greeted the order with surly passive aggression. He refused to obey, arguing that he and his men would be too exposed to enemy cannon fire. Again a furious Arnold turned to Captain Simeon Thayer, who, along with Captains Topham and Hurlbert, took the forward position.

Hanchet was not wrong about the danger. At one point a cannonball went right through the bed that Thayer and Topham were sharing, passing between the men.

Dr. Isaac Senter was given orders to take possession of the General Hospital on the banks of the St. Charles River. Senter was pleased with the facility, "a fine, spacious ward, capable of containing fifty patients, with one fire place, stoves, &c." The hospital's only drawback was its location, very near the walls of Quebec and the St. Roch gate. With the enemy so close, Senter did not dare take up residence in the building. Instead, he traveled to and from the hospital every day, within sight of the city walls, while the sentries on the wall took shots at him with their muskets as he passed.

On December 9, Montgomery sent out a fatigue party after dark to erect a battery on the height of the Plains of Abraham, about two hundred yards from the city. Cannon and mortars were also sent to St. Roch, and another battery was established.

The batteries were built with the materials at hand: sticks, dirt, snow, and ice. Fascines—bundles of sticks—were laid on the ground and covered with snow. Then large baskets woven from sticks, called gabions, were set up and filled with dirt and snow, "little, however, of the former," wrote Senter, "as it was almost impossible to procure any as the ground was very hard frozen." Then water was poured over the whole works and left to freeze.

With a nearly full moon illuminating the frozen countryside, the Americans struggled through the night to erect the battery, their clothes soaked through, their hands aching with the cold as they dug up snow and chipped away at the solid ground. Some of the men suffered frostbite.

For three nights the troops labored to erect the works and gun platforms. When dawn came on the third day, the works were complete. The stillness of the winter morning was broken by the flat boom of heavy artillery from the walls of Quebec, the whistle of round shot passing overhead, the thud of solid iron balls striking the ground and the works, throwing clods of dirt and snow and shattered gabions high in the air. The British artillery tore down the battery even as the Americans labored to build it up.

The earth, snow, and ice works were strong, but not "sufficient to repel the monstrous force of their 32's and 42's." One gun crew was wrestling their piece into place when a British shot pierced the breastwork, killing two men and wounding five. By the middle of the day,

Private Simon Fobes observed, "our heap of nonsense was completely battered to pieces."

Still, the Americans continued to fire on the city, not with any hope of breaching the walls but to keep the British on edge and, as Stocking wrote, to "amuse the enemy and conceal our real design." The firing seemed to Senter to have a psychological effect, "as they were (as usual) alarmed. Bells beating, dogs barking, &c." The British responded in kind, firing back at the Americans, although with little effect.

For all the American effort to unnerve the enemy—psy-ops, in modern parlance—Carleton would not be moved. When Montgomery sent a surrender demand under flag of truce, his flag, like Arnold's, was fired on.

The Guns of Fort Ti

While Arnold and his diminished force huddled outside the walls of Quebec, Philip Schuyler struggled along in Albany. Though he was spared most of the physical discomfort that Arnold and his men suffered—many visitors commented on the "elegant style" in which he lived—he certainly endured as much anxiety as he wrestled with problems of provisioning, troop strength, and a want of subordination.

New recruits continued to arrive at Albany to be forwarded to Canada, but to Schuyler's distress many of them lacked adequate clothing, shoes, or even muskets, all of which the ailing general struggled to provide.

In early December, the pudgy former bookseller-turned-artillery officer Colonel Henry Knox arrived in the area on a mission from Cambridge. With Washington's army holding the British under siege in Boston, the commander in chief needed only heavy artillery to make the enemy's position entirely untenable, and Knox had volunteered to get that artillery from Ticonderoga. Knox is generally given credit for the idea, though of course that was precisely what Arnold and Colonel Samuel Holden Parsons had had in mind when they recommended taking Ticonderoga seven months earlier.

On December 5, Knox began an inventory of the heavy guns at Fort Ticonderoga, French artillery left over from the previous war. Soon the colonel was on his way back to Cambridge, hauling fifty-eight cannons and mortars to the waiting army.

It is hard to appreciate the enormity of this task without understanding the size and weight of the guns involved. The smallest of the guns, eleven brass 4-pounders, were six feet long and weighed more than half a ton each. A majority of the guns, thirteen in all, were 18-pounders, each weighing forty-two hundred pounds, more than two tons of iron concentrated in a barrel nine feet long. The biggest gun that Knox took with him was a brass 24-pounder that weighed five thousand pounds.

In all, Knox's train of artillery weighed about sixty tons. This he and his men loaded in and out of boats and onto sleds, and dragged through blinding snowstorms and over precariously thin ice. His epic march through the frozen country with his "precious convoy" would be one of the few events in the history of the American Revolution that could rival Arnold's march to Quebec for sheer determination and will. Arnold, of course, did not have the burden of dragging heavy guns with him, but Knox was never beyond the reach of civilization and its concomitant aid and comfort.

On January 18, Knox's guns arrived at Cambridge and provided the American army with the heavy artillery they had been lacking. It was just over nine months since Fort Ticonderoga had been taken for exactly that purpose. On March 17, 1776, the British army evacuated Boston, driven out by the threat posed by the guns of Ticonderoga mounted on Dorchester Heights.

Behind the Walls

While Arnold and Montgomery huddled outside the walls of Quebec and prepared for an attack, Guy Carleton prepared for defense. Captain John Hamilton, of the frigate *Lizard*, sent his first officer, Lieutenant Thomas Pringle, back to England in the merchant vessel *Polly* to report on Quebec's precarious situation and request that reinforcements be sent. But that was an investment in the future. It would be half a year at least before those troops could arrive. In the meantime, Quebec was on its own.

One of Carleton's first acts after arriving in the city was to issue a proclamation that any man not willing to bear arms in defense of Quebec was to leave the city within four days and the Province of Quebec by December 1. It was a harsh move, but a shrewd one. The hundreds of men who left the city represented so many mouths that he did not have to feed, and a potential fifth column for the Americans about whom he did not have to worry.

Once he had collected all the men who would stand and fight, Carleton found that his force inside Quebec was not so insubstantial, at least not when compared with the ill-clad, ill-equipped, and poorly disciplined Americans outside.

While Carleton was still in Montreal, Lieutenant Governor Cramahé had assembled a motley army of more than thirteen hundred men. These included Maclean's two hundred Highland Emigrants, dressed in their civilian clothes, some wearing remnants of their French and Indian War uniforms; sixty-three Royal Fusiliers; and six members of the Royal Artillery in their blue regimental coats with red facings.

Augmenting that force now were more than three hundred officers, sailors, and marines from the *Lizard, Hunter,* and two armed sloops. These men enjoyed a much higher level of training and experience than the American forces. The two men-of-war had been laid up for the winter and their guns and stores moved into the city.

Added to the ranks of Quebec's defenders were seventy-four men from the various merchant vessels trapped in Quebec harbor. Lastly there was the established militia, uniformed in green regimental coats with buff-colored waistcoats and breeches, or in more casual winter attire, a sort of blanket jacket called a capote, leggings, and wool hat. Of the militia, two hundred were British and three hundred Canadian.

By the end of November, after Carleton was done threatening and cajoling, he had eighteen hundred defenders under arms, though part of them were citizens coerced into service. There were, altogether, some five thousand people within the walls of Quebec. Customs collector and temporary captain of militia Thomas Ainslie estimated that they had provisions for eight months, though Maclean felt that the provisions were "by no means adequate to maintain the number of inhabitants." Firewood was going to be a problem as well.

Throughout December the defenders and besiegers faced off, taking potshots at one another, locked in a virtual standoff. The Americans lobbed shells into the city, with little effect, and riflemen shot at anyone who moved on the walls. The British returned fire with the heavy guns taken from the naval vessels and mounted on the ramparts.

As the month dragged on, Ainslie began to doubt that the Americans would be able to attack. The weather was bitter. As it happened, the snow and cold of the winter of 1775–76 would be the worst in living memory. "This is no wall scaling weather," Ainslie wrote, "the night was clear & inconceivably cold—it is employment enough to preserve ones nose." Nor did he think that the Americans would be able to approach the walls carrying their crude scaling ladders while sinking up to their waist in the snow. Still, American deserters continued to show up in the city with reports of Montgomery's pending attack. Carleton and his officers slept in their clothes, ready to turn out at a moment's notice.

A Plan of Attack

In the third week of December, Dr. Senter noted the appearance of a new enemy in the American camp. "From this to the 23rd," he wrote, "no occurrences of consequence, except the small pox broke out in the army."

It is unclear whether Senter was being droll. One would expect an army doctor to recognize the significance of a disease that in the end would be far more deadly to the Americans than all the British muskets in Canada.

Smallpox was one of the great killers of the eighteenth century. A viral disease transmitted most often by personal contact, it revealed itself through chills, headaches, and back pain, followed by high fever, nausea, and frequent vomiting. After about four days, the fever would drop and pustules would begin to break out. By the third or fourth week the pustules would scab over and drop off, if the patient lived that long, which he or she generally did not.

Montgomery and Arnold knew that they would have to move soon. For one thing, many of Arnold's troops' enlistments would be up on December 31, and there was little chance of the men sticking around after that. (Back in Cambridge, General Washington was staring with open dismay at exactly the same deadline.) Even Montgomery, beloved and victorious, had failed to get his men to agree to stay for a full year, settling on a termination date of April 15, "which allows them time to plant their corn upon returning home."

The foot soldiers weren't the only ones eager to leave. Just days before the attack on Quebec, Montgomery wrote to remind Schuyler of his, Montgomery's, "determination to return home," and to say that he was assuming that "measures are taken to supply my place."

In the same letter, Montgomery warned of more trouble brewing. Though the men in general were in favor of an assault on the city, the captains of three companies of Arnold's detachment were "very averse from the measure." The leader of the malcontents was, of course, Hanchet, and with him were Captains Goodrich and Hubbard. (Abner Stocking, a private in Hanchet's company, gives a clue as to why Arnold was unpopular with some when he writes, "We had taken some disgust to our general, as he was for maintaining more rigid discipline than we were willing to submit to." Author and historian Kenneth Roberts wrote, "This passage sheds some light on Washington's aversion to New England troops.") Also involved in the controversy was Arnold's old nemesis John Brown, who now commanded 160 men and was angling to add those three companies to his roster.

Montgomery was so short of troops that the defection of three companies, he wrote, "threatens the ruin of our affairs." The general "wanted no persons with him who went with reluctance." The foot soldiers in the three companies, however, were not reluctant at all. They were driven by an esprit de corps that gave them an "earnest desire of going with the rest of their fellows who went through the woods," by which they meant the march through the Maine wilderness. Dr. Senter wrote to Arnold offering to lead one of the companies. Arnold thanked him, but told him that his services as a doctor would be needed more.

By mid-December, Montgomery had drawn up the basic outline of his plan to attack Quebec City, which was to wait for a stormy night, "the first strong northwester," then attack with two divisions, one at the Lower Town and another using scaling ladders to go over the walls of the Upper Town at Cape Diamond.

Montgomery now had only to wait and hope that a night of sufficiently thick weather occurred before January 1, 1776, when more than half of his army at Quebec was set to go home.

ON DECEMBER 27, Montgomery thought he had his night. In the midst of a fierce snowstorm, he ordered the men to muster in their assigned divisions according to his battle plan. But around midnight the storm broke and the moon came out, casting too much light for a surprise attack. The men were stood down.

Happily, one does not have to wait long for snow during a Canadian winter. On December 30, Montgomery's hoped-for blizzard blew up, the snow "outrageous, and the cold wind extremely biting."

A few days before, several Americans had deserted to the enemy, and Montgomery assumed that his attack plan had been compromised. Once again he changed his strategy.

Initially he had intended to attack the Upper and the Lower Town at the same time, going over the walls of the Upper Town with scaling ladders. Now he determined to launch two simultaneous attacks from opposite directions on the Lower Town, while Colonel James Livingston, leading the Canadian division that had captured Chambly, and John Brown, with his men, were to make a feint against the wall south of St. John's Gate and set fire to the buildings there. With attacks coming from four directions at once, Montgomery hoped that Carleton would divide his command to counter each, leaving every point weakly defended.

Such an attack was suggested by Quebec City's unusual configuration, situated as it is on a roughly triangular headland overlooking the St. Lawrence at the confluence of the St. Charles River. One leg of the triangle, running northeast to southwest along the St. Lawrence, was protected by the steep, virtually unassailable cliffs of Cape Diamond.

From the city's southwest corner, the formidable wall that Arnold and Montgomery had been facing for a month across the Plains of Abraham ran almost due north over the open country behind the headland before turning east, then southeast along the heights above the St. Charles River. The wall thus protected two sides of the city; the third side was protected by the Cape Diamond cliffs, more daunting than any wall.

The Upper Town sprawled over the high ground atop the cliffs; the Lower Town occupied a strip of shoreland at the eastern apex of the headland. One main road, with a heavily guarded gate, connected the wharves and warehouses of the Lower Town with the residences, government buildings, churches, and fortifications of the Upper Town.

From the American position on the Plains of Abraham, west of the city, there were two ways to reach the Lower Town without passing through the Upper Town. From the north, one could move through the streets of the suburb of St. Roch, then along the narrow cobbled road between the city wall and the St. Charles River. From there a street called the Sault au Matelot ran down to the Lower Town.

To the south of the city, a steep path at Cape Diamond led down to Wolfe's Cove, at the bottom of the cliffs, where one could walk along the riverfront far below the Cape Diamond bastion, then, after some distance, around to the Lower Town.

Montgomery hoped that those two routes would permit a pincer movement on the Lower Town, from where he planned to carry the attack through the main gate to the Upper Town. The defenders of Quebec, of course, were perfectly aware of this possibility and had had ample time to prepare for it. Across the roads that led to the Lower Town, they had erected wooden barricades set at right angles to the walls on the north side of the city and the cliffs on the south. The barricades were designed to stop exactly the sort of march around the city's perimeter that Arnold and Montgomery were intending.

Arnold and Montgomery, in turn, were aware of the barricades and planned accordingly. With one detachment consisting of about six hundred men, Arnold would work his way around the northern perimeter, taking the route through St. Roch. Morgan's riflemen would form the lead company, followed by an artillery company under Captain John Lamb with one brass 6-pounder fieldpiece pulled on a sled. Various companies of musket men would follow, including the indomitable Thayer and Topham and the malcontents Goodrich and Hubbard, who in the end decided to join the attack.

Major Meigs's company was to form the rear, but in fact Dearborn's company came last, because his men, being quartered across the St. Charles River, were late in getting their orders.

Montgomery's division, about three hundred men, would follow the route south around Cape Diamond and hook up with Arnold in the Lower Town, where they would attack together. Meanwhile, Livingston and Brown would make their feint against the western wall of the city south of St. John's Gate, about halfway between the Cape Diamond bastion and St. Roch. Livingston would fire rockets as a signal for the four American columns to move out.

It was a dangerous and difficult plan, "rash and imprudent," as Private Abner Stocking, who had marched with Arnold to Quebec, later described it. The officers who gathered in a council of war on the night of December 30 understood that, and a sense of foreboding hung over them. Montgomery was "extremely anxious," according to Dr. Senter, and the others seemed to share his mood. But they had no choice. In less than twelve hours, Arnold's troops would begin melting away, their enlistments up. The officers agreed unanimously to go forward with the attack.

Around four o'clock on the morning of December 31, the troops assembled, Montgomery's on the Plains of Abraham, Arnold's at St. Roch. With many of the American soldiers wearing captured British uniforms, they needed a way to distinguish one another from the enemy. They had earlier decided to affix hemlock sprigs to their hats for that purpose. Now to the sprigs they added pieces of paper with the words "Liberty or Death" written in bold letters.

At five o'clock that morning, Livingston's rockets rose into the air, and the troops advanced.

Arnold's Attack

Arnold and Montgomery's divisions had to move along the walls of the city, making their way over narrow, ice-covered pathways in the dark, at times with steep precipices on the other side falling away to the rivers that bordered the town. The storm was in full fury, with a wicked northwest wind biting exposed skin and driving the fast-falling, wet snow before it, making for bad visibility and treacherous, miserable conditions, conditions they hoped would hide them from British sentries. The men marched with heads down to protect their faces "against the imperious storm of wind and snow," and with the tails of their coats over their flintlocks to keep the priming dry.

At the very head of Arnold's division was an advance guard of thirty men called the "forlorn hope," that less-than-optimistic eighteenth-century term for the men destined to be first through the breach. This division was led by Arnold himself and included Eleazer Oswald.

The suburb of St. Roch was a tangle of alleys, roads, and buildings huddled beneath the looming walls of the city. The men marched in single file through deep snow. Once through the suburb, they began skirting the wall along the north side of the city, passing by the Palace Gate, one of the main entrances into Quebec. By then the British were on to them.

Soldiers on the ramparts fired on the column as it slogged through the storm. All that Arnold's men could see of the enemy were the red and orange flashes of priming and powder, bursts of light in the dark. Rifleman John Henry recalled, "we received a tremendous fire of musketry from the ramparts above us. Here we lost some brave men, when powerless to return the salutes we received."

The first barricade, a high wooden wall erected across the road and manned by thirty militia and two small cannon, stood at the head of the Sault au Matelot. Arnold's plan was to bring up the 6-pounder and blast a few rounds into the wooden barricade. With the defenders hopefully dead, scattered, or unnerved, the "forlorn hope" would charge the barricade with the scaling ladders they carried with them, swarming up and over the obstacle, while Morgan's men marched around the outer end of the barricade on the river ice if possible.

That was the plan.

Unfortunately, the snow that was supposed to hide the attackers' movements proved more hindrance than asset. The 6-pounder, though not a big gun, still weighed more than a ton, and the artillerymen were attempting to haul it on a sled through a slashing blizzard, with snow rapidly piling up and choking the narrow roads. It proved impossible, and the gun was abandoned well before the first troops reached the barricade.

Arnold and his forlorn hope, followed by Lamb's artillerists (now serving as infantry) and Morgan's riflemen, pushed on for the barricade at Sault au Matelot. Behind them the main body of the division, struggling to keep up, soon became lost, "there being no road, the way dark and intricate," Meigs wrote, "among stores, houses, boats and wharves." All the while the column was "harassed . . . with a constant fire of the enemy from the walls, which killed and wounded numbers of our men." The snow, falling fast and thick, obscured the footprints of the lead companies, giving the main body no path to follow.

As the bulk of his troops blundered around in the dark, Arnold's forlorn hope approached the first barricade undetected. With his own cannon left behind in the snow, and scouts reporting no possibility of flanking the wall over the ice, Arnold prepared to mount a frontal assault.

Suddenly a volley of musket fire flashed from behind the barricade. One of the musket balls ricocheted off the cobblestone road and split in two. The bigger part struck Arnold in the left leg, below the knee, passing between the tibia and fibula and lodging near his ankle.

Arnold staggered from the blow, blood soaking his torn stocking and filling his boot. The Americans were trapped in the narrow road under the enemy's guns, with no place to hide. Their only choice now was to attack or retreat, and to retreat was unthinkable.

The fieldpieces behind the barricade opened up with a blast of light and noise, illuminating the road and the closely pressed buildings like a flash of lightning. Grape- and canister shot ricocheted off cobblestones and bricks. But as the guns were drawn in to reload, Arnold's hardened veterans surged forward with a collective shout, Morgan and Thayer leading the way.

The scaling ladders were set against the wooden barricade, and rifleman Daniel Morgan was the first to rush up. As he reached the top, a defender thrust a musket in his face and fired. The ball missed, but the muzzle flash burned Morgan's face and knocked him backward off the ladder, dropping him in a bank of snow.

For a moment Morgan lay stunned and motionless. Then he shook himself back to his senses, stood, and led his riflemen in another charge at the barricade. The woodsmen swarmed up and over the wall, Morgan himself dropping down to the gun platform between the barrels of the two guns, which deflected a thrust from a bayonet that would have run him through.

Most of the Quebec militia turned and fled, and those who did not were captured. The first barricade was taken, with the loss of one man killed and six or seven wounded, but among those wounded was Benedict Arnold.

Within the Walls

Around four in the morning, Captain Malcolm Fraser, of Maclean's Royal Highland Emigrants, had been making his rounds of the city walls. Out in the night, through the near blinding snow, he could see flashes of light, though he could hear no sound of guns. The sentries told him they had been seeing lights for some time along the Plains of Abraham and down by Cape Diamond.

Fraser, like everyone in the city, was braced for an attack, and he expected it to come on a stormy night just like this one. They had never before seen lights such as they were seeing now, and that was enough to alert Fraser that something was going on. He ordered the men to the ramparts under arms. Drums beat and bells rang, and "in a few minutes the whole Garrison was under arms," Ainslie wrote, "even old men of seventy were forward to oppose the attackers."

Quebec's defenders paraded miserably on the ramparts, muskets clutched in near frozen hands, peering through the driving snow, wondering what was happening out there in the dark. Then, an hour after Fraser had first seen the lights, two rockets soared into the sky, and everyone knew that this was the night.

Gunshots followed immediately on the heels of the rockets, as John Brown's men, hidden behind a rise eighty feet from the walls, opened up with small arms fire. Soon, a small detachment of American artillery-men in the St. Roch suburb began lobbing mortar shells into the city.

Montgomery had imagined that the great length of the walls around Quebec would make the city vulnerable, because Carleton would have to spread his men thin to cover them. This was true, but the British also enjoyed the benefit of being inside their defensive circle, which allowed Carleton to move men quickly from one point on the walls to another and to communicate with his various detachments. He used this to advantage.

The American deserters had alerted Carleton to Montgomery's plan to scale the walls at Cape Diamond. As the British expected, the Cape Diamond bastion and the walls by the St. John's Gate, just to the north, soon came under attack. Colonel Henry Caldwell, of the Royal Highland Emigrants, led a force of militia down toward Cape Diamond to reinforce the men there. But Carleton soon realized that those attacks were only diversions (the feints by Livingston and Brown), and he hurried the men off to where the real fighting was breaking out.

Along the northeast walls of the city, a division of sailors from the men-of-war anchored in the river huddled against the storm, cradling their unfamiliar muskets. Dimly through the black night, they saw Arnold's men hunched over against the wind, working their way around to the Lower Town. The sailors opened up "a dreadful fire of small arms" on Arnold's main body as they staggered along, trying to find their way.

Meanwhile, just northeast of Cape Diamond, Captain Barnfair, master of the *Fell*, and a handful of sailors and Canadian militia were hunkered down in a blockhouse that overlooked the southern approach to the Lower Town along the shores of the St. Lawrence. They had been drinking, but still they managed to load the four small cannon mounted there, and now, keeping an indifferent watch, they waited for the enemy's possible approach.

Montgomery's Attack

While Arnold and his men were still blundering through the alleys and wharves along the northeast wall of Quebec, Montgomery and his

New York troops worked their way around Cape Diamond, at the southwestern corner of the city.

The cape, according to Abner Stocking, "presents a precipice, the foot of which is washed by the river, where enormous and rugged masses of ice had been piled on each other, so as to render the way almost impossible." Montgomery's troops made their way along this path single file through the blinding snow, clambering over the great ice drifts that the St. Lawrence River had thrown up on the narrow beach.

Montgomery was leading the forlorn hope of his column, just as Arnold had taken the lead with his. For two hours he and his men struggled along the shore from Wolfe's Cove around the point of Cape Diamond. At last they came to the wooden barricade blocking the southern approach, a substantial stockade wall made of posts fifteen to twenty feet high and held together with stout railings. The barricade ran from the side of the cliff right to the water's edge.

Unlike the barricade at Sault au Matelot, however, the one Montgomery faced was undefended. Rather than scale the wall with ladders, Montgomery called for saws with which to cut their way through. The men cut through four posts, the telltale sound of their sawing lost in the howling wind. With the gap opened, Montgomery and two of his officers—his aide-de-camp Captain John Macpherson and Captain Jacob Cheeseman—stepped through.

A short way beyond the first barricade was a second one of similar construction. Again Montgomery opted to cut an opening close by the cliffs, this time sawing through the posts himself. The sawn posts were knocked aside, and Montgomery and his officers stepped through.

There Montgomery paused to let his soldiers, who were strung out along the path behind, catch up. About fifty yards ahead, dimly visible, he could see a blockhouse, a formidable structure two stories high, built right in the middle of the approach to the Lower Town, with just enough space for a cart to pass on either side.

This was the blockhouse manned by Barnfair and his sailors and a few Canadian militia. Montgomery led his men across the fifty yards of open ground, intent on assaulting and taking this last stronghold between him and the Lower Town. Drunk and taken by surprise, the sentries, "being chiefly Canadians, having given a random and harmless fire, threw away their arms and fled in confusion to the barrier."

The blockhouse would have fallen easily, except that one of the sailors, perhaps Barnfair himself, decided that he could not abandon the post without discharging at least one of the cannon that were already loaded. Making his way to the second floor, he grabbed up a linstock and shoved the glowing slow match into the powder in the touchhole. The gun went off, spraying grape- and round shot into the night, right into the advancing Americans.

Montgomery had just drawn his sword when a round of grapeshot hit him square in the head, knocking him back and killing him instantly. Also killed in the blast were Captain Macpherson and Captain Cheeseman, a sergeant, and a private.

With the three most senior officers dead, command of the division fell to Colonel Donald Campbell. A genuine leader in the vein of Daniel Morgan might have rallied the men and led them on to what would have been an easy victory over the sentries in the blockhouse, but Campbell was no such leader. He was not in the least inclined to continue the attack, and, without real leadership, his men weren't either.

Leaving Montgomery's body in the snow, Campbell found himself "under the disagreeable necessity of drawing off the troops (too ready to depart)." They retreated back the way they had come. One soldier would later write, "Campbell . . . was ever after considered as a poltroon in grain . . . ," and though Campbell was acquitted of wrongdoing at a later court-martial, he was forever loathed by his men for giving up the fight.

With Montgomery's troops in retreat, the British and Canadian defenders were free to concentrate themselves against Arnold's still advancing division.

The Fight in the Lower Town

The death of Montgomery deprived his men of bold leadership, but Arnold's division still had a number of talented and aggressive officers, including Daniel Morgan, Simeon Thayer, Christopher Greene,

Eleazer Oswald, and Henry Dearborn, who was still hurrying to the fight even as the first barricade was overrun.

With Arnold wounded, Morgan took command. He ordered one of his riflemen and the Reverend Samuel Spring, who had accompanied Arnold's men on the march to Quebec, to take Arnold back to the hospital. Reluctantly, and shouting encouragement to his men, Arnold draped an arm over each man's shoulder and was carried off, dragging his wounded leg behind, through a hail of musket fire from the walls above.

Morgan and his men needed about twenty minutes to secure the prisoners they had taken behind the first barricade, during which time Meigs and much of the main body, which had been lost, came up with the advance party. Now many of the Americans found that their muskets would no longer fire, the priming having become wet, so they tossed them aside and took up discarded British weapons.

Morgan went forward to reconnoiter the second barricade, and to his surprise found it undefended. He opened the gate in the wooden wall and stepped cautiously through. The narrow street was deserted. Seeing a chance for a quick advance into the Upper Town, he rejoined his men and tried to lead them forward, but the officers refused, insisting that they wait for Montgomery's division to join them as planned. "Our officers deem it proper," wrote Morison (in the present tense for heightened drama), "to suspend scaling the wall until the main body come up, at whose delay we are astonished."

The men waited in the bitter cold and violent storm, seeking what shelter they could find. Soon dawn began to break, and still Montgomery and his men had not arrived. With the cover of dark rapidly fading, Morgan knew that he had to get his troops moving against the second barricade. But now, rather than Montgomery's men, a force of British and Canadian troops met them. As the Americans advanced, Captain Anderson, a retired navy lieutenant leading a company of soldiers, stepped out through the gate. Anderson called for the Americans to surrender. Morgan raised his rifle and "answered the British captain by a ball though his head."

Anderson's men dragged the captain's body back through the barricade. But now other troops who had taken positions in the houses lining the narrow street opened up on Morgan's men from windows, and Anderson's men fired from a platform that allowed them to shoot over the top of the barricade. Morgan's troops charged the barricade with ladders, but a significant force of defenders had massed on the other side, and every attempt to swarm over the walls was thrown back. Morgan's men could not go forward, and soon they would learn that they could not go back.

Dearborn's Company

Henry Dearborn's men had missed the initial attack, but they hurried to catch up, rushing along the path by which Arnold had led his men. Along the way Dearborn met Arnold, who was being carried back to the hospital. Dearborn would later recall, "he Spoke to me and desir'd me to push on forward." Dearborn did that, and soon became hopelessly lost.

Carleton knew by now that he had the upper hand, and he was willing to risk sending men outside the protection of the city walls. As Dearborn struggled to find the main body of troops, Captain George Laws swept out of the Palace Gate to hit his division in the rear. Seeing the British troops in the gathering light, Dearborn was uncertain who they were, because most of the Americans were wearing captured British uniforms, and these troops "were dress'd like us."

One of the British soldiers hailed Dearborn and asked who he was. "A friend!" Dearborn answered.

"A friend to who?" the soldier asked.

"To liberty!" Dearborn answered. It was not the reply the British soldier was looking for. He replied "God damn you!" and stood to fire. Dearborn in turn aimed his own musket, charged with ball and buckshot, and pulled the trigger. Nothing happened. As with Morgan's men, Dearborn found that not "one in Ten of my men could get off our Guns they being so exceeding wet." Outnumbered, lost, and surrounded, Dearborn ordered his men to escape if they could. Many did, but many others, Dearborn included, were taken prisoner.

Morgan's men were now cut off and trapped between the first and second barricades. Finding shelter in various buildings, they continued to exchange fire with the British defenders. Morgan led his men back to the first barricade in an attempt to break out and retreat, but soon the troops that had taken Dearborn's men added their weight to the attack. Surrounded and outnumbered, their retreat cut off, a council of officers decided "to surrender prisoners of war," Meigs wrote, "which we did with great reluctance."

The End of Victory

The rockets that Colonel Livingston let off on the morning of December 31, 1775, signaled more than the start of the attack on Quebec. They also signaled the high-water mark of the American invasion of Canada, the closest that the Continental soldiers would ever come to realizing the dream of taking and holding the Province of Quebec and making Canada an ally in the Revolution. If not for the loss of Montgomery, the attack might well have succeeded, but with his death, the wounding of Arnold, and the surrender of about three hundred men—a third of the troops there—any hope of taking Quebec was effectively dashed, and with it any hope of possessing Canada.

The day after the Americans' defeat was the beginning of a new year, new in every way. For the English and Canadians sheltered behind the walls of Quebec, it would mean spring, supply ships, troop ships, and salvation. For the Americans, whose prospects had looked so promising just months before, it would mean a year of defeat, of falling back before the onslaught of Carleton's newly reinforced and seemingly unstoppable army.

Unstoppable, that was, until they were forced to contend with Benedict Arnold's navy.

Nearly all "portraits" of Benedict Arnold are based only on the artist's imagination. The Du Simitiere portrait, done while Arnold was military commander of Philadelphia, is one of the only portraits known to be done from life. It shows the stout, intense Arnold, his nose prominent—a feature that is often described by his contemporaries. (Fort Ticonderoga Museum)

In this reconstructed courtyard of Fort Ticonderoga, the double stairway in the middle of the far barracks, called the "Ethan Allen steps," is thought to be located where Allen and Benedict Arnold confronted Lieutenant Feltham and demanded the surrender of the fort. (Photo by author)

This monument commemorates Arnold and the men who fought at the Battle of Valcour Island. The southern end of Valcour Island, where the battle took place, is to the left of the monument. Little Island is to the right. (Photo by author)

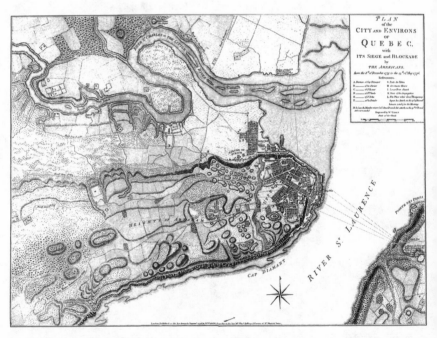

A map of Quebec at the time of the American siege from December, 1775, to May, 1776, drawn by British officer William Faden.

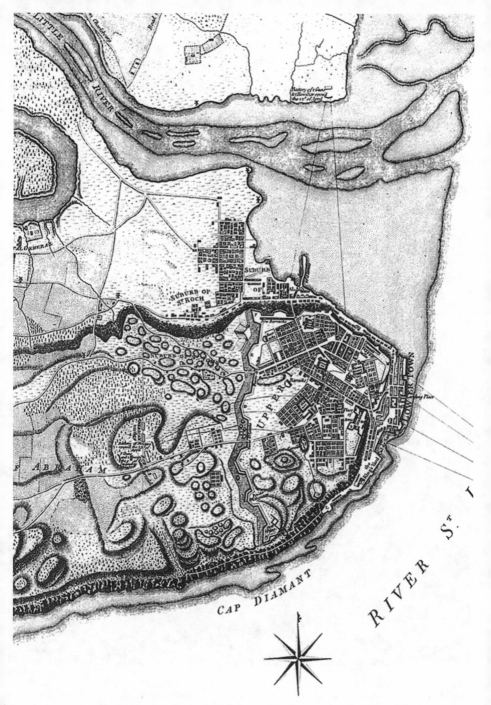

Detail of the Faden map. The Plains of Abraham, from which the Americans laid siege to the city, are to the left. The wall that ran across the point of land on which the city was located can be clearly seen, walling off the Upper Town. To the north and south of the city are the narrow routes taken by Arnold and Montgomery. The suburb of St. Roch is north of the city proper, just outside the walls. On the eastern end of the city, just below the label for the Lower Town, is the Cul de Sac, or Basin, Quebec's small harbor.

Major General Philip Schuyler was the scion of one of New York's oldest leading families. He was generally well liked by most, including Arnold, for his easy grace and considerate nature, though for some his sophistication smacked too much of the aristocracy. Schuyler was extremely competent, but ill health prevented him from playing a more active role in the northern campaigns. (Fort Ticonderoga Museum)

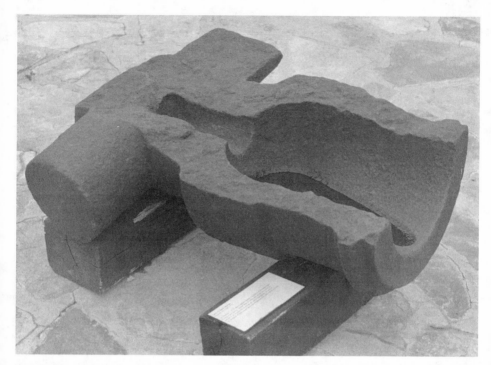

This mortar burst when engineer Jeduthan Baldwin test-fired it prior to mounting it aboard the gondola *Philadelphia*. (Photo by author)

Fort Ticonderoga looks across the water to Mount Independence. At the time of the Revolution, Mount Independence was cleared of trees and became the most significant American stronghold on Lake Champlain. (Photo by author)

E

D

River
au

Sable

Point au Sable

These Rivers
are almost choaked
with Sand & tho'
large can only

Receive Boat

in the Spring
& Canoes or

Batteaux in

the Fall.

Lake Champlain.

References

A. The Rebel Fleet. B. The line of Gun Boats

C. The Royal Savage run on Shore on a small Island

D. Retreat of the Rebels in the Night.

NB. The Ships are placed as during the

Action; Soon after which they again Anchor'd

with the Boats in the dotted line. E. The

Gun Boats are from 30 to 36 Feet long & 10, 16 or 18 Feet wide.

Lt. James Hadden's sketch of the Battle of Valcour Island. Hadden, an artillery officer with the British army, took part in the northern action in 1776 and 1777, including the Battle of Saratoga. At Valcour Island, Hadden commanded one of the gunboats. (Fort Ticonderoga Museum)

from their Comrades. Their Officers

were sent to Canada on Parole.

Sketch of the Action in Lake Champlain

River
Sala-
manac
Rapid
Rocky &
barded w
Rocks
without

Cummerland
Bay.

Cummerland Pt.

La Grande Isle

L'Isle de St. Michel.

Here the
French
sunk 4
Vessels in 1759

L'Isle de Valicour.

A

D

Carlton

B

Maria   Inflexible   C

Loyal Convert   Radeau

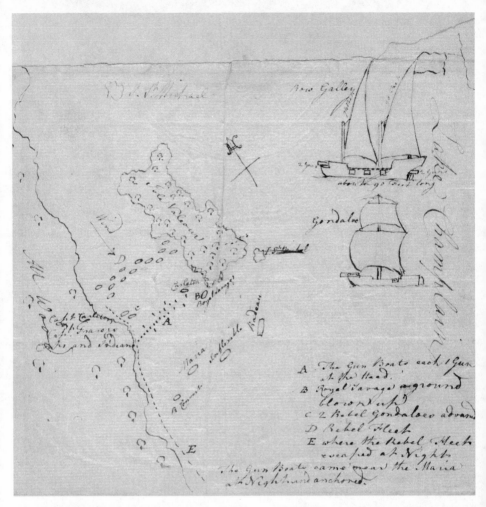

A sketch of the Battle of Valcour Island, from a letter written by British engineer Charles Terrot. Terrot includes quite accurate sketches of an American row galley and gondola. (Fort Ticonderoga Museum)

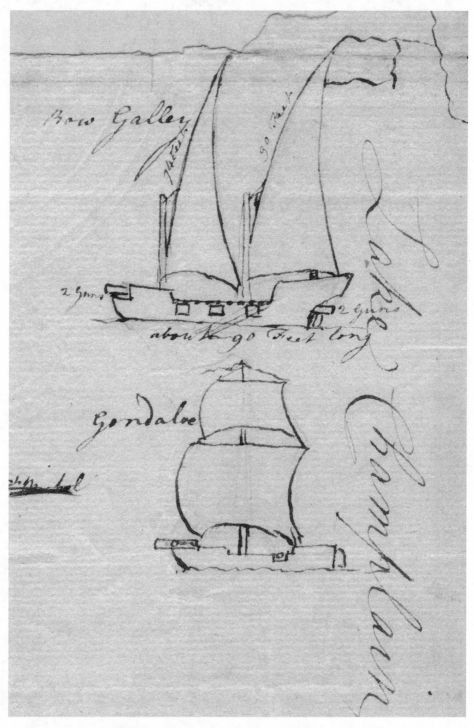

Detail of the Terrot sketch showing the careful drawings the engineer made of the odd-looking vessels he encountered on Lake Champlain. (Fort Ticonderoga Museum)

After nearly six hours of giving and receiving a brutal cannonade, the gondola *Philadelphia* sank at her anchor at Valcour Island. Here the row galley *Washington* is seen coming to the aide of the sinking vessel. In 1935, *Philadelphia* was raised from the bottom, and now is on display at the Smithsonian Institution in Washington, D.C. (Painting by Ernest Haas courtesy Lake Champlain Maritime Museum.)

Arnold's gondolas, essentially oversized bateaux, sailed best when running before the wind. The gondolas were put into service as fast as they could be finished, and spent months patrolling Lake Champlain before the climactic Battle of Valcour Island. In the background on the right, the schooner *Liberty* carries out her duty, carrying correspondence and supplies up and down the lake. (Ernest Haas painting courtesy the artist.)

Two of the row galleys and two of the gondolas exchange gunfire with the British fleet, while the sinking *Philadelphia* is assisted by the *Washington*. The wreck of the *Royal Savage* lies on the rocks on Valcour Island to the right, and beyond the island, the larger British ships look on, unable to get up into the fight. (Ernest Haas painting courtesy the artist.)

The *Congress*, Arnold's flagship at the Battle of Valcour Island, runs into Ferris Bay (now called Arnold's Bay) ahead of the British ships, which are too deep to follow. Battered from three days of fighting and unable to escape, *Congress* is beached and set on fire. (Ernest Haas painting courtesy the artist.)

Ferris Bay, now known as Arnold's Bay, is where the row galley *Congress*, with Benedict Arnold aboard, and four of the gondolas ran aground and were burned by the Americans before they could be taken by Guy Carleton's superior British naval force. The Americans briefly established a defensive position on the high ground in the middle of the picture against a possible British landing before marching off to Fort Ticonderoga. (Photo by author)

VIEW of the old FRENCH FORT, REDOUBTS and BATTERIES at TICONDEROGA on LAKE CHAMPLAIN and HIS MAJESTYS SHIP INFLEXIBLE also the PIERS Constructed with the Trunks of large Trees by the AMERICAN ARMY for the conveyance of their troops to Mount Independence. taken on the spot by H. Rudyard Lieut. Corps of Royal Engineers in the Year 1777

A view of Fort Ticonderoga from Mount Independence painted in 1777 by Lt. Henry Rudyard of the Corps of Royal Engineers. To the left is the ship *Inflexible*, built at St. John's in less than a month. To the right, the line of pilings are all that remain of the "great bridge" constructed by American engineer Jeduthan Baldwin. (Fort Ticonderoga Museum)

Fort Ticonderoga as seen from Mount Defiance. The fort sits on the peninsula to the left. To the right is Rattlesnake Hill, later called Mount Independence, and the site of major American fortifications. In 1777 Burgoyne mounted guns on the spot where this photo was taken and drove the Americans from Ticonderoga. (Photo by author)

One of Fort Ticonderoga's guns looks over Lake Champlain toward Skenesborough (Whitehall). Ticonderoga was built by the French to defend against British advances from the south, and thus was oriented the wrong way for Americans defending against the British coming from the north. (Photo by author)

Lake George looking south. Passage up the long, narrow lake was the standard route from Fort Ticonderoga to Albany. Burgoyne chose to go by land instead—a choice he came to regret. (Photo by author)

The Battle of Saratoga monument of Benedict Arnold marks the spot where Arnold was wounded on the last day of fighting. John Watts de Peyster, who erected the monument in 1887, could not bear to put the name of the traitor Arnold on the monument, so he dedicated it "In Memory of the 'most brilliant soldier' of the Continental Army." Likewise, Peyster would not put Arnold's likeness on the monument, so instead he put Arnold's boot in memory of the leg wound he suffered. (Photo by author)

1776

CHAPTER *17* *The Aftermath*

LIEUTENANT THOMAS PRINGLE, first officer of His Majesty's Ship *Lizard*, missed the battle for Quebec City.

On November 22, 1775, while all of Quebec was making ready for the looming attack by American forces, Pringle had stepped on board the merchantman *Polly*, anchored just off the city. In his hands was a bundle of letters, the last communication that the city would be able to send to England before winter ice sealed the St. Lawrence River from the sea.

It was a cold morning, with a glaze of frost on the ship's decks, spars, and rigging. The wind was light out of the west, a fair breeze for the downriver journey to the Gulf of St. Lawrence and, if the wind held in that quarter, across the Atlantic Ocean to England.

As the *Polly*'s crew made ready to sail, Pringle watched his old ship-mates from the *Lizard* prepare for a grueling siege they were sure would come. Three days before, the bulk of the American troops commanded by Benedict Arnold had left the walls of the city and marched upriver, but no one doubted that they would link up with Montgomery's men and return in force.

The *Lizard*'s crew "Clapd a Buoy upon the End of the Streem Cable and Slipt it," letting the anchor cable slide into the river as they hauled the frigate toward the protected water of the Cul de Sac. The *Polly* and the transport *Elizabeth* broke out their anchors and dropped down the river as the *Lizard* gently ran aground, her crew shoring her up with spare spars to keep her upright on the falling tide.

A council of war on November 16, having decided that the sailors were too important to the defense of the city to be allowed to leave, had laid an embargo on all merchant shipping currently at Quebec. Likewise, the men-of-war, with their heavy guns and holds full of needed supplies, from gunpowder to food and rum, were ordered to remain. But someone had to carry word of the beleaguered city's predicament to England. "I have sent the Polly on this Service," wrote John Hamilton, captain of the *Lizard* and the senior naval officer at Quebec, to navy secretary Philip Stephens, "as none of the King's Vessels could be spared." The *Polly's* hold was filled with a cargo of flax seed, the property of two local clerks whose loyalty to the king meant that they "would be hangd if they fell into the Rebel Hands." Hamilton spared their cargo by way of rewarding their loyalty.

Thomas Pringle would be the messenger. Hamilton wrote, "it is not in my power to give their Lordships so full & particular an Account of our situation as I would wish . . . ," so he was sending Pringle, "who can give a very clear & particular Account of the whole."

Pringle was from a prominent and wealthy Scottish family, the only son of Walter Pringle, a successful merchant and planter in the West Indies. Well connected and well liked by his superiors, Thomas Pringle seemed destined for advancement, and indeed he would end his days as a vice admiral of the red. The most important step in his long career, the leap from lieutenant to post captain, would come in another year as a result of the fighting on Lake Champlain.

The council of war had also ordered the St. Lawrence River pilots to sail for England, so that they would be available to pilot relief ships back in spring. They weren't the only ones making that late season crossing. A few weeks after the *Polly* and the *Elizabeth* arrived in England, the *London Chronicle* reported, "The American prisoners whom Mr. Brooke Watson brought over from Canada, are about 20 in number. Amongst them is Colonel Ethan Allen, who took Ticonderoga."

The passage across the gray seas of the North Atlantic in late November and early December was bitterly cold and dangerous, but it was also mercifully short, with a great and steady sweep of wind from west to east driving the *Polly* along. Just a little over a month after sailing from Quebec, Lieutenant Pringle stood in the elegant offices of the Admiralty at Whitehall in London, presenting his report and the letters he carried to the Lords Commissioners of the Admiralty.

Foremost among the correspondence was a letter from Guy Carleton to the American secretary written just two days before Pringle had sailed. The governor's grim closing prediction read in part, "I think our fate extremely doubtful, to say nothing worse"

When he wrote his pessimistic assessment, Carleton may well have felt that he and Quebec had been forgotten back home. That was not the case. The king, his cabinet, and Parliament were as eager to maintain ownership of Canada as the Continental Congress was to take it from them.

On September 25, 1775, while Montgomery had been laying siege to St. John's and Arnold had been struggling through the wilderness of Maine, five Irish battalions intended for Boston had been redirected to Canada, one to Halifax and four to Quebec.

Such a force would have changed everything, but by the time the orders arrived at Cork, Ireland, two of the battalions had already sailed for Boston. The other three were ordered to sail, and if they found the St. Lawrence frozen over, they were to go ashore and march overland to Quebec. Even those three battalions would have been enough to brush aside the American invasion, but after storm damage forced their transports back to Ireland, the battalions were rerouted again, this time to join an attack on Charleston, South Carolina. Carleton and Quebec, it was decided, would have to fend for themselves until spring.

The letter that Pringle carried from Carleton was addressed to American secretary William Legge, the Earl of Dartmouth. Carleton did not know, even as he was writing the letter, that Lord Dartmouth no longer held that post.

Like many inside and outside the government in England, Dartmouth hated the idea of making war on fellow Englishmen in America, and he dreaded the consequences. The king and Lord Frederick North, the prime minister, however, believed that only decisive and overwhelming military action would force the colonies back in line, and they wanted an American secretary who felt the same. They found their man in Lord George Germain, who became American secretary in November 1775.

Germain was not an ideal choice for Carleton. The two men disliked each other, and Germain thought that Carleton was probably exaggerating the danger to Quebec. "I take the General to be one of those men who see affairs in the most unfavorable light," Germain wrote to the Earl of Sandwich. Still, Germain (and more importantly King George III) did not want to see Quebec fall into rebel hands, and the new American secretary began immediately to plan for the city's defense.

John Montagu, the Earl of Sandwich, First Lord Commissioner of the Admiralty, was at his country home in Hinchingbrook when the news from Quebec arrived, and he did not feel that it warranted his returning to London. He wrote to Germain to assure him that Admiralty secretary Sir Hugh Pallisser would handle everything "as if I was on the spot." But Germain felt a greater sense of urgency. His first concern was sending a relief force to Quebec, one large enough to drive off the Americans but small enough that it could be organized quickly.

On January 4, 1776, Germain sent word to the Lords Commissioners of the Admiralty that it was "the King's Intentions that every Effort should be made to send Relief to Quebec as early as possible." Three victualers of 180 tons each, vessels designated to carry provisions, were contracted. Germain ordered the navy to provide a fifty-gun ship, two frigates, and a sloop-of-war, ready to sail by the middle of February.

In addition, Germain ordered two armed transports with provisions for three thousand men for three months, enough to supply the city of Quebec as well as the relief force. The ships would also need room to carry the 677 officers and men of the 29th Regiment of Foot, plus "half the Baggage, Camp Necessaries, and Women, belonging to a complete Battalion . . . ," a battalion on foreign service being allowed eighty tons of baggage and sixty women.

Numerically, the 29th would be slightly inferior to the American army outside Quebec, but the Americans were, from Pringle's report, ill equipped, exhausted, dispirited, starving, and increasingly falling victim to smallpox. The 29th, on the other hand, was a well-trained, well-equipped, disciplined unit and would be augmented by the sailors, marines, and guns of the men-of-war, not to mention the troops that Carleton already had behind the city walls.

This first wave, the "early fleet," as Germain called it, would be enough to lift the siege from Quebec, if the city had not already fallen to the rebels. Quickly assembled and deployed, the early fleet would buy time for the government to put together what Germain called "the second embarkation."

In November 1775, Captain Charles Douglas, the rotund and imposing master of the fifty-gun, fourth-rate ship of the line *Isis*, had been appointed third in command of naval forces in North America. Now Douglas, onboard *Isis*, was ordered to lead the first wave of relief to Quebec.

Germain issued specific instructions for the men-of-war. The fleet was to rendezvous at the Isle aux Coudres, in the St. Lawrence, about fifty miles below Quebec. If the river was still frozen, they were to find the nearest safe port and wait for clear passage. They were to gather intelligence regarding the situation at Quebec. If the city was still in British hands, they were to get word to Carleton that relief was on the way, then work upriver to Quebec as quickly as they could. If Quebec had fallen, they were to land the 29th Regiment on Isle aux Coudres and wait for the second embarkation.

As the relief squadron prepared to sail, Germain wrote a letter to Carleton explaining the tactical situation. The "small squadron of His Majesty's ships . . ." was "prepared with the greatest dispatch . . . ," but that was only the beginning. "Every effort is making to push forward the second embarkation of troops."

Even now, Germain was thinking not just of retaking Canada but of retaking Lake Champlain and Lake George and pushing south to Albany as well. Though Carleton held overall command of the forces in Quebec Province, Germain didn't want Carleton leading an attack up the lakes. Let Carleton govern Quebec; a more trustworthy military man could be found to lead troops south. For that task Germain tapped Major General John Burgoyne, who had returned from America the previous autumn and had used his time well, ingratiating himself with the ministry. Burgoyne would sail to Quebec with the second embarkation, the large force intended for the invasion of the colonies.

Burgoyne and Germain had spent many winter hours discussing the strategy of that invasion, though, in writing to Carleton, Germain did not commit his thoughts to paper. "Major-General Burgoyne will be so fully instructed in every point, in regard to the important services that are to be carried on," Germain wrote, "that it will be unnecessary now for me to say anything on that subject."

Outside the Walls of Quebec

On the first day of 1776, even as the British ministry in London actively prepared for the relief of Quebec, things were quickly falling apart for the Americans outside the walls of that city.

Benedict Arnold, a fragment of a musket ball lodged in his leg, had been carried bleeding from the head of his column into the General Hospital, where Dr. Senter "discovered and extracted" the jagged, broken bits of lead. In physical and emotional torment, Arnold awaited news from his division and from Montgomery's. From his hospital bed he managed to dash off a letter to Wooster in Montreal, apprising him of the "critical situation we are in" and urging Wooster to "give us all the assistance in your power."

Soon word came that Montgomery had been killed and his men had retreated.

One can imagine the personal hell in which Arnold now found himself. He was helpless, an invalid, a condition that in the best of times would have been insufferable for so active a man. Montgomery, whom he liked and admired, was dead, their plans in ruins, their chance to capture Quebec—the culmination of five months of near superhuman effort—gone.

With the fighting still going on, Arnold received word that Carleton had sent a small division outside the walls to capture the American battery in St. Roch that had been shelling the city. The battery silenced, Carleton's division was advancing toward the nearby General Hospital. Senter and others "entreated Colonel Arnold for his own safety to be carried back into the country . . . ," but Arnold would have none of it. "He ordered his pistols loaded," Senter wrote, "with a sword on his bed, &c., adding that he was determined to kill as many as possible if they came into the room." Privately, Arnold may even have been wishing that his life would end that way.

Arnold also ordered Senter, his aides, and the other wounded men to arm themselves. Captain Isaiah Wool then led a ragged column of stragglers and the still-ambulatory sick and wounded against the British advance, driving Carleton's men back to the safety of Quebec.

It was a tiny victory in an otherwise disastrous defeat, but for a day and a half Arnold did not know for certain just how disastrous it had been. On January 1 Senter wrote in his journal, "All in obscurity; no intelligence from the troops in the lower town." Then, on January 2, Major Return Meigs arrived at the hospital. Taken prisoner with Morgan and the rest, Meigs had been sent by Carleton under flag of truce to gather up the baggage and personal effects of the other officers and men to make their lives as prisoners of war a bit more tolerable.

Meigs explained to Arnold everything that had taken place after his wounding, how the troops had become trapped between the barricades with guns that would not fire because of the wet weather. Meigs gave Arnold an account of the killed and wounded. He assured Arnold that the prisoners were being "treated very humanely" and that Montgomery's body had been interred by Carleton with "every possible mark of distinction."

That done, Meigs gathered up his and the other prisoners' belongings and returned to captivity. He and his fellows would remain prisoners of war until May, when Carleton (whom Dearborn described as appearing "to be a very humane tender-hearted man") granted them parole. Some, such as Thayer and rifleman John Henry, would not be granted parole until August. They returned to their homes until they were officially exchanged for British prisoners, at which time most took up arms again in the fight for independence.

Arnold braced for a counterattack. Carleton had been too shrewd to risk an assault on the Americans when they were at full strength, but now he was in a position to possibly roll up Arnold and Montgomery's remaining seven hundred or so battered and dispirited troops. On January 6, the Americans began building a defensive breastwork of snow and ice. "We are in expectation every night that the enemy will come out upon us," Haskell wrote.

The outlook was as bleak as it had ever been. The enlistments for most of Arnold's troops were up, and men were leaving as soon as they found the means to return home. "[T]he troops," Arnold wrote to Wooster, "are dejected, and anxious to get home, and some have actually set off." Arnold himself was almost out of cash and food.

For Arnold, whose correspondence usually displayed an almost pathological optimism, that letter to Wooster was particularly dark. "For God's sake order as many men down as you can possibly spare. . . . I hope you will stop every rascal who has deserted from us, and bring him back," Arnold pleaded.

Despite his dire straits and the "excessive pain" of his wound, Arnold was still thinking about how Quebec might be taken—albeit not by him. "[Y]our presence here will be absolutely necessary," Arnold told Wooster, knowing that it would be two months at least before he himself would be in a position to command.

Weakened though the Americans might be, Carleton had no intention of venturing outside the walls, save for occasional armed forays into the suburbs to tear down houses for firewood. To deprive the British of this resource, Arnold began burning the buildings that surrounded the city. This sparring over combustibles would mark the extent of the military action during the bitter cold early months of 1776.

It was not until the second week of January that Philip Schuyler got word of the defeat at Quebec. He wrote to George Washington, saying, "My amiable friend, the gallant Montgomery, is no more; the brave Arnold is wounded." He went on to warn Washington that nothing would "prevent the most fatal consequences, but an immediate reenforcement." In that letter, and another sent at the same time to the Continental Congress, Schuyler requested that three thousand of Washington's men be marched to Canada.

But Washington was enduring troubles of his own. Enlistments for his troops, like Arnold's, were running out, and the soldiers, discouraged by dull siege work, were going home. As those troops were leaving, recruiters were scouring the country for new men. Thus Washington found himself replacing an entire army, even while carrying on the siege of Boston. "It would give me the greatest happiness," Washington replied to Schuyler,

> if I could be the happy means of relieving our fellow-citizens now in Canada . . . but it is not in my power, since the dissolution of the old Army. The progress of raising recruits for the new has been very slow and inconsiderable . . . In short, I have not a man to spare.

The Continental Congress was not blind to the need for more troops in Canada, despite the callous ignorance that Arnold would come to believe characterized their attitude toward military matters. Even before Congress learned of the failed attack on Quebec, it had ordered that nine battalions, about sixty-five hundred men, be raised for the fighting there. Two would come from the men already serving under Wooster and Arnold, and the others from New Hampshire, Connecticut, and New York, as well as one made up of Canadian citizens.

Unfortunately, the Continental Congress did have a penchant for believing that simply passing a resolution authorizing a thing would somehow make it so. In fact, the battalions were not nearly as quickly forthcoming as Arnold and the others huddled around Quebec might have wished.

As for Canadian allies, Wooster wrote, "they are not persevering in adversity . . . they are not to be depended upon, but, like the Savages, are extremely fond of choosing the strongest party," which, in early 1776, did not appear to be the Americans.

By early January, word of Arnold's heroic march to Quebec was spreading through the colonies, and he was being lauded as a hero. On January 10, in recognition of that effort, Congress voted to make "Benedict Arnold, Esq., Brigadier-General for the Army in the Northern Department."

Two days after Congress passed the resolution, and exactly a month before Arnold would find out about it, Colonel James Clinton arrived at Arnold's headquarters to take command. Arnold had asked Wooster to come down from Montreal, but Wooster had his hands full with administrative duties and sent Clinton instead. Arnold, still hurting from his wound and now gout ridden, gladly resigned his command, "until my wound will permit my doing my duty."

CHAPTER *18* *A Frozen War*

IF PHILIP SCHUYLER had known about the fleet bound from England, and Germain's hope of attacking up the lakes, he would not have been the least surprised. Since taking command of the Northern Department, Schuyler, like Arnold before him, had focused on the idea of building watercraft to stop that very thing.

But Schuyler enjoyed one advantage over the British in that he already had a small fleet of ships on Lake Champlain. The American squadron consisted of four vessels: the schooner *Liberty*, taken at Skenesborough; the sloop *Betsey*, renamed *Enterprise*, which Arnold had taken at St. John's; and the *Royal Savage* and the *Revenge*, the two partially completed schooners that Montgomery had acquired when he, in his turn, had captured St. John's.

It was not a formidable force, but it was enough to secure American control of the lake. With that issue settled for the present, and with the outcome in Canada hanging in the balance, Schuyler in the early days of 1776 was thinking foremost of moving troops and supplies up and down the lakes. His first concern was maintaining and augmenting his fleet of bateaux, those ubiquitous boats of the north country that were so well suited for transport over inland waters.

By late 1775, Schuyler had built nearly a hundred bateaux, and he continued to have more built as the boats wore out or were destroyed or abandoned by troops who had used them to cross the lakes on their way home from the northern front. Additionally, Schuyler paid a penny per foot to oar makers, who produced hundreds of oars and paddles. The Continental Congress had directed that he build a number of bateaux "not exceeding one hundred," though Schuyler wrote to Washington that "a much greater number are necessary . . . Congress have stinted me." He kept the work going in the early days of 1776.

In an effort to help, Congress ordered that shipwrights from New York and Philadelphia be sent to work on the boats, but at Schuyler's request that order was rescinded. The bateau was a boat from the north country, Schuyler explained, and "one Albany shipwright will do nearly as much of that kind of work as two that are not accustom to it."

Instead, Schuyler contracted with local boatbuilders, drawing up a contract for building "Batteaus other Vessels or Buildings" as the commanding officers might direct. They were "To begin their Work at sunrise and Continue at it til sunset excepting one Hour at Breakfast and one and a half Hours at Dinner." They were to bring their own tools and would be provided, per day, one and one quarter pounds of beef or pork, one and a half pounds of flour, and half a pint of rum, which served as a welcome lubricant for all the men in the northern theater.

Whereas Schuyler was thinking only of bateaux to move troops and materiel, the Continental Congress was thinking also of naval defense, particularly on the St. Lawrence River, which they hoped would remain in American hands for some time. The most expedient means for getting a naval force on the St. Lawrence was to build one in that neighborhood. Because Schuyler was already building boats, Congress wrote to him expressing a wish that he "assist General Wooster" in an effort to "construct the Armed Boats to be kept there."

But Schuyler knew that the lakes were not the place for that. The falls on the Richelieu River prevented large vessels from traveling between Lake Champlain and the St. Lawrence, as the British would learn. Schuyler wrote John Hancock, president of the Continental Congress, that "It never entered my thoughts to build gondolas on Lake Champlain, as I well knew that they could not, without great danger, if at all, be got into the St. Lawrence."

Schuyler further informed Congress that "we have very good ship-carpenters here, yet none are acquainted with the construction of galleys." If Congress wanted galleys like those that Pennsylvania was building for the defense of the Delaware River, Schuyler suggested, then Congress should send him some men from Pennsylvania to oversee their construction.

The production of bateaux went forward under Assistant Deputy Quartermaster General Hermanus Schuyler, most likely a distant cousin of Philip Schuyler. Hermanus set up shop at Fort George, at the southern end of Lake George, about fifty miles from Albany, the launching point for men traveling north by boat.

The first job was to erect boathouses in which to build the vessels, the severe weather making it impossible to work outdoors. By late January, Hermanus Schuyler could report that "the carpenters go on very well bought [both] sides of the work house is bourded to morrow day are to begin at the rest." Schuyler sent men out in teams of six or seven to cut timber.

Two boathouses were finished by the middle of February, one of them 170 feet long and 30 feet wide, the second 42 feet by 33 feet. At Philip Schuyler's urging, Hermanus worked the men hard. Hermanus assured the general, "I push all that I can I have the carpenters to take their breakfast by candle."

And their output was impressive. By the beginning of March, Hermanus Schuyler reported that "the Carpenters make twenty four beatois in Eight day Every two days they turn out Six by Next Tuesday I houp to have forty Eight dun." By the end of the month, he wrote that "in twelve days we shall have all the old & new Beattous dun if head [had] but pitch."

Supplies were a problem, especially in winter, when shipping had to be done by sleigh, so that many sleighs were employed hauling provisions to Canada. Hermanus's correspondence with Schuyler, echoing Schuyler's correspondence with the Continental Congress and the New York Provincial Congress, sounded a constant cry for more nails, oakum, pitch, blacksmith supplies, blacksmiths, and all the other sundry skills and materials that went into boats.

The only thing they had plenty of was lumber, as long as they were willing to use it green.

A Commission to Canada

The siege of Quebec devolved into dull routine. On February 12, Arnold wrote to Congress, "nothing has occurred worth notice." The sum total of reinforcements was 175 additional men who had arrived from Montreal. Sickness was starting to take a toll, with about two hundred men down. Of those, nearly fifty had smallpox. By the end of February, that number would double.

The suffering of besiegers and besieged was made worse by the brutal Quebec winter. "Exceeding cold . . . ," Private Caleb Haskell wrote in his diary, then a few days later, "The weather almost unendurable by reason of the cold," and later still, "There is little stirring by reason of the cold." The Americans sheltered themselves in the houses scattered around Quebec, but sentry, picket, and patrol duty required constant forays into the bitter outdoors, night and day.

Although the fight for Quebec had turned into a waiting game for the besieged and the besiegers, it was also a race between the Continental Congress and Parliament to see who could get reinforcements there first. It was clear that Quebec, and all of Canada, would go to the side that could first bring significant force to bear.

Ice was the key. The St. Lawrence River was frozen, preventing British transports from pushing up to Quebec City. Lakes George and Champlain were frozen as well, and although they could be crossed in that state, deep snow made them mostly impassable. The war in Canada resembled a frozen tableau, waiting for spring.

With the death of Montgomery, command of the forces in Canada had fallen to David Wooster, a situation with which no one, including Wooster, was pleased. On February 17, Congress resolved that "Major-General Lee be directed to immediately repair to Canada to take upon him the command of the Army of the United Colonies in that Province." This news was greeted with great enthusiasm. Charles Lee, the foul-mouthed major general of dubious hygiene who had served as a regular British army officer, was certainly the most experienced general officer in the Continental army, and considered by many to be its best.

Major General Philip Schuyler, commanding the northern theater from Albany, was well pleased with this decision. He and Wooster had been much at loggerheads, and Schuyler had informed Congress that "matters are got to such a height between us, that either he or I must immediately quit this department." Now Wooster would be Lee's problem.

With Lee's arrival, Schuyler would be heading for New York City, though he felt he could not leave until "all is in a proper train for the Northern Service," which could not happen until the lakes were clear of ice. Schuyler hoped "a change of air" would be beneficial to his chronic poor health. "[T]he frequent letting of blood," he complained, "which is necessary for my disorder, weakens me much."

Wooster was also pleased. "I am very glad to hear that General Lee is coming into this Province," he wrote, and suggested that it might be a good idea to send "one or two other Generals with him." If there was one point on which Wooster and Schuyler agreed, besides their desire to see Lee in command, it was the need for a substantial army in Canada. The present troop strength was nowhere near adequate to conquer that country, or even to hold what had already been won.

Neither general entertained any delusions that the British would fail to reinforce their Canadian garrison as soon as the ice went out on the St. Lawrence. "I can hardly doubt but that the enemy will send a very formidable body of troops into Canada . . . ," Schuyler wrote to John Hancock. Wooster echoed that sentiment, saying, "I am of the opinion that we shall need a real army in this Province, a nominal one will not answer the purpose."

At the same time that Congress ordered Lee to Canada, it also ordered a committee of three—two congressmen and a private citizen— to travel there as well. As usual, Congress had big plans, and the instructions to the commissioners called for a comprehensive and patronizing approach to the Canadians. The commission was to "Explain to them the nature and principles of Government among freemen," and how effectively the American system adhered to those principles. They were to try to "stimulate them, by motives of glory, as well as interest . . . ," to join with the Americans in the fight for liberty. When, at last, the Canadians were ready to join the cause, then the commissioners were to assure them that "it is our earnest desire to adopt them into our Union as a sister Colony."

It was a measure of how little the members of the Continental Congress understood the situation in Canada that they could have drafted such instructions. The men chosen to execute this dubious commission, however, could hardly have been better qualified. The commissioners from Congress were Samuel Chase, of Maryland, and Benjamin Franklin, of Pennsylvania, whose reputation and diplomatic skills could not fail to impress Canadians. The private citizen was Charles Carroll, of Carrollton, Maryland, possibly the wealthiest man in America.

Carroll was a good choice not just for his wealth but for his religion. As a Roman Catholic, it was hoped that he could reassure Canadian Catholics, who feared religious oppression under the Protestant Yankees. "[T]he anathemas of the [Catholic] Church," John Adams wrote, "are very terrible to our friends in Canada."

The Canadians had cause to fear. Wooster, in Montreal, had not helped matters, coming down hard on the Catholic Church to the point of forbidding Christmas celebrations, which until the nineteenth century were abhorrent to Protestants. Protestant Americans found Roman Catholic practices completely alien. John Fassett, after attending mass out of curiosity, called it "the strangest thing that ever I see in my life. Their Ceremonies are beyond what I can express." Henry Livingston was amazed at how solemnly Canadians "go thro the round of follies their absurd religion calls upon them to attend."

Carroll was not only Catholic, he had been educated in France and spoke French fluently. To further enhance his standing, he took along his cousin, John Carroll, a Jesuit priest.

Far from resenting or fearing congressional intrusion, the officers in the Northern Department were delighted to hear that the commissioners were on their way. "I am exceedingly happy to learn that the gentlemen Commissioners will be here soon," Schuyler wrote. No doubt he hoped that the commissioners would strengthen his influence with Congress.

But Congress giveth and Congress taketh away. Eight days after directing Lee to Canada, Congress resolved that he not depart until further orders. A third front was opening up with a possible British attack on Charleston, South Carolina, and Congress was considering Lee to command Charleston's defense. Finally Lee was sent south, and on March 6 the Continental Congress announced the appointment of Major General John Thomas "to the command of the forces in Canada."

Thomas was a Massachusetts native and a doctor by trade who had served as a physician and army officer in the Lake Champlain region and in Canada during the French and Indian War. Liked and respected by George Washington and Charles Lee, he had, just days before his promotion, commanded the troops that fortified Dorchester Heights, overlooking Boston, and trained the guns from Ticonderoga on the British. Now Congress was ordering him north.

CHAPTER *19* *The Early Fleet*

ON FEBRUARY 15, 1776, Lieutenant John Enys, of the 29th Regiment of Foot, mustered his company on the parade grounds of the Chatham Barracks east of London. American Secretary George Germain had determined that the early fleet would sail for Canada in mid-February, and the 29th was bound for the relief of Quebec.

It was a smart unit, the men dressed in white waistcoats and breeches and black gaiters. Their regimental coats were red with yellow facings, and they wore black cocked hats with white lace trim. The grenadiers, taller than the other men, looked taller still with black fur busbies on their heads.

The company marched from the barracks to the rattle of drums played by the 29th's distinctive drummers, Black men who wore yellow regimental coats with red facings, the inverse of those worn by the troops. The town of Chatham overlooked the estuary of the River Medway, near the head of navigation, and at a nearby quay the men boarded a tender that would carry them down the Medway to the Royal Navy anchorage at the Nore Lighthouse, near the mouth of the Thames Estuary. There the soldiers clambered up the rounded sides of the transport that would take them to Plymouth, on the southwest coast of England, to join with their naval escort, then on to Canada. Hauling their baggage and muskets below, they tried to settle into the alien, confined world of a sailing ship.

Enys did not join them. Having received permission to travel to Plymouth by land "in order to settle some business," he returned to Chatham, then continued on for Plymouth the next morning. Reaching Plymouth Sound, Enys found a host of ships riding at anchor, pitching in the short chop and straining at their cables. Among the usual crowd of fishing boats, merchantmen, coastal traders, and men-of-war were the two ships he was looking for, the frigate *Surprize* and the sloop-of-war *Martin*. What he did not find was the rest of his company. Delayed perhaps by contrary winds, the transport from the Thames would not arrive until March 17, more than a month after the troops had gone aboard.

The other ships of the fleet were more fortunate, though not one sailed in February. The fifty-gun *Isis*, under the command of Captain Charles Douglas, slated to be flagship of the squadron in the St. Lawrence River, sailed from Portland on March 11. The frigate *Triton*, the armed ships *Bute* and *Lord Howe* (serving as troop transports), and the hired store ships sailed on March 16. Each ship carried its assigned contingent of the 29th, with the bulk of them, nearly four hundred men, shipping aboard the *Bute* and the *Lord Howe*. The *Lord Howe* was commanded by Lieutenant Thomas Pringle, who was returning to Quebec four months after leaving the city.

Once Enys's company of the 29th arrived at Plymouth, "no time was lost" dividing the men between the two ships waiting to take them to Canada. Enys shipped aboard the frigate *Surprize* along with two fellow army officers and twenty-seven privates.

Eager as they were to go, however, the wind did not cooperate, but kept the ships bottled up in Plymouth Sound. Impatiently, the ships' masters and crews waited for the shift that would allow them to heave their cables short, break out their anchors, and work their way down the sound, south to the Atlantic.

The ships were crowded, but not unbearably so. This was only the advance expedition, a small portion of the men whom Germain intended to drop like a sledgehammer on the rebels in Quebec. Even as this early fleet was preparing to sail, Germain was organizing the second embarkation, the massive fleet and army intended to sweep the Americans from Canada and chase them down Lake Champlain to the Hudson.

Finally, on March 21, the wind blew fair for clearing Plymouth Sound. For more than a month the enlisted men had been living in the confines of the ships while Enys and his fellow officers had lodged ashore. Now the officers hurriedly packed their gear and scrambled out to the ships as sails were loosened and capstans rigged and manned.

At four that afternoon, His Majesty's frigate *Surprize* and sloop-of-war *Martin* won their anchors, sheeted home topsails, and got under way. Around noon on the following day, the two men-of-war left the Lizard, England's southwesternmost point, astern and shaped a course for the Cabot Strait, between Newfoundland and Nova Scotia. They were ten days behind *Isis*.

The first part of the passage was fast. "It was Impossible to have had better weather than we had all this Month . . . ," Enys wrote from on board *Surprize*. But fine weather never lasts long in the North Atlantic in early spring, and on April 1 a storm forced the frigate to heave to. For two days the *Surprize* rode out the gale under deeply reefed sails while wind screamed through the rigging and huge Atlantic swells passed under her, or broke with torrents of green water across her decks. Enys did not record how the landlubbing soldiers fared, but they could not have been happy.

On April 8, *Surprize* struck soundings off the coast of Newfoundland, where she found herself among icebergs and in thick fog. The heavy mist froze on the rigging until "the Ship Appeared as if Rigged with Ropes of Cristal Near four times their usual diameter." Enys found the sight pretty but the result "far from . . . pleasant"; the crew had to beat the lines for hours to free them from the ice and allow the sails to be trimmed.

On April 12 *Surprize* raised the island of St. Pierre, off the southern coast of Newfoundland, and approached the Cabot Strait. The frigate had gained nine days on *Isis*, which had passed that way the day before.

At about the same time, *Isis* encountered a solid field of ice stretching as far as the eye could see, blocking the Gulf of St. Lawrence west of the Cabot Strait. It seemed unlikely that the ship would be able to get through. Had the fleet left a month earlier, as Germain had envisioned, it would have been impossible.

Douglas, in command of *Isis*, "steer'd on Sundry points of the Compass" looking for a passage through the ice. Failing to find one, he decided to see "what effect, the running down a large piece of Ice, of about 10 or 12 feet thickness, would have upon the Ship." Carrying all the sail that she could bear, *Isis* sailed directly at the sheet ice, making about five knots. The cutwater and the heavy, bluff bows slammed into the ice, sending a shudder the length of the ship and, to Douglas's delight, smashing the ice to pieces with no substantial damage done to the vessel.

Thus encouraged, and thinking it "an enterprize, worthy of an English ship of the line, in our King and Country's sacred cause, and an effort due to the gallant defenders of Quebec . . . ," Douglas plunged on through the frozen gulf, making westing and leaving bits of his ship's bottom sheathing and cutwater on the broken ice astern. They made a good twenty-four miles before they encountered a snowstorm and found themselves frozen in place.

For "9 days of unspeakable Toil," according to Douglas, *Isis* battled her way through the ice, putting "in Practise various expedients" to break through. On April 18 the ship could run only two to three times her length before becoming stuck fast. When that happened, the crew "Box'd her off," backing the foresails to make the ship sail in reverse, then, once free of the ice, braced the foresails around and made as much headway as they could before becoming stuck once more.

The following day they made a bit more progress until once again being frozen in. Again they tried backing and filling the sails, and even shifted pig iron ballast in an effort to break free, but nothing would work. Finally they stowed the sails and remained where they were.

At four o'clock the next morning, they hit on another idea. With the wind blowing fair, they furled the sails to the yards with weak rope yarn and hoisted the yards aloft. When all was ready, the men hauled on the sheets, breaking the rope yarns, so that all the sails were set in the same instant, the studding sails being set quickly as well. The hope was that this evolution would jerk the ship free. It did not.

Finally, around nine o'clock in the morning, the ice around *Isis* broke up of its own accord, enough for the heavy ship to get underway. She managed to log a few miles that day, backing and filling, until she was once more frozen in.

Some miles astern, the *Surprize* began to encounter drift ice in the Cabot Strait. With the wind building, the frigate was forced to heave to during the night, but the pilot felt that they would find clear water once they worked free of the strait and into the Gulf of St. Lawrence.

To their disappointment, they found instead the same endless ice field that *Isis* had encountered. Like Douglas, Captain Robert Linzee of *Surprize* tried smashing through it, and met with good success. Unlike Douglas, however, who was willing to scatter shards of his vessel over the ice, Linzee, in the less stoutly built *Surprize*, had the crew make up fenders of old rope, and nail a three-inch-thick plank to the bow to prevent the ice from cutting into the hull. They made progress, but by nightfall the frigate was again frozen fast.

For more than a week, the ships smashed their way through the ice, sometimes making headway, sometimes stuck firm. Even the heavily built *Isis* was eventually forced to put fenders around her bow, though these were torn free by the ice. While the ship sat motionless, Lord Petersham of the 29th Regiment marched his soldiers onto the frozen Gulf of St. Lawrence and drilled them.

Enys and his fellow officers on board the *Surprize* found ways to amuse themselves during the painfully slow passage. They melted ice for drinking water and found it surprisingly fresh and considerably better than the shipboard water stored for a month or more in casks. They also experimented with a "Machine for distilling Salt Water fresh" using the steam from the cooking pots. On April 20, Enys wrote, "Saw an immense Number of Seals and as the Ship was Still fast i[n] the Ice, we amused ourselves by killing them."

Slowly, doggedly, the early fleet fought its way through the Gulf of St. Lawrence, every day taking them a few miles closer to the American army in Quebec.

Waiting for Spring

By the end of February, Arnold reported that "my wound is entirely healed and I am able to hobble about my room." Now a brigadier general, he resumed command of the troops in Quebec from Colonel Clinton, but he was still hoping for a more experienced officer to assume overall command. Specifically, he hoped that Congress would send Charles Lee.

As February yielded to March, the weather began to ease. On March 4, Haskell reported "Uncomfortable weather; in the evening we had heavy rain." Whereas before ice and snow had stopped men and supplies from moving through the Champlain valley to Canada, now it was a lack of ice that posed a problem. By the first week of March, Schuyler had collected seventy-six sleds at Albany with which to send supplies and cannon to Montreal and Quebec, but by then the ice was too thin. "Some horses and one man have already been drowned on Lake George and Lake Champlain," he wrote. Now they would have to wait for the ice to break up enough to allow bateaux to cross the lakes before men and supplies could move north again.

Quebec City was still buried under five feet of snow in late March, but fresh American troops were trickling in and Arnold was preparing for action. He spent the latter part of the month establishing a battery of four guns on Point Levi and another battery of eight guns, one howitzer, and two mortars on the Plains of Abraham. This activity did not go unnoticed behind the walls of Quebec. "A hot firing began this morning in the city upon our men at Point Levi," Haskell observed.

Arnold wrote that he hoped the batteries "will have the desired effect"—to compel Carleton's capitulation—and "in case they fail we have ladders, &c. for a storm." He was also preparing fire ships to send against the small fleet anchored in the harbor.

Arnold's army, although smaller than he had hoped for, had grown to 2,505 men, and his troubles had grown in proportion. Of the troops he had, 786 were sick, 616 of them with smallpox.

Even more annoying to Arnold, 425 of the smallpox victims had contracted it from self-inoculation, a not-uncommon practice at the time. A pustule on a patient in the early stages of smallpox was pricked, and the matter inside the pustule scooped out. This was administered to the person being inoculated through a small puncture in the arm. After suffering a mild case of smallpox, the inoculated person was then immune to the disease. Crude as it was, this eighteenth-century smallpox inoculation was effective, with only one person in a thousand dying from the inoculation itself.

Self-inoculation would become standard in the Continental army, but for all its benefits, it was a controversial practice during the early stages of the war. Some swore by it. Others, such as Benedict Arnold, despised the practice.

Among those of his men who were self-inoculated, 271 were Green Mountain Boys, led by Seth Warner, whom Wooster had requested to continue with the army for a short-term enlistment. This in no way pleased Arnold. Because the self-inoculees reported for duty sick, Arnold figured that "the publick will incur an expense of at least twenty pounds for each of those people who will not, on an average, have done ten days' service to the 15th April, to which time they are engaged." That the "people" in question were Green Mountain Boys did not temper Arnold's opinion.

An additional problem that plagued Arnold in Quebec City and Wooster in Montreal was money, or, more specifically, a lack of hard currency. The Canadians' desire to help the Americans had always been in direct proportion to the latter's ability to pay in specie, or coin, as Arnold had discovered when he first emerged from the Maine wilderness. By the spring of 1776, specie was in critically short supply, and Canadians were not inclined to accept paper currency.

It was a serious conundrum for the Americans. Still focused on the need to win Canadian hearts and minds, they also needed supplies. Desperate, Arnold issued "a Proclamation, giving our paper money currency; promising to exchange it in four months for hard cash [a promise he could not have been at all certain of keeping] at the same time declaring those enemies who should refuse it." The proclamation had the desired effect—Arnold was able to purchase what he needed—but "the greater part of the people" took the currency grudgingly, and Canadian relations deteriorated further.

On April 1 the new commanding officer arrived at Quebec, but it wasn't John Thomas. Rather, it was David Wooster, coming down from Montreal. Three months before, Arnold had begged the pompous and contentious Wooster to relieve him, but now Arnold's fellow New Havenite arrived just when Arnold no longer needed him. That afternoon, Arnold and Wooster rode the lines, and Arnold briefed Wooster on the strategic situation. Wooster, for his part, showed little interest in anything that Arnold had to say.

The day after Wooster's arrival, Arnold's battery on Point Levi opened fire on Quebec, but on that same day Arnold reinjured himself. Hoping to lure Arnold into attacking, Carleton staged a false prison break within the walls of Quebec, complete with shouting and gunfire. Hearing the alarm, Arnold raced to his horse and leaped into the saddle, but the horse reared and fell on Arnold's wounded leg. For the next ten days, the restless Arnold was once again confined to bed.

David Wooster was not given to consultation in any event, and with Arnold injured he was able to dismiss his junior officer completely. "General Wooster did not think proper to consult with me in any of his matters," Arnold wrote to Schuyler.

Injured and under the command of an officer who scorned his help, Arnold felt useless, for him the most unbearable of circumstances. Thinking he could accomplish more as commander at Montreal than he could as second in command at Quebec, Arnold asked Wooster's permission to take that post, a request that Wooster "very readily granted." On April 12, Arnold rode away from the camp outside Quebec, leaving behind the men he had led through the wilderness and his long-held dream of entering that city in triumph.

CHAPTER *20 The Commission to Canada*

ON THE DAY that Arnold left the siege of Quebec to take command at Montreal, the new commander of the American forces in Canada, Major General John Thomas, was waiting for ice-out near the south end of Lake George.

Thomas had arrived too late to cross the frozen lakes by sleigh, but too early to get over the ice-choked water by bateau. With Thomas were about eleven hundred men, troops sent to augment the forces in Canada, also waiting for the opportunity to move north. Philip Schuyler, at small, crumbling Fort George, advised John Hancock that "General Thomas is seven Miles from this place where I have advised him to remain untill the Lake opens as we have scarcely room to lay down at this place."

Although it would have been possible to march troops to Quebec, Schuyler feared that with spring coming on, Quebec would be reinforced by the British before Thomas and his men could get there. It would be faster to wait for the water route to open up.

The commissioners—Benjamin Franklin, Samuel Chase, and Charles Carroll—also on their way to Canada, were stuck for the same reason. They had arrived at Albany on April 7 after an overland trip from Philadelphia to New York, followed by a boat journey up the Hudson. General Schuyler—"a man of a good understanding improved by reflection and study," as Carroll described him—had met them at the landing and entertained them "with great civility" at his Albany home.

Two days later the commissioners left Albany for the Schuyler family seat thirty-two miles north. Traveling by wagon, they were joined by General Schuyler, his wife, and two daughters, "lively, agreeable, black eyed girls," according to Carroll, an astute and thorough observer and diarist. Also in the carriage was General Thomas, on his way north to meet his troops at Lake George.

On April 11, Schuyler and Thomas traveled the remaining twenty-two miles north to Lake George, both eager to send men and supplies over the lake in bateaux the moment the ice was out. The commissioners remained behind with "the amiable family of General Schuyler." The following day an early spring storm blanketed the region with snow. On April 16, with a foreboding of crisis, and unwilling to wait any longer to assume the command to which he had been appointed just over a month before, General Thomas set out across Lake George, his bateau crew forcing a path through the thinning sheet of ice.

An Arduous Journey

By April 19 the ice had receded enough for the commissioners to follow Thomas, but just barely. Heavily bundled against the cold, the four men and General Schuyler clambered into two bateaux and settled on the thwarts. The bateau men took up oars, and in the bow of each boat another man stood with a long pole to fend off the large chunks of ice that bobbed in the lake like miniature icebergs, and potentially just as dangerous. "[W]e were delayed considerably in getting through the ice," Carroll wrote, "but with the help of tentpoles, we opened ourselves a passage through it into free water."

They spent the night on the lake, each boat being rigged with a tentlike awning. The next morning they reached Lake Champlain and Fort Ticonderoga, where they remained while their boats were made "ready and fitting" to carry them north over the lake. On April 24 they were underway again.

The trip down the lake, if cold, was not unpleasant, and the commissioners slept comfortably in their bateaux, under the awnings made up for them, on beds they had brought from Philadelphia. Still, it was another hardship in what was proving to be an arduous journey for the seventy-year-old Franklin. "I have undertaken a fatigue that at my time of life may prove too much for me," he had written from Saratoga.

On April 27 they reached St. John's, where they inspected the works captured by the late Richard Montgomery more than half a year before. They sent an express rider to Arnold in Montreal for carriages to carry them the rest of the way, and that night slept in the home of Moses Hazen, on the east side of the river about a mile north of the fort.

Hazen, a Canadian and longtime resident of the St. John's area, was the Loyalist who had spoken to Arnold during the first capture of St. John's and carried word of that event to Carleton. Since then he had thrown in with the Americans and now held a colonel's commission in the Continental army. Wooster had left Hazen in command at Montreal when he went to Quebec, and when Arnold arrived to take over at Montreal he sent Hazen to command at St. John's. Hazen's house, which now served as a tavern, had suffered at the hands of passing troops, particularly British troops who did not care for his choice of allegiance. "[I]n short," Carroll wrote, "it appears a perfect wreck."

The commissioners spent the next day at Hazen's house as bateaux loads of the soldiers who had been waiting for ice-out at the south end of Lake George passed on their way to reinforce the garrisons in Canada. Then, on April 29, the commissioners loaded themselves into the carriages sent from Montreal, though a shortage of carts—or an excess of baggage—forced them to leave some of their personal effects behind. "I have never traveled through worse roads," Carroll wrote of the eighteen-mile trip to La Prairie, "or in worse carriages."

The commissioners arrived that same day at La Prairie, three days behind General Thomas, and crossed the river to Montreal. There to greet them at the landing was Brigadier General Benedict Arnold, along with a number of his officers—Thomas having already pushed on for Quebec—and some of the leading citizens of Montreal. Hoping to impress upon the skeptical Canadians the importance of these men sent by the Continental Congress, Arnold and his officers paraded the commissioners to Arnold's headquarters while guns from the citadel roared out a salute.

Arnold had organized a multistage reception. At headquarters the commissioners were presented to more of Montreal's civic leaders, who "were crowding in to pay their compliments," as Father John Carroll observed, after which the commissioners were escorted to another apartment to take tea with "a large number of ladies, most of them French." The exhausted men were then taken to an elegant dinner, followed by "singing of the ladies, which proved very agreeable," Father Carroll observed, "and would have been more so if we had not been so much fatigued with our journey."

Finally, Arnold and some of the other gentlemen conducted the commissioners to the home of Thomas Walker, perhaps the finest residence in Montreal, where they were to lodge. "I suffered much from a number of large boils," Franklin would later write of his sojourn in Montreal ". . . [M]y legs swelled and I apprehended a dropsy."

The next morning the three men met again with Montreal's citizens, but this time for business, not pomp and ceremony. The commissioners heard about the lack of hard currency, deteriorating relations between Americans and Canadians, the smallpox sweeping through the army, and the hundreds of men leaving at the end of their enlistments or deserting beforehand. Affairs in Canada, the commissioners realized, were much worse than they had imagined.

Men and Bateaux

Brigadier General John Thomas had been even more eager than the commissioners to get to Canada. Like every other officer in the Northern Department, he worried about "a reinforcement of the Ministerial troops, as there is the utmost reason to suppose there will be, as soon as the navigation of the river will permit."

Regarding his own troop strength, he hardly knew what to expect. At the time of his appointment, Congress had told him he would have six thousand troops in Canada. While traveling north, Thomas had known that he had eleven hundred men waiting near Fort George, but in Albany he received a report suggesting that the troops already in Canada would "be much short of an equal number." Fearing that he would have to fight a substantial British army with two thousand men, Thomas had written a plaintive letter to Washington before leaving Albany, asking the commander in chief's opinion regarding the number of men needed. It was, in fact, a tacit request for more. "[S]hould the Ministerial troops there be reinforced . . . ," he wrote, "so small a number must be thought to be inadequate for the defense of that quarter."

Schuyler was able to assuage Thomas's worst fears, but only slightly. He advised Thomas that the number of troops in Canada "would be much short of five thousand," which the two men agreed was the minimum number necessary for the defense of Quebec Province. It was this nightmare scenario that propelled Thomas through the drift ice of Lakes George and Champlain to reach his new command.

He arrived at Montreal on April 26, ahead of the commissioners and also the troops he had left at Fort George, whom he expected to reach the St. Lawrence in a few days' time. In Montreal he met with Benedict Arnold and other officers to get a sense for "the state of our Army before Quebeck, and in other parts of the Province of Canada," discovering, as the commissioners would four days later, that the situation was indeed dire.

In the waning days of 1775, Richard Montgomery had convinced the men whose enlistments were up to continue on until April 15, after which they could return home in time for spring planting. That agreement had saved the winter army, but now it was coming back to bite Thomas just as the spring campaign season was about to begin. "I find that the troops who engaged only to the 15th of April are mostly on their return home," Thomas wrote from Montreal, "and cannot be prevailed upon to continue longer in this country." The new commander now realized he would be lucky to have four thousand men once those who were on their way arrived at their posts.

The Continental Congress described troop strength in terms of regiments, not numbers of men, the unspoken assumption being that a regiment at full strength would comprise some 730 men. The reality was quite different. Of the five regiments that passed through Fort George on their way to Canada in mid- to late April, including those that had been waiting for ice-out with Thomas, the largest numbered just five hundred men, and the smallest, led by Colonel Van Schaick, numbered only seventy-five men. Thus the deployment of five regiments, which should have consisted of 3,650 men, actually totaled only around thirteen hundred. "I find the regiments are very incomplete," Thomas complained. This problem would be compounded with every regiment that marched north.

To make matters worse, Thomas found that he had only two weeks' provisions for his men and no chance of buying more from the Canadians. The only artillery officers he had were John Lamb's men, now prisoners of war in Quebec. "I should have been happy could I, consistent with the truth, have given a more pleasing account of the state of affairs in Canada," Thomas wrote to Washington, "but it is my duty to represent the facts as they are."

Neither Washington nor Congress was insensible to the deficiencies in the Northern Army. In late April, by order of Congress, Washington dispatched another four regiments under the command of Brigadier General William Thompson and six under Major General John Sullivan to further reinforce Thomas. The total troop strength in Canada would ultimately be about six thousand men, though more than fifteen hundred of those were sick and unfit for duty. Still, for all the complaining by officers in the northern theater, this number represented a major commitment to Canada on the part of the Continental Congress and Washington, reducing Washington's own mid-May troop strength in New York to just 8,880, with 6,923 effectives.

Washington reminded Schuyler that he should "make every preparation at Albany for expediting the troops to Canada." That suggestion might well have rankled Schuyler, who had advocated a massive bateau-building program, only to be limited by Congress to one hundred boats. By the time he heard from Washington concerning the new regiments, most of his bateaux were in Canada, having been used to send the first wave of troops, stores, artillery, ordnance, and the commissioners and Thomas down the lake.

"I have only twenty new ones left, and thirty-seven of those built last year," Schuyler informed the commander in chief, "the whole of which will carry no more than fifteen hundred." The little fleet of ships on

Lake Champlain was enough to carry five hundred men, but Schuyler's appeals for sailors had gone unanswered, and the vessels remained at anchor with no crews to sail them.

Schuyler wasted no time ramping up his bateaux construction, and soon was turning them out at a rate of four per day. On May 4, Thompson's brigade arrived at Fort George, much to Schuyler's chagrin, because he did not have the boats he needed to send them on to Quebec. A want of bateaux, as well as foul weather, kept the soldiers camped around the southern part of Lake George.

Men were sent down the lake to Canada as boats became ready, but Schuyler knew that his troubles were not over. Sullivan's brigade was due at Albany anytime and would need transportation overland from Albany to Fort George. Schuyler had wagons enough to move Sullivan's troops and gear or to carry supplies for the men in Canada, but not both. It was, in Schuyler's words, a "truly distressing dilemma." He called on the Albany committee to round up all the wagons they could find, offering the wagon drivers three pounds ten shillings per trip.

That transportation should be such a problem was not due to any want of effort on Schuyler's part. "General Schuyler does everything, indeed much more than I thought was in the power of man to do, in forwarding the troops and provisions," Thompson wrote to Washington. Getting men and supplies to Canada was a herculean task for anyone, let alone a man suffering from chronic illness and chronic shortages.

By May 7, all of Thompson's troops were on their way to Quebec.

"Not the most trifling service can be procured . . ."

When Franklin, Chase, and Carroll discovered the truth of the Americans' situation in Canada, they abandoned their original mission. The want of hard currency and the miserable state of the army had so compromised the colonies' standing in Quebec Province that coaxing the Canadians into the American fold was an impossible task.

In their first report to Congress, written two days after their arrival in Montreal, the commissioners wrote,

It is impossible to give you a just idea of the lowness of the Continental credit here, from the want of hard money and the prejudice it is to our affairs. Not the most trifling service can be procured without an assurance of instant pay in silver and gold.

By way of example, the commissioners discovered that the express rider they had sent from St. John's requesting carriages from Montreal had been stopped at La Prairie because the ferryman refused to accept the rider's Continental dollars. If a friend of the Americans, a Mr. McCartney, had not happened by and changed a paper dollar for silver, the carriages would never have been sent.

It was a sobering lesson in the economics of occupation, but one that American military leaders in Canada had been trying for months to make Congress understand. Arnold, Montgomery, Wooster, and Schuyler had written Congress on that point. Moses Hazen, who, as a Canadian, was well positioned to understand the Canadian mind-set, had urged Congress in person to send a respectable army, led by able generals and provided with "a suitable supply of hard cash." Commenting on the time when hard money had been available, Hazen wrote of his fellow Canadians, "The ready assistance which they gave us on all occasions, by men, carriages or provisions, was most remarkable."

By the time the commissioners arrived, that remarkable assistance had evaporated. The Americans' cash had dwindled, but their need for provisions had remained, forcing them to take by force what the Canadians would not sell for paper money. "The peasantry in general have been ill-used," Hazen wrote,

> . . . promised payment, from time to time, yet they look upon such promises as vague, their labor and property lost, and the Congress and the United Colonies as bankrupt; and (what is a more material point) they have not seen sufficient force in the country to protect them.

The Canadians, after being made "with the point of the bayonet" to sell provisions cheaply and for useless American paper currency, and being subject to occasional looting, had abandoned any pretense of support for the American cause.

Benedict Arnold seconded Hazen's assessment. Faced with that reality, the commissioners concluded that "till the arrival of money, it seems improper to propose the Federal union of this Province with the others." Instead they began to serve as ad hoc military advisors. On the day after their arrival, they attended a council of war with Arnold, Moses Hazen, Colonel John De Haas, and the volunteer Prussian brigadier general Baron de Woedtke, with whom they had sailed to Albany. Most of the points upon which the council agreed were plans that Arnold had already put into motion.

They resolved to establish a battery near the Falls of Richelieu to prevent enemy vessels from ascending the river, though Arnold had ten days before sent a lieutenant to Crown Point to bring up a number of heavy guns for just that purpose. The council also agreed to build six gondolas at Chambly, just below the falls, though again Arnold had already ordered that work begun, being of the opinion that a few armed boats north of the falls would "effectively secure the pass, as no ship larger than a frigate can go up."

Arnold had a small fleet of captured vessels at Montreal with which to defend the St. Lawrence, and earlier he had attempted to bring two boats down from St. John's to augment the force. A row galley had been "driven over the fall and stove to pieces." The passage of a gondola, perhaps the *Schuyler* or the *Hancock*, had been a bit more successful, though the boat was "cut to pieces" and was "in a shattered condition." Prior to the commissioners' arrival, Arnold had ordered material to repair that boat and build more, but the attempt had reinforced Schuyler's belief that nothing much larger than a bateau could run the rapids on the Richelieu.

Arnold now sent Colonel Hazen to Chambly to oversee the French carpenters and bateau men hired to build the gondolas, giving Hazen specific instructions on how the boats should be built. Previously, Arnold had sent Colonel Bedel and two hundred men to a post called the Cedars, about forty-five miles upriver from Montreal. A small British garrison comprising the 8th Regiment was stationed to the west, and Arnold feared that they would march to the relief of the city.

Five days after that council of war, the commissioners were, if anything, even less optimistic about America's position in Canada. Writing to Congress, they concluded that if hard currency could not be forwarded immediately, "it would be advisable, in our opinion, to withdraw our Army and fortify the passes on the lakes."

As it happened, on the very day they wrote those words, the British were making the decision for them, 130 miles down the St. Lawrence at Quebec.

CHAPTER 21 *"God of Armies, Help Us"*

WHEN MAJOR GENERAL JOHN THOMAS arrived at the camp outside the walls of Quebec on May 1, he, like the commissioners, discovered that things were even worse than he'd thought. Smallpox was not just a problem but a full-blown epidemic. Thomas found only nineteen hundred men at the post, and of those only a thousand—a little more than half—were fit for duty. The rest were invalids, due mostly to smallpox. Of those fit for duty, three hundred were men whose enlistment had run out on April 15, "many of whom refused duty, and all were very importunate to return home."

Additionally, Thomas found no more than 150 pounds of gunpowder and provisions for six days. Procuring supplies from the French inhabitants was like pulling teeth, eighteenth-century style.

Thomas and his officers decided to play the one hand they had left, an American brigantine named *Peggy*. The *Peggy*, coincidentally owned by Benedict Arnold, had become trapped for the winter at Quebec, and Arnold himself had ordered her converted into a fire ship. On the night of May 3, the *Peggy* got underway, with her crew hoping to get in among the shipping near the Lower Town and set it, and perhaps the town itself, ablaze. Those men fit for duty were arrayed under arms outside the city, ready to capitalize on any panic brought on by the fire ship.

Unfortunately, Quebec's defenders, suspicious of the strange vessel, fired into her. The gunfire ignited the *Peggy* while she was still two hundred yards from the harbor entrance, and she blew up before she could do any harm to the city.

On May 5, Thomas called a council of war with General David Wooster and all the field officers in camp. They were not an optimistic bunch.

The council agreed that the arrival of any British men-of-war would deny the Americans use of the river. Before that happened, it was essential to get the sick and the artillery and supplies away from Quebec and up to Three Rivers (now Trois-Rivières), and to move the army "further up the river as soon as it could conveniently be done, to secure some posts where there would be a prospect of resisting with some success."

That evening Thomas received word that a convoy of fifteen ships was on the St. Lawrence, 120 miles downriver from Quebec. This was the early fleet, on its way to lift the siege of the city, though in fact the lead ships were much closer than the messenger thought. Still, the core of the information was correct. The British were coming.

The next morning the American forces began loading their sick and their artillery into bateaux for transport upriver. In the middle of that operation, which placed the army in an awkward and vulnerable position, the first five British men-of-war arrived. From that moment on, the American adventure in Canada, which had looked so hopeful at first, began to quickly unravel.

The Relief of Quebec

On April 21, the *Isis* at last broke clear of the Gulf of St. Lawrence ice field and passed between the Gaspé Peninsula and 140-mile-long Anticosti Island, at the mouth of the St. Lawrence River. That night, in a blinding snowstorm, the fourth-rate ship stood into the river. *Surprize,* a much faster ship than *Isis,* was less than a day behind.

As *Surprize* made her way up the St. Lawrence, Captain Linzee tried to go ashore to find out the state of things at Quebec, but a thick fog forced him to lie to for several days. When the fog began to clear, *Surprize* spotted another ship coming up with them. Not knowing what ship it was, Linzee ordered his own ship cleared for action.

Lieutenant John Enys was impressed by the evolution.

It is Surprizing to see how Active and Cleaver the Sailors are at this Work. It was quite finished before I thought they had time to begin it and looked pretty enough all bulkheads and births being knocked down so that She appeared fore and aft a compleat double Battery without the Smalest obstruction from one end to the other.

The unknown ship, however, turned out to be the sloop-of-war *Martin*. Still hoping to gather intelligence, Linzee sent his first officer ashore. Enys went with him, hoping to see "a Savage which I expected to See leaping from Hill to Hill in the Manner Goats do in England." All he got for his troubles, however, was a bitterly cold boat ride and some dubious information from the only Canadian they encountered, "who as a picture of poverty beggar'd all description . . . every part of his dress being the work of his own family. . . ."

It was not until May 3 that *Isis* reached the rendezvous at Isle aux Coudres, sixty miles below Quebec. "There (bringing a fair wind with them)," Douglas wrote, "first the Surprize then the Martin joined us." At the island the British ships secured pilots, and on May 5 Douglas ordered *Surprize*, "a remarkably good sailor," to push on to Quebec.

Also on the St. Lawrence, and not far behind the relief force, was the British frigate *Niger* and three transports carrying the 47th Regiment. General Howe, aware of Carleton's predicament, had ordered the troops up to Quebec as soon as he thought the ice would allow passage, and *Niger*, then at Halifax, was ordered to escort them up the river.

Surprize ran through the treacherous traverse at the downriver end of twenty-mile-long Isle d'Orleans, and in the afternoon saw people ashore, apparently leaving church. By way of greeting, Linzee raised the colors and fired a gun to leeward, hoping that it would encourage some of the locals to come aboard the frigate. Instead it had the opposite effect, sending the Canadians running for shelter.

That night Linzee anchored six miles below Quebec, unwilling to go closer in a dying breeze without knowing the strength of the American batteries. The frigate's crew cleared for action and prepared for towing off fire rafts, fearing that the rebels might drift them down on the strong current.

The next morning, May 6, at first light, *Surprize* was underway again, and by six o'clock the beleaguered people of Quebec caught sight of her coming upriver. Thomas Ainslie wrote that "a vessel appear'd turning P[oint] Levi to the inconceivable joy of all who saw her: the news soon reached every pillow in town, people half dress'd ran down to the Grand battery to feast their eyes on the sight of a ship of war displaying the Union flag."

This was the moment that the desperate soldiers and Loyalist citizens of Quebec had been awaiting for five long months. They hoisted a signal to indicate to the *Surprize* that it was safe to close with the city, and the frigate dropped anchor in the basin just seven weeks after leaving Plymouth, England.

As soon as she was anchored, Captain Thomas Mackenzie, of the *Lizard*, took a boat out to the ship and escorted Linzee and some of the officers of the 29th ashore. Soon after, orders were sent out for the soldiers and marines on board *Surprize* to disembark. As they were doing this, the ponderous fifty-gun *Isis*, twice the size of the next largest ship at Quebec, stood in slowly under topsails, rounded up, and let go her best bower. With her was the little sloop-of-war *Martin*. No sooner were their anchors set than they began landing their marines and soldiers, including the 29th's Grenadier Company, about two hundred troops in all.

Within the city, Carleton found his own troops "much improved and in high spirits." Not caring to remain besieged a moment longer, he mustered his troops under arms and led them out of the St. Louis and St. John's gates, where they were joined by the soldiers and marines from the ships, about 850 men in total, and advanced "to see what those mighty boasters were about."

The Americans were about running, and not much else. "[T]he Rebels abandoned the place," Enys wrote, "and that with so great precipitation that they even left a field peice Loaded in the field with only a Nail put into the Vent which was easily drawn from thence." A few shots were fired, and Enys thought briefly that the rebels had formed up in the woods at the end of the Heights of Abraham, but it was soon clear that they were gone. At the American headquarters at Holland House, Colonel Maclean found General John Thomas's dinner sitting by the fire, which the British soldiers proceeded to eat.

The siege of Quebec was over, and the reconquest of Canada had begun.

"The most terrible day . . ."

As soon as the ships dropped anchor, Canadian civilians who had been providing grudging assistance to the American army abandoned them entirely, and "would neither furnish us with teams nor afford us the least assistance," Thomas wrote, "but kept themselves concealed." As the loading of supplies and the sick and wounded went on, Thomas gave orders for the men to hold themselves in readiness to march at a minute's notice.

The Americans had only one fieldpiece and no entrenchments, or anyplace where they might have taken a defensive position. Once the troops landed from the ships and Carleton sallied forth from the city, there was no choice but to run.

The American retreat from Quebec came close to being a rout, though some order was maintained. Colonel Elisha Porter wrote that "when the Enemy were within about 80 Rods of us we had orders to Retreat Slowly & in good Order (which we did)."

Porter's men and the others making up the rear guard formed in the first woods they came to and held off the British advance until the remainder of the army had filed past. Most likely this was the resistance that Enys had observed. Finally they too marched off, retreating fifteen miles upriver, where they halted for a few hours' rest before marching through the night.

They got away with their lives but little else. Two hundred of the sick were left behind to be taken prisoners of war. Nearly all of the artillery, stores, and the men's belongings were abandoned or captured on the river by the men-of-war. (The commissioners in Montreal were later informed that some of the baggage was plundered by Americans whose enlistments were up. "We are informed," the commissioners wrote, "that the men who, from pretended indisposition, had been excused from doing duty, were the foremost in the flight, and carried off such burdens on their backs as hearty and stout men would labor under.") A gondola and an armed schooner were also captured, along with two tons of gunpowder that Schuyler had struggled to forward to Quebec.

The men-of-war wasted no time continuing upriver, blasting the retreating army with heavy broadsides. "This is the most terrible day I ever saw," wrote Reverend Ammi Robbins on May 7. "God of armies, help us. Three ships came near by us, firing as they came, and our boats and people in a scattered condition, coming up. Distress and anxiety in every countenance."

The disorganized and scattered army paused at Deschambault, where Thomas called another council of war to pose the question, "is it prudent for the Army in its present situation to attempt to make a stand at this place?" The answer was an unequivocal no. With few supplies and the frigates already upriver of the Americans and able to cut them off, it was clear that Deschambault was no safer than Quebec.

The council agreed that the army should move farther upriver to Sorel, on the south side of the St. Lawrence and right at the mouth of the Richelieu, the route back to America. Thomas, however, would stay behind with five hundred men until he received word from Arnold at Montreal. If supplies could be forwarded to Deschambault, Thomas would stay and attempt to hold that post.

Benedict Arnold, when he heard of the council of war's decision, did not agree with it. He felt that Deschambault, where the swift, narrow river and high bluff afforded a good opportunity to hold off British men and ships, should be held. If it could not be, Arnold felt that the army should instead abandon Canada entirely, fall back to Isle aux Noix, and worry about keeping the British from invading America. "I tremble for the fate of our scattered, sick, starved and distressed Army," he wrote to Schuyler. Eager for action, he left Montreal on May 10 to join the army at Sorel, with the intention of taking a gondola to Deschambault if his presence there could be of any help.

With supplies so low—Thomas's men were on half rations—any troops sent from the colonies without provisions would be more burden than help. Thomas therefore sent orders back to Sullivan's brigade in Albany to remain there until supplies could be sent up. Unfortunately, selfless devotion was not always the order of the day. When Schuyler met up with one regiment bound for Canada, he ordered them to unload their heavy baggage from the bateaux to make room for barrels of pork, "acquainting the officers and men with the distress our people labored under in Canada." As soon as Schuyler was gone, the officers dumped the pork out of the bateaux and reloaded their baggage.

The commissioners in Montreal heard about Thomas's retreat on May 10. A week and a half after their arrival in Canada, they knew that their mission was over. "We are afraid it will not be in our power to render our country any further services in this Colony," they wrote to John Hancock, President of the Continental Congress.

The next day, Benjamin Franklin set off for home. Charles Carroll wrote in his journal, "The doctor's declining state of health, and the bad prospect of our affairs in Canada, made him take this resolution." Father John Carroll accompanied Franklin to help him on the arduous journey back to Philadelphia.

Charles Carroll and Samuel Chase decided to remain in Canada awhile longer, and Arnold, for one, welcomed their authority. Writing to Chase, he acknowledged that the commissioners' original task was now impossible, but he added, "Your presence, however, is absolutely necessary, and I am rejoiced to hear your determination of staying." Indeed, Chase and Carroll, by virtue of their office, assumed the supervisory role of the Congress as a whole. "We have no fixed abode," they wrote to Schuyler, "being obliged to follow your example and become Generals, Commissaries, Justices of the Peace; in short to act in twenty different capacities."

Thomas remained at Deschambault for six days, hoping each day to receive provisions, entrenching tools, and sundry other supplies. When they did not come, he pulled his troops from Deschambault and the town of Jacques-Cartier and marched the starving, half-naked men to Three Rivers, intending to eventually return to Deschambault and make a stand there.

What Thomas and his fellow American officers did not know, however, was that a much greater force than the one that had driven them from Quebec was on its way from England. Carleton did know this, and he knew that it was in his best interest to await its arrival and attack with overwhelming numbers, rather than attack the Americans now at Three Rivers, while the British and American armies were at close to equal strength. When contrary winds prevented Carleton from moving supplies by water, he pulled the 29th and 47th regiments back to Quebec and left a Canadian guard to watch the enemy. He could afford to wait.

Arnold arrived at Sorel on May 12 and began to organize the "sick, starved and distressed Army," and to rebuild the battery that commanded the river. Overseeing that work was engineering colonel Jeduthan Baldwin, who wrote in his diary, "19 Sunday. this is Observd but all the men at work that can be employed with tools at three breastworks."

Baldwin, forty-four years old, had seen service in the French and Indian War and had gained his only hands-on experience in military engineering as the designer of the American defenses around Boston. He would have considerable opportunity to practice his newfound trade over the course of the next year, and would prove to be one of the shining lights in an officer corps that was not always distinguished by talent, diligence, and zeal.

Smallpox continued to devastate the army. The epidemic was spreading so fast that Arnold, who had vigorously opposed inoculation while outside Quebec, now began to organize a systematic program of inoculation, an initiative that was supported by the commissioners and other officers.

By May 16, General Thompson and his men had made it north to the St. Lawrence. Thompson and Colonel Arthur St. Clair, of Pennsylvania, stopped at Montreal to meet with the commissioners; then they too joined the army at Sorel.

Major General John Thomas arrived the following day, having left about eight hundred men at Three Rivers. He was not happy with Arnold's inoculation program. Colonel Porter wrote, "17th Orders from Genl. Arnold for 119 of my Regt to Innoculate immediately which was done Genl Thomas arriv'd in ye Afternoon—he was much displeas'd with ye Order—order'd them to Stop." In fact, Thomas ordered the death penalty to anyone who inoculated.

The Cedars

On the day Thomas arrived at Sorel, a column of British regulars and Canadians with a contingent of Indians, a total of about three hundred men under the command of Captain George Forster, was marching from the west to liberate Montreal, just as Arnold had feared. To get there, they would first have to take the Cedars, where Arnold had earlier sent Bedel's division. After a brief siege, Forster forced the garrison to surrender, and a few days later he surrounded and captured the relief column that the commissioners had sent to their aid.

When word of the disaster at the Cedars reached the commissioners, Arnold was recalled from Sorel and dispatched with one hundred men to try to catch Forster and liberate the prisoners.

Arnold entrenched at La Chine, thinking that Forster would have to come that way, but when Forster got word of Arnold's force, he retreated west with his prisoners. Upon learning that, Arnold began a hard march after them while his bateaux followed, forcing their way up the swift-moving river. At six o'clock in the evening on May 25, his main force arrived at the little fort of St. Ann's, at the fork of the Ottawa and St. Lawrence rivers, just in time to see the enemy's bateaux removing prisoners from an island, possibly L'Ille-Cidieux, three miles off. The boats disappeared up the Ottawa River, bearing off the captive Americans.

"Words cannot express our anxiety, as it was not in our power to relieve them," Arnold wrote. When their bateaux finally caught up with them, the American relief force pressed on but was unable to approach the shore where Forster's troops were now entrenched. The Americans retreated to wait for daylight and a renewed attack.

But Forster had his own problems. He was not sure he could control his Indian forces; nor could he—as a British officer—countenance "the customs and manners of the savages in war . . . of putting their prisoners to death." Before such a thing could happen, making him responsible for a massacre, he hoped to rid himself of the prisoners. He sent an officer to Arnold under flag of truce to negotiate a deal.

Arnold thought the offer disingenuous, and wondered how Forster could on the one hand induce the Indians to hand over the prisoners but on the other fail to stop them from stripping the men naked or murdering them. Nonetheless, when Forster agreed to equal terms— he would release his prisoners in exchange for the American army releasing the same number of British prisoners—Arnold also agreed. It was a minor victory for the Americans, the last they would get in Canada.

CHAPTER **22** *"An Army Broken"*

EVEN AS LORD GEORGE GERMAIN had been organizing the ships to carry the 29th Regiment to Quebec, he was also putting together "the second embarkation," the force intended to reclaim Canada.

From the start, Germain had been thinking beyond simply saving Quebec. He intended to mount an offensive move from Canada, and that meant a push up Lake Champlain. In late March he wrote to General William Howe in Boston, who had overall command of the army in America, to say that he hoped the army in Canada "will be able to advance into the other Colonies, by the Passage of the Lakes, and accordingly every proper preparation has been made here, that can give Facility to such a Plan." Germain did not yet know that Howe had evacuated Boston after Washington's army had mounted batteries on Dorchester Heights using the cannons transported from Ticonderoga by Henry Knox.

Part of the preparations, of course, included boats. As early as January 1776, the Admiralty office began considering "The Size or Dimension of the Sloops proposed for the Navigation of Lake Champlain," as well as the design of boats to be sent in frame to Canada. The Admiralty referred to the vessels as "Batteaux," perhaps believing this to be the accepted name for any boats used on the lakes, though in fact a bateau was "a sort of Vessel unknown in this Country." But the frames that would eventually be sent across the Atlantic were not for bateaux in the north country sense.

After some consideration, the Lords Commissioners of the Admiralty decided on two armed sloops of about ninety tons each and "at least four hundred Batteaux from 36 to 40 feet in length." The Admiralty began immediately to arrange for materials and craftsmen to be sent to Quebec to build the vessels. The frames, or "ribs," of the vessels were fashioned in England and shipped to Quebec. The only things the Admiralty did not send were timber and planking, there being plenty of both in the virgin forests of Canada.

As for men, Germain intended to send eight regiments then stationed in Ireland, comprising about five thousand men. In the beginning of the year, England had signed treaties with a smattering of German states to provide soldiers for the war in America. Five thousand of these "Hessian" mercenaries were also slated for Carleton's forces in Canada.

Once these troops were secured, their transportation became the next big obstacle. Germain was forced to move the German units in two divisions, and he warned Carleton that, "on account of the difficulty of procuring transports," he could not say for certain when the second division would depart.

The problem was greater than just getting these troops to Canada. Germain's aggressive approach toward ending the rebellion meant a great increase of troops for every theater in America—particularly, more troops for William Howe to counter Washington's main army. Before evacuating Boston, Howe had written to Germain, "I apprehend the rebels would not have less than 10,000 men on the side of Rhode Island, and perhaps 20,000 in the province of New York to act against General Carleton on one hand and the New York corps on the other." Germain accepted Howe's estimate, though in fact Washington's effectives numbered only about seven thousand, and the number of men arrayed against Carleton would not exceed six thousand, fewer than forty-five hundred of whom were fit for duty.

Along with ten thousand men for Carleton, an additional sixteen thousand men—twelve thousand of them Hessians—were being sent to Howe, and seven regiments, including two that had been intended for Quebec, were heading to Charleston. The logistics were staggering, and the fact that England had the resources to achieve such a thing should have given any American patriot pause.

In the first week of April, while *Isis*, *Surprize*, and the other ships carrying the 29th Regiment were approaching the Canadian coast, two massive convoys were assembling to carry the troops of the "second embarkation" to Quebec. This was the army intended to drive the Americans from Canada and follow them up the lakes to the Hudson River.

The thirty-two-gun fifth-rate *Pearl* and the frigate *Carysfort* sailed from Cork, Ireland, that week with forty-one ships in convoy, carrying seven battalions of British troops. The military bands struck up their martial tunes, but the drama of the moment, with music in the air and a great fleet of ships loosening sail and winning their anchors, could not make the troops crammed on board forget that they were leaving behind all they knew and were sailing to war in a strange wilderness country thousands of miles away.

Setting their massive topsails to a steady northeast wind, the ships stood out into the open sea, shaping a course for Canada. On board the transport *Friendship*, Sergeant Roger Lamb stood at the rail and watched his native Ireland disappear below the horizon. Though he, too, was caught up in the excitement of getting under way, still he appreciated the gravity of the circumstance. "[T]he idea of being separated, perhaps forever, from parents, friends and country," he wrote, "penetrated my bosom with a pang which nothing could remove at the moment." It was an emotion that no doubt played through the hearts and minds of thousands of soldiers scattered among the fleet.

Lamb's convoy was just part of the mobilization. Another five ships, not ready in time, were to sail with the frigate *Tartar*, and less than three days later, another thirty-two ships carrying German soldiers would sail from Plymouth for Quebec. For the Germans, fighting in a war in which they had no personal stake, in a sparsely settled country whose language they could not speak, the feeling of isolation and homesickness was even worse than it was for the British troops.

The ships in this convoy included the thirty-two-gun men-of-war *Juno* and *Blonde* escorting eight ships filled with ordnance and twenty troop transports carrying the 21st Regiment, as well as three thousand German troops from Hanau and Brunswick.

On board the *Blonde* was Major General John Burgoyne, appointed second in command of the British and German forces in Canada. Burgoyne was fifty-four years old, older than most men of his rank. As a young captain he had eloped with Lady Charlotte, the daughter of the Earl of Derby, whose angry father had cut her off financially. Burgoyne had sold his commission to support his new bride in her accustomed style and to pay his gambling debts. After living more than six years in

France, the couple had returned to England, where Charlotte's father forgave her and Burgoyne purchased a captaincy, likely through Derby's influence.

Burgoyne was a good self-promoter, but he was a good soldier as well, and he rose quickly. He had put considerable thought into the way the war in America was being waged. Prior to being sent to Canada, Burgoyne had written and submitted to the cabinet an insightful report entitled "Reflections upon the War in America."

Although Burgoyne was sent to Canada as second in command to Guy Carleton, it is possible—even likely—that Germain intended him to take the lead in military matters. Germain was no fan of Carleton, and may have considered the governor too timid as a leader of troops. Certainly by August 1776, Germain had decided that Burgoyne should lead the offensive up the lakes. He sent orders to that effect to Canada, instructing Carleton that he should turn over military operations to Burgoyne and return to Quebec to concentrate on "restoring Peace, and the establishing of good order and legal Government in Canada," which was essentially busywork.

Germain sent these orders by a Captain Le Maitre, an aide to Guy Carleton whom Carleton had sent to England with dispatches. Le Maitre traveled three times to the Gulf of St. Lawrence but "had the Mortification to find it impossible to make his passage to Quebec, and therefore returned to England."

Why Le Maitre could not get to Quebec is unclear, but he likely knew that the orders he carried would lead to Carleton's replacement as military commander, and out of loyalty found reasons to fail to deliver them. Whatever the reason, the orders never reached Carleton, and the governor continued to lead the military effort in Canada. Burgoyne would have to wait until the 1777 campaigning season to put his ideas for the conquest of America into effect.

"This critical juncture . . ."

Anxious to retain Canada, the Continental Congress wrote to General Thomas on May 24, pointing out that if the army was to retreat from that country, "the loss of Canada will not be all; the whole frontiers of the New England and New York Governments will be exposed." During the year since the taking of Ticonderoga, which Congress had initially wanted to abandon, the delegates had come to understand that Lake Champlain was the highway to invasion from the north.

In addition to the regiments already sent to Canada, Congress ordered six thousand militia to be raised and sent north, though it was generally agreed by the commanders there that if the militiamen had not already had smallpox, they would do more harm than good. Congress also assured Thomas that it had "tried every method to collect hard money for the Army in Canada, without success." That being the case, the delegates sent "all the hard money that was in the Treasury . . . the sum of sixteen hundred and sixty-two pounds, one shilling and three pence, in three bags . . . ," equal to a little more than four thousand dollars.

Thomas, however, was no longer in command. On May 20, he ordered the troops at Three Rivers, starved of provisions, to fall back to Sorel. Writing to the commissioners in Montreal, he informed them that unless extraordinary steps were taken to relieve the men, "it will not be possible to keep the Army together." Then John Thomas fell victim to the disease that had crippled half his army.

Colonel Elisha Porter at Sorel wrote, "21st. Genl. Thomas broke out with Small Pox & in the Morning resigned the command to Genl. Thompson. NB no meat for 3 Day."

In the same vein, Jeduthan Baldwin wrote, "Genl. Thomas Sick & not one barrel of provision in the Store & the men at half allowance for several Days past, & no sertainty of any coming soon, was truly distressing." The troops were left even more miserable by a stretch of severe weather, suffering through cold, wet nights with little shelter. The men infected with smallpox were crammed into barns, "and not the least thing, to make them Comfortable."

Though Thomas had turned over temporary command to Thompson, he wrote to Major General David Wooster and asked him to assume overall command of the army in Canada. For the commissioners, already frustrated with Wooster, this was too much. On May 27 they wrote to John Hancock, their last letter from Canada, saying that with the fate of the army and the country at stake, "we think it a very improper time to conceal our sentiments."

Samuel Chase and Charles Carroll then let loose. "General Wooster, is, in our opinion," they wrote, "unfit, totally unfit, to command your Army, and conduct the war." They suggested that the Connecticut general be recalled.

The week before, the two commissioners had traveled from Montreal to Sorel and Chambly to inspect the troops, and were horrified by what they discovered. The American forces were in complete disarray. They found, as Lewis Beebe, a physician posted at Chambly, wrote, "Parts of different Reg^ts. arrived from Sorrell, all being ignorant of their destination, but very few general orders, and they usually countermanded within a few hours of being given."

In their letter to Hancock, the commissioners laid out the unhappy truth:

> We cannot find words strong enough to describe our miserable situation: you will have a faint idea of it if you figure to yourself an Army broken and disheartened, half of it under inoculation, or under other diseases; soldiers without pay, without discipline, and altogether reduced to live from hand to mouth. . . . Your soldiers grumble for their pay; if they receive it they will not be benefitted, as it will not procure them the necessities they stand in need of.

The commissioners did not know about the 1,662 pounds hard money on its way, but they would not have been mollified if they had. Congress, they noted, owed the troops and the inhabitants of Canada more than ten times that amount.

Perhaps the most valuable knowledge the commissioners came away with was an understanding that an army could not be made up of men on short-term enlistments. The army needed real discipline, and that would not happen, they wrote, until,

> soldiers can be enlisted for a term of years, or for the continuance of the war. . . . No duty must be expected from soldiers whose times are out, let their country stand ever so much in need of their services: witness the unfeeling flight and return, at this critical juncture, of all the soldiers, and a greater part of the officers, who are entitled to be discharged.

George Washington had learned a similar lesson in January while struggling to reconstitute an army that had dissolved even while holding the British in Boston under siege. Reminding his countrymen of the difficulty, he wrote that "we have disbanded one army and recruited another within musket shot of two and twenty regiments, the flower of the British army."

For all the romantic notions, then and now, of the citizen-soldier, the minuteman called to arms to defend his country, it became clear to those fighting the war that only a professional army could win, not a rabble biding its time until discharge. It was a change that would come, and it would be one of the most profound differences between the mob that retreated from Canada in 1776 and the army that stood up and beat Burgoyne in 1777.

On May 29 the commissioners left Montreal for the last time, traveling to Chambly for a council of war with Arnold, Wooster, and the other general officers and field officers. John Thomas was also at Chambly, having left Sorel on May 21.

The council of war was held on May 30. The officers and congressmen did not come up with any bold plan but rather concluded that the army would try to hold the country between the St. Lawrence River and Sorel if possible, and prepare for an orderly retreat from Canada if necessary.

The next day the commissioners left for St. John's, arriving on June 1. There they met Major General John Sullivan, who had just arrived from Albany with fourteen hundred men. Also at St. John's was David Wooster, his bags packed, on his way home to Connecticut.

It would be another week before Congress received the letter from the commissioners complaining of Wooster's incompetence and immediately recalled him from Canada. By then Wooster was already gone.

On June 10 the commissioners were back in Philadelphia, where they received the approbation of Congress for "the restoration of order and discipline" in Canada.

CHAPTER *23* *Three Rivers*

WHILE ATTENDING THE May 30 council of war at Chambly, Brigadier General William Thompson received intelligence that Carleton's forces, about eight hundred strong, had moved up from Quebec to take the position at Three Rivers recently abandoned by the Americans. Still technically in overall command, Thompson hurried back to Sorel and ordered Colonel St. Clair, with six to seven hundred men, to march to Three Rivers and "endeavor to surprise the enemy posted there, making prisoners of as many as possible, and cutting off all who oppose you."

When John Sullivan, who was senior to Thompson, arrived at St. John's and discovered that Thomas was "down with the smallpox, without the least prospect of a recovery," and that Wooster was packed to go, he realized that "the command devolves upon me." In half a year, the troops in Canada had been under the command of Schuyler, Montgomery, Wooster, and Thomas. Now it was Sullivan's turn.

Major General John Thomas had seemed to be on his way to recovery. His physician, Lewis Beebe, reported, "G. Thom:ˢ remained exceeding well . . . and every Symptom appeared very favorable." But the recovery did not last long, and on June 2, Beebe wrote, "this morning a little after the first dawnings of the day Genˡ. Thomas expired . . . ," just thirteen days after contracting smallpox.

Setting out from St. John's to tour his theater of operations and "find with certainty where the enemy is, and what they are about," Sullivan stopped briefly at Chambly, only to discover that Thomas was dead. Elisha Porter wrote that "about noon Genl Sullivan arrivd but could not attend Ye Funeral—he went off to Montreal soon."

Sullivan was thirty-five years old, a successful lawyer from Durham, New Hampshire, a descendant of Irish nobility. He had been a major in the local militia and a delegate to the Continental Congress before his appointment as one of eight brigadier generals. He had served under Lee at the siege of Boston and had led a successful expedition against Fort William and Mary, near Portsmouth in his home colony.

George Washington wrote to John Hancock expressing his opinion of Sullivan, which was largely favorable. He warned, however, that Sullivan "has his wants, and he has his foibles." The foibles, Washington felt, were "manifested in a little tincture of vanity, and in an over-desire of being popular, which now and then leads him into some embarrassments."

That vanity was evident in the high opinion that Sullivan cultivated of his own abilities and popularity. Despite all the difficulties encountered in Canada by officers such as Arnold, Montgomery, and Thomas for more than half a year, Sullivan wrote to Washington, "I may venture to assure you and the Congress that I can, in a few days, reduce the Army to order; and . . . put a new face on our affairs here, which a few days since seemed almost impossible."

In Sullivan's mind he was already halfway to taking Quebec, with the Canadians rallying to his standard. "It really was effecting," he wrote, "to see the banks of the Sorel lined with men, women and children, leaping and clapping their hands for joy to see me arrive."

Learning of the British advance on Three Rivers and of Thompson's having sent St. Clair's regiment there, Sullivan ordered Thompson to march with an additional two thousand men, take over the command, and, if feasible, attack.

By the end of his first week in Canada, however, Sullivan was feeling a little less certain of his ability to put a new face on things. He wrote to Washington asking that either Washington himself or Charles Lee come and take command, certain that that would be the key to winning Canada. It was too late, of course, and events were already in motion that would spell the end of America's northern incursion, even before Washington had a chance to reply.

The Second Embarkation

Like the first fleet that George Germain had sent for the immediate relief of Quebec, the convoys from Cork and Plymouth enjoyed a relatively easy crossing, with fair wind, until April 19. On that day they joined together, the Plymouth fleet coming up as the Cork fleet lay becalmed. J. F. Wasmus, a German surgeon sailing with the Plymouth convoy, noted that "Our fleet is quite respectable now and incl. the frigates consists of 79 sailing ships, all of them 3-masted: a truly beautiful sight similar to a glimmering city." For a few days they sailed together, until contrary winds scattered them again.

By May 4, while *Isis* and her companions were on the last leg to Quebec, the Cork fleet found itself among icebergs off Newfoundland. William Digby, a lieutenant of grenadiers with a poetic bent, observed that they were "formed in the most romantic shapes, appearing like large castles." (With a soldier's prejudice, he also described the transport's captain as "a good seaman and an agreeable companion, which does not always follow.)

After nearly piling up on Cape Race, the southeastern tip of Newfoundland, the fleet made the St. Lawrence River by the second week of May. The ice that had so hampered the passage of Douglas's ships across the gulf was finally gone.

By the end of May, thirty-nine transports, including Digby's and the men-of-war *Carysfort* and *Pearl*, had arrived at Quebec. No sooner did the ships anchor in the Cul de Sac than Carleton ordered them to continue upriver, which they did, the wind holding fair until they arrived at Port Neuf, about forty miles below Three Rivers. This was the moment that Carleton had been waiting for. Now at last he had men enough to protect Quebec and attack the rebels, and he wasted no time going on the offensive.

With the transports wind-bound, the troops were ordered ashore to cover the rest of the distance by land. "We were about 500 men," Digby wrote, "and more, we hoped, not far in our rear—all in great spirits on leaving the ships." The soldiers had been almost two months on shipboard, and were no doubt delighted to feel solid, unmoving ground beneath their feet.

Nor would they be disappointed about the arrival of more troops. By June 1 more transports had arrived, as well as the *Juno* and the *Blonde*, carrying Burgoyne and the other high-ranking officers. On

June 2 Carleton wrote to Germain that the regiments from Ireland under Brigadier General Simon Fraser and Burgoyne's troops from Plymouth had mostly arrived.

Joshua Pell, one of the officers, wrote in his journal, "1st June we disembark'd at Quebec and march'd immediately in quest of the Rebels." Pell and his men were heading for Three Rivers, where Digby and the others with him arrived on June 6. "Troops were joining us fast," Digby wrote. The British had field artillery as well. The next day, ships carrying Fraser's men worked their way upriver to join the troops already there.

Sergeant John Lamb was also part of the expedition sent to Three Rivers, "the general rendezvous of the army." Carleton, he observed, "found himself at the head of twelve thousand regular troops." John Sullivan and the Americans did not know it, but they were no longer advancing on a small force. They were attacking the vanguard of the army sent to drive them from Canada.

The Attack at Three Rivers

On the evening of June 6, Thompson and his men set off in bateaux from Sorel to link up with St. Clair. They met at Nicolet around midnight but judged it too late to continue. The next evening they set off again, crossing the St. Lawrence and landing about nine miles above Three Rivers. About 250 men were left to guard the boats while the rest advanced on the town. Their plan was to march through the night and hit the surprised British at daybreak.

Thompson split the American forces into five divisions, planning to attack the British from four directions while holding one division in reserve. But the Americans were misinformed or purposely deceived by locals regarding the number of British troops in the town and how they were arrayed. Local guides led the columns toward Three Rivers in a roundabout way that left them still marching well past dawn, fully exposed to British guns.

It hardly mattered whether the guides' actions were borne of incompetence or treachery. The result was the same. The sloop-of-war

Martin and the armed transports in the river opened up on the American columns, sweeping them with broadsides. The Americans had only small arms with which to fire back. In an effort to avoid the ship's guns, Colonel Maxwell marched his column inland through a swamp, which, after three hours of wading through waist-deep mud, seemed worse than the broadsides.

When at last the Americans were able to launch their attack, they discovered that they faced not eight hundred men but thousands of British and Hessian soldiers, well entrenched and supported by artillery, led by Brigadier General Fraser.

The American troops were exhausted, having lost two nights' sleep, and "from the badness of the ground" were unable to form up and carry out a coordinated attack. Hopeless as it was, they advanced to within eighty yards of the British lines before being caught in a cross fire from the fieldpieces and the fleet. "We had no covering, no artillery, and no prospect of succeeding, as the number of the enemy was so much superior to ours," one participant wrote.

Thirteen years after the French and Indian War, many of the British troops—including Digby and Lamb—had never been in combat before. Lamb began to appreciate the seriousness of the situation "when the bullets came whistling by our ears." The old combat veterans in his unit assured him that "there is no danger if you hear the sound of the bullet, which is fired against you, you are safe, and after the first charge all your fears were done away."

Lamb quickly discovered the truth of this. Despite the inexperience of some of the British and German troops, their discipline, training, equipment, leadership, and numbers far surpassed anything that the Americans could throw at them.

The fighting was hot, a wild and desperate exchange, with the Americans caught between British artillery on shore and the guns of the ships on the river and facing a vastly superior force. No troops could have stood long under such conditions, and soon the Americans were in full retreat, with the enemy in pursuit. The British, making use of their naval support, sent transports to land men upriver and cut off the American escape.

With the road along the river covered by the men-of-war's guns, the Americans made a disorganized march through woods and swamps. About two hundred soldiers were captured, including William Irvine, second in command, and General William Thompson himself. (With acid British condescension, Carleton referred to him as "Mr Thompson whom I think they call a major-general.")

The retreating column arrived within a mile of the landing, only to find that the British were there before them and the boats were gone, the guards having rowed off before they could be taken. With the enemy covering all the ferries across the river, the Americans were trapped on the north shore of the St. Lawrence. The exhausted men found a spot of high ground, posted guards, and slept.

The remnants of Thompson's command were saved only by Carleton's innate caution. The next day the British governor ordered his troops, now spread out along the river, to fall back to their original posts. The Americans made their way unmolested back to Sorel, "repulsed, and not beaten."

The Final Retreat

In Montreal, Benedict Arnold, who was trying to hang on but also preparing to leave, sent the heavy baggage and the sick, along with a large cache of stores he had commandeered, down to St. John's. "The junction of the Canadians with the Colonies," he wrote to Sullivan, "is now at an end. Let us quit them, and secure our own country, before it is too late." Arnold had forwarded every man he could spare to support the attack at Three Rivers, reducing his garrison to about three hundred troops.

Then, on June 14, the British fleet, thirty-six sail by Sullivan's count, appeared off Sorel. Even Sullivan could see that his army was beaten. He called a council of war, and all present agreed that they should abandon Sorel. The American army decamped and made its way up the Richelieu River just hours ahead of the British grenadiers and light infantry.

In a grossly self-serving letter, Sullivan assured Washington that he personally had wanted to make a stand at Sorel, but "to my great mortification, I found myself at the head of a dispirited Army, filled with horror at the thought of seeing their enemy." He went on to explain how all of the events prior to his arrival—the retreat from Quebec, the disaster at the Cedars (he did not mention the battle at Three Rivers, the most serious defeat)—had served to kill the men's will to fight. There was nothing left but to fall back from the enemy.

As the Americans were retreating, the British fleet came to anchor in the St. Lawrence River off Sorel. A blue ensign broke out at the mizzen peak of the *Blonde,* a signal for the men to begin disembarking, and the light infantry and grenadiers were ferried ashore. The Americans had abandoned their camp just two hours before. Their campfires were still burning in the fire rings.

The next morning the 9th and 31st battalions, with six 6-pounder field guns, landed under the command of General Burgoyne. Around nine o'clock the British army, some four thousand strong, marched off in pursuit of the rebels.

Sullivan hurried his men to Chambly, but Chambly was as vulnerable as Sorel, and the enemy was on their heels. Making no attempt to hold the town, they hauled baggage and stores up the rapids in bateaux and burned the three gondolas that had been constructed there, as well as the other vessels and the garrison building, "leaving nothing but ruin behind."

Panic began to creep in among Sullivan's troops. When a false rumor spread that the British were closing in, "it had the effect of sending great Numbers of officers and Soldiers upon the run to St. Johns, & Some to the Oile of Noix & others could not be Stopt till they got to Crown point."

Sullivan, in the chaos of his retreat, failed to send word of what was happening to Arnold in Montreal. Unaware that Sorel had been abandoned, Arnold on June 15 sent his aide, James Wilkinson, with an express to Sullivan. Crossing the St. Lawrence, Wilkinson and his small band ran smack into an advance guard of British forces at Varennes, moving on Montreal. Before they were spotted, Wilkinson and his men leaped a fence, raced into the woods, and made their way back to their boat. By five that afternoon they were back in Montreal, where Wilkinson warned Arnold of the danger.

By seven that evening, Arnold had his entire garrison loaded aboard bateaux and crossing to Longueuil and La Prairie in a driving rain. Even as the Americans were evacuating, British transports were working their way up the river to Montreal. "[H]ad not the wind failed," Carleton wrote to Germain, "this column might have arrived at Longueuil the same night, and about the same time with Mr. Arnold and the remainder of the Rebels."

It took Arnold all night to round up the thirty carts needed to transport the sick, the baggage, and supplies to St. John's. As they were leaving, Arnold could see British ships on the river near Montreal, and locals told him that the British now occupied the city. Arnold led his men to St. John's, destroying bridges behind them. "The number of the enemy is very considerable," he wrote to Sullivan.

By June 17, Arnold and his men had met up with the others, and all that was left of the American army in Canada was gathered at St. John's. Another council of war was held, and it was agreed that St. John's could be easily cut off by the enemy and the Americans trapped, just as the British had been the previous October. Crown Point, it seemed, was the only safe place left to them. The sick and the stores were loaded into bateaux and sent to Isle aux Noix, then the troops began stripping the garrison of everything they could carry. Arnold had the frames of a few vessels being built there taken apart, numbered, and sent to Crown Point.

When the bateaux returned from Isle aux Noix, the men still at St. John's set the rest of the fortifications on fire, piled into the boats, and pushed fifteen miles upriver. With all but one bateau gone, Arnold and Wilkinson rode two miles down the road toward Chambly to reconnoiter the head of the British column. After watching the enemy's rapid approach, they rode back to St. John's and removed the saddles and tack from their horses. Then Arnold, unwilling to leave anything of value behind, shot his horse and insisted that the reluctant Wilkinson do the same. Wilkinson climbed into the boat with Colonel Jeduthan Baldwin and a few others, then Arnold "pushed the boat off with his own hands." Arnold was the last American soldier to leave Canada.

As the Americans were making for Isle aux Noix, two British columns were closing on St. John's from Montreal and Chambly. The advance guard of Major General Phillips's column, approaching from Longueuil, arrived at St. John's on the morning of June 19, only to find that Burgoyne's troops, whom Arnold had observed, had taken possession of the fort the night before. The garrison buildings and the boats that the Americans had left behind were still in flames.

The American army paused in their retreat at Isle aux Noix, and soon the low, wet island, overrun with troops, became a hellish place. From nearly every tent sick and dying men called out for help, but there was nothing to be done. A barn was crowded with men dying of smallpox, their still-living bodies infested with maggots. "No mortal will ever believe what these suffered unless they were eye witnesses," Beebe wrote.

Leaving Isle aux Noix and going any farther up the lake would mean officially abandoning Canada, and Sullivan did not want to be responsible for such a thing. Instead, he looked for orders from Schuyler, Washington, or Congress.

While the effective men remained at Isle aux Noix, the sick were carried up to Crown Point. John Trumbull, who would go on to become one of America's foremost painters, was then a colonel serving at Crown Point, and was there to receive the invalid troops as they arrived. He recalled,

> ... it is difficult to conceive a state of much deeper misery. The boats were leaky and without awnings; the sick being laid upon their bottoms without straw, were soon drenched in the filthy water of that peculiarly stagnant muddy lake, exposed to the burning sun ... with no sustenance but raw salt pork, which was often rancid, and hard biscuit or unbaked flour; no drink but the vile water from the lake, modified, perhaps, not corrected, by bad rum, and scarcely any medicine.

Along with the sick, Sullivan sent Benedict Arnold to confer with Schuyler. Arnold arrived at Schuyler's headquarters at Albany around midnight on June 24, the first time he had been out of Canada since the previous November. Arnold carried dispatches from Sullivan describing the circumstances of the army and asking for orders.

Schuyler recognized immediately that Isle aux Noix was a bad place to make a stand. In addition to being low and swampy, it was even more vulnerable to siege than St. John's, because the British had only to cut off the water routes to the island, which they could easily do. Batteries erected on the nearby shores could easily sweep the entire island with round shot.

"I wish you had complied with your Council of War, and retreated as far south as Crown Point," Schuyler wrote to Sullivan. Polite as ever, Schuyler assured Sullivan that he "would not have presumed to order" a retreat to Crown Point, but would have waited for Washington's reply, "if I had not thought the danger of remaining at Isle-aux-Noix too great." Without directly ordering him to do so, Schuyler made it clear that he wanted the army back at Crown Point.

That was enough for Sullivan, though he still made a pretense of surveying other possible places at the north end of the lake to make a stand, which he had no intention of doing. By July 2, the American army of the Northern Division was back at Crown Point. Carleton, Burgoyne, and the British forces were at St. John's. The only thing standing between the two armies was twenty-five miles of the Richelieu River and eighty miles of Lake Champlain.

And there the British advance halted, because the British lacked the means to move their men up the lake. Sergeant Lamb wrote, "We could not for want of boats urge our pursuit any farther." The American retreat had been made possible by Schuyler's frenetic program of bateau construction and the handful of larger vessels they had captured. Had it not been for the lake, and the inability of the British regulars and the Hessians to cross it, there would have been nothing to stop Carleton and Burgoyne from pushing south all the way to the Hudson.

Only one rational strategy remained to the Americans, and the desperate officers at St. John's had agreed to it unanimously. "They were fully of the opinion," Sullivan wrote, "that (in the present unhealthy state of the Army) it would be best to remove to Crown Point, fortify that post, and build armed vessels to secure the navigation of the Lake."

The next fight the British and Americans had in the Champlain valley would not be contested by armies. It would be a naval battle.

CHAPTER *24* *Birth of Two Fleets*

WITH A HUNDRED miles of water separating the American and British armies, the most intense fighting in the Champlain valley in the latter half of June was taking place between Major General Philip Schuyler and Major General Horatio Gates.

Gates, like Major General Charles Lee, had been born in England, though he lacked even Lee's minor pedigree. Gates's parents had served as butler and housekeeper to the Duke of Leeds, a connection that helped get Gates into the British army at a young age. He rose to the rank of major, serving in Canada during the French and Indian War. He and Washington had fought together with General Edward Braddock at the Battle of Monongahela, where Gates was wounded.

Lacking the money or connections to rise higher than major, Gates quit the British service and, with help from his old comrade George Washington, bought a plantation in Virginia. At the outbreak of the Revolution, he was appointed brigadier general and served with Washington at Cambridge.

On June 18 John Hancock informed Washington that, after "the most unfortunate death of General Thomas," Congress had appointed Gates to command in Canada.

Since the time when Schuyler, because of his poor health, had turned over military command to Montgomery, there had been effectively two leaders in the Northern Department—Schuyler in Albany, coordinating men and supplies, and one of a series of generals in Canada overseeing military operations. It was an arrangement that seemed to work, and no doubt Washington envisioned its continuance when he ordered Gates "to the very important command of the troops of the United Colonies in Canada." Washington used the phrase "in Canada" repeatedly in his orders to Gates. Unfortunately, by the time Gates arrived at Albany, there were no more military operations in Canada.

Gates was under the impression that he had command of all the troops in the Northern Department, regardless of where they were, but Schuyler disagreed. "If Congress intended that General Gates should command the Northern Army, wherever it may be, as he assures me they did, it ought to have been signified to me . . . ," he wrote to Washington. Schuyler would not serve under Gates, whose commission was more recent than his. Gates was the darling of the New England contingent in Congress, and the long-running animosities between New England and New York played a part in the friction between the two. The two men agreed, however, to let Congress settle the matter.

Congress did settle things, after a fashion, a few days later, informing Gates that it had intended to "give him the command of the Troops whilst in Canada" but did not intend to "vest him with a superior command to General Schuyler whilst the Troops should be on this side [of] Canada." Hancock wrote to Schuyler and Gates "recommending to them to carry on the military operations with harmony."

Incredibly, the men did just that, more or less, though the animosity between them never died. Gates wrote to Washington assuring him that he would obey Schuyler's orders and that the two major generals would "go hand in hand to promote the public service." Thus agreed, the two maintained the balance of power earlier established between Schuyler and the commander in Canada, except that the commander, Gates, was now at Ticonderoga.

John Sullivan, however, was less sanguine about Gates's appointment. Though Gates had considerably more military experience than Sullivan, his commission was more recent, which should have made him Sullivan's junior. Sullivan read in Congress's decision an implication that he "was not equal to the trust they were pleased to repose in me," in which case honor demanded that he resign his post. But if that was not the case, and Congress was simply putting a junior ahead of him, then he still felt compelled by honor to resign his post, which he did.

Benedict Arnold welcomed Gates's elevation. He and Gates had corresponded during the Canadian campaign, and the two men had a mutual respect. Their correspondence in the spring and summer of 1776 showed nothing but courtesy and genuine good will. Their friendship would last another year before turning very sour indeed.

The American plan for defense, formulated in those last, desperate days at St. John's, had been to fortify Crown Point. On July 7, however, a council of war was held there, consisting of Schuyler, Gates, Arnold, Sullivan, and de Woedtke. They agreed that Crown Point was "not tenable" and should be abandoned.

The men had their eyes on a new post, the high bluffs directly across the river from Ticonderoga, known to locals as Rattlesnake Hill. A few days before, Colonel John Trumbull had been sent to examine the ground and gauge its suitability. He found "an almost level plateau" fifty to seventy-five feet above the lake and surrounded on three sides by sheer cliffs, with a natural landing place for boats on the north side and good ground for a road in the east. Trumbull reported that it was "finely adapted for a military post."

That being the case, the officers agreed that the sick and wounded should be sent to Fort George, far away at the southern end of Lake George, and that the fit troops should "retire immediately to the strong ground on the east side of the Lake, opposite Ticonderoga."

Not everyone agreed. In an extraordinary move, a group of junior field officers held their own council, then drafted a letter to Schuyler listing seven reasons why Crown Point, and not Ticonderoga or the high ground to the east, should be garrisoned.

Washington, too, was unhappy with the generals' decision, and expressed to Gates his "sorrow at the resolution of your Council, and wish that it had never happened." Washington felt that abandoning Crown Point was as good as giving up the lake, because he was sure that the British would occupy the fort and keep the Americans bottled up to the south.

Schuyler told the field officers that he was not at liberty to discuss his fellow generals' reasons for their decision, but he assured them that the reasons were good ones, better than the ones presented for staying, and that was an end to it. To Washington, however, he offered a fuller explanation, pointing out that Crown Point was a peninsula, which meant that the enemy could too easily land above the fortification and cut it off. Separately, Gates assured Washington that the place was a wreck anyway. In the end Washington admitted that he knew nothing of the area personally and could not really speak to it, but he did fear "the Observations of the Field Officers . . . will be too well Verified."

Arnold spent the next week and a half at Crown Point, forwarding men and supplies up the lake.

The British Navy in the Woods

The British army had driven the rebels from Canada "with much less trouble than was expected on our embarking from Great Britain." They literally could not march fast enough to catch up with the fleeing Americans.

But now the marching was over, and the British were looking to the lake, where naval superiority—not numbers and training of soldiers— would decide the issue. Aware of the four ships the Americans had already—three of which had been taken from the British, and one from a Loyalist—they knew they needed a force at least equal to that. Digby observed, "How to pursue them over Lake Champlain was our next thought, and the tediousness that threatened our operations necessary for so great an expedition was far from pleasing."

Happily for them, England was the greatest maritime power on Earth, and a respectable naval force was just a few miles away on the St. Lawrence, manned by seamen who were second to none in skill and experience. Carleton would not have to beg for shipwrights and sailors as Schuyler did. Still, the British faced a huge task. Digby felt that they would be ready to move up the lake in seven to eight weeks, proving that the Americans had no monopoly on unrealistic projections.

They wasted no time getting to work, not even waiting for the Americans to be gone. On June 3, four days before the battle of Three Rivers, Lieutenant William Twiss, of the Royal Engineers, was ordered to that town to oversee the building of "King's Boats" or "Royal Boats." These boats were flat bottomed, and their bows were square, "resembling an English Punt." Each one could carry thirty to forty men with supplies.

On June 14, even before Arnold had abandoned Montreal, Lieutenant Dacres, of the *Blonde*, was put in charge of "the Boats, Vessels, &c going on the Lakes with the Army." A week later, Carleton asked Charles Douglas, who had hoisted his commodore's broad pennant, to give orders for forwarding all the men and materiel that could be found for "the building of armed Vessels for the Lake."

For the command of vessels on Champlain, Douglas proposed a force of seven commissioned officers and two hundred sailors, with one officer to be commander in chief. For that post he chose Thomas Pringle, captain of the armed ship *Lord Howe* and the officer who had delivered Carleton's correspondence to the ministry the previous year, departing just as Quebec was closed down by the siege. Pringle was well known to the officers in Quebec Province and well connected within the Admiralty.

Finding sailors was more of a problem for Douglas, because he had only enough to man the vessels that were on station in the St. Lawrence. He considered pressing men from the numerous transports still on the river, but decided it would "never due on this occasion." Instead, he opted to strip *Lizard* (which was in poor condition from spending the winter in the ice and being shot at by rebel cannon) and *Isis* of their crews, and take drafts from the other frigates.

Feeling that sailors and petty officers for the lake service should be volunteers, the commodore offered a pay increase to encourage them. "No considerable time, is to be lost herein," Douglas wrote, "As it is hoped a sufficient Strength of Craft will shortly be in readiness . . . for Lake Champlain."

The British had vessels enough on the St. Lawrence to form a fleet on the lake, but getting them over the rapids in the Richelieu River posed a significant challenge. Arnold had destroyed a row galley and nearly destroyed a gondola trying to get them down the rapids near the height of the spring runoff; getting vessels up the river in summer would be harder still. Douglas ordered Lieutenant John Starke, of the schooner *Maria*, and Edward Longcroft, who had spent the winter in Quebec and now had command of the captured rebel schooner *Brunswick*, to lighten their vessels enough to get them to the foot of the rapids at Chambly. That was as close as they could get to St. John's by water.

Captain Harvey, of the sloop-of-war *Martin*, was sent to Sorel to see whether camels—floats that could be partially submerged, lashed along either side of a vessel, then pumped out to raise the vessel up—would enable them to move six armed, flat-bottomed vessels up the rapids. The experiment was a failure. If any large vessels were going to travel from Chambly to St. John's, they would not be doing so by water.

Guy Carleton remained at Chambly, overseeing preparations. With the river unnavigable by anything larger than a bateau, Carleton called on the naval officers for supplies "required for Transporting the armed Vessels from Chambly to St. John's, by land." At the same time, to address the shortage of boats to transport troops, Carleton and Douglas asked that the masters of the transports and ordnance ships on the St. Lawrence give up their longboats "for want of readier craft." The longboat was the largest of a ship's boats, and typically could carry thirty to fifty men. Douglas estimated that those of the fleet in the river could transport as many as eighteen hundred men with equipment and provisions for ten days.

The shipmasters, doing "honor to their Country," agreed to leave their longboats behind, but in the end it seems that few of them actually did. Douglas hoped they would also leave their carpenters, at least those "whose ships are not leaky," but it seems that not many of those stayed behind either.

On July 7 the portly Commodore Douglas made his way on board the schooner *Maria* at Chambly to confer with John Starke. The schooner was still at the foot of the falls, and the men considered how to get it the twelve miles to St. John's, most of which was rapids. Because the ship could not go by water, the men decided, it would have to be hauled over land. Douglas issued orders for Starke, working under Pringle's direction, to cooperate with the engineers and sundry other army officers so that "the Hull of His Majts Schooner which you Command may be transported by Land beyond these rapids."

The navy men were unsure what would be required to accomplish this. The ship would have to be stripped of its contents, of course, and the masts and rigging taken out. If that proved insufficient, and if transporting her required "taking down of the said Schooner near to the very Waters edge as she now floats, leaving nothing but the Timbers standing," Starke was authorized to allow her to be stripped "to within two streaks [strakes] of her present line of floatation."

In other words, Starke was to remove her planking to the waterline if necessary. The same orders were given to Longcroft, of the schooner *Brunswick* (which may have been the same schooner later called *Carleton*). Additionally, the American gondola *Convert*, captured on the St. Lawrence and renamed *Loyal Convert*, was disassembled and hauled around the rapids.

The arms race on Lake Champlain was under way.

CHAPTER **25** *The Gondolas of Skenesborough*

THE AMERICAN DEFENSIVE strategy for Lake Champlain had two prongs—find and fortify the strongest possible land-based position, and build a fleet to oppose the British on the lake.

The first part commenced in June when the council of war chose the high ground across the narrow stretch of water from Ticonderoga as a defensive position. The second part had, in fact, been under way for some time, thanks to Philip Schuyler's long-held appreciation of the need for naval superiority on the lake.

All through the winter, Schuyler had been building bateaux at Fort George to move the army to and from Canada. As the weather began to improve, he had geared up for more ambitious boatbuilding, and he knew that the facilities at Fort George would not suffice.

For one thing, vessels built at Fort George had to be hauled over the three-mile carry to Lake Champlain, which was tolerable for bateaux but impractical for larger vessels. Skenesborough, however, was on Lake Champlain itself, and it boasted sawmills, a forge, and other facilities courtesy of the former royal governor of New York and former prisoner of war Philip Skene.

In mid-April, around the time that Arnold was taking command at Montreal and the commissioners were waiting for the ice to go out on Lake George, Philip Schuyler had sent Hermanus Schuyler to Skenesborough to begin turning the town into a shipbuilding community, something quite unknown in the near-wilderness of northern New York. Hermanus met with local leaders and arranged for men to mend bridges and cut open the roads to the town "so as Troops can go along very clever."

The boats that Philip Schuyler had in mind were of a type commonly employed in Europe as shoal-water naval vessels. They were called, properly, "gondolas," though in America the name was often rendered as "gundalow" or some similar variant. American gondolas were generally flat bottomed, though they were sometimes built with a slight deadrise, giving the bottom a broadly V-shaped cross section. They were essentially large, open boats, sharp at the bow and stern, framed and planked with white oak, and they could be propelled by oars or by a square mainsail and topsail set on a single mast.

The gondola *Philadelphia*, like the other, larger gondolas that Schuyler built, was mostly decked over. In two places, approximately a third of the way aft from the bow and a third of the way forward of the stern, the decking was open down to the bilge, dividing the deck into forward, midships, and after sections. Hermanus Schuyler described the first two gondolas he built as being "50 foot long and 15 foot beam & 4 1/2 deep," making them a bit smaller than the gondolas *Hancock* and *Schuyler*, which had been built the previous summer. Each gondola was armed with a 12-pounder aimed forward over the bow and a single 9-pounder on each broadside.

Even as Hermanus Schuyler was preparing to build gondolas at Skenesborough, bateaux construction continued apace. By the beginning of May, Philip Schuyler informed John Hancock, president of the Continental Congress, that he was "under the necessity of building a number of Batteaus far Exceeding what Congress ordered." He had completed 130 boats and, if that was not sufficient, intended to build upward of two hundred or more.

As soon as the shipyard at Skenesborough was ready, work began on the gondolas. Hermanus Schuyler, who had returned to Fort George, was ordered back to Skenesborough to carry out Philip Schuyler's orders to "do every Thing in your power to forward the Building of the Gundaloes." Philip Schuyler gave Hermanus explicit instructions to fire any diseased, drunk, or lazy workers and to keep the sawyers going night and day, along with tips on how to ensure that the "Sawyers may not play Tricks" in counting the sawn logs, and how to guard against fire.

On June 12, as John Sullivan, in Canada, was preparing to abandon Sorel, Hermanus Schuyler wrote to Philip Schuyler that "one of the Gundalows is so far forward as having stem & stern rais'd tomorrow they will begin to put in the knees." With so much timber felled over the winter months—about 120 logs cut and waiting to go to the sawmill—Hermanus was unsure what to do with the men who had been felling trees. "I should be glad to know what to do with the wood cutters," he wrote, "whither to send them to Lake George or sett them about other business."

As Philip Schuyler prepared for the defense of the lake, major military and political events were transpiring elsewhere. In mid-April George Washington had marched his army from Boston to New York City, where he expected the British to strike next. He was right. On June 29, forty-five British ships bearing ten thousand troops anchored inside Sandy Hook, in the outer reaches of New York Harbor—an imposing sight to the fewer than seven thousand fit-for-duty American soldiers dug in on Long Island and Manhattan.

By the end of August, some thirty-two thousand British and German soldiers would assemble under the overall command of General William Howe, supported by a fleet of nearly four hundred ships—the largest naval force of the eighteenth century—under Howe's brother, Admiral Richard Lord Howe. Howe's army was larger than Philadelphia, America's largest city, with thirty thousand people. Opposing Howe's army after a summer of desperate recruiting would be an American army of some twenty thousand, many of them too sick to fight.

In Philadelphia on June 7, Richard Henry Lee, of Virginia, presented a resolution to the Continental Congress calling for America to declare its independence from Britain. Congress reacted by forming a committee of five delegates to draft a declaration. The five included Benjamin Franklin, still ill and exhausted from his journey to Quebec, as well as Roger Sherman, of Connecticut; Robert Livingston, of New York; John Adams; and Thomas Jefferson, who would write the draft.

And to the north, in Quebec Province, the situation was rapidly deteriorating.

With the British driving American forces from Canada, Schuyler's anxiety regarding gondolas to defend Lake Champlain increased still further. On June 22 he wrote to Hermanus Schuyler admonishing him for not reporting more often and urging greater speed and efficiency.

"Early rising, a Close attention to the Orders I have Given, which direct a strict and sharp look out, upon Every Body Employed under You, will forward the Work with Expedition & Oeconomy."

On June 28, Hermanus reported that "the one Gundalow is laust [launched] yesterday and will be finished to morrow . . . ," and the second would be launched the day after. He wrote to Colonel Cornelius Wynkoop, at Fort Ticonderoga, asking him to send hands who could help deliver the gondolas from Skenesborough to the fort, but Wynkoop replied that he had "not men enough to keep a Sufficient Gard." Schuyler was forced to retain the men who had just delivered barrels of nails and rum instead.

For all of Philip Schuyler's concern over the pace of building at Skenesborough, by the end of June he was feeling somewhat encouraged about the situation on the lake. "We have, happily, such a naval superiority on Lake Champlain that I have a confident hope the Enemy will not appear upon it this Campaign . . . ," he wrote to Governor Trumbull in Connecticut.

Despite this premature and unwarranted optimism, Schuyler went on to inform the governor that Congress wanted more vessels built, and he needed more shipwrights to build them. He asked Trumbull to send two companies of twenty-five shipwrights to be paid at the same rate as men currently employed in the public service, about fifteen dollars per month. Schuyler would soon find out that shipwrights were not to be had for that amount.

By July 1, the first two gondolas had been sent off to Ticonderoga and the next two had been set up on the stocks. Captain Henry Bradt, the lead shipwright, told Hermanus Schuyler that "we'l be able to Launch One every week, if we have good weather." Eight days later, Hermanus reported that three gondolas were on the stocks, one of them already planked.

Boatbuilders for the Lakes

One of the most pressing issues for the many parties involved in the shipbuilding—Schuyler, Gates, Washington, the colony of New York, and the Continental Congress—was the dearth of qualified ship-wrights on Lake Champlain. This problem had been plaguing Schuyler from the beginning, but now, with the British in Canada in overwhelming numbers and Congress insisting that a fleet be constructed, the problem was becoming a crisis.

In June, George Washington wrote to Schuyler from New York saying that shipwrights "cannot be now had, every one qualified for the Business, being employed here." With the money to be made working on privateers in their hometowns, qualified shipwrights had little incentive to leave for the uncertainties of a frontier post hundreds of miles away.

On July 3, the Continental Congress voted to give its Marine Committee the power to contract for shipwrights to go to Skenesborough. In order to attract men, Congress laid out generous conditions. The men would be paid thirty-four and two-thirds dollars per month, more than twice the pay of a Continental navy carpenter, though, unlike the navy men, the carpenters on Lake Champlain would not have to go to sea or expose themselves to possible shipwreck or enemy gunfire.

Additionally, the shipwrights on the lake were to receive one and a half rations of food and half a pint of rum per day. Their pay would start when they signed their employment contract, and they were allowed a day's pay for every twenty miles traveled. The shipwrights were, as historian William Fowler noted, the highest-paid men in the naval service. Only Commodore Esek Hopkins, the top-ranking officer in the Continental navy, was paid more.

The same day that it approved the new pay rate for shipwrights, Congress voted to "resolve itself into a committee of the whole, to take into their farther consideration, the Declaration [of Independence]."

"Sometimes I dream . . ."

As the chief engineer at Ticonderoga, Colonel Jeduthan Baldwin was a busy man. On July 8 he described one day's work, writing, "went to Ticonderoga, with Genl. Schuyler & Genl. Gates, Viewd the grounds on the East Side ye Lake with Col. Trumbull on one Hill, took 26 Carpenters with me to repair ye Vessels & the Saw Mill at Skeensboro."

With the return of the army, Ticonderoga and the surrounding posts had gone from being little more than a way station for troops moving north to the center of activity for the Northern Army. Most of the fit men sent from Crown Point were posted at Ticonderoga; others were ordered up to Rattlesnake Hill to begin clearing away the "primeval forest," as John Trumbull called it. On July 11, the surveying ended and the work began, with Baldwin and two hundred men struggling in pouring rain to clear a road to the top of the hill and dig a well. "Very wet," Baldwin reported.

Although the gondolas were being built in Skenesborough, their rigging and fitting out was to be done at Ticonderoga, and artisans needed for that work were sent on to the fort. The orderly book of Samuel Van Vechten at Fort George records blacksmiths sent to Skenesborough and armorers and gun-carriage makers to Ticonderoga. He writes, "Mr. Noah Nicholls with the Wheelrights are to remain at Ticonderoga under the direction of Coll. Baldwin, Chief Engineer."

Gun carriages were a problem. Many had been abandoned in Canada, and now men were needed for the specialized work of building new ones. "We have to be sure a great train of artillery," John Trumbull wrote to his father, the governor of Connecticut, "but very few of them are mounted on carriages, and materials and conveniences for making them are very slender." Arnold, at Crown Point, sent to Ticonderoga "eight wheelwrights and gun-carriage makers."

All these were the responsibility of engineer Jeduthan Baldwin. An entry in his journal gives an idea of the number of specialty trades represented at Ticonderoga. After complaining that he had to do the job of a quartermaster general, Baldwin went on:

> I have the intire direction of all the House & Ship Carpenters, the Smiths, Armourers, Roap makers, Wheel & Carriage makers, Miners Turners, Coalyers, Sawyers & Shingle makers, which are all together 286, besides the direction of all the fateagueing parties, so that I have my hands & mind constantly employed night & Day except when I am a Sleep & then sometimes I dream.

A New Nation

On July 4, the Continental Congress approved the revised draft of the Declaration of Independence. It had taken more than a year of political and military struggle before the colonies were ready to make that move.

Even after the Battle of Bunker Hill, moderates in Congress had persuaded that body to send the "Olive Branch Petition" to King George, looking for a peaceful resolution to the conflict, one short of independence. The king had refused even to read it, and instead had declared the colonies in rebellion. More troops, including the hated German mercenaries, were sent to quash the Americans.

In January 1776, Thomas Paine had published "Common Sense," which laid out in simple terms the argument for independence. The tract sold more than a hundred thousand copies in just a few months, an astounding number given that the entire population of the colonies, including slaves, was just two and a half million, and an indication of how ready the colonists were to embrace a break from the mother country. Half a year later, Paine's arguments became America's.

News of the Declaration reached Ticonderoga on July 16. Colonel Elisha Porter wrote in his journal, "this Morning we rec'd the Agreable News of Independenancy being declared by the Congress About Noon 2 or 3 Kettles of Brandy Grog evidenced our Joy of the News."

The men on Lake Champlain were far from the center of things in Philadelphia or even New York, where Washington's army was dug in. News traveled slowly and unreliably to the northern outposts. In their isolated and often miserable circumstance, the men easily lost sight of the war's purpose.

The news they received on July 16 helped bring it into focus again. It was only an announcement of the Declaration, not the actual stirring words that Jefferson had penned, but the news alone was a great tonic for men suffering for a cause that might have been growing increasingly obscure in their minds.

By the third week in July, the new fortification on the high ground across from Ticonderoga still had no name. Ensign Bayze Wells wrote, "ordered to our New incampment Acrofs the Lake . . . no name for it as Yet this incampment was A howling Wildernefs when we Began to Clear it." Baldwin called it simply "the East Point."

Then, on Sunday, July 28, Colonel St. Clair read aloud, for the first time at that northern post, the Declaration of Independence, and Jefferson's stirring words "That these United Colonies are, and of Right ought to be Free and Independent States." St. Clair ended it with, "God save the free independent States of America!" The men followed with three cheers.

"It was remarkably pleasing to see the spirits of the soldiers so raised, after all their calamities . . . ," one observer wrote. And now there was an event worthy of lending its name to the new bastion. Rattlesnake Hill became Mount Independence.

CHAPTER **26** *The Summer of 1776*

THE BRITISH ARMY had built two ships at St. John's the year before, but the Americans had taken them before they could do their builders any good. Now, once again, St. John's became a shipbuilding center, this time on a scale never before seen there. While some vessels were hauled overland from Chambly, shipwrights at St. John's began working furiously to assemble gunboats sent in parts from England and to build others from the keel up. Surgeon Wasmus, visiting St. John's, observed, "many workers of all types about and the camp of the English and Germans makes this desolate place very lively."

Perhaps the most unusual of the gunboats was the *Thunderer*, a radeau—a flat-bottomed, nearly flat-sided, square-bowed, ketch-rigged boat, much like a modern-day barge with two masts. This hull shape had the advantage of simple construction, without the complicated curves of a bateau or a gondola. She was quite large, more than ninety feet on deck with a thirty-three-foot beam. Her flat bottom, which gave her great stability, and wide deck made her an ideal gun platform, and with her six 24-pounders and six 12-pounders she would be the most powerful vessel on the lake. Unfortunately, the same properties that made her a good platform made her an unwieldy sailor, a problem that would soon become evident.

By the second week in July, an officer from the 31st Regiment wrote to a friend in England, "What will seem most surprising to you is, that we are now hauling three large armed Vessels over Land, for twelve Miles, to the Lakes."

Watching these vessels being moved overland must have been unlike anything the men had ever seen. They were not small ships. They were about sixty feet long, and sitting on dry land they would have stood about fifteen feet to the top of the gunwale. Even with their planking stripped away to the waterline, they were enormously heavy and unwieldy.

Most likely the stripped-down vessels were held up by cradles of the type used to support a ship prior to launch. Trees cut from the ubiquitous forest and stripped of their branches formed huge rollers along the miserable road over which the vessels had to be moved. Teams of oxen were yoked to the boats' massive wood frame. Teamsters cracked their whips and shouted in English and French. The animals dug their hooves into the muddy road, and slowly, foot by foot, the partially built ships, weighing many tons, moved through the twelve miles of forest from Chambly to St. John's.

Soon after they began moving the schooner *Maria*, the British discovered that the road from Chambly was too soft to support her weight, even with the planking partially removed. Rather than repair the road, which would have been too time consuming, it was decided to strip the vessel down even further. Because the frames of large vessels were made up of several parts that could be disassembled, the planking and frames could be removed right down to the floor-heads, the very lowest part of the frames attached to the keel.

Thus disassembled, the vessel would have looked more like a shallow, open Viking longship than an eighteenth-century schooner, but such was required to get *Maria* and the other two vessels over the barely adequate roads of the Canadian frontier.

While the schooners were moving over land, Carleton ordered Douglas to take apart and send to St. John's a ship that was being built at Quebec. This one, which would later be named *Inflexible*, weighed 180 tons, almost twice the size of the *Maria*. She was not a schooner but rather a ship—square rigged on all three masts—and would be by far the most impressive vessel on Lake Champlain.

Carleton tapped Lieutenant John Schank, master of the armed ship *Chanceaux*, to command *Inflexible*. While at Quebec, *Chanceaux*'s carpenter was sent on shore for "marking the Timbers, on purpose to be taken to pieces and sent to St. Johns." That work consumed two days, after which the frames were taken apart and dropped in the river, then towed out to where they were loaded aboard boats.

For transportation, Schank had thirty longboats from the transports that would soon sail for England. It took most of August to get *Inflexible*'s disassembled hull from Quebec to the new shipyard at St. John's.

Once the frames and timbers were on their way, Douglas sent *Chanceaux* down to Sorel so that her guns, sails, anchors, and other equipment, being "remarkably well adapted," could be transferred to *Inflexible* once she was finished. *Chanceaux*'s crew would go as well.

While the fleet was under construction, the soldiers prepared for the part they would play. Lieutenant Hadden's orderly book records the instructions:

> The Commanding Officers of Corps will take every opportunity to exercise the Troops in the use and management of the Boats, [the soldiers would be rowing themselves—there were not nearly enough sailors for that task] in Embarking, Rowing, Landing and forming with Celerity; also in attacking and boarding Boats, or Armed Vessels, that they may be expert in those Exercises should the Rebels be foolish enough to attempt opposition on either Element.

Skenesborough

On July 10, Colonel Thomas Hartley returned to Crown Point. He had been dispatched by John Sullivan to reconnoiter the lower part of Lake Champlain and gather intelligence concerning the enemy. Hartley learned secondhand that the British were actively building a fleet, "three sloops and two schooners at St. John's, which they expected would be soon finished."

The news was hardly surprising, merely confirming what was expected, but it underscored what was at stake. There was an arms race under way, a race for naval superiority on Lake Champlain, and to the winner would go the invasion route into New England and perhaps ultimate victory in the war.

Arnold was still at Crown Point, forwarding men and supplies to Ticonderoga and Fort George, when Hartley reported to him. Sending Hartley's report to Gates, Arnold noted that he, too, believed that "the enemy have a number of vessels in forwardness, and will exert themselves in building."

Though Arnold had no official connection to the American ship-building effort, it was clearly on his mind. He made a list of the artisans in his command who could be of service in that department, dividing the ship carpenters into gangs of fifteen and sending them along with oar makers to Skenesborough. (Oars had many uses and were constantly in demand. In August the bateaux master was sent to area encampments to collect them. A general order was issued saying, "Neither Officer or Soldier is for the future to use any of the oars for any purpose than they were designed for, Proper poles must be cut for to carry provisions & baggage.")

Arnold was one of the most experienced mariners in the theater, perhaps second only to Jacobus Wynkoop (not to be confused with Colonel Cornelius Wynkoop), who was commodore of the fleet. Toiling at Crown Point, Arnold might well have been thinking that his proper place, the place where he could be most effective, was running things in the naval line.

Gates shared Arnold's concern about the British naval effort, and soon he too was thinking that Arnold should have a hand in the boats' construction. "I am anxious to have you here as soon as possible," Gates wrote from Ticonderoga, "as maintaining our naval Superiority is of the last Importance." Gates did not mention in what capacity he needed Arnold, but his frustration with the slow pace of boatbuilding was starting to show. "I hourly expect one, or two more Gondolas, from Skenesborough and labour in all my Power to get them rigged, and armed," Gates complained.

Manpower was one problem, materials another. There was plenty of wood in the area, if the boatbuilders did not mind it green and the sawyers could cut it into planks fast enough, which they could not always do. But virtually every other kind of naval store was lacking. A list of items needed for fitting out the vessels, drawn up by Schuyler's secretary Richard Varick, includes just about everything that could not be made out of wood, as well as some things that could but required special skills. On the list were seventy anchors and hawsers of various sizes, coils of rope from one and a half inches to six inches in diameter, rat-line cordage, two hundred double blocks (pulleys with two sheaves), three hundred single blocks, marline, spun yarn, fifty hourglasses, ten spyglasses, forty "small Colours (Continental)," pots, wooden bowls, pistols and cutlasses, one dozen hand speaking trumpets, six fishing nets, and on and on.

What they needed was a well-stocked chandlery, the sort of conve-nience that could be found in any seaport town where ship chandlers competed aggressively for business, but such a thing was utterly alien in the barely settled regions of upper New York, two hundred miles from the nearest salt water.

Near the end of the second week in July, Brigadier General David Waterbury arrived at Ticonderoga to head up the five thousand Con-necticut troops who were being sent to the Northern Army. Gates, eager to see more happening at Skenesborough, had sent Waterbury to take charge there, instructing Hermanus Schuyler to "act in con-junction with General Waterbury, and do your utmost, with his com-mand and assistance, to forward the publick service." Waterbury had been with Montgomery at St. John's, and, like Arnold, was an experi-enced mariner with some familiarity with ship construction.

Waterbury was not sent to Skenesborough to take over shipbuild-ing, though the longer he was there the greater the role he would play in that business. Initially he was to take command of the Connecticut militia and put them to work at the most needed tasks, the first of which was to clear and repair the notoriously bad road from nearby Cheshire's Mill to Fort Edward to allow carriages to travel that way and for "the conveyance of provisions and stores."

Likewise, Wood Creek, which connected ultimately to the Hudson River (and is now part of the route of the Champlain Canal), was to be cleared and opened for boat traffic. The troops would build and garri-son "some little works" for the defense of Cheshire's Mill and Skenes-borough Mill, mostly against Indians, particularly those allied with the British, who were still a threat to the local settlements. And the troops were to assist with the construction of ships whenever muscle more than skill was needed.

While Waterbury saw to keeping roads and waterways open, Hermanus Schuyler supervised the bustling shipyard. Huddled along the bank at the narrow, southern tip of Lake Champlain, the mills, forges, and slipways were abuzz with the sort of industry that Philip Skene had always envisioned for his eponymous town, though in support of a cause he abhorred.

Soon after Waterbury arrived at Skenesborough, he wrote to Gates, "I think the business is going on very lively, according to the number of men." He was probably right—Hermanus Schuyler was likely getting as much work as he could from his shorthanded gangs—but the work was certainly not "lively" enough for Gates's liking. "I . . . am baffled by the Laziness of the Artificers, or the Neglect of those, whose Duty it is to see them diligent at their Work . . . ," he complained to Arnold.

Nor did anyone seemed overly satisfied with the boats being produced at Skenesborough. The model that everyone seemed to have in mind was the row galley being built in Philadelphia for defense of the Delaware River, though one wonders how many men in the Northern Army had actually seen this boat. Philip Schuyler had written on several occasions for shipwrights familiar with its construction to be hired for Lake Champlain, but by July 1776 none had been sent. So, starting with the *Hancock* and the *Schuyler* in 1775, Schuyler built what he was able to build—gondolas, whose construction was well known locally and not very different from that of oversized bateaux.

But Gates was unenthusiastic about these. "The Gondolas General Schuyler has Order'd to be built," Gates wrote to Hancock from Ticonderoga, "as he has no model to direct him, are in nothing but in name like those at Philadelphia, the Rigging and Artillery are all to be Fix'd here, and when done, they seem to be Vessels very unwieldy to move, & very indifferent for the purpose intended."

By the middle of July, Gates reported that two gondolas were finished, though it is unclear whether he meant simply that the hulls had been constructed or that the vessels were rigged as well. Certainly the list of "Articles wanted immediately for the Vessels and Gondolas on Lake Champlain," written five days later, is almost identical to the earlier one, suggesting that there was still a desperate need for supplies, rigging material in particular. Spyglasses and half-hour glasses were no longer on the list, but frying pans had been added. (Examples of the latter two items were found aboard the wreck of the gondola *Philadelphia* when it was recovered in 1935.)

John Trumbull wrote to his father, "It is true that we build a thing called a gondola, perhaps as much as one in a week; but where is our rigging for them, where are our guns?" The Americans, of course, did not necessarily have to build gunboats fast, they just had to build them faster than the British. "[I]f the Enemy gives us time to do all this, it will be well, if not, This wretched Army will probably be yet more unfortunate," Gates observed.

By the end of July, Congress's offer of generous wages to shipwrights began to pay off, and experienced boatbuilders started arriving at Skenesborough. On July 20, Waterbury wrote, "This moment there is a part of a company of carpenters from Connecticut arrived. The remainder is at Cheshire's and I shall send a boat for them tomorrow morning."

The carpenters at Cheshire's could not get to Skenesborough by land. Along with their other difficulties, the troops and boatbuilders had been plagued by rain. The day before the carpenters arrived, it rained so hard that two men at Mount Independence drowned in their tent.

Three days later, Cornelius Wynkoop arrived at Skenesborough, sent by Gates "to forward and oversee the business now going on at the Place he thinking it did not Go forward as fast as it should." Wynkoop reported that another twenty-nine carpenters had arrived, but none of Waterbury's Connecticut militia, whose help was needed at the sawmills.

By July 24, one hundred shipwrights from Massachusetts and Pennsylvania were reported on their way. By the end of the month, there were two hundred boatbuilders at Skenesborough, turning out armed vessels as quickly as they could, with several boats on the stocks at any given time.

But even that good news was not enough to give General Gates any comfort.

CHAPTER *27* *A Most Deserving and Gallant Officer*

HORATIO GATES was frustrated by more than just the pace of ship-building; he was frustrated as well by the inactivity of the existing fleet. For three months Jacobus Wynkoop had had command of the Lake Champlain fleet, which now consisted of the little schooner *Liberty*, the sloop *Enterprise*, the schooner *Royal Savage*, and the schooner *Revenge*, which may have been the second vessel captured at St. John's with the *Royal Savage*.

In the early months of 1776, there had been no one to command the vessels, and no one was very tempted to take the position. Unlike a blue water naval command, the lakes offered little chance for glory and no chance for prize money, just a dull job in a wilderness backwater, promising headaches and little else.

The Continental Congress had selected Major William Douglass as commodore of the little fleet. Douglass, however, was holding out for a better assignment. As the months dragged on, he did not report for duty, or even officially accept the post, and no one was sure whether he would.

Finally, in frustration, the New York Provincial Congress recommended Jacobus Wynkoop, whom they claimed "was bred a mariner . . . " for the post. Wynkoop, a captain in the 4th New York Continental Regiment, was fifty-one years old. He had served "in the last two wars, by sea and by land," and fought in a number of engagements, a record he never tired of flaunting.

On May 7, Schuyler ordered Wynkoop to "immediately repair to Ticonderoga and take the Command of all the Vessels on Lake Champlain," which he did. They had wasted more than four months dithering over command of the fleet, and with the growing threat from Canada, it was not time that they had to spare.

In the first half of Wynkoop's tenure, while the American army was in Canada, transportation had been a bigger priority than naval superiority, so the guns had been removed and the vessels "employ'd as Floating Waggons." By the first part of July, however, the fleet was at anchor at Ticonderoga, unarmed and rendered inactive by a want, mostly, of carriages on which to mount the guns.

Gates wrote to Arnold, "I labor continually to get the Commodore to Crown-Point with the Vessels." At Crown Point, Gates figured, the vessels might do some good if the British came up the lake. Gun carriages were built at Ticonderoga, and by July 16 the *Royal Savage* mounted ten guns, 4- and 6-pounders, with the other vessels waiting to be rearmed as well.

Once *Royal Savage* was fitted out, Gates sent her, with Wynkoop in command, to Crown Point, where the commodore was to get instructions from Arnold as to where best to cruise. Gates was, he informed Arnold, "intirely unacquainted with the Lake below Crown Point," having never been beyond that post.

What's more, Gates knew nothing about ships, and he was starting to appreciate the fact that Arnold did. "I wish you were here, to give directions for putting our whole Squadron a Float," he wrote to Arnold; "it seems to me they are very Tardy About it, but I am intirely uniform'd as to Marine Affairs."

Hermanus Schuyler, David Waterbury, and Cornelius Wynkoop had been dispatched to Skenesborough to move things along, but still Gates felt that boat construction dragged. Finally, on July 22, Gates made the obvious decision. Benedict Arnold, he knew, was a hard-driving, dedicated officer with maritime experience, so Gates sent him to Skenesborough "to expedite the building of the gondolas."

Arnold arrived at Skenesborough the next day to find that Hermanus Schuyler had just sent off the fourth completed gondola to Ticonderoga, though a shortage of anchors, cordage, and blocks prevented them from being put in sailing condition. Schuyler reported that two additional gondolas would be ready in a few days but were hampered by shortages of materials. The carpenters stood in need of oakum, files, bar iron for bolts, grindstones, and "About A Tun of Rum."

"Spanish row galleys"

Arnold found not just the two gondolas under construction, but a small cutter that would be named *Lee*, built from the frames that he had numbered and sent down from St. John's.

On a fourth slipway, framed and planked up on one side, was one of the row galleys that had been so often discussed. Hermanus Schuyler referred to it as a "Spanish row galley" or just "Spanish galley," and Arnold called it "a row galley, on the Spanish construction," perhaps because the galley as a vessel type was so strongly identified with the Mediterranean.

A galley was about twenty feet longer than a gondola—about seventy feet on deck—but the differences between the two vessels were much greater than that. Although a gondola was decked over in places and carried a sailing rig, it was essentially an oversized rowing boat, with the flat bottom, nearly flat sides, and the pointed bow and stern of a bateau.

A galley, on the other hand, was a small ship in the manner of a schooner such as the *Royal Savage*. (After the British captured the galley *Washington*, they added a bowsprit and square sails and turned her into a brig.) A galley was round bottomed and square sterned with a fair amount of tumblehome (meaning that the sides sloped inward toward deck level, so that the boat was wider near the waterline than on deck), all of which made the vessel considerably more difficult to build.

Like the more conventional man-of-war, a galley was constructed with a raised quarterdeck and a proper gun deck, as opposed to the partial decking of a gondola. Whereas the guns on board a gondola fired over the gunwales, the guns on a galley were rigged to gunports cut in bulwarks, as in a larger man-of-war. A gondola had only an awning to shelter the crew while not under way, there being no "down below" area on board this shallow vessel. The officers on board a galley, by contrast, were presumably quartered in temporary cabins below the quarterdeck, and the crew in the hold below the full weather deck, with five feet of headroom between deck beams.

A galley had two masts stepped and was rigged with triangular lateen sails, which made it much more weatherly than the flat-bottomed gondola, with its square course and topsail. A galley also carried considerably more firepower than a gondola, though not as much as Arnold hoped for. He had intended for the galleys to be armed with 24- and 18-pounders, but in the end only 18-, 9-, and 6-pounders were available.

The "Spanish row galleys" were in every way much closer in design to the galleys built in Philadelphia for defense of the Delaware River, the vessels that everyone seemed to feel must be emulated.

When Arnold arrived at Skenesborough, he found a gang of shipwrights under a Captain Winslow just arrived from Connecticut. Recognizing that the row galleys would be much more effective in battle than the gondolas, he instructed Winslow to begin work on a second one to his specifications—sixty-nine feet on deck and eighteen feet on the beam, with a depth of hold of five feet.

Arnold planned to set the Pennsylvania and Massachusetts carpenters to work on three additional galleys, which he hoped to have done in just three weeks, with plans for four more after that. He told Hermanus Schuyler that ten gondolas would suffice. From now on, Arnold wanted to concentrate on larger vessels.

Gates was delighted with Arnold's zeal and effort, and by the end of the month had ceded all naval operations to him. Writing to Washington on July 29, Gates said,

> General Arnold is just returned from [Skenesborough] where he has been exerting his utmost diligence in forwarding the vessels constructing there. Our little fleet already built is equipping under his direction, with all the industry his activity and good example can inspire. As fast as they are fitted, they are sent to Crown Point . . . As soon as all the vessels and gondolas are equipped, General Arnold has offered to go to Crown Point and take the command of them. This is exceedingly pleasing to me, as he has a perfect knowledge in maritime affairs, and is, besides, a most deserving and gallant officer.

In an effort to reinforce the correctness of their earlier decision, Gates also pointed out to Washington that whoever had the superior naval force had control of the lake, regardless of who possessed Crown Point.

"The Vessells cannot be Compleated untill . . ."

Historians have tended to credit Benedict Arnold with the direct supervision of the Champlain fleet's construction, but in fact he spent little time in Skenesborough. He was, rather, something of a cyclone of activity, spinning between Skenesborough, where the ships were building, Ticonderoga, where they were fitting out, and Mount Independence, where the chief American defenses were under construction. Typical of Arnold, wherever important work was taking place, he was there.

By the end of July, Skenesborough was filling with competent and experienced boatbuilders. Once Arnold had lit a fire under them, he had only, as he wrote to Schuyler, to give "such directions as I thought necessary, and orders to begin four row-galleys, nearly of the construction of those built in Philadelphia."

Arnold, Gates, Schuyler, and Varick, among others, were still engaged in a desperate scramble for naval stores. Gondolas were stuck on the stocks and could not be launched for want of oakum to caulk the seams. The lack of sailcloth, blocks, and cordage was still critical. Arnold, writing to Schuyler for those and other things, reminded the major general that "The Vessells cannot be Compleated untill the Blocks & Cordage arives."

Arnold also reminded Schuyler of a list he had compiled of other gear they still lacked. Fearing that the landlubbing Schuyler would not appreciate the need for such things as tar brushes and bolt-rope needles and palms, Arnold wrote, "many of the articles in my List, tho' trifles Are absolutely necessary, & cannot be procured here."

Schuyler and Washington hoped to find naval stores in Albany, where shipping along the river supported chandleries on shore. With William Howe's army in New York and his brother Richard's fleet blocking the Hudson, shipping was largely at a standstill, and the generals felt that supplies should be available.

Benedict Arnold offered the names of two Connecticut merchants, former associates from his days in commercial sail, who could provide cordage and sailcloth. In Poughkeepsie, shipwrights were building two of the frigates recently ordered by the Continental Congress. The half-built ships were under constant threat from the British navy, however, and even if they were completed, they could not leave the Hudson as long as the British held New York. Schuyler felt that the material furnished for their construction could be better used at Ticonderoga.

George Washington, no great fan of the frigates, agreed that the vessels on Lake Champlain were a much higher priority. Schuyler instructed Varick to write to the "Gentlemen at Poghkeepsie, who have the Direction of Building the Vessels there," to send on any supplies that could not be had at Albany.

Varick did, but was informed that the yard in Poughkeepsie had almost none of the items he needed save for blocks. The cordage and sailcloth on hand had already been cut for use on the frigates. But Varick learned that the quartermaster at New York would be able to send up most of what was needed.

Sailors and Marines

With the need for shipwrights largely met, Arnold, Schuyler, and Gates turned to the next manpower problem—qualified and experienced sailors—one of the many areas in which the British enjoyed a potentially decisive advantage. For Arnold, who had spent a good part of the summer of 1775 asking for naval stores and sailors to be sent to Lake Champlain, the experience must have been like déjà vu. As he had the previous year, he reiterated the need for real sailors. He wrote to Schuyler, "we must have them our Navigation without them will be useless, — Soldiers, or Landsmen will by no means answear without a number of Seamen In each Vessell."

The most expedient means of obtaining sailors was to draft them out of the Northern Army. Gates issued a general order for 348 seamen and marines to be recruited from the four brigades, but that effort yielded only 70 men.

Arnold estimated that he would need at the very least three hundred more men than that, along with experienced captains for each vessel. He considered sending to Connecticut for seamen, but he did not believe that any could be hired for the six and two-thirds dollars per month offered by Congress. He had been informed that sailors could not be engaged for less than ten dollars per month above the standard wage.

It was the same problem that Arnold had experienced the year before, and the same problem he encountered when looking for shipwrights—the lure of the privateers. Privateers were offering sailors easy discipline and the chance to make a small fortune in prize money. Though Congress specified that at least one-third of a privateer's crew be made up of landsmen so that sailors would be available for other duties, it did little good.

Also competing for sailors were the fledgling United States Navy as well as the little navies that most of the thirteen states had established for their own coastal protection. Though not as tempting as the privateers, these still offered a chance of prize money, in which a portion of the sale of any captured vessel was doled out to the crew, a standard practice in all navies at the time.

The fleet on Lake Champlain, by contrast, offered "no prospect of makeing reprisals on the Lake, but rather Fatigue & Danger," according to Arnold, in a realistic assessment of their recruiting problems.

As with the shipwrights, Congress hoped that higher wages would be a sufficient incentive, so they offered an additional eight shillings above the pay to which enlisted men were already entitled to anyone who would serve in the Lake Champlain fleet. Arnold asked Schuyler to send to Connecticut or to Washington's army for two to three hundred more sailors, and he requested that Varick issue a warrant on the paymaster general for a thousand pounds to pay the bounty offered seamen.

With frustrating slowness, the crews of the vessels filled out, but they would never be the experienced, professional mariners that Arnold hoped for.

CHAPTER *28* *The Fleet Comes Together*

By the end of July, the *Royal Savage* and the *Liberty* were at Crown Point. The *Enterprise* was nearly fitted out at Ticonderoga and would be going off soon, followed by four of the gondolas, rigged and ready for service. Arnold was at Ticonderoga, but he intended to return to Skenesborough to "accelerate the business" there.

Part of the delay in Skenesborough was due to someone, probably Arnold himself, coming up with the idea of mounting mortars on board two of the gondolas. The mortar was a short, squat gun used to hurl an exploding projectile in a high arc, generally to bombard a fixed fortification. The gun required a steady platform and careful adjustment of aim, elevation, and fuse timing, making it useless in a naval battle with vessels in constantly shifting positions. The mortar could be and often was used, however, on board a solidly anchored ship to shell positions on shore. Most large navies of the time had vessels specifically built for this purpose.

It is likely that Arnold, who later told others that he planned to take the fleet right up to St. John's, was intending to use the mortars on the shipyard there, putting a stop to British shipbuilding before it could become a threat.

David Waterbury wrote to Gates apologizing for the delay in getting the newest gondola up to Ticonderoga, explaining that "they had much more to do than they expected to complete the platform for the mortar." The new gondola, possibly the *Philadelphia*, was made "as strong as she could be made" to withstand the tremendous downward recoil of the heavy gun.

On July 30, Cornelius Wynkoop wrote to Gates that a gondola was on its way to Ticonderoga, "which the carpenters have named after me." (If so, the name was later changed, because there is no record of a gondola named *Wynkoop*.) The next day the gondola arrived at the fort, and the ubiquitous Jeduthan Baldwin set a 13-inch mortar on the specially built platform. The mortar was one of the guns that Henry Knox had dragged from Ticonderoga to Cambridge. The well-traveled cannon had since been returned to Ticonderoga, then sent up to Canada, then hauled back to Ticonderoga again.

Around sunset the mortar was tested, with nearly fatal results. As soon as the gun was fired, the 13-inch shell split, sending shrapnel screaming over the gun crew's heads. At the same time, the mortar itself burst, the upper part flying twenty feet in the air. "[T]he peice that blowd of weighd near a ton," Baldwin wrote, adding that he "was nigh & saw the men fall when the mortar burst." Incredibly, no one was killed or even hurt.

The next morning, Baldwin test-fired the other 13-inch mortar, and "she burst Just in the same mannar." They were the only two mortars at Ticonderoga, having been hauled over hundreds of miles "at an immence cost altho they were worth nothing," and Arnold was forced to abandon any hope of using them in a preemptive strike.

The Fleet Takes Shape

The early part of August saw a torrent of letters from the quill pen of Philip Schuyler's secretary, Captain Richard Varick, as he scoured New York and Connecticut for supplies for the fleet. He sent out requests for "Oakum . . . pitch . . . Anchors, Cables, Rigging, Cordage, Military & Naval Stores . . . ," also dispatching an express rider to Connecticut to buy sailcloth and cordage from the merchants whom Arnold had recommended.

Varick sent to forges in the New York towns of Livingston Manor and Salisbury for "Swivel & Grape, [and] double headed & Chain Shot"; the latter were two types of ordnance designed to disable ships' rigging. From the shipyard in Poughkeepsie where the frigates were being built, he scrounged slow-match fuses and six dozen large sails, bolt rope, marline needles, twine, blocks, and oakum. On Schuyler's orders, Varick wrote to George Washington for a number of articles.

From the shipowners and merchants in Albany and Schenectady he obtained all the anchors, cables, and cordage that could be had. Soldiers guilty of minor infractions were sentenced to the tedious job of making or "picking" the oakum by means of teasing the fibers out of a strand of old rope.

To Skenesborough, Varick sent iron and grindstones, pitch, tar, steel, oakum, bellows, and other blacksmith tools. Ship carpenters continued to arrive, and Varick sent them on to Hermanus Schuyler with what had become a boilerplate warning and admonition. Shipwrights were put on notice that, "in the present state of Affairs," they might not receive everything they had been promised, but they would be compensated eventually. Varick informed them that General Schuyler was confident they would do their job anyway and not let petty jealousies, "the Bane of Every Service," interfere with their duty.

On August 6, returning to Skenesborough from Ticonderoga, Benedict Arnold was well pleased with what he found. "[T]he Gallies much forwarder than I expected, three will be launched in a Fortnight . . . the Carpenters are Very Industrious, & spirited . . . ," he informed Gates.

The galley *Congress* was already launched, less than a month after the keel had been laid. The three others—*Washington, Schuyler,* and *Lee*—were nearing completion (the *Schuyler* would at some point undergo a name change to *Trumbull*). This extraordinary effort was thanks mostly to a corps of skilled shipwrights driven by an energetic and thoroughly professional officer, Benedict Arnold.

The frenetic pace of building soon outstripped the supply chain, in particular the production of iron spikes and milled wood. There were twenty-five blacksmiths at Skenesborough at the beginning of August, but tools enough for only four forges. And the sawmills, for various reasons that included excessively wet weather, were having a hard time keeping up with the demand for planks.

Two gondolas, numbers seven and eight, were on the stocks when Arnold returned to Skenesborough. Earlier he had set the total number of gondolas at ten, but now, with a shortage of planks threatening the construction of the galleys, Arnold gave orders to halt construction of the smaller vessels, as they "retard the Building of the Gallies, which are of more Consequence."

The next day the *Congress* was sent down the lake to Ticonderoga for fitting out. The results of Varick's efforts were evident in the cache of naval stores now available there to complete the vessels. Arnold praised Varick's work to Philip Schuyler, saying that the captain "has been very active and industrious in procuring the Articles for the Navy, many are arrived at Tyonderoga, and proper Steps taken to procure the others."

By August 11, three of the gondolas had joined the *Congress* at Ticonderoga, where they were rigged prior to being sent north to Crown Point. A few days later, Waterbury informed Gates that the three galleys were planked up on the outside but that work had come to a near halt. Most of the shipwrights were now waiting for planks for the ceilings (the interior sheathing) of their vessels. The mill at the shipyard, however, was flooded after a week of heavy rain and unable to produce the planks. Instead, Waterbury set the idle carpenters to work framing up two more galleys. Gates ordered Waterbury to man the three galleys after their launching with a regiment of Connecticut troops and sail them to Ticonderoga, leaving Cornelius Wynkoop in command at Skenesborough.

As it turned out, the first half of August represented the high-water mark of American ship construction, when the astounding frenzy of building at Skenesborough reached its peak. Toward the end of the month, shipbuilding activity slowed as an ominous new threat emerged—disease.

It was not, in this instance, smallpox. The army retreating from Canada had been so ravaged by that disease that Gates and Schuyler had made eradicating it a chief priority. Every man sick with smallpox was sent to Fort George, and a scrupulous effort was made to prevent anyone from reinfecting the army at Ticonderoga.

Typical of their effort was the furious reaction of Waterbury and Gates to the discovery that a company of carpenters hired in Rhode Island "at prodigious Wages" had inoculated themselves. The carpenters were stopped before they arrived at Skenesborough. Gates asked

Governor Trumbull to have the governor of Rhode Island "Dismiss them immediately, pay they do not deserve a penny."

So successful were their efforts to eliminate the disease that, by the end of August, Gates could inform Washington, "Small-Pox is now perfectly removed from the Army."

Thus it was not smallpox that was striking down the shipwrights at Skenesborough, but fever and "ague," a term that referred to various malaria-like diseases, the symptoms of which were chills, sweating, and fever. Waterbury (who had injured a leg, which laid him up for a few days) reported that "the business has been much retarded by so many of the carpenters being sick. . . . I have been very uneasy myself that the galleys are not completed before now."

Waterbury could only watch as the pace of ship construction dropped off to a crawl, and predicted launch dates passed with the galleys still on the stocks. Sick carpenters began to apply for discharge, eager to get away from that place. Gates forwarded carpenters from Ticonderoga up the lake to Skenesborough to replace those who were leaving, and the ranks of soldiers were scoured for men with woodworking skills.

By the end of the month, the galleys were still on the ways. "I cannot get the galleys off according to your Honour's expectation," Waterbury informed Gates on August 30. He hoped, he said, to launch one the next day, and looked forward to being on the lake himself, per Gates's orders, and away from Skenesborough. "I never saw so much fever and ague in my life as there is at this post," he wrote.

Even Benedict Arnold could not have expedited the construction of the galleys. But as it happened, Arnold was no longer overseeing construction. Rather, he was doing what he did best, taking the fight to the enemy.

"Men of Firmness, & approved Courage . . ."

During the first few days of August, Arnold was distracted from other duties by the court-martial of Moses Hazen, whom he had accused of disobeying orders with regard to his handling of provisions commandeered in Montreal while the army was retreating from Canada.

Unfortunately for Arnold, the court was made up of junior field-grade officers, many of whom nursed petty grievances against Arnold and were more inclined to side with their fellow field officer. Hazen, furthermore, had cultivated friendships with many of the officers who sat in judgment of him. The results were predictable.

During the second day of trial, the court badgered Arnold's chief witness and finally disallowed his testimony. Arnold was furious and let it be known. Elisha Porter, who sat on the court, wrote in his journal, "rec d much abuse from Genl Arnold which produced a spirited repri-mand from ye President." When the court acquitted Hazen, Arnold was neither subtle nor delicate in his outrage. The court, feeling that its honor had been sullied, informed him that "nothing but an open acknowledgment of your error will be conceived as satisfactory."

Arnold was not about to acknowledge any error, but he was ready to give members of the court satisfaction in the traditional way. He as-sured them that "as soon as this disagreeable service is at an end . . . I will by no means withhold from any Gentleman of the Court the satis-faction his nice honor may require." But Arnold got no takers on that offer. Instead, the court informed Horatio Gates that it wished to try Arnold for contempt.

On August 10, Porter "Dind with Colo Hazen with the Members of the Court Marshal," a cozy little reunion among friends. Two days later the court ordered Arnold's arrest, but by then Gates had had enough and dissolved the court. Gates then wrote to John Hancock asking that Congress look into the matter against Arnold. Recognizing that Arnold could be a hothead, he suggested to Hancock, with mar-velous eighteenth-century delicacy, that the "warmth of General Arnold's temper might possibly lead him a little farther than is marked by the precise line of decorum to be observed before and to-wards a Court-Martial."

That said, Gates told the president of Congress that the country "must not be deprived of that excellent officer's service at this impor-tant juncture." Arnold, in Gates's opinion, was more important than the sensibilities of the junior-grade field officers.

Throughout this business, Arnold continued to move between Ticonderoga and Skenesborough, driving the shipbuilding effort, but even that was not what he really wanted to do. As early as the second week in August, he was eager to take command of the fleet and get under way down the lake, and Gates was eager for him to do so.

Horatio Gates had lost patience with the aging Jacobus Wynkoop. "I think the Commodore seems slow," he wrote to Arnold, "& wish he may retain all the prowess for which he says he was so Famous last War." For the coming fight, Gates wanted the fleet "Commanded by Men of Firmness, & approved Courage," and in his opinion that was not Wynkoop.

Though the fleet had showed some activity, it was less than auspicious. On July 27, Bayze Wells recorded that he was sent from clearing land on Mount Independence over to the lake "in order to work on Board Gundalow Providence under the Command a Cp^t Simmons [Isaiah Simonds]," an exchange of duties he was probably happy to make. On August 4 the small fleet, consisting of the flagship *Royal Savage*, the *Enterprise, Revenge, Liberty,* and a smattering of gondolas, set sail down Lake Champlain.

A few days later, the *Providence,* one of the gondolas completed and on patrol, suffered a serious mishap while exercising her guns. Captain Simonds ordered five guns fired. The gun crews fired the 12-pounder on the bow, then the larboard (port) 9-pounder, and Simonds ordered the two guns loaded again.

On the order to reload, a seaman named Solomon Dyer sponged out the muzzle of the bow gun to extinguish any sparks left from the last firing. Dyer apparently was not thorough enough, however, and he paid for that oversight. As he rammed a fresh gunpowder cartridge down the muzzle, the cartridge "went of While he Was Standing before the Mouth of the Cannon," Wells wrote, "which Blew Boath his hands & one nee almoft of and Likewife the Sprung Rod Part or all of it went through the Left Part of his Body at the Root of his arm Blew him overboard we could not find him untill 7th." When Dyer's mangled body finally rose to the surface, his shipmates recovered it and gave him a funeral ashore.

Comedy followed tragedy a few days later when Wynkoop, looking down the lake through his glass, saw what he was sure was the enemy fortifying a position on shore. He ordered his boatswain to call the other officers for a council of war aboard the *Royal Savage*, where they considered what action to take. Finally Captain Isaac Seamon, of the schooner *Revenge*, climbed aloft to reconnoiter the enemy position. Only then was it discovered that the "enemy" that Wynkoop had seen was in fact a flock of white gulls.

Small wonder that Gates was eager to put Benedict Arnold in command.

CHAPTER *29* *Arnold in Command*

ON THE SAME day that the crew of the gondola *Providence* buried their shipmate Solomon Dyer, Horatio Gates issued formal orders for Benedict Arnold to take command of the fleet.

Gates gave Arnold two choices of where to position his vessels. "Upon your Arrival at Crown-Point," he wrote, "you will proceed with the Fleet [of] the United States under your Command, down Lake Champlain to the narrow Pass of the Lake, made by the Split Rock." Split Rock was a long way from the enemy, just twenty miles down the lake from Crown Point. Oddly, the other choice Gates gave Arnold was very near the enemy indeed, the narrows made by Isle aux Tetes (now Ash Island), which was north of the Canadian border in the Richelieu River. (Isle aux Tetes, or Island of the Heads, had been so named when, in 1694, an Abenaki war party had defeated a band of Mohawks there and placed their heads on stakes around the island's perimeter.) Gates might possibly have been confused about the geography of Lake Champlain. It would happen again.

Gates was careful to rein in Arnold's more aggressive tendencies, making it clear that Arnold was to go no farther down the lake than his orders indicated, and that he was to take no risks with the precious fleet. "It is a defensive War we are carrying on; therefore, no wanton risque, or unnecessary Display of the Power of the Fleet, is at any Time, to influence your Conduct." Arnold was, however, to drop hints within the fleet that the real plan was another invasion of Canada. Gates felt that such suggestions would help bolster the fleet's morale.

If the British were to come up the lake, Arnold was to defend the pass at which he was stationed "with such cool determined Valour, as will give them Reason to repent their Temerity." To further check

Arnold's ardor, Gates forbade him from leaving the fleet to participate in any scouting mission or small-boat attack.

Gates's orders were, by his own description, no more than "the great Outline of the Service, which your Country expects from the Rank and Character you have acquired." Knowing nothing of naval matters, Gates did not presume to give specific instructions concerning the management of the fleet. That he left up to Arnold.

Manning the fleet was an ongoing problem. General orders went out to the various regiments of the Northern Army with quotas of men to be drafted for the ships, all of whom would get extra pay for the duty. Arnold requested "as many Seamen as those Corps can furnish . . . ," though a majority of the men sent would be landsmen with no maritime experience.

On Arnold's recommendation, a Connecticut sea captain named Seth Warner (not the Seth Warner of Green Mountain Boys fame) was asked to raise a company of sailors. Governor Trumbull agreed to pay them a twenty-dollar bounty along with a premium for bringing their own blankets, guns, and cartridge boxes, and the sailors were allowed to sign up for a short (five-month) enlistment. Even with those enticements, however, Warner was able to attract only eleven sailors. Warner himself would end up as captain of the galley *Trumbull*.

Along with sailors, Arnold was on the lookout for other specialists, in particular a surgeon. The new commodore did not think it prudent to sail without one, and he informed Gates that the want of a surgeon and a few other articles prevented the fleet from getting under way. Hearing that the surgeon's mate from St. Clair's regiment had a decent medicine box and was willing to join the fleet, Arnold asked that he be sent, "or someone who will answer to kill a man Secundum Artem [by his art or skill]." Arnold wrote to Dr. Thomas Potts at the hospital at Fort George urging that no time be lost in sending a surgeon. He also asked Potts to send him a patient, Robert Atkinson, "an exceeding good Pilot for this Lake," once he was well.

Benedict Arnold arrived at Crown Point to take command of the fleet on the evening August 15. Along with the sloop *Enterprise* and the three schooners, four gondolas were fully operational. The gondolas, most of them likely named for the communities from which the ship-wrights who built them hailed, were the *New Haven, Providence, Boston,* and the oddball, *Spitfire.* Each carried three carriage guns and eight swivels and was manned by a crew of forty-five.

The gondolas *Connecticut* and *Philadelphia* were still at Ticonderoga, being rigged.

Also fitting out at Ticonderoga was the *Lee.* Though referred to as a row galley, she was rigged unlike any of the others. Rather than twin la-teen sails on two masts, *Lee* stepped a single mast with a square course and topsail, a boom-and-gaff driver, and two headsails rigged to a bowsprit. (This was, in fact, a cutter rig, and the British who captured the *Lee* called her a cutter.)

In her hull shape and deck arrangement, however, she was much like the other row galleys, though much tubbier, being twenty feet shorter but almost the same beam. It was this similarity, no doubt, and the fact that she could be propelled with sweeps, that led the Americans to call her a row galley. She mounted one 12-pounder, one 9-pounder, and four 4-pounders, giving her only a little more firepower than a gondola.

"Commr in Chief of the Fleet on Lake Champlain . . ."

On August 17, the fleet had its first genuine alarm, but the only gun-fire turned out to be Jacobus Wynkoop firing on his own vessels.

Colonel Thomas Hartley, in command of the nominal force still left at Crown Point, had sent a party of soldiers about seven miles down the lake to act as guards for the oar makers working in the woods. Around two in the afternoon, Hartley spotted a large fire, the previously arranged signal that meant the enemy was approaching. He reported it to Arnold, who immediately dispatched Hartley with one hundred men to cover the guards' and oar makers' retreat if necessary.

Arnold also sent word to Captain Isaac Seamon, of the *Revenge,* and Captain Premier, of the *Liberty,* to sail seven to eight miles down the lake, then report back what they discovered. The schooners' crews turned to immediately, weighing anchor and setting sail. One of the schooners fired a swivel gun as a signal to get under way, and the signal was returned by the other.

Jacobus Wynkoop, on board the *Royal Savage* and still, as far as he knew, in sole command of the fleet, was startled by the sound of the guns and even more startled to see two of his vessels getting under way without orders. Certain that the schooners "ought not move without his immediate orders ... and fearing that some design had been formed by the Captain of the said Schooner, or their crews to go over to the enemy," Wynkoop ordered a swivel gun fired to bring them to.

The schooners immediately came to anchor again, and Wynkoop sent his first officer over to collect the captains and bring them to the flagship. Seamon was still ashore, but Premier came aboard *Royal Savage* and presented Wynkoop with Arnold's orders.

Now Wynkoop was more surprised than ever. He wrote immediately to Arnold, assuring him, "I know no Orders, but what shall be given out by me." Gates and Arnold likely did not know—but Wynkoop had not forgotten—that after the confusion with Douglass, Wynkoop had agreed to serve only as commodore, "not being willing to act in a subordinate capacity."

A furious Arnold replied with a blistering note. "[Y]ou surely must be out of your senses," he wrote,

> to say no Orders shal be obey'd but yours ... you are much mistaken, and if you do not suffer my Orders to be Immediately complied with by sending the Captains of the Schooners to obey them I shall be under the disagreeable necessity, of Convincing you of your Error by Immediately Arresting you.

Arnold reinforced his claim to authority by signing the note, "B Arnold B[rigadier] Genl & Commr in Chief of the Fleet on Lake Champlain."

With that clarified, Arnold expected to see the schooners get under way immediately. When they did not, he took a boat out to the *Royal Savage* to confront Wynkoop. Arnold began by explaining why the schooners had to be sent out. Wynkoop, understanding at last, issued fresh orders to the captains that were virtually identical to Arnold's except for sending the schooners eight to ten miles down the lake rather than seven to eight, and he sent these orders under his name alone.

That done, the two officers discussed the command confusion, Arnold reminding Wynkoop that he had "aquainted you some time since that the Commander in chief had Appointed me to take command of the Navy of the Lakes." What's more, Arnold said, Wynkoop had "receiv'd and executed" Arnold's orders "for some time past." Indeed, the month before, after *Royal Savage* had been rearmed, Gates had sent her to Crown Point with orders for Wynkoop to receive instructions from Arnold.

When Arnold showed Wynkoop his orders from Gates, the reality of the situation began to dawn on Wynkoop and "brought him so far to reason." But Wynkoop continued to insist that he would not take orders from anyone, save for general instructions from the commander in chief, and if that was not to be the case then he would give up command of the fleet.

Both men wrote to Gates that evening with similar accounts of what had taken place, expressing a general understanding that Wynkoop would leave if he was not wanted as commodore of the fleet. Gates, however, after his months of frustration, was not inclined to forgive Wynkoop his mistake. He wrote to Arnold ordering him to "Instantly put Commodore Wynkoop in Arrest and send him prisoner to Head Quarters at Tyonderoga," and to tell the other officers that the same fate awaited anyone who did not obey Arnold's orders.

Gates also wrote to Schuyler, informing him of what had transpired and revealing some of the frustration he felt with Wynkoop. "Many Officers of rank in this department say, he is totally unfit to command a single vessel." Gates hoped that Schuyler would, "without Scruple, forthwith dismiss him the Service."

By the time Arnold received orders to arrest Wynkoop, his attitude had softened. Though he could not disobey a direct order, he could at least make the arrest respectful. He sent Wynkoop a copy of Gates's order for arrest, telling him, "In Compliance of the above Order, I do hereby put you in Arrest, of which you will take notice and govern yourself accordingly." He ordered a boat and crew to convey Wynkoop to Ticonderoga at a time that "will be most agreeable."

The next day Arnold wrote to Gates informing him that he had ordered Wynkoop to headquarters. He did not say that he had arrested Wynkoop, telling Gates rather that none of the other officers had disobeyed an order and that Wynkoop genuinely believed that neither Arnold nor Gates had authority over him. "He now seems convinced of the Contrary, & sorry for his disobedience of orders," Arnold wrote. He asked that Wynkoop "be permitted to return home without being Cashierd."

Gates was not mollified. When Arnold's letter arrived at Ticonderoga but Wynkoop did not, Gates fired off another note to Arnold along with a copy of the arrest order, professing his surprise to find his orders "not . . . complied with by the Arrival of Mr. Wynkoop at the Post." Gates had dropped the title "Commodore" he had used the day before.

When Wynkoop did at last arrive at Ticonderoga, Gates sent him on to Schuyler, and Schuyler sent him home. Wynkoop wrote a long letter to Congress, outlining what had happened and asking that Congress "grant him such Relief as he is in Justice entitled to," a plea that Congress essentially ignored. The next year, Wynkoop would be back on the lake and once again in command of the fleet.

Underway

On August 23, Horatio Gates sent Dr. Stephen MaCrea to fill the high-sounding office of First Surgeon of the Fleet. Arnold was happy to have him. Impatient to be under way, Arnold had decided to sail on "the first fair wind even without a Surgeon."

Gates informed Arnold that the gondola *Connecticut*, being fitted out at Ticonderoga, would be delivered to Crown Point that day, and that one row galley, by which he meant the *Lee*, would soon follow. The gondola *Philadelphia*, under the command of Captain Benjamin Rue, had joined the fleet three days earlier. Still short of sailors, Arnold filled out the crews with men drafted from Hartley's regiment.

Finally, around sunset on August 24, the entire fleet, under the command of Brigadier General Benedict Arnold, hove up their anchors and set sail to run down the lake before a southerly breeze. In the van sailed the flagship *Royal Savage* and the sloop *Enterprise*. With Wynkoop gone, Arnold took command of the flagship, though he would later ask Gates to send another captain for her. "[I]n case any Accident should happen to me," Arnold explained, "the present Master is not fit for the Command in Chief, tho a good man in his present Station." He likely felt as well that he could be a more effective commodore of the fleet if he did not have the added burden of commanding one of its vessels.

Next in sailing order went the gondola *New Haven*, under the command of Samuel Mansfield, and the *Boston*, whose captain was named Sumner. Following were the *Providence* and the *Spitfire*, the latter commanded by Philip Ulmer. After those went the *Philadelphia* and the *Connecticut*, which had just joined the fleet that morning under the command of Joshua Grant. Bringing up the rear were the schooners *Revenge* and *Liberty*.

They must have made an impressive sight, sailing north in a line two abreast, ten vessels of what Bayze Wells called "Sail of the Line," though any British seaman would have laughed to hear that motley collection elevated to the status of England's mighty line-of-battle ships.

Certainly the Americans were impressed with the force they had collected. Philip Schuyler informed John Hancock, "We are however so much a Head of the Enemy in our Naval Force, that I do not apprehend they will be able to equal our strength this Campaign . . . ," and his sentiment was echoed by others in the Northern Department, including Horatio Gates and Colonel Anthony Wayne who had come to Canada as part of General Thomas's brigade. No one, it seemed, had any idea what they were up against.

CHAPTER 30 *A Line of Battle*

ARNOLD'S SHIPS covered only about four miles on their first day, coming to anchor "in A Line of Battle had Good anchorage in 4 fathom water," according to the newly minted lieutenant Bayze Wells, who cultivated a lofty vision of his little fleet.

The next morning they got under way half an hour after sunrise, with overcast skies and a southerly wind. On the schooners' decks, gangs of men hauled on peak and throat halyards as the flogging sails were raised and hauled taut. Aloft, the topmen laid out on the yards and cast gaskets off the square sails, the tightly furled canvas tumbling down and hanging in disorganized bunches of cloth.

On board the gondolas, the big square mainsails were loosed and the topsails hoisted away, the sails lifting to the favorable breeze as men hauled on braces to trim them. The forty-five or so men on board each of the gondolas must have been grateful for the sounds of canvas snapping and filling and the gurgle of water around the stem. Had the wind been out of the north, the schooners might have been able to tack against it, but the flat-bottomed gondolas could not have. The gondola crews would then have been in for a long, hard pull to windward, creeping north under the power of the twenty-foot sweeps. If the wind had been at all brisk, even that would have been impossible.

As the fleet continued north down the lake, the wind became shifty, blowing northerly around noon, then swinging into the south again by two in the afternoon. By four o'clock the fleet had sailed through The Narrows and passed Split Rock. At seven o'clock they came to anchor for the night along an open stretch of the western shoreline about seven miles north of Split Rock, where, according to Wells, they "Set a Watch and Prepared for the Enemy."

The enemy that arrived that night was not the British, but that age-old nemesis of sailors, foul weather. A violent wind blew up from the northeast, driving rain before it, lashing the ships and setting them to pitching hard at the ends of their anchor cables. Dawn revealed an ugly storm that looked likely to get worse. Arnold, realizing that the vessels could not weather a hard blow on that exposed lee shore, sent his boat through the fleet, passing the order to be ready to sail for a sheltered anchorage by two that afternoon.

An hour before their appointed departure, the wind suddenly built in force. Arnold knew that they could wait no longer; it was time to go. He fired a gun as the signal to get under way, and the schooners and clumsy gondolas heaved up their anchors and set their close-reefed sails. The "hard gale made an amazeing Sea," Arnold reported. All the vessels except the *Spitfire*, which was closest to land, were able to claw off the shore into more open water.

As the *Spitfire* struggled for sea room, the mounting waves drove her closer and closer to the western shore of the lake. The gondolas were awkward sailers in the best of conditions, but now, with a big sea running, a strong headwind, and a lee shore, those defects seemed likely to prove fatal for the *Spitfire*. Arnold climbed into a small boat—a bold, even reckless act in those conditions—and rowed over to the gondola. Shouting against the gusting wind, he ordered Ulmer to anchor again, furl his sail, and ride it out. It was the only way to prevent *Spitfire* from being driven ashore, although Arnold held little hope that even at anchor the vessel would live through the storm.

With *Enterprise* in the lead, the fleet sailed south again, running before the northeast wind, retracing its route past Split Rock and through The Narrows, making for the shelter of Buttonmould Bay. The straining canvas proved too great a load for *Connecticut*'s rig. Halfway to the bay, her mast went by the board, collapsing with a great, rendering crack and smothering the bow under canvas and torn cordage.

As the crew heaved and slashed at the shattered gear, struggling to clear away the wreckage, the wallowing, dismasted gondola was taken in tow by *Revenge*. The *Enterprise* went aground as she was luffing up to run into the bay, but, stranded on the muddy shallows, she served as a marker for the rest of the fleet, which sailed around her and came to anchor in the relatively sheltered water. At five o'clock the *Enterprise* refloated and anchored with the others.

All the next day the fleet lay pinned in Buttonmould Bay by a fierce northerly wind and driving rain. Arnold, never one to waste a moment, sent a scouting party ashore to find out whether the locals had any intelligence from St. John's or word of what was happening in New York. For more than two months, General Howe's army, said to be thirty thousand strong, had been encamped on Staten Island, while Washington's men across the harbor on Long Island waited nervously for the ax to fall. Rumors spread like smallpox through the Northern Army. Arnold and his men were eager for real news.

All through the next day the storm continued unabated. On board the gondolas the men huddled miserably under canvas awnings, finding scant shelter from the wind and blowing rain. Word somehow reached the fleet that the *Spitfire* had foundered. Then, to everyone's amazement, the gondola appeared that evening, standing into the bay and coming to anchor, having "rode out the Storm, tho exposed to the rake of Cumberland Bay . . . Fifty miles long." Arnold had fully expected to hear that she had sunk or been driven ashore, but the only loss was the bateau they had been trailing astern.

The storm passed, but for two more days the wind continued out of the northeast, keeping the fleet trapped in the bay. Arnold invited all the captains and lieutenants ashore for a social gathering, where they competed at target practice and enjoyed a roast pig, wine, punch, and cider. The officers toasted the Congress and General Arnold and named the nearby point of land Arnold's Point.

This was Arnold at his best—jovial, friendly, always in command but not the martinet that his enemies accused him of being. The gathering on Champlain's shore was a "moſt Genteel feaſt," as Wells put it, providing a great boost to the esprit de corps for the fleet's officers.

The officers would have been less inclined toward celebration, however, had they known that even as they were enjoying themselves on the eastern shore of Lake Champlain, Washington's army on Long Island was being outmaneuvered and rolled up by Howe's overwhelming force. As it happened, the storm that nearly sank Arnold's fleet had swept east, soaking Washington's miserable, defeated men, but also preventing the ships of the British navy from sailing into the East River and cutting off the American retreat from Brooklyn. Washington's brilliant nighttime evacuation across the river to Manhattan, facilitated by John Glover's maritime regiment from Marblehead, Massachusetts, saved the army from complete destruction—but it would not have been possible without the storm that battered Arnold's flotilla.

Riding at anchor in Buttonmould Bay, Arnold and his men knew nothing of that. Finally, on September 1, the wind swung around to the south—a fair breeze on which, once again, to head down the lake. By four that afternoon, the fleet was under way back through The Narrows, coming to anchor west of Split Rock.

Gondolas and Galleys

On August 31, Jeduthan Baldwin, writing in his journal, managed to mix up ship types when he recorded "the Lee Gundalo & a Row Galley Saild from [Ticonderoga] Down the Lake." He meant the row galley *Lee* and the gondola *New Jersey*, which arrived at Crown Point the next day. There Thomas Hartley loaded a supply of biscuit on board and procured a pilot in preparation for sending them down the lake to join the others.

All through the month of August, Waterbury and Hermanus Schuyler had been predicting the imminent launch of the three big galleys on the stocks, but by month's end the boats remained high and dry. "The sickness of the carpenters at Skenesborough has delayed our row-galleys," Gates explained to Governor Trumbull, "and the misfortune General Waterbury met with in wounding his leg, contributed not a little thereto." Fever and ague were indeed at the heart of the problem; those carpenters who weren't sick wanted to go home before they became so. Many were trying to sell their tools before they left, but there were not enough carpenters left at Skenesborough to buy them. Even Hermanus Schuyler had fallen ill and petitioned Waterbury for leave to go home to recover.

In early August, with the shipyard operating at its peak, Arnold had envisioned at least eight row galleys completed by the end of summer. Less than a month later, Gates informed Schuyler that "it will not be possible for the carpenters to finish more than one galley, after those now on the stocks are launched; and to do this, they must put all the healthy men they have into one gang, and discharge the rest." That one galley—possibly the one started while the carpenters were waiting for ceiling planks—would become the *Gates*, and she would be finished too late to be any help that year.

The three galleys that were nearly done and waiting to go down the ways were of slightly different sizes. The *Congress*, built by a lead carpenter from Philadelphia named Thomas Casdrop, was seventy-three feet on the keel and nineteen feet on the beam, with a six-foot hold. The *Washington*, build by a Massachusetts shipwright named Titcomb, was sixty-five feet on the keel with a nineteen-foot beam and a five-foot ten-inch hold.

A shipwright from Connecticut named Winslow built the *Trumbull*, the smallest of the three. She was sixty feet on the keel with a beam of ten feet and a hold of five feet three inches. The differing sizes would suggest that none of the vessels was built to a specific plan, rather crafted as the lead shipwrights saw fit, to Arnold's general specifications for a "Spanish galley."

On September 1, thanks to Schuyler's and Varick's efforts, a large store of cordage, blocks, cables, and other material for rigging arrived at Ticonderoga. It had earlier been suggested that matters could be expedited by sending some sailors to Skenesborough to begin rigging the ships in the shipyard, but, given the sickness there, Gates and Waterbury now agreed that it would be best to deliver the unrigged vessels to Ticonderoga as soon as possible.

The *Congress* was finally launched on September 1 and the other two shortly after. *Congress* arrived at Ticonderoga on September 10, followed the next day by the *Trumbull*. Gates reported to Schuyler, "General Waterbury and two of the row galleys are now here; the third is hourly expected from Skeen."

In that letter Gates also mentioned to Schuyler, "I am astonished at the calumnies that go to Congress against general Arnold." Gates, who would eventually become one of Benedict Arnold's biggest detractors, added, "I am confident the Congress will view whatever is whispered against General Arnold as the foul stream of that poisonous fountain, detraction." In retrospect, it would be clear how such "calumnies," and the ugliness surrounding the Hazen court-martial, were the start of the intrigue that would eventually wear Arnold down and lead him to orchestrate his own fall from grace.

The arrival of rigging supplies at Ticonderoga offered renewed hope that the row galleys would soon join Arnold in defense of the lake, but the hope was false. There were still not enough supplies to complete all the vessels waiting there, and ironwork was also in short supply.

By the latter part of September, Schuyler was still pleading with the shipwrights in Poughkeepsie, writing that "the row Gallies which are the Greatest Strength of our Naval force on the lake cannot be Equipp unless we are furnished with the Cordage." The struggle to finish the galleys would go on until they were nearly too late to do any good.

"[T]he Whole was Done in order and Good Difsepline . . ."

In early September, rumors about the disastrous Battle of Long Island reached the Northern Department, and everyone was shaken by the "great and awful event . . ." and worried that a similar rout could happen to them.

On the morning of September 2, Arnold received intelligence that the enemy was just four miles down the lake. He sent a boat through the anchored vessels with orders to clear for action, and, according to Wells, "we Roufed all hands up and Prepared for Battle on yᵉ Shorteſt Notice."

But that alarm, like others before, turned out to be nothing, and soon the fleet was once again pushing north, "under way with a Fresh Southerly breeze & expect to be at Ile Ta'te before night," where they hoped to gather intelligence regarding the enemy. Far astern they spotted two vessels, which Arnold correctly guessed were the *Lee* and the *New Jersey*, coming to join them.

The next day the fleet fired its first shots in anger. Standing down the lake with a fresh breeze, the vessels arrived at Cumberland Head around one o'clock in the afternoon. Picket boats sent out in advance spotted about twenty men on shore and opened up on them with swivels. Arnold sent some riflemen ashore to search for the enemy, but they found nothing. It was the Americans' first indication that the woods at the north end of the lake were swarming with British soldiers and Canadians and Indians allied with the British. It was a lesson that Arnold learned immediately, but others, to their peril, did not.

A few days later, Gates sent a lieutenant with seventy men down the lake to Arnold, together with a letter expressing the hope that Arnold would release Hartley's men, because Hartley was eager to have them back. Gates also sent a chart of Lake Champlain and word that he had appointed General David Waterbury not as captain of a galley but as second in command of the fleet. Third in command would be Colonel Edward Wigglesworth, an experienced seaman and former artillery officer from Massachusetts.

Gates had thus far avoided giving Arnold specific instructions on how to run the fleet, but now he began to yield to the temptation to micromanage. He told Arnold that, with the two additional officers, he would be able to divide his fleet into three columns, "yourself in the centre, General Waterbury on the right, and Colonel Wigglesworth on the left."

By the middle of the first week in September, Arnold and his ships were at Windmill Point, where Lake Champlain narrows into the Richelieu River, just below the Canadian border and twenty-six miles from St. John's. The fleet was encountering more and more of the enemy. At Isle aux Tetes, just north of Windmill Point, Arnold and his men found several hundred men encamped; they made a quick retreat at the sight of the American fleet.

The British of course knew they were there, and sent boats upriver from St. John's in the hope of luring the Americans into a trap, but Arnold would not be tempted any closer to the main body of the enemy. Instead, he sent two scouting parties into the woods to discover what they could of British strength at St. John's.

To further prepare his fleet for battle, Arnold ordered men to take their ships' boats ashore to cut sticks and lash them into fascines.

These were to be fastened along the low sides of the gondolas to give added protection against boarders and small arms fire, a function performed by hammocks and netting on larger ships.

Arnold's orders specified that all the boats should go ashore at the same time, but Sumner, of the *Boston*, forgetting the lesson of Cumberland Head, sent his boat in alone. No sooner had the men waded ashore than the woods and undergrowth seemed to explode with gunfire. Bullets whistled overhead, and the stunned Americans found themselves "attacked by a Party of Savages, who pursued them into the Water."

The "savages" were led by a British lieutenant named Scott, who called for the fleeing Americans to surrender. Scott had been sent with a party of Indians to take an American prisoner so that the British might gain some intelligence of the rebels' actions. He and his native allies had actually paddled undetected through the American fleet the night before. At daybreak they had taken cover on shore right where the *Boston*'s boat landed.

The surprised Americans tumbled into the boat, but before they could pull out of range, three were killed and six wounded.

Arnold turned the heavy guns of the fleet on the woods, which sent the enemy running. He then sent a party ashore to see what they could find. They came up with a laced beaver hat and a button bearing the markings of the 47th Regiment.

In the excitement of firing at a real enemy, the *Royal Savage*'s gunner tried to ram an oversized ball into the muzzle, and it lodged halfway down. When the excitement had ended, the gun was sent ashore to be fired in case it should blow up, but the charge managed to dislodge the ball with no mishap.

Soon after the Americans had "fired a few Shot" at the enemy, the row galley *Lee* and the gondola *New Jersey* arrived. The assembled fleet saluted the new arrivals with a single gun from each ship fired one after another, alternating between the left and right sides of the line of ships, Bayze Wells noting that "the Whole was Done in order and Good Difspline." *Lee* then returned the salute.

Incredibly, at Crown Point, eighty miles south, Hartley heard the distant guns and reported "a very heavy cannonading down the Lake

all this Morning it is undoubtedly between our Fleet and the Enemy."
Word of the gunfire sent an alarm racing through the men at Ticonderoga and Mount Independence, who were anxiously awaiting the
appearance of the enemy, which they believed to be imminent. Hartley requested that Gates send reinforcements to Crown Point, and
Gates issued orders that all troops should hold themselves in readiness
for attack. Baldwin recorded, "all hands at work at Daylight prepairing
our batteries against the worst."

When Schuyler heard from Gates about the gunfire, he wrote to
Hancock and to Washington, telling them that "it is most probable
that the enemy are attempting to cross the lake." Schuyler asked that
militia and a supply of cartridge paper be sent north at once.

Hartley dispatched a boat with Lieutenant John Brooks on board to
find the fleet and see what was going on. Meanwhile, everyone waited
for whatever might happen next.

South from St. John's

While the Americans at the south end of Lake Champlain had been
pushing hard to prepare their fleet, the British at the north end had
been pushing equally hard. Like the Americans, however, the British
had encountered problems and setbacks.

As July turned to August, Commodore Charles Douglas began to realize that the "terraqueous Expedition" would not be taking place as
quickly as he had hoped, due to the "Magnitude of the Enterprize." It
did not help that the British were constantly fighting the prevailing
wind and current while moving supplies up the St. Lawrence and
Richelieu rivers from Quebec to Chambly. On top of that, some of the
craftsmen began to suffer from dysentery. Douglas hoped to have the
fleet finished by "some time in September."

In the second week of August, a division of the army was sent upriver to Isle aux Noix, where they found a tombstone marking the
graves of two American officers and two privates who had been surprised, killed, and scalped by Indians sympathetic to the British during the American retreat from Canada. The tombstone, which said

that the men were "Not Hirelings But Patriots," had clearly been set up for the benefit of the British and Hessian troops following in the Americans' wake. The epitaph read:

Sons of America rest in quiet here
Britannia blush, Burgoyne let fall a Tear
And tremble Europe sons with savage race,
Death and Revenge await you with disgrace.

Judging by the number of journal entries that made mention of the tombstone, it had its intended effect.

By mid-August, the convoy carrying the second wave of German troops arrived at Quebec. Of greater interest to Douglas, however, were the twenty shipwrights from Glasgow, Scotland, and ten house carpenters from Portsmouth, England, who were also aboard, and who were sent on to St. John's as quickly as possible.

On September 2, Lieutenant Digby returned to St. John's from Isle aux Noix in time to see the launching of the schooner *Carleton*, "complete in guns, &c, &c." The British, fearing an American attempt to take the vessel, posted an officer and twenty-four men aboard her every night, with six men in a cutter patrolling the river.

Carleton's captain would be James Richard Dacres, lately first officer of the *Blonde*, who had been overseeing the boats on the lake. Thirty-six years later, Dacres's son, also James Richard, would find his place in naval history as captain of the British frigate *Guerrière* when she was defeated by the USS *Constitution* in the War of 1812. But James the younger would not be born until five years after the end of the American Revolution. Thanks to Arnold's fleet, he was nearly not born at all.

In early September, the British encampments were much alarmed by the near approach of the American ships. A canoe full of Indians had observed Arnold's vessels at the mouth of the Richelieu, and Arnold's salute of the *Lee* and the *New Jersey* didn't go unnoticed either. The gunfire had the same effect on the British camp that it did on the Americans. "[W]e very distinctly heard 13 or 14 cannon shot . . . ," Digby wrote. "All hands were ordered to throw up more works."

To the surprise of the British troops, however, the Americans did not appear. A few days later Digby noted that the British "gave over all thoughts of their coming down to attack us, and the building of our vessels went on with great dispatch at St. John's." Douglas was amazed and delighted, as well he might be, by the unprecedented speed with which the *Inflexible* was coming together, and he was at last confident that she would be ready in time to move with the expedition. Douglas wrote Captain Pownoll, of the *Blonde*, that *Inflexible*'s prowess would give the British "domination of Lake Champlain beyond a doubt."

CHAPTER *31* *A Place to Make a Stand*

IN A REPORT to Gates written from Windmill Point, Arnold expressed concern over a letter he had received from his old acquaintance Samuel Chase, the congressman from Maryland and one of the commissioners who had been with Arnold in Montreal. Chase was troubled by the attacks on Arnold's character stemming from the Hazen affair, the same situation that Gates had written Schuyler about. "I cannot but think it extremely cruel," Arnold wrote to Gates, "when I have sacrifised my Ease, Health and great part of my private Property in the Cause of my Country to be Caluminated as a Robber and thief, at a Time too when I have it not in my Power to be heard in my own Defence."

That sort of complaint was not at all uncommon among the officers in the Continental army. Schuyler, for one, was forever reminding people of the great sacrifices he made for his country, as did other officers. Still, it hinted at Arnold's growing frustration with the politics of military service. Unlike other officers, including Gates, who took every opportunity to run to Philadelphia and huddle with congressmen, Arnold had not been out of the combat theater since marching from Fort Western, Maine, nearly a year before. Such dedication to fighting, at the expense of political connections, would do him no good in the end.

Arnold now had twelve vessels in his fleet, and he moored them across the narrow part of the river, with the *Royal Savage* and the *Lee* in the center, the *Revenge* and *Liberty* on the flanks, and the gondolas in the middle, so close that even a bateau could not sneak past. Unlike many of his fellow officers, however, Arnold harbored no delusions about the possible strength of his adversary or the weaknesses of his own force.

"We have but very indifferent men, in general," he complained to Gates, adding that a "great part of those who shipped for Seamen know very little of the matter." Worse, his men were starting to fall sick, and he had to send back to Ticonderoga twenty-three men "who will be of no service for some time." If he discovered that the enemy's fleet was greatly superior to his own, Arnold intended to head back up the lake to Cumberland Head or Schuyler's Island and wait for the arrival of the much-anticipated row galleys. He pleaded, again, for real sailors to be sent down the lake.

Soon after Arnold had arranged his fleet in line across the river, men aboard the guard boats and flanking vessels could hear the sound of trees being cut on the nearby shores and see lights moving through the woods at night. Arnold concluded that the British were constructing batteries from which they could deliver a lethal cross fire. Around noon on September 8, with a convenient northerly wind, the fleet stood up the lake and came to anchor again on the west side of Isle la Motte.

As they came to anchor, Lieutenant John Brooks arrived by boat from Crown Point and came aboard the *Savage*. He had been sent by Hartley to find out what the cannonade had been about, but the strong northerly wind had slowed his trip down the lake.

No doubt he told Arnold that everyone at Crown Point and Ticonderoga was in a state of near panic wondering what had happened. Arnold wrote a quick note to Gates explaining that everything was all right and that the gunfire had been no more than the "few Shot" the fleet fired at the Indians. Sheepish, perhaps, about the brouhaha he had caused, Arnold did not mention the thunderous multigun salute. He did take the opportunity to ask Gates to send warm clothing for his men.

The following day, Colonel Wigglesworth arrived on a boat from Ticonderoga with sketchy news concerning the Battle of Long Island. Arnold was pleased to see Wigglesworth, calling him "a gentleman of whom I have a good opinion." Arnold sent word back to Gates that he intended to make his stand at Isle la Motte, because that place was "the best in the Lake to stop the enemy," and was also fairly well protected from strong wind, with good holding ground and nearby sheltered harbors for the gondolas to duck into if a gale blew up.

Along with the letter, Arnold sent back the pilot Robert Atkinson "to guide the row galleys down the lake, and another twenty-two men sick with ague."

On the same day, in Philadelphia, the Congress resolved that wherever "the words 'United Colonies' have been used, the stile be altered, for the future, to the 'United States.' "

"A Remove to the Island Valcouer . . ."

Horatio Gates wrote to Arnold giving his approval of Arnold's decision to move south to Isle la Motte. In doing so he put his self-professed ignorance of the lake on display by warning Arnold to be careful that the British did not cut off his retreat by fortifying Point au Fer. Arnold politely thanked him for his approval and pointed out that the fleet was moored "five Miles to the Southward of Point aux Fire," and out of reach of any possible shore batteries.

Arnold told Gates that he still had little intelligence regarding the enemy's naval strength. One man from each of the scouting parties that Arnold had sent out had returned to report the enemy's strength at Isle aux Noix at about a thousand men "and no Water Craft except Batteaux." Arnold had no word from St. John's on the state of the British fleet building there until he spoke to a deserter from Colonel Maclean's regiment, who reported two or three schooners or sloops along with gondolas and floating batteries.

With his imperfect knowledge of the enemy, Arnold was careful not to be caught napping. The two small schooners were kept on patrol above and below the line of moored vessels, while guard boats were rowed around the anchored craft and half of each crew was kept on deck and under arms at all times.

But even as Gates was congratulating Arnold on his decision to make a stand at Isle la Motte, Arnold was having second thoughts. "If I hear nothing from St. Johns, soon, I design makeing a Remove to the Island Valcouer untill joined by the Three Gallies," he told Gates. The advantages of Valcour, Arnold explained, were that if the Americans succeeded in their attack, the British could not escape, and if the Americans were bested, their retreat would be "open and Free."

In the end, though Valcour was indeed an excellent choice, none of Arnold's enumerated reasons turned out to be true.

In a further effort to gain intelligence, Arnold dispatched a Frenchman named Antoine Girard, who, for fifty dollars, agreed to go to St. John's and spy for the Americans. Arnold did not know that Girard had earlier been caught near Ticonderoga, where he was thought to be spying for the British. Girard returned from his spying mission in what Arnold thought was a suspiciously short amount of time, bearing a British pass from Isle aux Noix. His report on British naval strength was essentially accurate, but Arnold, even without knowing the man's past, felt that the British had put him up to making a false report. He arrested Girard and bundled him off to Ticonderoga, accusing him of being a double agent.

Soon after, Lieutenant Whitcomb, the leader of one of Arnold's scouting parties, arrived with two prisoners in tow, an ensign and a corporal of the 29th Regiment. (Due to the irregularity of Continental troops, the prisoners at first had refused to believe that Whitcomb was a soldier.) When Arnold heard their accounts, which were similar to the others he had heard, including Girard's, he was finally willing to acknowledge with some certainty that he was up against a powerful enemy. "I am inclined to think . . . ," he informed Gates, "that the Enemy will soon have a considerable naval Force."

Faced with that reality, Arnold asked Gates to send 6- or 8-inch howitzers, as well as slow match, grape-, and chain shot. He told Gates that he planned "first fair Wind to come up as high as Ile Valcour."

Up the Lake

When Arnold got his northerly wind, he shifted his fleet up the lake as far as Baye St. Amand, a cove just north of Cumberland Head with good holding ground in seven and a half fathoms and well protected from a north wind. Before leaving Isle la Motte, they were joined by the eighth and final gondola, the *Success*, commanded by Captain Lee. The gondola's name would later be changed to *New York*, but the name *Success* continued to crop up.

While the fleet moved south, *Liberty* was ordered to cruise around Isle la Motte until two in the afternoon, then join the others. As *Liberty* was standing up the lake, a Frenchman came down to the shore opposite the island and hailed the schooner, indicating that he wanted to be taken on board. The *Liberty*'s master, Captain Premier, recalling the earlier ambush, approached the man with caution. He sent in a boat, the crew backing it toward shore with swivel guns loaded and slow match lit.

Not willing to get too close, the crew ordered the Frenchman to swim out to them, but the man waded only as deep as his chest before claiming that he could not swim. When he realized that the boat crew was not going to come any closer, he waded "back and give three Cahoops." On that signal "three, or four, hundred, Indians, Canadians & Regulars rose up and fired." The storm of musket balls wounded three of the men in the boat, but the others fired their swivels and muskets into the enemy while the *Liberty* blasted away with broadsides of grapeshot. Soon the enemy retreated inland.

This was yet another reminder of the dangers ashore. The edge of the lake was swarming with Indians, and on her way to rejoin the fleet, the *Liberty* spotted two to three hundred with birch bark canoes on the western shore. Such a highly mobile and easily concealed force posed a significant threat to the American fleet, particularly to the boats carrying supplies and correspondence up and down the lake. Arnold sent *Liberty* as an escort for the boats heading back to Ticonderoga.

When Arnold wrote to Gates from Baye St. Amand, hints of his mounting frustration and the stress under which he was laboring began to creep into his letter. He asked again that seamen and gunners be sent, and wondered on paper why the galleys were not yet done. "I wish the Workmen could all be employed, on One Gally & finish her first, that Something might be Added to the fleet I cannot help thinking that they are hindering each other." If the British were going to attack at all that year, Arnold believed it would be in the next week, and the addition of the galleys could well decide the thing.

Gunpowder was another concern. The crews of the fleet exercised every day at their great guns, but it was dumb show only. The shortage of powder prevented them from live-fire exercise (perhaps another reason why Arnold failed to mention his wasteful salute of the *Lee*).

Last, Arnold complained again about the quality of his men. "The Draufts from the regts at Tionderoga, are a miserable Set . . . ," he wrote, suspecting, perhaps with good reason, that the regimental commanders had pawned off their worst men on the fleet.

The Gunboats of Autumn

Although camp life at Ticonderoga and Mount Independence was no vacation, life aboard the American fleet was likely much worse. The onset of autumn brought with it violent storms—"an exceeding hard gale here the 20th, and a prodigious sea," Arnold wrote. Later he would write, "We have continual gales of wind, and the duty very severe," and that from the man who had spent the previous winter outside Quebec.

Funneling between the Adirondack Mountains to the west and the Green Mountains to the east, the wind would come screaming down the length of the long, narrow lake, often driving cold rain before it. Bayze Wells's journal contained entry after entry about the foul weather: "Fryday 13th Sep^{tr} this Day the wind South Very Strong . . . Sabbath 15th Sep^{tr}, wind shifted to the Nortweſt thare held Very Strong . . . Tueſday 17th this Day the wind at South and Rain . . . Fryday 20th Sep^{tr}, A more Winde night I scerce Ever Knew."

The air grew colder, so much so that the Americans began to wonder whether the season was already too far advanced for a British offensive. The conditions were perhaps bearable for the men on board the schooners and the sloop, with cabins and a lower deck to shelter them, but the gondolas were essentially big, open boats with only an awning overhead and the fascines and possibly a lee cloth to protect them from the weather. Forty-five men were crammed aboard vessels about fifty feet long. None of the men in the fleet was adequately clothed.

Fever and ague were sweeping though the close-packed crews. Wells, aboard the *Providence*, reported that Captain Simonds was sick, and Wells himself often complained of illness and other discomforts. "[A]bout Six P.M. Mr Tiffany and I Bath^d for the Itch with Brimstone tallow and tar mix together and Lay in our Cloaths." Wells attempted this cure for "the Itch" twice more.

On September 20, Wells wrote that "An∫el Fox was Cabb^d twelve Strokes on his Naked Buttucks for sleeping on his watch." Two days later Ananius Tubbs received the same punishment for the same offense. It was not a severe punishment, not for so serious an offense as sleeping on watch, and not when compared with the usual naval punishment of a dozen lashes on the back with a cat-o'-nine-tails. No doubt Arnold, who could probably claim more experience than any other officer in the Continental army when it came to leading men through extreme adversity, understood that men could be pushed only so hard.

Everyone was near the limit of his endurance, and still the British did not come.

CHAPTER *32* *The British Head South*

AFTER SENDING two boats to explore the anchorage between Valcour Island and the western shore of Lake Champlain, Arnold, on September 24, "Gave A sailing Signal about Seven A.M. the whole fleet hove up Imediatly and Stood up the Lake." They anchored near the south end of Valcour, between the island and the shore, in six fathoms of water with good holding ground. The fleet was "as near together as possible, & in such a form that few Vessells can attack us at the same Time, & then will be exposed to the fire of the whole fleet." Bayze Wells referred to the place as "St Antonies Bay."

The schooner *Liberty* was not with the fleet. Carrying the three men wounded in the ambush of her boat crew, she had sailed south for a refit at Ticonderoga. The *Revenge* was kept cruising the lake.

The day after taking position at Valcour, Arnold invited his captains and lieutenants to dinner ashore on the island, much as he had at Buttonmould Bay. "A mo∫t agreable Entertainment," Wells reported.

Arnold kept the men training with the cannons. Certain that they would soon be in battle, he decided to use part of his precious powder supply for live-fire exercises. An empty cask was anchored about a mile out, and each gun crew was allowed to fire a single round at the target. After they secured the guns for the night, the wind increased and it began to snow. The gun crews would get just one more chance to practice with loaded guns before they had to use them in earnest.

Horatio Gates wrote to Arnold to reassure him that "no man Alive could be more Anxious for the Welfare of you & Your Fleet, than General Waterbury, & myself . . . ," and that they were exerting every effort to get the galleys finished. Arnold never received those soothing words. The *Revenge*, cruising the lake, spotted the boat carrying the messenger and closed with it. The messenger, taking the *Revenge* for a

British vessel, destroyed the letters and papers while the schooner was still some distance off.

The next word that Arnold had from Gates was delivered by Captain Seth Warner, aboard the galley *Trumbull*, which joined the fleet at Valcour Island on September 30. Gates could sense Arnold's bleak mood, and his letter was part pep talk and part explanation, with a carefully modulated dose of reality. Gates told Arnold that the *Trumbull* "carries a fine reinforcement of seamen, and besides, is herself a considerable addition to your squadron." The other galleys would be coming soon, but they were still in need of twenty coils of rope to finish the rigging, and only a fraction of the powder that Arnold had asked for had arrived, "so economy is the word." Gates concluded that "more cannot be done than is done to despatch them."

Arnold was delighted by the arrival of the *Trumbull* and was encouraged by Gates's letter, but those good feelings dissolved once he understood the reality of the situation. Rather than "a fine reinforcement of seamen," which Arnold took to mean at least a hundred sailors, he found that Warner had the crew only for his own row galley and not one man more. The *Trumbull* was "not half finished or rigged; her cannon are much to small."

The stress that Arnold was enduring, holding his command together while waiting for the arrival of a superior enemy, was eating away at him. Writing back to Gates, he was unequivocal about his mounting disgust and frustration. "I hope to be excused (after the requisitions so often made)," he wrote on October 1, "if with five hundred men, half naked, I should not be able to beat the enemy with seven thousand men, well clothed, and a naval force, by the best accounts, near equal to ours."

It may have been frustration talking, but Arnold seemed to believe that negligence, not a genuine lack of supplies, was holding back the fleet. He pointed out that he had ordered rigging for eight galleys, the number he had originally envisioned, so it seemed odd to him that there was not enough even for three. "I am surprised by their strange economy or infatuation below," he wrote to Gates. "Saving and negligence, I am afraid, will ruin us at last."

Given the increasingly bitter weather and his men's inadequate clothing, Arnold did not think he could stay at Valcour Island beyond another two weeks. Along with his letter to Gates, he sent another list of needed supplies, which he petulantly headed, "Articles which have been repeatedly wrote for." They included double-headed, grape-, and chain shot; iron for langrage (fragments fired like shrapnel from a cannon) and twenty-seven other items ranging from caulking irons to "50 swivels with monkey tails." The last two items were "Clothing for at least half the men in the fleet, who are naked," and "100 seamen (No land-lubbers)."

On October 2, a gale blew up out of the south that battered the ships at anchor and swung the *Royal Savage* into the *Providence*, forcing *Providence* to pay out the full length of her anchor cable to keep clear. The gale blew all through the next day before tapering off after dark. Then the rain set in.

On Sunday, October 6, around noon, the row galley *Washington* arrived, commanded by John Thatcher. Also on board was David Waterbury, whom Gates had appointed second in command of the fleet. Of greater interest to the men, the *Washington* also carried a barrel of rum for each gondola. An hour later the *Congress* joined the fleet.

At the time that the row galleys had sailed from Ticonderoga, Gates had not received Arnold's litany of complaints, so the letter that Waterbury carried did not address them. Rather, Gates told Arnold that the *Liberty* would be sailing the next day, and the fourth row galley, the *Gates*, was due at Ticonderoga from Skenesborough.

When Gates did receive Arnold's letter of October 1, his reply was terse and defensive. He assured Arnold that every sailor at Ticonderoga had been sent up and that those requested from New York had not arrived, and he didn't think they would. "[A]s to the Equipment of the Trumbull," he wrote, "I am not answerable for any Deficiency, General Waterbury, who had the Intire Management of Rigging and Arming The Gallies, will satisfy all your Questions of that Head." Every article that Arnold had requested had been put aboard the *Liberty*, Gates said, except those that were simply not available. He pointed out to Arnold that "where it is not to be had you, & the Princes of the Earth must go unfurnish'd."

Gates was concerned by Arnold's talk of abandoning Valcour Island and moving the fleet up the lake. He urged Arnold to consult with Waterbury and Wigglesworth on when best to come south, but was certain that the three officers' "Zeal, for the public Service, will not suffer You to return One Moment sooner than in prudence & Good Conduct you Ought to."

When Arnold replied on October 10, his tone was much more conciliatory. Though he expressed surprise that in the four months he had been asking for sailors, two hundred at least could not have been found, he did not blame Gates for that, but rather "the good People below." He expressed satisfaction with the clothes that Gates had sent, and discussed what ships might be built next for the defense of the lake.

Arnold assured Gates that he would consult with the other commanders. "We cannot at Present Determine how long it will be requisite to remain here," he wrote.

As it happened, the next day the British would determine that for him.

The British Underway

Commodore Douglas was mostly pleased with the fleet building at St. John's. He felt that the gondola, by which he most likely meant the *Loyal Convert*, "cuts a very good appearance." At the same time, design flaws in the radeau *Thunderer* were starting to show themselves. "The Radeau would be more formidable did she carry her Six Battering 24 pounders below a bit higher . . . ," the commodore observed.

By the end of September, the schooners *Maria* ("so called after lady Maria Carleton," Digby wrote) and *Carleton* had been reassembled after being taken nearly apart for transporting around the rapids. On September 27, they sailed from St. John's to Isle aux Noix, where they anchored to wait for the rest of the fleet. Thomas Pringle, in command of the fleet, chose *Maria* as his flagship.

Advance units of the army continued to move closer to the Americans. Brigadier General Simon Fraser's brigade moved about six miles upriver from Isle aux Noix to Rivière la Colle, while the 1st Brigade shifted from St. John's to Isle aux Noix. The Brunswick troops, under the overall command of Major General Friedrich Riedesel (spelled phonetically by the British as "Redhazel"), left Montreal and moved up to St. John's.

Preparing to cross the lake, Digby wrote, "We were all provided for the cold weather . . . with warm clothing such as under waistcoats, leggings, socks, &c, &c and smoking tobacco was counted a preservative of the health." This was in sharp contrast to the half-naked American troops they had driven from that place.

The radeau *Thunderer*, built new from the keel up, was finished about the same time as the schooners and prepared to sail. Two companies of the 29th Regiment were ordered on board, as well as fifty men from the Hessian Artillery, for a total of three hundred men, not including the sailors. There was apparently room for only 150 men below, because Lieutenant Hadden specified in his orderly book that half the men "must be supposed on Deck all night." Presumably they took turns. Hadden further noted that "The Stern will be for the Officers, and the forepart for the Sailors." Those instructions might have been necessary for soldiers, but not for the sailors, for whom it was standard shipboard protocol.

Thunderer's gun crews were made up of a mix of British and German troops, save for those manning the 12-pounders in the bow and stern, which were served entirely by Hessian artillerymen under the command of Captain Georg Pausch. Pausch and his men had only recently arrived in Canada with the second convoy of Hessians, and they were still learning. A few days before, Pausch had written in his journal, "This afternoon, at 5 o'clock, I practiced with the English Cannoniers firing with English cannon, and in the English fashion. It went off very well . . . Yet I do most sincerely wish I had my own cannons."

The crowded conditions on board *Thunderer*, however, made for uncomfortable living. It rained hard during the Germans' first night aboard, and Pausch had his men stand guard on deck in shifts so that each could get some rest below. Finding that there was no room even for his baggage, Pausch had it sent back to Montreal. "All the Englishmen," he wrote, "on account of this overcrowding were unpleasant companions."

With no wind the following day, *Thunderer* had to be kedged up the river. An anchor was lowered into a boat and set out ahead of the ship, then the ship was hauled up to the anchor and the process repeated. "This worked splendidly," Pausch reported, with the flat-bottomed radeau being particularly suited for such an evolution.

It soon became clear to everyone that there were too many men on board the radeau, and the Germans were off-loaded at Isle aux Noix. Pausch was given command of two of the gunboats crewed by British sailors, their cannon to be manned by his Hessian artillerymen. Before setting out, Pausch made certain that his men were provided with fourteen days' rations of salt meat and a German favorite, toasted or burned biscuit, which they called *Zweibach.*

By October 5, the entire British fleet, save for *Inflexible*, was ready to go. Lieutenant Digby, who had been sick, hitched a ride from Isle aux Noix to Rivière la Colle aboard the *Loyal Convert.* "The floating Battery (Thunderer), Maria and Carleton sailed with us," he wrote, "and our little voyage was pleasant." The *Maria*, with Burgoyne on board (who, according to Digby, was "idolized by the army"), managed to run aground but was towed off with no damage.

The fleet came to anchor at Rivière la Colle, about six miles south of Isle aux Noix, where the ships cleared for action and continued to wait for *Inflexible*'s arrival. On October 7 the army advanced even farther up the lake, with Fraser's brigade moving up to Point au Fer and the 1st Brigade advancing from Isle aux Noix to Rivière la Colle.

The planned order of ship and boat movements up the lake called for three small boats to go first as scouts, followed by the larger men-of-war in line of battle. Behind them would come the twenty or so gunboats mounting 24- or 12-pounders in their bows, then the grenadier companies in flat-bottomed boats. The rest of the army in bateaux would follow.

For some time the soldiers had been drilling at the oars and maneuvering their boats into formation. A single gun was the signal for them to form eight boats abreast; two guns meant that the boats should form in line ahead. "This had a pretty effect," Digby observed, "as our men were all expert at rowing."

Pretty it may have been, but the commanding officers soon realized that it was dangerous as well. If the American fleet somehow eluded the British men-of-war and got in among the boats, the rebels with their heavy cannons would slaughter the all-but-defenseless British and German soldiers. Instead it was decided that, in the event of a naval fight, the troops would be landed to await the outcome.

Autumn was advancing, and the leaves were well along in the change from summer green to fall reds, browns, and yellows, as Digby and his fellow soldiers pitched their tents on Point au Fer and waited for the *Inflexible* to come up. They feasted on deer and pigeon and enjoyed the stunning beauty of that part of the world.

By October 9, while Arnold, at Valcour Island, was beginning to think that the British would not come at all, the entire fleet, save for the big ship, was gathered at Windmill Point. Fully loaded, *Inflexible* drew too much water to navigate the river from St. John's. Her guns, eighteen 12-pounders weighing in total about twenty-seven tons, were sent up by boat, to be placed back on board once the sloop-of-war was in the lake, where "a ship of the line would have water sufficient."

Finally, on October 10, *Inflexible* was up with the fleet and ready to sail. She had been launched on September 29. German surgeon Wasmus, apparently a stranger to shipbuilding, marveled at the "sled-like machine" on which *Inflexible* slid down into the river. Once she was anchored and floating, "there sounded a cry of hurrah, done 3 times by the sailors and workmen."

The men who built *Inflexible* had reason to cheer; their accomplishment was nothing short of astounding. Even the task of dismantling, moving, and rebuilding the schooners paled in comparison to the extraordinary effort of putting *Inflexible* together.

The schooners were smaller, carried simple fore-and-aft rigs, and were already finished and fitted out before being dismantled. *Inflexible*, on the other hand, was no schooner but a fully rigged ship, square rigged on three masts, and she had been no more than a partially framed hull when she was taken down at Quebec and moved to St. John's.

Her keel had been laid there on September 5. Her frames were then set up, and she was planked inside and out, decked, and caulked. Then her hatches were put in place, her interior was fitted out, and twenty-four days after her keel was laid she was launched. It is unlikely that she had even her lower masts in place when she went into the water, but four days later she was completely rigged, shrouds and back-stays set up, ratlines hitched to the shrouds, yards crossed and sails bent on, running gear rove off. *Inflexible* was twenty-eight days from first spike to setting sail.

According to Douglas, the shipwrights' work was no more than twelve men's labor for sixteen days. The rest of the work was accomplished by sailors working under the supervision of Lieutenant John Schank.

Impressive as she was—Digby said, "it certainly was a noble sight to see such a vessel on a fresh water lake . . . "—one could argue whether she was worth the effort. Had Carleton put his resources toward finishing the other vessels more quickly, he would have been able to meet Arnold before the Americans had their row galleys finished, and he would have launched his attack up the lake with more time left in the campaigning season. But Carleton was ever cautious, and wanted the overwhelming strength that *Inflexible* represented, and so it was not until the second week in October that the British fleet set out.

With a fair wind, the ship, schooners, radeau, gondolas, gunboats, and longboats headed up the lake in search of their equally heterogeneous enemy, the only force between them and Fort Ticonderoga.

CHAPTER *33* *The Battle of Valcour Island*

THE AMERICANS knew they were coming.

From Tuesday, October 8, to Thursday the tenth, the wind had been out of the south, and the Americans who were huddled behind Valcour Island may have felt able to relax just a bit, knowing that the powerful British fleet could not get up the lake in the face of that wind.

Then, on the morning of October 11, the wind came around out of the north. It was a clear day, the finest kind of crisp autumn weather, the leaves on the hardwoods brilliant with color. The men on the gondolas and row galleys could see snow on the mountains to the west.

Valcour Bay, where the fleet had been anchored since September 24, was really just the channel between Valcour Island and the western shore of Lake Champlain, made wider by a shallow harbor on the island near its southern end. This area of water was just under a mile and a quarter at its widest, with good holding ground for the ships' anchors in water three to ten fathoms (eighteen to sixty feet) deep.

Despite the fleet's defensive, "back against the wall" position, the Americans were unlikely to get trapped in a dead end. Sailing directions for Valcour Island written a few years after the battle would say, "let the Wind blow from any Quarter, you may always Sail out upon the Lake." That was possible because the channel between Valcour and the mainland was deep enough along its entire length for ships to pass. Arnold had chosen well. His position was as close to holding entrenched high ground as one could get in a naval battle, with an escape route in the rear.

Valcour is not a particularly tall or steep island, but it is heavily wooded and tall enough that the American fleet was hidden from any ships coming down past Cumberland Head. By the same token, however, a lookout on Valcour Island was not in a good position to see up the lake toward Isle la Motte or the approaches from Canada. On the morning of October 11, therefore, Arnold sent out a guard boat, likely just before dawn, to keep an eye to the north.

Between seven and eight that morning, the guard boat was back, pulling hard for the fleet. The boat crew fired a gun as an alarm and reported the news for which Arnold and his men had been waiting for more than a month—the British fleet was underway.

"A most pleasing sight . . ."

On October 9 the British fleet had moved from Isle aux Noix to Point au Fer. Digby, still with the army at Point au Fer, described it as "a most pleasing sight to the Army. Their decks were all cleared and ready for immediate action." The British apparently were enjoying a northerly wind at their end of the lake, while it blew southerly by Valcour Island, not an unusual occurrence on Champlain. On October 10 the British were able to move up to the southern end of Isle la Motte.

Thomas Pringle, commodore of the fleet, had chosen the schooner *Maria*, commanded by Lieutenant John Starke, as his flagship. General Guy Carleton joined him on board, a decision that did not sit well with everyone. Digby, who was no great fan of Carleton's, wrote that "many blamed his hazarding himself on an element so much out of his line." What's more, with Pringle in command, there was really nothing for Carleton to do "except proving his courage," which Digby claimed no one doubted in any event.

It is not entirely clear whether the British knew the whereabouts of the American fleet, but Carleton did receive some intelligence regarding Arnold's position on the evening of October 10. Dr. Robert Knox, Carleton's personal physician and Inspector General of the Hospitals, who sailed with Carleton aboard *Maria*, claimed that Carleton was told that "Mr Arnold had a fleet of 16 ships in cumberland bay."

Lieutenant John Schank, in command of *Inflexible;* Edward Longcroft, who had been in command of the schooner *Brunswick* but now commanded the *Loyal Convert;* and Starke, of the *Maria*, claimed that Pringle "had information . . . the night before" that the American fleet was anchored behind Valcour Island. (Days after the battle, Thomas Pringle would write a brief and self-serving report in which he mentioned himself, Dacres of the *Carleton*, General Carleton, and no one else. That letter was printed in the *London Gazette*, the means by which officers' deeds were brought to public notice in England. The following year, after reading it, Lieutenants Schank, Starke, and Longcroft coauthored a scathing reply, refuting most of Pringle's claims and giving their version of events. Thus two of the most important accounts of the action from the British perspective are in complete disagreement—a dilemma for historians.)

Whether or not Carleton knew the exact location of the fleet, he certainly knew that Arnold was in the neighborhood. Through most of September, the American fleet had been conspicuous in its presence at the north end of the lake.

Carleton had intended originally to move his army up the lake with the fleet, landing the troops when a naval battle seemed imminent. Now, sure that Arnold was close, he revised that and opted to hunt down the American fleet and bring it to battle before embarking the bulk of his army in their vulnerable boats. Leaving Burgoyne at Point au Fer and Riedesel at St. John's, with the army split between those posts and Isle aux Noix, Carleton ordered the fleet to prepare to sail.

Relative Force

Along with its larger ships, the British fleet included twenty or so gunboats, each with a single gun in its bow, ranging from 9- to 24-pounders. Each gunboat was manned by seven artillerymen to work the gun and eleven sailors to work the boat, all under the command of an artillery officer. The boats each carried fifty round shot and thirty case shot, the latter being tin canisters filled with musket balls. Along with the gunboats were four longboats, also with carriage guns in the bow, and another twenty-four longboats carrying provisions.

This fleet was manned by eight officers, nineteen petty officers, and 670 seamen detached from the St. Lawrence fleet and the transports, a pool of skilled manpower that would have made Arnold swoon with envy.

Hadden reported that "a large Detachment of Savages under Major Carleton also moved with the Fleet in their Canoes." Major Carleton was Thomas Carleton, Guy Carleton's younger brother. He and his Indians were not expected to be part of a naval fight, but rather to occupy the adjacent shores and harass the Americans.

All told, the British fleet mounted a total of about eighty-nine guns on approximately thirty-four vessels. The Americans carried somewhat less, seventy-eight guns, not counting swivel guns, on fifteen vessels. But these numbers were deceiving, because the cumulative weight of the shot fired—the weight of metal, as it was known—was a crucial factor in naval strength, and there the British were far ahead of the Americans. The British guns were bigger, and altogether the fleet fired a weight of metal of more than a thousand pounds, whereas the American fleet fired just over six hundred.

The larger vessels of the American and British fleets, with their guns arranged in broadside, could bring only half their guns to bear at any one time. But the brunt of the fighting on the British side would be carried out by the gunboats, with their single guns forward, which could always bear on the enemy. For the gunboats there would be no disengaged side.

Arnold's gondolas each mounted three big guns. In their bows they carried 9- or 12-pounders, with a 9-pounder to port and another to starboard. It might have been possible for the bow gun and one broadside to find a target at the same time, but never all three. Thus more than a third of the American guns would not bear on the enemy during the fight, making the Americans' odds that much worse. The Americans, some of whom for months now had assumed that the British would never be able to match their force on the lake, were about to find out how wrong they were.

The British Invasion from the North

At first light the British fleet won their anchors and set sail. Captain Pausch and his Germans kept out of the way and watched as blue-jacketed British sailors laid out the running gear and sweated the halyards on board the two gunboats he now commanded, which he erroneously called "batteaux."

The gunboats, like Arnold's gondolas, were designed to move under sail or oar, but on the morning of October 11, "with favorable wind," Pausch wrote, they "got very early under sail. At 5 o'clock in the morning, we received orders to get in readiness for an engagement."

Pringle does not seem to have arranged the fleet in any particular order as they set sail up the lake. Perhaps he felt that the careful arrangement practiced earlier was no longer necessary, because they no longer had the army to protect.

Around half past nine the fleet passed Cumberland Head and looked into Cumberland Bay, where, according to Knox, "to our great mortification, we cou'd discover no ships." Whether they knew it or not, they were just seven miles from the American fleet and less than an hour from coming to grips with them.

The Battle Begins

After hearing the report from the guard boat's crew, Arnold sent a scouting party to the north end of Valcour Island to "See which way the fleet was a going . . . ," whether they would pass down the east side of Valcour Island, as he hoped, or swing around into the channel between the island and the shore and come up behind the Americans.

Arnold then called a meeting with his chief officers—General David Waterbury, second in command, and Colonel Edward Wigglesworth, third—who joined Arnold aboard the schooner. Arnold asked for opinions on how the battle should be fought.

Waterbury contended that the "fleet ought to Com to Saill," stand out of the harbor, and meet the enemy, "Not Ly Where We Shold Be Surrounded." Waterbury's concern, apparently, was that the British would divide their force. One division might approach between the island and the shore and attack the American fleet from astern, while another would come the other way around the island and hit the Americans from the front. The American fleet would be trapped between them, caught in a cross fire with no escape route.

It was a valid concern, and the British may well have contemplated such a move. Hadden would later complain that racing into battle lost to the British fleet "the opportunity of going in at the upper end of the Island and attacking the whole at once." (Here and in other places, Hadden confused upper and lower on the lake. He meant that the British lost the chance to go in at the lower, northern end of the island and get behind the American fleet.) But Arnold had to weigh that possibility against the near certainty that his fleet would be crushed in a ship-to-ship duel on open water. Sallying forth would mean throwing away all the advantages of their position in Valcour Bay and gain them nothing. If the British did try to come up behind, the scouts at the north end of the island would warn him well before they arrived.

Arnold declined Waterbury's suggestion, and the council of war was over. It was time to prepare to fight. Arnold moved from the schooner *Royal Savage* to the galley *Congress* and made that vessel his flagship. He also sent Wigglesworth out in a yawlboat to observe the enemy's movements. Then he ordered the *Royal Savage* and the galleys *Trumbull* and *Washington* under way and formed his gondolas into a defensive line.

"One of the Enemies Vessels was discover'd . . ."

The first contact between the British and American fleets occured around eleven that morning as the British fleet was passing down the east side of Valcour Island. Dr. Robert Knox was aboard the schooner *Carleton*, and, in a letter describing the battle, he would make the somewhat dubious claim to have been the first to spot an American ship at the south end of Valcour Island. That vessel, which Knox and the others saw, was the *Royal Savage*.

Why Arnold sent out the schooner and galleys is unclear, unless it was to lure the British into a fight and prevent them from simply bypassing the fleet. At ten o'clock Wigglesworth returned and reported that the British fleet was running down the east side of Valcour Island. "[A]t my return," Wigglesworth wrote, "the three galleys and two schooners were under sail standing across the lake, between the island

and the main." No sooner had they seen the British fleet coming than they hauled their wind and began to beat back to the American line of battle in Valcour Bay.

Not only did Pringle give no particular instructions regarding the sailing order of the fleet, he seems to have given no orders regarding the manner in which his fleet would attack. Rather, like a pack of hounds, they all went in chase of the Americans. "The pursuit of this vessel was without order or regularity . . . ," Hadden would later recall, lending credence to Pringle's officers' accusations of "neglect . . . proceeding from want of capacity or want of inclination."

To get at the Americans, the British had to run past the south end of Valcour Island, come around, and work their way to windward in the face of the rebels' fire, which is what made Arnold's position such a good one. The gunboats came in first. Because they were able to move under oar, they were not as hampered by the strong northerly wind as were the larger ships, and they plunged into the fight with their bow guns blasting away.

The galleys *Congress*, *Washington*, and *Trumbull*, rigged with weatherly lateen sails, managed to make it back to Valcour Bay and take their place anchored in the line of battle before the shooting started. Not so *Royal Savage*. The schooner, never a good sailor, was struggling to get to windward, just like the British ships. Pascal De Angelis, serving under his stepfather, Seth Warner, on board the *Trumbull*, was three days shy of his fourteenth birthday. He watched as the schooner "Misstayed Several times and could not Git up to the Line."

Missing stays—failing to turn her bow through the wind while attempting to tack—the schooner fell more and more to leeward, right into the fire from the gunboats. The well-trained British and German artillerymen loaded and ran their big guns out, firing at close range into the struggling American schooner. *Inflexible*, too, according to Schank, managed to hit her with her 18-pounders.

As *Royal Savage* tried to gather way, her mast was damaged and her rigging cut up, making her even more unmanageable. Twelve- and 24-

pound round shot slammed into her hull—a hull not built to stand that sort of abuse—and continued to tear her up aloft. Unable to get up with the American fleet, mauled by the gunboats, the schooner was run hard aground on the southwestern tip of Valcour Island by her captain, David Hawley.

With the schooner lost, Hawley and most of his men jumped overboard and splashed ashore. The British gunboats turned their fire on the escaping men, but in doing so made themselves a target. Hadden, in command of one of the gunboats, wrote, "this firing at one object drew us all in a cluster and four of the Enemies Vessels getting under weight to support the *Royal Savage* fired upon the boats with success."

The gunboats were just asking to be decimated in that formation. The officer commanding the boats (who, unlike Pringle, was exerting tactical control) gave orders for the boats to form a line across the bay, facing the crescent-shaped American line of battle. That maneuver, Hadden wrote, "was soon effected tho' under the Enemies whole fire and unsupported, all the King's Vessels having dropped too far to Leeward."

It was still before noon when the fight devolved into a brutal slugfest between the American ships and the British gunboats and longboats. "Our attack with about 27 batteaux . . . ," wrote Pausch, who, with Hadden, was part of the line, "became very fierce; and after getting to close quarters, very animated."

Arnold wrote, "the engagement, became General, & very warm." As the gunboat fleet jockeyed, they found that they were most effective keeping about seven hundred yards off the American line. At that distance their big guns were extremely effective. Any nearer and the American grapeshot could sweep through the tight-packed crews.

Hadden referred to the fight as "unequal combat," and no doubt it appeared so to the men in the open boats, facing the gondolas and galleys, the schooner *Revenge,* and the sloop *Enterprise.* But it was not as unequal as it seemed. The gunboats had nearly thirty guns at work, some of them 24-pounders. The American fleet had no guns of that size. Their biggest guns were 18-pounders, and they had only four of those.

Moreover, not all the American guns would bear; probably no more than forty-eight or so could be brought into action. De Angelis observed, "the Enemy Fleet attaced ours with Great fury and we Returned the fire with as Great Sperit and Viger and the most Desparate Canannading."

The fight, for the moment, was nearly even, and that was entirely because Arnold's positioning of his fleet had deprived the British of the use of their most powerful ships, the ships that Carleton had insisted on spending his entire campaign season building.

CHAPTER *34* *"The Battle was Verrey Hot"*

WHILE THE BRITISH gunboats kept up their furious duel with the Americans, the rest of the British fleet struggled to get their guns into play.

No eighteenth-century vessel, not even a schooner, was much good at clawing to windward. Doing so was even more problematic for a square-rigged ship such as *Inflexible*, and the problem was made worse by the confined space in which the fleet had to sail. The ships lost speed and momentum and were set farther to leeward every time they tacked or wore around. (To "wear ship" was to shift tacks by means of jibing—turning away from the wind—rather than tacking—turning into it. Though this maneuver gave up more distance to windward, it was sometimes the only way to coax a clumsy sailing vessel from one tack to the other.) The tacks had to follow in rapid succession on the narrow lake, so it was nearly impossible to make progress into the wind.

The ship least able to work to windward was also the most powerful in the British fleet—the radeau *Thunderer*. She was a fast ship down wind, typical of a flat-bottomed vessel. Hadden would later record the ship making more than nine knots in a fair breeze, an impressive speed. But a flat-bottomed vessel is particularly inept working to windward, when a deep keel is needed to keep a ship from slipping sideways down wind. *Thunderer*, having run past Valcour Island, simply could not get back.

Lieutenant John Enys, who was on board the radeau, wrote, "our fleet . . . were obliged to tack in order to get into the Bay. This rendered the Vessel I was on board totally useless. . . . We fired some few Shot at the time we first Saw their fleet but believe it might have been just well lett alone."

Lieutenant Edward Longcroft managed to work the *Loyal Convert* up into the fight, perhaps with the sweeps, she being essentially a large gondola. Passing to the east of the line of British gunboats, Longcroft inserted his little ship into the middle of the furious gunfire, but the lieutenant had more in mind than simply joining the line of battle. Acting on his own initiative, apparently without orders, Longcroft meant to take back the *Royal Savage.*

The *Loyal Convert* crawled slowly through the wicked fire of the American guns. After taking the ship as close to the island as he could under sweeps, Longcroft and his boarding party clambered into the ship's boat and pulled for the stranded schooner.

Not all of the *Royal Savage*'s American crew had disappeared onto Valcour Island, but those still aboard quickly surrendered as Longcroft and his men swarmed over the ship's low sides. The British sailors grabbed the rammers and sponges abandoned by the Americans, manned the *Savage*'s 6- and 4-pounder broadside guns, and turned them on the American fleet.

Jahiel Stewart, watching the action on *Royal Savage* from the sloop *Enterprise,* saw "the Regulars boarded her and fire from her to our fleet & the battle was verrey hot." The American fleet now concentrated its fire on the *Royal Savage,* which no doubt made a better target than the gunboats. Longcroft and his men continued to fire back as grape- and round shot swept past them, tearing up bulwarks, masts, rigging, and men. Meanwhile, Longcroft sent men into the great cabin to see whether anything there was worth taking.

Finally, Longcroft could see that his position was untenable. He had too few men to refloat the *Royal Savage,* and no help was coming. Dead and wounded were strewn across the shattered deck, and the *Loyal Convert,* which had not anchored, was getting set farther and farther downwind. Half the men in the boarding party had been killed by enemy shot. Longcroft and his survivors abandoned the American schooner and climbed back into the longboat. Once again they rowed through the storm of gunfire to return to their own vessel.

While the ships and boats battled one another with their great guns, Major Carleton's Indians landed on Valcour Island and on the mainland and began to fire on the Americans with muskets. The long range prevented them from doing any real damage, but they may have wounded or killed some of the ships' crews, as well as some of the stranded crew of the *Royal Savage*. Gunners on board the *Washington* swept the woods with cannister shot to drive them off.

Still the larger vessels continued their struggle to get into the fight. At one point the *Inflexible* clawed within range of the line of gunboats "and fired several broadsides with much effect . . . ," according to Schank. But she could not maintain her position due to the northerly wind, and for some reason did not come to anchor, and soon she was once again out of the fight.

The American Fleet

Under the continuous, numbing blasts of heavy guns, the scream of grapeshot passing overhead, and the splintering, jarring crush of round shot striking home, the American fleet was taking an awful pounding.

Benedict Arnold paced the gun deck of the *Congress*, peering out at the enemy's line through the blinding, choking cannon smoke. Feeling the "want of Seamen & Gunners," Arnold personally aimed most of the guns "with good execution," he felt.

At the center of the line, more conspicuous than the gondolas, *Congress* attracted much of the incoming shot. With each blast of her broadside guns, the little ship shuddered along her whole length. Passing round shot gouged two sections from her mainmast and damaged the main yard. Iron balls slammed into her sides, smashing holes through the green wood in a dozen places.

But the other ships in the fleet did not get off much easier. The gondola *New York* was swept again and again by enemy fire until all her officers save Captain John Reed were killed. When one of the gun captains touched his slow match to the touchhole of his aging gun, the barrel burst, sending shards of thick, hot metal whipping through the closely packed men. Sergeant Jonas Holden was injured in the arm and side, and Lieutenant Thomas Rogers was killed. The explosion must have done little to encourage the men working the remaining two guns.

The *Philadelphia* was struck again and again until, finally, she began to sink at anchor. The *Washington*, like *Congress*, was extensively cut up, "hulled a Number of Times, her Main Mast Shot thro. . . . both Vessells are very leaky & want repairing." *Washington*'s captain, John Thatcher, and master were wounded, and the first lieutenant was killed.

The *Trumbull*, too, took her share of the enemy's shot. Round shot struck the galley's mainmast about halfway up, shattering the wooden spar. The top half leaned over until the remaining bits of standing rigging snapped under the load, then the mast plunged to the deck below. Its lower half, still standing, was badly smashed, the shot having "shivered it almost to peases."

The *Trumbull* also received a 12-pound shot in the stern and twenty to thirty other hits. Splinters of white oak were blown from her sides to become airborne projectiles, as dangerous as the enemy's shot. According to young Pascal De Angelis, "our Wounded were Leiut. Camfeild. Boatswain Cone. Gunner Simmons. James Timberlake a seamon Sam[l]. Anderson and 8 more Slightly Wounded But Timberlake and Anderson are dead." Still the crew worked the guns as fast as they were able. By the end of the fight, *Trumbull* was all but out of round shot for her 12- and 18-pounders.

Jahiel Stewart was aboard the sloop *Enterprise*, which was serving as the hospital ship. Boat crews pulled through the gunfire collecting the wounded and taking them to the sloop. Stewart recorded in his journal, "they brought the wounded abord of us the Dockters Cut of great many legs and arms and See Seven men threw overboard that died with their wounds."

As green as they were, entirely inexperienced in naval combat, the Americans put up a terrific fight. Pausch, a seasoned professional artilleryman, was impressed. "The cannon of the Rebels were well served," he wrote, "for, as I saw afterwards, our ships were pretty well mended and patched up with boards and stoppers."

The Schooner Carleton

For two hours the gunboats traded fire with the Americans before one of the British fleet's larger vessels could work its way up. It was the schooner *Carleton*, under the command of Lieutenant James Dacres. Tacking up to the fight, she passed through the British gunboats near the Valcour Island end of the line and most likely came to anchor about five to six hundred yards from the enemy.

The *Carleton* then opened up with her broadside of six 6-pounders, and "immediately received the Enemies whole fire which was continued without intermission for about an hour." The schooner was closer to the Americans than the gunboats and made a larger target, and the rebel gunners took full advantage of that. Just like Longcroft on board the *Royal Savage* earlier, the *Carleton* endured a terrible beating.

"[O]ne of the Regular Skooners Came up verrey bold . . . ," Stewart wrote, adding that "we Cut her Rigen most all away & bored her threw and threw."

Soon after the *Carleton* engaged, Lieutenant Dacres was wounded and knocked unconscious. Dacres had brought two midshipmen with him from the *Blonde*. The first, Robert Brown, had his right arm shot off, but incredibly he survived. With Dacres and Brown wounded, the second midshipman assumed command. This was Edward Pellew, just a teenager, who would go on to become one of England's greatest frigate captains during the Napoleonic Wars and end his days as Admiral Viscount Exmouth. As it happened, Benedict Arnold nearly deprived the British navy of one of its greatest officers.

Pellew's first act was to stop the men from throwing Dacres, whom they thought dead, overboard. Pellew continued to fight, keeping his men at the guns despite the withering fire from the Americans. The *Carleton*'s deck resembled a slaughterhouse, with half her crew killed or wounded. When her battered hull began to fill with water, Pellew knew that the schooner could not remain where she was.

The midshipman most likely ordered the anchor cable slipped and sail set. The sailors not working the guns sorted out the torn rigging and shattered gear and hoisted away on the halyards, but in attempting to get under way, the *Carleton* hung in stays, pointing into the wind like a weathervane, unable to turn. Pellew raced out onto the bowsprit, completely exposed to the enemy's fire, and hauled the jib over in an attempt to get the schooner's head around.

Even that was not enough. Luckily, Schank, on board the *Inflexible*, saw the *Carleton*'s danger and sent two of his boats to tow her off. Passing through the line of gunboats and the heavy cross fire, the *Inflexible*'s boats took up the *Carleton*'s towline and pulled the schooner's head around to tow her south and out of the direct fire.

Before they could get clear, however, the towline was parted by enemy shot. Pellew again risked his life going forward to pass a new hawser. At last the *Carleton* was towed out of range. She was the only one of the big British vessels to closely engage that day, and she paid a heavy price for the honor.

"How do you like a sea fight?"

Once again the sailors and artillerymen on board the gunboats carried the fight for the British navy. The Hessian Artillery officer Lieutenant Dufais was commanding the second of the two gunboats under Pausch's command. As the Americans turned their attention back to the gunboats, a round shot drove through Dufais's powder magazine, and the gunpowder exploded.

Pausch was sighting down his gun, taking aim on the Americans, when his sergeant called his attention to the blast. In the smoke that hung like a blanket over the combatants, Pausch could not tell who was aboard the gunboat. As he watched, another explosion sent an ammunition chest flying through the air, and when the wind rolled the smoke away he recognized his own men "by the cords around their hats."

The gunboat was on fire, and Pausch turned his own boat out of the line to rescue the crew. By the time he got there, Dufais's gunboat was sinking fast. Another gunboat, commanded by an English artilleryman named Smith, also drew up to the foundering boat and took off Dufais and two others, while the rest of Dufais's crew—nine cannoneers and nine sailors—crowded into Pausch's boat.

With those eighteen men, along with Pausch's crew of ten cannoneers, ten sailors, one sergeant, one drummer, and one boy, the gunboat was dangerously overloaded. "In what a predicament was I?" Pausch wrote. "Every moment I was in danger of drowning with all on board, and in the company, too, of those I had just rescued."

But by then it was around five in the afternoon. Evening was coming on, and the fighting would soon end for the day.

By several accounts, the flagship *Maria* managed to get off a few guns at the rebel fleet, but for most of the battle she remained about a mile astern of the gunboats, near the western shore of the lake. At first she was hove to under topsails, then Commodore Pringle gave orders for Lieutenant Starke, her commanding officer, to bring her to anchor. Starke, furious about being kept so far from the fight, refused. It was bad enough that they were making no effort to get *Maria* into the fight. To anchor so far away was, according to Starke, "an act truly unbecoming on such an occasion."

Pringle, in his official report, wrote that "the Carleton schooner . . . by much perseverance, at last got up to [the gunboat's] assistance," but "none of the other vessels of the fleet could then get up." This, however, was hotly disputed by Schank and Longcroft, who insisted that they had joined the fight and openly wondered why Pringle had not.

The *Maria*, they claimed, "was the best sailor" in the fleet, and certainly before the fight the schooner had been considered the most weatherly of the British vessels. That was perhaps why Pringle had chosen her for flagship over the more powerful *Inflexible*. It does seem odd, therefore, that the *Carleton* had been able to work her way up to the fight but the *Maria* had not. The disgruntled officers wrote that Pringle "was the only person in the fleet who showed no inclination to fight." Their implication was clear; they thought that Pringle was a coward.

According to Knox, at about one that afternoon, just at the time when, in Pausch's words, "this naval battle began to get very serious," General Carleton expressed an opinion that the *Maria* was not close enough to the action. At that moment an 18-pound round shot whistled over the boom on which Knox and Carleton were leaning. Carleton turned to Knox and asked, "Well, Doctor, how do you like a sea fight?" But the *Maria* never moved closer.

The First Day's Fighting Ends

By dusk the British gunboats were nearly out of ammunition. They and the American fleet had been pounding away at one another without letup for six hours. For all that, the British crews suffered only twenty casualties, many of them from the explosion on the German boat, which was the only vessel lost. Hadden credited the gunboats' low profile for their remaining largely unscathed.

Pringle, seeing no reason to continue the fight, consulted with Carleton, and the two officers agreed to withdraw the gunboats and the *Carleton*. Pringle implied in his report that he ordered the boats to pull back, though the three officers who challenged him claimed that his signals "were confused and not understood" and that it was Carleton's aide-de-camp, acting on his own, who gave the order.

However it happened, the gunboats began to break off the engagement and fall back to a point just beyond the range of the American guns. As the wind eased, the *Thunderer* was at last able to come up within range. Pausch noted the effort of his Germans manning the howitzers, writing, "Any way, the two 4 pounders did their best, in firing at the frigates of the enemy."

As the British withdrew, Carleton sent a party on board the stranded *Royal Savage* to set her on fire in case the Americans had any thoughts of towing her off. Soon after, the fire reached her magazine and she exploded, and what was left of her continued to burn through the night.

Pringle, by his own account, ordered the boats and ships to "anchor in a line as near as possible to the Rebels, that their retreat might be cut off . . ." Schank and his fellow officers scorned the result. They claimed that the *Maria* weighed anchor and shifted to a spot half a mile from the place where she had been anchored during the battle, with *Inflexible* anchored beside her and *Carleton* even farther away. With the vessels arranged in that way, the right flank of the British line was to the east of Petite Island, at the southern tip of Valcour. To the west was a gap at least a mile wide between the left flank of the British line and the western shore of the lake.

Hadden wrote that "the Boats having received a small supply of Ammunition were unaccountably order'd to Anchor under cover of a small Island without the opening of the Bay."

"We Come by them undiſcovered . . ."

As the fighting tapered off, the battered gondola *Philadelphia* filled with water and sank. Captain Rue and the survivors among his crew climbed on board the *Washington*, which was in only slightly better shape. Incredibly, *Philadelphia* was the only American vessel lost, though all the fleet had been severely mauled. Arnold's initial estimate of his casualties was about sixty men out of 760, an 8 percent casualty rate.

Arnold called a council of war with Waterbury and Wigglesworth. Their situation was grim—"every Vessells Ammunition being Nearly three forths spent. & the Enenmies greatly Superior to us in Ships, & Men . . . " was how Arnold described it. Their battered fleet would not withstand another pounding such as it had endured that day, and there was no question that dawn would bring a resumption of the fight, this time—in all probability—with the larger British vessels engaged.

The only choice, Arnold felt, was to retreat, to slip away, and Waterbury and Wigglesworth agreed. It was a bold and risky idea, just the sort of thing that appealed to Arnold. The question remained, which way to go—north around Valcour Island, or south, straight through the enemy's anchored fleet?

Several factors came into consideration. The wind was dying but still northerly, and that would make it more difficult for the fleet to go north, requiring the vessels to use sweeps alone and no sail. What's more, Arnold most likely did not care to feel his way around the north end of the island in the dark. His choice was to go right through the British fleet.

Wigglesworth, in *Trumbull*, would lead the way. About seven that evening, word went to the ships of the fleet. De Angelis wrote, "about half after 7 oclock We Received orders from General Arnold to Get Ready and Proceed up through the enemies fleet and Lead the van

With Cornal Wigglesworth on Board and Carry a Lanthorn att our Starn."

At about half past eight, the *Trumbull* weighed anchor, set her shredded foresail, and ran out the sweeps so the weary men could row, moving the galley faster than she could sail in the fading wind. "It being calm," wrote Wigglesworth, "we row'd out clear of the Enemy without being discovered."

They went about their work as quietly as they could, with orders given in low voices and every evolution carried out with care so that no sudden noise would alert the enemy. (Hadden would report that the oars of Arnold's vessels were muffled—wrapped in canvas where they passed through the tholepins—but how he knew that, other than by guessing, is uncertain.) To the Americans' advantage, everyone's hearing on both sides had undoubtedly been dulled by the incessant and numbing blasts of the guns.

One by one the American vessels fell in, sailing and rowing along the western shore of the lake. Behind *Trumbull* went the gondolas in a ragged line, the men pulling wordlessly at the long sweeps, the awkward boats moving silently through water strewn with wreckage and the bodies of the dead.

On board the *Enterprise*, Stewart wrote, "we histed [hoisted] Sails & put out our oars & maid all the Speed we could and they did not give us one gun nor we Did not fier one at them." With each vessel following the shaded stern lantern of the one before, they moved undetected through the British lines. In the darkness, the *Enterprise* managed to go aground, but she was quickly hauled off and got under way again.

Last of all followed the galleys *Washington* and *Congress*, with Waterbury and Arnold on board. Arnold had shifted his flag to *Congress* but had not had time to shift anything else, and now he could only watch as his papers, clothes, and personal effects went up in flames in the great cabin of the *Royal Savage*. He did not know that Longcroft's boarding party had collected his papers, and they were now in British hands.

In his report, Pringle would claim that his effort to keep the Americans at bay was "frustrated by the extreme obscurity of the night." No one else made mention of poor visibility, however, though the night was dark and moonless. Perhaps the still-burning *Royal Savage* impaired British night vision, but in fact Pringle's poor positioning of his fleet was the chief factor allowing Arnold and his ships to escape. Certainly Schank, Starke, and Longcroft put the blame squarely on Pringle, claiming that it was "not . . . the extreme obscurity" but the mile-wide gap between the left flank of the British line and the western shore of the lake that allowed the enemy to wriggle free.

Hadden, an artillery officer and landsman and therefore more disinterested than the disgruntled lieutenants, wrote of the Americans' retreat, "this, the former position of the Gun Boats wou'd probably have prevented." Had Pringle arranged his ships in the manner he claimed, the Americans could not have slipped through undetected.

Throughout the dark hours, the British sailors and artillerymen slept at quarters, ready to resume the fight at any alarm. But when dawn came at last, they saw to their astonishment that there would be no fight. The Americans were gone.

CHAPTER 35 *South Wind and Open Water*

HADDEN, FOR ONE, was impressed. He wrote, magnanimously, "This retreat did great honor to Gen'l Arnold who acted as Admiral of the Rebel Fleet." The mere reference to Arnold by his military title, and not "Mr.," displayed more respect than the British were generally wont to give. If Carleton and the rest were inclined to praise Arnold for his bold escape, however, they kept it to themselves.

Arnold's intent was simply to put as much distance as possible between the British fleet and his own. He hoped to make it to Crown Point, where he could be resupplied with ammunition for another stand.

The dying northerly breeze on the evening of the battle was an indication that a wind shift was coming, and as the Americans sailed and rowed through the dark, it did. Wigglesworth wrote, "At 12 o'Clock the wind breezed up at So.[south]," dead foul for the fleet. Suddenly the Americans' tortured escape became that much harder.

The row galley *Washington*, bringing up the rear, had the hardest time of it. Waterbury wrote, "the Wind Came Right a hed and So I Went to turning to Windward all Night and I did Not Gain any for My Vesel Was Very Dull." By "turning to Windward," of course, Waterbury meant tacking, but he was able to make little progress against the wind. The *Washington*—probably never the nimblest of vessels, particularly close hauled—was even clumsier with her rigging and sails shot up and water leaking into her battered hull.

The next morning, October 12, between about ten and eleven o'-clock, the *Washington*'s sails gave out entirely. The bolt ropes—reinforcements around the edges of the sails—had been shot through, and with those gone, the sails could not handle the pressure of the wind and split "from foot to hed."

The *Trumbull*, which had led the way through the British fleet, passed Schuyler's Island in the morning and continued south, coming to anchor at Ligonier Point, about six miles beyond, around ten o'-clock. The *Trumbull* had made good time, certainly better than the *Washington*, though, like the rest of the fleet, she had suffered a beating. At Ligonier Point, Wigglesworth decided to "wait for the fleet & stop our leak & sew out M$^{n.}$ Mast, which was shot in two."

The rest of the surviving American fleet came to anchor at Schuyler's Island, the sailing vessels arriving first. The battered gondolas, with their bone-tired crews rowing against the southerly wind, arrived piecemeal during the day. The *Washington* was among the last to limp into the anchorage. Schuyler's Island was just ten miles south of Valcour, but it had taken the fleet more than twelve hours to get there, working against the stiff wind gusting over their bows.

Once at anchor, Arnold penned a note to Gates informing him of the action and the mauling the British had inflicted. "On the whole I think we have had a Very fortunate escape, & have great reason to return, our humble, & hearty thanks to Almighty God for preserving. & delivering so many of us from, our more than Savage Enemies." He reported his intention to get to Crown Point as quickly as he could, asking that Gates send ammunition to that post and dispatch a dozen well-manned bateaux to help tow the fleet in case the wind persisted southerly.

Arnold did not wish to remain at Schuyler's Island any longer than necessary to stop the ships' leaks as best they could and repair the *Washington*'s sails. From where they rode at anchor, the Americans could see the British fleet under way, sailing hard to get up with them and continue the battle.

By that time, however, Arnold's men had been awake more than thirty hours, during which they had fought desperately for six hours without intermission, then spent the night sailing and rowing to escape their enemy. The sailing vessels *Enterprise* and *Revenge*, whose crews likely had done less rowing than the others (and in the case of the hospital ship *Enterprise*, no fighting), were probably the first to get under way again. They drew abreast of the *Trumbull*, still anchored at Ligonier Point, around sunset.

Arnold, in the *Congress*, was under way again by two that afternoon, but the *Washington* did not get under way until a little before sunset, and then only slowly. Around that time, Wigglesworth, aboard the *Trumbull*, reported that the two galleys were "about 2 Legs. [two leagues, or six miles] to Leeward."

The gondolas were in bad shape. Lightly built to begin with, they had been shot up and now were starting to come apart. Sometime during the previous night, the *Spitfire* had sunk, and the *New Jersey* was taking on water fast. By the morning after the battle, with the British fleet coming up on them, it had been clear that not all the gondolas were going to escape. Bayze Wells, aboard the *Providence*, wrote, "the Enemy Came hard again∫t us So that we ware Oblig^d to Leve three Gondolas and make the be∫t of our way with boats."

Unable to sail against the southerly wind that persisted throughout the day of October 12, the remaining gondolas "made thare E∫cape this Day by Rowing all night," their second night at the oars. Around midnight the *Boston* passed *Trumbull*, still at anchor and making repairs. An hour later the *Providence* likewise passed the galley, and her captain, Isaiah Simonds, informed Wigglesworth "that the Enemy had pursued us & had taken 1 gondola, viz, Capt. Grimes," of the *New Jersey*. The report was a bit premature. The *New Jersey*, which was taking on water fast, had been abandoned by her American crew but would not be discovered by the British for another day.

The *Trumbull* got under way at last around one-thirty on the morning of October 13. Standing off the New York side of the lake on a starboard tack, she crossed to the eastern shore. It was the only course she could sail. Once again the wind had increased, still from the south, exactly the direction the Americans were trying to go.

Frustrated Pursuit

At daybreak on October 12, the British were more than a little surprised to find only flotsam bobbing in Valcour Bay. Knox, aboard the flagship *Maria*, wrote, "to our utter astonishment under the cover of ye night Mr Arnold sailed thro' a part of the fleet, and in the morning we saw them 3 leagues ahead."

The same fresh southerly breeze that hampered the Americans' flight to Crown Point also frustrated the British pursuit. The wind was moderate at first, and, after weighing anchor and making sail, the British fleet was able to beat into it—and, according to Hadden, made considerable progress in the chase.

That did not last, however. The wind continued to build, kicking up a severe chop on the lake. Even a landsman—artillery officer Lieutenant John Enys, on board the *Thunderer*—recognized that conditions were not good. The *Inflexible*, he wrote, was "in Some danger," though he did not know the reason. (He may have overheard the sailors discussing it and missed the technical nuance.)

The problem with the *Thunderer* was more obvious. The radeau carried leeboards, which resembled side-mounted swing keels, on her port and starboard sides. Lowering the leeward-side leeboard helped to keep the vessel from drifting sideways, but, according to Enys, the leeboards carried away, which made the radeau heel hard in the rising wind and slide rapidly off to leeward. The water began to pour "into her lower parts," perhaps through her gunports, which were only four and a half feet above the waterline. It was soon clear that *Thunderer* would not be beating to weather in that kind of wind.

The rest of the British fleet, the schooners and the *Loyal Convert*, did their best to get up the lake. With their sails sheeted tight and straining in the wind, they tacked south, their bluff bows smacking into the chop, sending sheets of cold lake water flying aft and making the vessels stagger and shudder along their whole lengths as if they were once again firing broadsides at an enemy.

Finally, "the violence of the wind and a great swell" forced the ships to come to anchor. The Americans were in full view only ten miles away, yet still beyond reach. The only comfort for the British was knowing that the southerly wind would probably prevent the Americans from getting away.

The Death of the Fleet

All through the dark hours of the morning of October 13, the American fleet slogged south to Crown Point. Sometime during the night the wind began to moderate, which allowed them to make better progress. *Congress* made ten miles over the ground during the night before she, along with the *Enterprise* and perhaps some others of the fleet, came to anchor again.

About an hour after sunrise, the British fleet was in sight. Stewart, on board the *Enterprise*, wrote that "we manned all our oars with three men to an oar and the generals boat Came up and ordered us to make all the Speed we could to ty [Ticonderoga]."

Congress was just twenty-eight miles north of Crown Point, and *Trumbull* was closer still. Despite having been the last to get under way the previous night, *Trumbull* was farther up the lake than the other two row galleys. Wigglesworth reported, "In the morning on Sunday, 13th, the Hospital Sloop & Revenge were ahead & the two galleys in the rear & the rest of the gondolas rowing up in Shore & the Enemy's fleet in chase of us, the wind dying away."

Arnold sent a boat to *Trumbull* and ordered Wigglesworth to wait for the rest of the fleet to come up, most likely so that the galley could serve as an escort for the slow, vulnerable gondolas. Wigglesworth did so by "stretching across the lake," tacking back and forth across the lake as the other vessels closed with him.

The *Washington* had spent the night rowing and sailing up the lake. Sunrise found her about eight miles south of Schuyler's Island, halfway between a cluster of four small islands called Four Winds Islands or The Brothers, and about two miles astern of Arnold and *Congress*. The *Washington*, "a dul Sailer" and leaking fast, was the rearmost of the American fleet. The rest of the ships, Waterbury observed, were scattered over a distance of about seven miles as they raced pell-mell for the presumed safety of Crown Point.

And the British were close behind.

During the night of October 12, the British fleet had come to anchor, unable to make way against the strong southerly wind. Early in the morning of the thirteenth, however, they, like the Americans, found the weather beginning to moderate. Hadden wrote that "the Fleet proceeded, the Boats using their oars to make head against the Wind." A number of the American ships had anchored, under the assumption that the British were also at anchor. "Tho' the British Fleet gained but little by a contrary conduct," Hadden wrote, "that little enabled them to overtake the Enemy next day."

Arnold's fleet fell victim that day to the capricious winds of Lake Champlain. Soon after sunrise, Arnold observed that the "Enemy's Fleet were very little way above Schuyler's Island, the Wind breezed up to the Southward so that we gained very little by beating or rowing, at the same time the Enemy took a fresh Breeze from the N.E." In other words, while the American fleet was bucking contrary southerly winds, the British, just twelve miles or so north, were getting a favorable northerly breeze that was driving them toward their enemy.

As the sun climbed above the Green Mountains, the men on board the *Washington* found the British disturbingly close, just three to four miles astern and "a Going three feet to our one." With the galley "So Much torn and dul," Waterbury did not see much chance of getting away. He dispatched his ship's boat to Arnold to ask the general's permission to send the *Washington*'s wounded up to Ticonderoga by boat, then run *Washington* ashore and blow her up.

Arnold sent back word that Waterbury should by no means destroy his ship. He urged Waterbury to get up to Split Rock as quickly as he could, and there the fleet would make a stand.

By this time the northerly wind that had brought the British up had reached the American fleet as well, and Waterbury tried to make the most of it. He had his men wrestle out two square sails that had been meant for the gondolas, and set them as topsails above his ragged lateen foresail and mainsail.

It did no good; the British schooners and the *Inflexible* were just too fast with the wind astern. The chase went on for several hours, and the *Washington* managed to make it about five miles south of Split Rock before the enemy began to fire into her.

Waterbury could not fire back. He had brought his ship close by the eastern shore of the lake, and if he turned to port in order to bring his stern guns to bear, he would run aground. Turning to starboard to bring his broadsides to bear would have allowed the British to catch up that much quicker.

It was a moot point, in any event. *Washington* had taken such a beating that her weakened sides would not stand up to the recoil of her cannons. Waterbury wrote that the galley "was so Shatered She was Not able to Bare fiering." Around nine that morning, Waterbury surrendered the *Washington*.

The British took the galley into their service, and despite her damaged condition put her almost immediately to work. By October 20 she was carrying General Burgoyne to Isle aux Noix, and the next day she carried General Riedesel from there to Crown Point.

Waterbury endured a fair amount of criticism in the following months for surrendering without a fight. In a letter written to Horatio Gates a few months after the incident, he defended his decisions, arguing that he had been abandoned, and that "I found No Vesel to Make any Stop for Me But all Made the Best of thare Way for Crown Point." As to why Arnold had fired on the British while he had not, Waterbury claimed that neither he nor Arnold was able to hit the enemy, and "I all ways thought it Best to fier Somthing Near an Enimy or Not fire at all."

Arnold, for his part, did not censure Waterbury's decision to surrender, despite the fact that he himself fought nearly to the death. In his report to Schuyler, Arnold appeared satisfied that his second in command had had no choice but to strike his colors, stating simply, "The Washington Galley was in such shattered Condition and had so many Men killed and wounded she struck to the Enemy after receiving a few Broadsides."

Arnold's Last Stand

Carleton and Pringle wasted little time securing Waterbury's surrender. The *Congress* was only a mile or so ahead, along with four of the gondolas. The British fleet cracked on with all the sail they could carry to catch up with the other Americans.

The *Maria*, the fastest sailor and the least damaged, came up with *Congress* first, slamming the already battered vessel with grape- and round shot. Soon the other ships were in the fight as well, and the last act of the three-day battle was under way.

Arnold and the men of the *Congress* put up a ferocious fight, more so than was appreciated even in contemporary accounts. The galley was quickly surrounded, with the *Maria* alongside and the *Inflexible* and the *Carleton* under her stern. Forty-four British guns, with a combined weight of metal of 372 pounds, were pitted against *Congress*'s eight big guns and ten swivels throwing a mere 82 pounds.

The *Carleton* may have been well chewed up from the fighting at Valcour Island, but the *Inflexible* and the *Maria* were largely unscathed, their crews relatively fresh. The *Congress*, on the other hand, was battered and low on ammunition, and her crew had endured a demanding two days with little rest.

Despite this, the *Congress* fought for "five glasses," or two and a half hours, while the rest of the American fleet tried to make their escape. Though Pringle's detractors claimed that he kept the *Maria* "a greater distance when abreast of the Congress galley, than any officer inspired with true courage . . . would have done," Arnold reported that all three vessels were within musket shot, which meant point-blank range for their heavy guns.

The ships passed through The Narrows, their cannon and swivels blazing away as *Congress* shifted tacks to bring her broadsides to bear. The weary men aboard the galley hauled on the train tackles and ran their guns out gunports chewed up by enemy fire. Grapeshot whistled past, and solid iron balls slammed into the galley's hull.

The running fight took the *Congress* and her adversaries across the mouth of Buttonmould Bay. The British "kept up an incessant Fire on us . . . with Round and Grape Shot," Arnold reported, "which we returned briskly." During the entire two-and-a-half-hour battle, the *Congress* covered only about four miles, which would suggest that the British were not simply chasing a fleeing vessel. Against overwhelming numbers, Arnold was making a stand.

During the fight, four more of the British fleet came up, possibly four gunboats, and joined the attack. On board the *Congress*, the first officer and three men were killed, and the ship was all but destroyed, "the Sails Rigging and Hull . . . shattered and torn in Peices."

By noon the *Congress* had fought all she could, but Arnold had no intention of surrendering. Battling their way up the lake, they had overtaken four of the gondolas—the *Boston, Providence, New Haven,* and *Connecticut.* The gondolas, swept up in the running fight, found themselves outgunned and caught in a hopeless situation. Arnold turned the bow of the *Congress* east, into a small bay south of Button-mould Bay, known then as Ferris Bay and now as Arnold's Bay, and the four gondolas followed him in.

Benjamin Kellogg lived near the shore of Ferris Bay. According to his daughter, Sally, on the morning of the battle "we saw the shipping a-coming in shattered condition." Sally's mother and siblings, along with another family, gathered up what they could carry and threw it into a bateau floating in the bay, eager to get away from the fight that was heading toward them.

"We shoved out into the Lake and fell in between Arnold's fleet and the British fleet," Sally recalled. "The . . . foremost of the British ships played away on the shattered vessels of Arnold's fleet, but happy for us the balls went over us. We heard them whis."

Kellogg and his family made it to Fort Ticonderoga, then on to Bennington. The next year, Benjamin Kellogg would participate in the Battle of Bennington, a precursor to the fighting at Saratoga.

One by one, the *Congress* and the galleys ran ashore in Ferris Bay ("All tho I was keep from that privlage," Waterbury noted). The flat-bottomed gondolas ran nearly to the shoreline before their bows grounded on the sandy bottom. The men tumbled over the low sides, splashing into the cold water. Farther out, the deeper *Congress* took the ground, and the men climbed more carefully down her sides and into the water. Last of all came Benedict Arnold.

After taking off the small arms, which was all they could save, the Americans put the vessels to the torch. Flames spread along the decks and up the splintered masts and tarred rigging, catching on the canvas sails. Above it all, the ensign of the United States, the Grand Union flag, still snapped at the mastheads of the five vessels. They had not struck their colors.

A mile or so away, hove to on the lake, the British fleet continued to fire on the Americans, sending round shot screaming over the water and plowing up the dirt onshore. Arnold led his men up the steep banks that ringed the eastern end of the bay and deployed them in a line to defend against a British landing, but the British did not come. For the moment, they were done with Arnold's fleet.

Satisfied that his vessels were engulfed and would not be extinguished, Arnold gathered up his men and took to the woods, trudging toward Crown Point just a few hours ahead of a party of Indians that had been sent to cut them off. They had beached their vessels just ten miles short of their goal.

Arnold's fight had been witnessed from the *Trumbull.* "I thought it my duty to make sail and endeavor to save the Trumbull galley if possible," Wigglesworth wrote. She was still making her way to Crown Point when, about half past twelve in the afternoon, De Angelis wrote, "we saw a Great Expultion and supposed as General Arnal was aboard of the Galley that he ordered them blown up." As the fire reached the powder magazines, the ships exploded, rolling flames high into the air and scattering shards of burning wood and debris over Ferris Bay.

Dr. Knox, who watched the death of the American fleet from the *Maria,* would soon after claim that Arnold had burned the ships with the wounded still aboard. Knox might have seen the body of one of the men killed in the fight and accidentally left on board blown into the air when one of the ships exploded, but, if so, Knox was apparently the only one to see it, because no other witness recounted that grisly sight.

Knox, of course, had no way of knowing whether anyone left aboard the American ships was wounded or dead. Of those who would have known—the men in Arnold's fleet—none mentioned any of the wounded having been left to die in the flames, a thing that certainly would have attracted their notice. Nonetheless, the odious claim that Arnold burned the wounded with the ships was repeated among the

British and would gain some traction among Americans after Arnold's treason four years later.

The *Trumbull*, the one remaining galley, was pursued by the British fleet as she raced for Crown Point. "We double manned our oars and made all the sail we could, and by throwing off our ballast got off clear," Wigglesworth wrote. She managed to reach Crown Point about half past one that afternoon. Pringle, for some reason, ordered his vessels to remain to windward and not continue the pursuit, and, thanks to that decision, *Revenge* and *Enterprise* also reached Crown Point, around sunset. With them was the *New York*, the only surviving gondola in American possession, living up to her original name, *Success*.

On that same day, Enys reported, "a party of Canadians found a Gondola named the Jersey on the opposite Side of the Lake." Abandoned by the Americans, the *New Jersey* in the end did not sink, and instead joined the British fleet.

The *Lee* was run up the Onion River and supposedly set on fire, but, if she was, it did not take. A few days after the battle, she was discovered there and brought up to Crown Point, then in British hands, where she also became part of the British fleet. The *Liberty* was at Ticonderoga when the fighting began at Valcour Island, and never participated in the fight. The same was true of the row galley *Gates*, which was not completed in time for the battle.

Arnold had sailed with his fleet from Crown Point on August 24. Now, less than two months later, he and his men returned on foot, camping in the woods across from that post before continuing on to Ticonderoga. Benedict Arnold's navy was shattered just three and a half months after its conception, when he and the other general officers of the Northern Department had agreed to abandon Crown Point and concentrate on building a naval force.

The navy was gone, but its real effects had yet to be felt.

CHAPTER 36 *End of the Campaign Season*

THE LOSS OF the American fleet induced panic among the American troops at Ticonderoga and the local population loyal to the American cause. As what remained of Arnold's navy gathered at Crown Point, it was clear to Thomas Hartley, in command of the small garrison there, that he would be shortly overrun.

Jahiel Stewart, on board the *Enterprise*, wrote that "we Came by Crown-point and Set it on fier." There was no reason to stay. The men set fire to all of the buildings that would burn and moved by boat and land south to Ticonderoga.

On October 14, around four in the morning, Arnold and his men reached Ticonderoga. Arnold was exhausted, having had almost no sleep or food for nearly three days. But soon he had recovered and threw himself into preparations for Carleton's inevitable attack on the fort. "[W]e are busilly employed in compleating our Lines Redoubts," he reported to Schuyler, "which I am sorry to say are not so forward as I could wish."

On the same day that Arnold returned, a number of boats came up from the British under flag of truce. John Trumbull was sent to find out what they wanted. On board the boats were David Waterbury and about 110 prisoners taken by the British. Carleton had given them their parole and sent them to Ticonderoga.

The fort began to fill not just with soldiers but with civilians, such as Benjamin Kellogg and his family, who feared the coming fight. Jeduthan Baldwin wrote in his journal,

> Some of the Inhabitants ran Some 5, Some 7 or 8 Miles in the woods with women & Children in the greatest distress, leaving all there Housel stough [household stores?] Cloathing &c to the enemy, or to the flames. A Mellancholly Sight that was Seen at Ticonderoga, but may Expect a

more Mellancholly Seen to morrow or soon. God prepair us for it & grant us a Compleat Victory over our Enemy.

Everyone expected Carleton, with his massive and well-equipped army, to fall immediately on Ticonderoga, and preparations were made to resist him. All of the guns that had carriages were mounted and positioned, and blacksmiths and carpenters were set to work making carriages for those that did not. "Our Men work with life & Spirits this Day," Baldwin wrote, "which shows a determined resolution to defend this place to the Last Extr."

On October 15, Benjamin Rue, captain of the gondola *Philadelphia*, and sixteen of his men made it into camp. After their boat had sunk under them, Rue and the others had boarded the *Washington*. Before Waterbury surrendered, they left the ship in a bateau and rowed ashore, making their way by land to Ticonderoga.

As the days passed, the men continued to work feverishly and wonder when the British would attack. Colonel Anthony Wayne wrote to his brother-in-law, "The whole body of the enemy are now within two hours march of us—and we expect to see them every moment." Then, borrowing from Shakespeare's *Henry V*, he added, "The Contest will be Warm and bloody—they out number us—but if we are to die, we are enough—and if we Conquer the fewer the men the Greater the share of Honour."

Carleton's Autumn Blues

With the lake cleared of the rebel fleet, Carleton's ships and gunboats began to arrive at Crown Point and disembark soldiers. The facilities were not all they might have been, however. The old, burned-out barracks and crumbling walls from the last war were still there, and the Americans had done little to improve them. Rather than repair the old works, they had thrown up hastily constructed new works closer to the water's edge, and these they had burned on hearing of the British approach. Carleton's advance troops were set to making fascines to build up the crumbling walls, and they began preparations to get the burned-out barracks in order for occupation.

Back at the Canadian posts near the mouth of the Richelieu River, the rest of the army waited anxiously for word of events. On October 12 rumors started swirling around the camps about the naval battle that had taken place, but nothing definite was known. The men stared south through their telescopes, hoping to see a British vessel returning with news.

Finally, on October 14, a canoe was seen pulling for the camp on Point au Fer, and as it drew closer the men at that post recognized Sir Francis Clark, Burgoyne's aide-de-camp. He was waving a flag with thirteen red and white stripes, an American ensign, perhaps from the *Royal Savage*. Clark brought authentic news of the battle, and it was greeted, according to Digby, "in three huzzas, and the joy expressed by the whole, gave evident signs of their satisfaction on so important a victory."

Benedict Arnold, it seemed, had won some grudging admiration among the British troops. "Sir Francis," Digby recounted, "also informed that general Arnold who acted as commodore, after finding all was lost some how escaped on shore, after behaving with remarkable coolness and bravery during the engagement . . . how great an acquisition his being taken would have been to us, as he is certainly a brave man." It was high praise indeed from a military that had little respect for the fighting qualities of the Yankee Doodles, a big step up from Carleton's dismissal of Arnold as a "horse jockey."

Clark also carried Carleton's orders for the troops to strike the camp immediately, board the boats, and make their way to Crown Point. That being done, the army arrived at Crown Point and Chimney Point, across the lake from Crown Point, at various times between October 17 and 20.

It was not the entire army, however, just the advance corps and the 1st Brigade that had been posted at Point au Fer. There were not bateaux enough to move the rest of the force from Isle au Noix and St. John's.

Guy Carleton, after all he had endured at the hands of the rebels—the loss of Ticonderoga, St. John's, and most of Canada, and the brutal siege of Quebec—was at last where he wanted to be, standing on Crown Point with a powerful army under his command. But now he was not so sure about his next move.

The weather was bitterly cold already and would get much worse. Crown Point was no place for an army to winter. Writing to General Howe, Carleton said, "I fear the want of time (the severe season is approaching fast) to put it in a proper state of defense, and of materials to put it in a condition to lodge the Troops, provisions and stores, which would be necessary to leave there, will force us back to Canada."

Fort Ticonderoga would be a tolerable place to winter, but Carleton did not think that place could be taken easily. What intelligence he could gather suggested a huge garrison there, some estimates running as high as twenty thousand rebel soldiers—a huge overestimate but one that gave Carleton pause. If a frontal attack would not work—and thoughts of Abercromby's failed assault of 1758 must have crossed Carleton's mind—then it would mean a siege, and the British general was not prepared for that. Once winter set in, the supply line from Canada would be precarious, and the spring melt would make it even more so.

The British army had finally made a thrust down into the United States, reversing the trend of the previous year. Now, according to Enys, "they all Stood without doing anything Material."

"Mr. Carleton has Not Yet Made Us a Visit . . ."

Work did not slow at Ticonderoga and Mount Independence. The civilians who had flocked to the fort were sent up the lake to Skenesborough. Baldwin continued to see gun carriages made, and on October 17 he began construction of a boom to stretch across the lake from Ticonderoga to Mount Independence, to prevent shipping from coming up beyond that point. Plans for construction of a bridge between the strongholds were approved by General Gates. The Americans, apparently, did not think they would be leaving Fort Ty anytime soon.

Since Carleton had first taken Crown Point, the wind had remained southerly, "so that the Enemy could not come with there Vessels from Crown Point," Baldwin wrote, "Since they came there to fight us at this place."

A few days later, Baldwin recorded that "nothing material has happined this Day, only hear of great Success at New York." That success was Washington's minor victory at the Battle of Harlem Heights, which had taken place more than a month before. As it happened, the day after Baldwin made that entry, Washington would abandon Manhattan and suffer a serious defeat at the Battle of White Plains.

The wind was certainly hampering Carleton's advance, but it was not entirely to blame for the British absence, because the gunboats and bateaux could have rowed the seventeen miles with no great hardship, and there were land routes as well. On October 25, General Arthur St. Clair wrote to a friend, "Mr. Carleton has not yet made us a visit which surprises me very much. His passing the Lake and defeating our fleet was to very little purpose if he rests there."

Finally, on the morning of October 28, the enemy appeared—a few gunboats pulling for the fort. Bayze Wells wrote, "in the morning our Enemies Apierᵈ at the three Mile Point three Boats with a Carrage Gun in Each bow one of which Came Within Cannon Shor of our North Eaſt Battery and of our Rogalleys which Gave them Several Shots."

Alarm guns were fired, and men grabbed up muskets and ran to their stations. One of the gunboats pulled to within a mile of the fort, but the British were sounding the water, not launching an attack. After American round shot began dropping around them, they hauled off and returned to Crown Point. Later that day a flotilla of seventeen boats appeared below the fort, to what end no one could tell. They returned to Crown Point without doing anything.

What the Americans did not know was that the first few boats carried none other than General Guy Carleton and his senior officers, who wanted to take a closer look at Ticonderoga and get a sense for what it would take to drive the rebels out. Satisfied that they had learned what they needed to, they returned to Crown Point.

And still the Americans waited. A British deserter coming in on November 1 told the Americans that Carleton had ten thousand men and eight hundred Canadians and Indians (a greatly inflated figure) and would be attacking Ticonderoga soon. After this intelligence, the men were ordered to "have 3 Days provision ready Cooked and to ly on their arms ready."

Then, on November 3, Baldwin noted that "a Scout came in & Reported that the Army had left Crown point." The next day brought confirmation. Incredible as it seemed, after six months of fighting aimed specifically at retaking Ticonderoga, Carleton had loaded his army back on board their transports and returned to Canada after getting within seventeen miles of his goal.

Winter Quarters

On November 2, Digby wrote matter-of-factly, "We embarked in our battows and long boats for Canada."

The campaign season was over. The men at Crown Point were already suffering from the cold. On November 2, Jahiel Stewart recorded, "This morning the snowe was verrey heard [hard]." He was told the snow at Crown Point was over a man's shoes. The British were in no position to maintain a siege of Ticonderoga through a bitter northern winter. They would try again next year.

The decision to abandon Crown Point and return to Canada did not seem to have upset the men who had followed Carleton south. Most, like Digby, recorded the fact in their journals without comment. Enys wrote, "we reimbarked to return to Canada as did the rest of the Army." Hadden, never shy about expressing an opinion, negative or otherwise, simply said that Carleton altered "his determination about repairing the Works &c. at Crown Point, the Stores were sent Back, and the whole Armament returned abt. the 13th, 14th or 15th Nov. 76." The men were probably relieved to find that they would not be spending the winter huddled outside the walls of Ticonderoga or in half-built barracks at Crown Point.

As they passed through St. John's on their way north, the troops found the works there much improved, as well as a dockyard with a new twenty-four-gun ship going up on the stocks. The British were already preparing for the campaign season of 1777.

CHAPTER *37* *Winter Quarters*

WITH THE END of Carleton's advance up Lake Champlain and the withdrawal of British and Hessian troops to Canada in early November 1776, the campaign season for that year was at an end, and there would be no chance of another British incursion from the north until spring. Near the end of the month, Horatio Gates wrote to John Hancock, "Lake Champlain is closed with ice, as low as Three-Mile Point, so all is secure in that quarter until the beginning of May."

The militia gathered at Fort Ticonderoga were no longer needed and were consuming great quantities of provisions, so Gates and Schuyler agreed to dismiss them. They also granted furloughs to homesick regulars, so that by the end of the month there were no more than fourteen hundred troops left at the fort.

To the south, George Washington did not enjoy the advantage of an enemy withdrawn to winter quarters. By mid-November, William Howe had driven Washington's army out of New York and across the Hudson River, and he kept on driving. Howe pushed Washington clear across New Jersey to Trenton, on the Delaware River.

As the American commander in chief raced to keep ahead of the overwhelming British force, he watched the bulk of his army melt away, starting with about two thousand militia who left for home, their enlistments expired.

On December 7, Washington ferried his weary troops across the Delaware River to the Pennsylvania side after destroying any boats he could not use. For the moment he was safe, with the ice-choked river creating a barrier between his army and that of the enemy, but Washington now had fewer than three thousand effectives, many of whom would be leaving at the end of the month. American military fortunes had never been lower. It was in reference to this period that Thomas Paine wrote the famous words, "These are the times that try men's souls."

Aware of Washington's problems, and knowing that Ticonderoga was safe for the season, Congress ordered Schuyler to send several regiments to augment Washington's army. Schuyler was way ahead of them. After hearing of Howe's victories in New York, Schuyler had ordered the furloughed regiments to remain in Albany in case they were needed. On December 3 he informed Congress, "I ordered seven [regiments] of the regular troops to join his Excellency General Washington. The last of those embarked yesterday at Albany under the command of General Gates." Impressive as that sounded, the seven regiments amounted to only about six hundred men.

Still, from all the middle colonies men marched to join Washington's diminished army across the river from Trenton, until at last the commander in chief's forces numbered about six thousand effectives. With those troops, on Christmas night 1776, Washington crossed the Delaware River and rolled up the surprised Hessian soldiers in Trenton. It was one of the boldest and most successful offensives of the Revolution, and the boost that that victory gave to the flagging morale of the nation might well have saved the cause of American independence.

Horatio Gates was not with Washington at the Battle of Trenton, however. Always an advocate of defensive action, Gates argued that, rather than attack, Washington should retreat farther. When Washington dismissed this advice, Gates used a purported illness as an excuse not to join the nighttime attack. Gates was coming to the opinion that he, not Washington, should command the Continental army, an opinion supported by several prominent New England delegates to the Continental Congress.

In the face of the British army's looming threat to Philadelphia, the Continental Congress had removed itself to Baltimore. Soon Gates was there as well, lobbying friendly congressmen for his cause. Washington's stunning success, however, robbed Gates of his argument that the present commander in chief was unfit for the job, and that issue, at least for the present time, was settled. But Gates was also concerned with another officer whom he saw as a competitor and a growing threat to his own reputation—Benedict Arnold.

Arnold Heads South

Benedict Arnold did not fight at Trenton either, though Washington's bold strike would have appealed to his nature even as it did not appeal to Gates's.

For nineteen months Arnold had served with the Northern Department virtually without respite. It had been fifteen months since he had seen his boys and his sister, Hannah, all the family left to him, and he was eager to see them again. Horatio Gates, writing to John Hancock from Albany, said, "General Arnold, who is now here, is anxious, after his very long absence, to see his family, and settle his publick accounts." But Gates knew Arnold, and added, "Should the motions of the enemy make his presence necessary below, I know his zeal for the service will outweigh all other considerations, and induce him to take the route that leads them."

Gates was right. Rather than traveling to New Haven, Connecticut, Arnold determined to follow Gates to Pennsylvania and join Washington's army there. Before he could leave, however, another matter required his attention. Moses Hazen, with whom Arnold had been tangling for half a year, now brought slander charges against Arnold.

The court of inquiry found that Arnold had, indeed, insinuated that Hazen had sold rum belonging to the army and pocketed the proceeds, but the court declined to order any kind of reprimand for so trivial an issue. That ended the matter for Arnold, but not for the Hazen/Easton/Brown cabal.

Arnold headed off to Washington's camp in Pennsylvania, but a few days short of his destination, a messenger found him on the road and delivered a note from the commander in chief.

Governor Trumbull of Connecticut had sent word to Washington that a large fleet of British transports had been sighted off New London. The militia had been assembled to defend the state, but

Trumbull requested that Washington send a few experienced general officers to command them. Washington chose the elder Major General Joseph Spencer as senior officer, and Arnold as the man from whom he expected real action. "I have full confidence," Washington wrote in closing, "in your exerting yourself in this as upon former occasions."

It turned out that the British objective was not in Connecticut but in Rhode Island. On December 8, British general Henry Clinton landed seven thousand troops in Newport virtually unopposed, capturing the city and the surrounding countryside. No one knew what Clinton's next move would be, but Washington hoped that the forces under Spencer and Arnold could at least offer some resistance.

By happy coincidence, Arnold's new orders would take him through New Haven on his way to assuming his post. He continued on to Washington's headquarters, where he remained for three days, conferring with the commander in chief. Then, leaving Washington just days before the Battle of Trenton, Arnold rode to New Haven for a long-delayed reunion with his sister and his three boys.

Arnold's visit was a brief but happy one. He was pleased to find his family well, his boys healthy and delighted to see their father again. Perhaps just as satisfying, Arnold was greeted by the pro-Revolutionary population of New Haven as a conquering hero, a man of great stature and reputation. If part of Arnold's motivation for service was to erase the shame that his father had brought down on the Arnold family name, here was proof that he was succeeding.

After a little more than a week at home, Arnold was on the road again, riding for Providence, where the troops collected to defend Rhode Island were mustered. The soldiers under Arnold's and Spencer's command were little more than raw militia, untrained, inexperienced, and a third fewer in number than the British forces they stood against. Fortunately for the Americans, Clinton had no plans beyond holding Newport as a safe harbor for the British navy. Even the fire-eating Arnold did not care to attack with so few men and so inferior an army, and the winter and early spring of 1777 passed without significant military action. John Trumbull, who had accompanied

Arnold from Ticonderoga, wrote, "The enemy were quiet in Newport, and we in our quarters near Providence."

On a personal level, however, Arnold received yet another in the series of blows that would eventually induce him to abandon the American cause and join the British. On February 19, Congress promoted five brigadier generals to the rank of major general. Arnold, despite being the most senior of all the brigadier generals and having a record superior to most, was not one of them.

A number of factors conspired in Arnold's being passed over. In the face of Howe's advancing army, the Continental Congress, in a fit of panic, had granted Washington extraordinary powers. Now they were rethinking that decision and reasserting their own authority in a number of areas, including the promotion of officers. Washington's patronage, which Arnold had looked on as a great benefit, may well have hurt his chances with a Congress that was determined to remind the commander in chief who was actually in charge.

Another goal of Congress was to spread promotions among the various states, the better to promote political harmony. Connecticut already had two major generals, Israel Putnam and Joseph Spencer, and Congress did not feel that they needed another. David Wooster, the former commander in Canada and Arnold's fellow New Havenite, was also passed over, though he, like Arnold, was senior to all those who were elevated. (Wooster, however, had been dismissed from the Canadian leadership on the advice of the commissioners sent to Montreal, and could not have been surprised to be passed over. Knowing this, Arnold was justified in viewing his own grievance as singular.)

On top of those considerations, moreover, were the numerous complaints that Arnold's enemies, most notably John Brown, had lodged with Congress, stretching back to the first capture of Ticonderoga.

No officer and gentleman of the time would have tolerated such an insult as being passed over for promotion, and certainly not Arnold. Writing to Washington, who was as incredulous as Arnold over Congress's decision, Arnold informed the commander in chief that he would resign his commission, as "I can no longer serve my country with honor."

Ticonderoga

If the battlefield was quiet in Rhode Island during the winter of 1776 and 1777, it was nearly moribund around the frozen outposts of Fort Ticonderoga and Mount Independence. With Gates's departure, command of the fort devolved to Colonel "Mad" Anthony Wayne, who was finding little outlet for his aggressive nature. "In the present debilitated state of the garrison," he wrote to Gates, "we can do little more than mount the proper guards, keep out the usual scouts, and find firewood."

Wayne complained about the neglect that Ticonderoga was suffering, and feared that the fort "will be left an easy prey to the enemy . . ." when the next campaigning season began if something was not done to provide the post with more men and supplies.

Colonel Jeduthan Baldwin took advantage of the slack time to visit his home in Brookfield, Massachusetts. By the end of February, he was back at Ticonderoga, however, active as ever. Among his projects was a hospital for Mount Independence, a blockhouse, and plans for a fort.

Most ambitious of all was what Baldwin referred to as "the Great Bridge," a floating bridge from Ticonderoga to Mount Independence, anchored to twenty-two massive caissons that were assembled on the ice, then sunk to the lake bottom when the ice was cut out from under them. Even the jaded British and Hessian troops were impressed by this engineering feat.

Throughout the winter and spring, Wayne continued to fret over the coming campaign season, his requests to be relieved of command due to ill health ignored. Mindful of how Arnold's fleet had preserved Ticonderoga the year before, Wayne tried without success to bring attention to rebuilding the shattered fleet. "I cannot forebear mentioning my surprise at the total neglect of the navy," he wrote to Hancock. Wayne felt that "in the course of eight weeks we could build vessels sufficient with those we already have to command the lake."

But Wayne's suggestions went unheeded, and no new naval construction was undertaken. Nor would it have mattered, because the enemy's naval force on Lake Champlain was now so superior that no construction the Americans could realistically have undertaken was going to catch up with them.

1777

CHAPTER *38* *The Road to Saratoga*

To AMERICANS engulfed by the Revolution, 1777 was the Year of the Hangman, because the three sevens resembled a tiny row of gallows. It would certainly prove to be a deadly year, particularly in the war's northern theater.

When word of the Canadian campaign of 1776 reached England, the king and his ministers were pleased, and the men responsible for the British victories were well rewarded.

Lieutenant Thomas Pringle, who had held the rank of master and commander during the Battle of Valcour Island, was elevated to post captain, as was Lieutenant Thomas MacKenzie, who had endured the long siege of Quebec. Lieutenants Dacres, Schank, and Starke were promoted to the rank of master and commander, and all the midshipmen with sufficient service time were promoted to lieutenant.

Captain John Hamilton, of the frigate *Lizard*, who had spent the winter aiding the defense of Quebec, was awarded five hundred pounds and made a baronet. Charles Douglas also received a baronetcy. Guy Carleton, who had been in overall command of every part of the action, was knighted.

Within the ranks of the army, no one seemed displeased with Carleton's decision to abandon the campaign before taking Ticonderoga. Digby wrote, "I am positive every officer in the army, if called upon, would acquit him of acting imprudently in retiring from that place to winter in Canada."

George Germain, however, did not see it that way. Never a big fan of Carleton, Germain was displeased to learn that Ticonderoga had been left in American hands. When he discovered that American troops from Ticonderoga had augmented Washington's forces in the Battle of Trenton, his displeasure deepened to resentment. In March 1777, Germain wrote to Carleton, saying,

335

I have had the Mortification to learn that upon your repassing Lake Champlain, a very considerable Number of the Insurgents finding their presence no longer necessary near Ticonderoga, immediately marched from thence & joined the rebel Forces in the province of New York & Jersey. That unexpected Reinforcement was more particularly unfortunate for us, as it enabled the Rebels to break in with some degree of success upon parts of the winter Quarters that were taken up by the army under the Command of Sir. Wm Howe.

Germain blamed Carleton for inadvertently contributing to Washington's stunning victories at Trenton and Princeton, which gave new life to the American cause when it was needed most. Germain had a point, but in the early months of 1777, he could not have anticipated the real fallout from the action on Lake Champlain the year before.

When, during the 1776 campaign, John Burgoyne received word that his beloved wife, Charlotte, had passed away, Carleton had granted him permission to sail for England, which he did even before Carleton abandoned Crown Point. The start of 1777 found Burgoyne luxuriating in the hot springs of Bath, England, a gathering spot for the wealthy and powerful, and no doubt indulging his love of the gaming table. Since his return to England, he had not been entirely idle, however. While seeing to personal and family matters, Burgoyne had also spent time further ingratiating himself with George Germain. Prior to leaving for Bath, Burgoyne wrote Germain a note, selflessly proclaiming, "I humbly laid myself at his Majesty's feet for such active employment as he might think me worthy of."

Burgoyne already had in mind the active employment he hoped to secure. Soon he was at work on "Thoughts for Conducting the War from the Side of Canada," in which he described in detail his plan for an invasion up Lake Champlain.

The following spring he would get his chance.

Rank and Honor

In mid-April, Benedict Arnold left Providence, Rhode Island, and rode for Philadelphia, where the Continental Congress was again sitting. He intended to settle his accounts and resign his command.

On the way he stopped in New Haven to spend time with Hannah and his boys, and he was still there when word reached him that a column of sixteen hundred British light infantry and five hundred Loyalists had landed near Fairfield and were marching inland with the intention of capturing military goods stored in Danbury, "the greatest Magazine the Rebels had ever collected . . . ," as one British officer put it. Leading the troops was William Tryon, the former royal governor of New York.

On April 26 the British column reached Danbury, where they found four thousand barrels of beef and pork, five thousand barrels of flour, and great quantities of other materiel, from coffee to tents to wagons. Putting it all to the torch, and the town of Danbury as well, the British then marched off toward Ridgefield, en route to their waiting ships.

As soon as Arnold heard the news, he saddled his horse and rode out of New Haven through a driving rain. With him were a handful of local recruits as well as his old Canadian comrade and sometime rival Brigadier General David Wooster. The men arrived at Bethel, four miles from Danbury, at two o'clock the next morning. There they found some six hundred militia and regulars under the command of militia general Gold Silliman. At first light, with rain still falling, Arnold and Silliman led five hundred of those troops on a quick march to Ridgefield to head off the British retreat.

Wooster, with a hundred men under his command, remained behind to harass the rear of the British line as they marched. Around eleven in the morning, he struck, attacking with "astonishing temerity," according to a British officer there. When the British wheeled and counterattacked, Wooster ordered a retreat, knowing that a full-blown engagement would be suicide.

Just as Wooster passed the order, a musket ball tore into his belly, and he slipped from his horse onto the field. His son, who was serving with him, ran to his side as the British troops overran the American defenders. Wooster's son, in the words of a British officer, "behaved remarkably well, refused Quarter & dyed by the Bayonet." David Wooster, left for dead by the British, was eventually carried from the field. He hung on for another five days before he, too, died.

Meanwhile, Arnold and Silliman had beaten the British to Ridge-field and threw up a breastwork of dirt, logs, and wagons across a re-stricted part of the road down which the British would march.

Tryon's column, two thousand strong, came upon the hastily built works around three in the afternoon. Thinking that the Americans would not stand against such overwhelming odds, Tryon launched a frontal assault, but the Americans held their position "with more Ob-stinacy than skill," according to a British officer. With Arnold riding the line and keeping the men steady, the Connecticut militia stood and flung the British back.

Finally, Tryon sent out flanking parties to get around the breast-works. The militia men, seeing that they would be surrounded, began to panic and run. Arnold raced his horse back and forth, trying to or-ganize the men, until finally the animal collapsed under him, shot nine times.

For an awful moment, Arnold lay pinned under the horse. Accord-ing to one report, a British soldier ran at him with fixed bayonet, shout-ing, "Surrender! You are my prisoner!" To this Arnold is supposed to have calmly replied, "Not yet," drawn a pistol, and shot the man.

With darkness coming on, Tryon halted his weary men for the night, and Arnold, finding another horse, headed out into the sur-rounding countryside, rallying men for the next day's fighting. When morning came, he led his troops to a place about two miles north of Norfolk, where he hoped to intercept the British column marching for the coast.

Alerted to Arnold's presence by Loyalists, Tryon altered his route, and the best Arnold could do was to harass the flanks and rear of the British column as it marched. In this the Americans were aided by a few pieces of artillery, three 6-pounders, served by Arnold's old friends John Lamb and Eleazer Oswald, who had recently been paroled after their capture at Quebec.

Arnold, on horseback, was as conspicuous as ever, riding along the moving front, driving the reluctant citizen-soldiers on, "exposing him-self almost to a fault." A bullet passed through the collar of his coat, and his replacement horse was shot out from under him.

Tryon's harried men at last reached the coast, where fresh troops were sent ashore to cover their embarkation. The raid was without doubt a British victory, but the Americans had showed that such raids could not be carried out without a price, and Arnold once again displayed his battlefield courage and leadership.

And the Continental Congress took note. After ordering the quartermaster general of the army to procure a new horse for Arnold, they dismissed papers submitted by Horatio Gates on behalf of John Brown. These papers, which included a slanderous handbill that Brown had printed, charged Arnold with a litany of abuses. The Congress found that the handbill "cruelly and groundlessly aspersed in publication" the general's character. Then, as John Adams put it, for "his vigilance, activity, and bravery in the late affair in Connecticut," Congress promoted Arnold to major general.

Congress did not, however, return Arnold to his former seniority, leaving him junior to those who had been promoted before him. Arnold found this unacceptable and was still determined to resign unless he could get his seniority restored. He traveled to Philadelphia and spent weeks lobbying for his proper rank, trying to settle his accounts, and seeking a reimbursement of the considerable personal fortune he had spent in Canada to feed and clothe his men. In June he accepted temporary command of a small force around Philadelphia, but soon he was back in the city, continuing his efforts.

It was no use. The Continental Congress, hypersensitive to any second-guessing of civilian control of the military, did not care to revisit Arnold's rank yet again. On July 11, a dejected Arnold handed in his resignation, unaware that Washington had just sent an urgent request for his services in the north.

"If General Arnold has settled his affairs," Washington had written,

and can be spared from Philadelphia, I would recommend him for this business, and that he should immediatly set out for the northern department. He is active, judicious and brave, and an officer in whom the militia will repose great confidence. Besides this, he is well aquainted with that country . . .

Once again the British were pushing down from Canada, and Arnold once again set aside his differences and rode to the defense. The war in the northern theater had resumed.

The Return of John Burgoyne

On May 6, 1777, the frigate *Apollo* let go her anchor below the cliffs of Quebec and was warped into the Cul de Sac. On board was General John Burgoyne. This time there would be no miscommunication, no orders undelivered. Burgoyne himself carried Germain's instructions to Carleton. Carleton was to defend Quebec with three thousand men, and the advance into the United States would be entirely Burgoyne's responsibility.

Just over a week after arriving in Quebec, Burgoyne continued up the St. Lawrence and the Richelieu reaching St. John's soon after, where his army of more than seven thousand British and Hessian soldiers was prepared to embark. Wintering over in Canada had done the soldiers no harm; indeed, six months of drilling in camp and acclimating to this new country had left them "in the greatest health, and much improved."

Burgoyne was pleased with what he saw and immediately set about organizing his offensive. On June 14 the first of his regiments climbed into longboats and bateaux and proceeded up the Richelieu to Lake Champlain under protection of the British fleet.

Britain's naval force on Lake Champlain in 1777 was not just superior, it was overwhelming. All the ships that had defeated Arnold's fleet the year before—the *Maria, Carleton, Inflexible, Thunderer, Loyal Convert,* and the others—were still there, together with the new vessel completed at St. John's over the winter, the *Royal George,* a ship of 384 tons and twenty-six guns, now the most powerful vessel on the lake. Also with the British fleet were the prizes taken from the Americans: the row galley *Washington,* the cutter *Lee,* and the gondola *New Jersey.*

To oppose the British fleet, the Americans had only the remnants of Arnold's navy: the row galleys *Trumbull* and *Gates* (the latter having not been ready in time for Valcour Island), the sloop *Enterprise,* the schooners *Liberty* and *Revenge*, and the gondola *New York*. Together they mounted less firepower than the *Royal George* and the *Inflexible* alone.

The American fleet was commanded by Jacobus Wynkoop, the crotchety French and Indian War veteran whom Arnold had replaced the year before. Arnold had bemoaned his lack of sailors in 1776, but the situation now was even worse, the American ships being manned by skeleton crews. The *Gates*, intended to carry a crew of eighty men, carried only forty. The *Trumbull* carried twenty-four. At the Battle of Valcour Island, the *New York* had had a crew of forty-five men; now she had eleven.

The Americans would have stood no chance in a battle with the British fleet, so they did not even try. Instead the fleet was kept behind Jeduthan Baldwin's bridge and boom and had no access to the lake north of Ticonderoga. Burgoyne's fleet and transports were free to sail unchallenged.

On June 25, advance British forces took Crown Point, and over the next five days the rest of the army moved up the lake together with baggage, supplies, and Burgoyne's massive artillery train. In just ten days, Burgoyne had moved as far up the lake as Carleton had during the entire campaign of 1776. Burgoyne, of course, did not have Arnold and his fleet to contend with, and his success bore out the long-held belief that naval superiority, not the possession of Ticonderoga, was the key to military dominance of the Champlain region.

Burgoyne's only concern now was reducing Ticonderoga and moving on to Albany.

The Taking of Ticonderoga

In early June, Arthur St. Clair had replaced Anthony Wayne as commanding officer at Ticonderoga. St. Clair had been promoted to major general for his service at the Battle of Trenton, one of the five men promoted over Arnold.

On June 20, as Burgoyne was preparing for his push up the lake, Philip Schuyler, still in overall command of the Northern Army, arrived at Ticonderoga and held a council of the general officers there.

Their conclusions were grim. Fewer than twenty-five hundred troops were fit for duty, and the "fortifications and lines on Mount Independence are very deficient." Ticonderoga, situated by the French to resist a move from the south, was not ideally placed to defend against an attack from the north. Despite that, the generals agreed that "both posts [Ticonderoga and Mount Independence] . . . ought to be maintained as long as possible . . . ," and that Schuyler should immediately apply to Washington for reinforcements. In the event of one or the other post having to be abandoned, they would give up Ticonderoga and make their stand at Mount Independence.

Five days later, a scout boat returned to Ticonderoga with news of the enemy landing at Crown Point, and St. Clair knew that the moment had come. In his letter to Schuyler, who had returned to Albany, St. Clair concluded, "Everything, however, shall be done that is possible, to frustrate the enemy's designs, but what can be expected from troops ill armed, naked and unaccoutered?" Had he known, he could have added "and outnumbered more than three to one."

On July 2, Burgoyne began deploying his men, sending columns overland from Crown Point to surround and invest Ticonderoga and Mount Independence. British troops skirmished with Americans holding the lines around Ticonderoga, but the fighting did not develop beyond that. Burgoyne was tightening the noose and had no need to risk a frontal assault. With his next move he checkmated St. Clair.

Looming over Ticonderoga to the southwest was a six-hundred-foot-tall hill traditionally known as Sugarloaf Hill but renamed Mount Defiance. The year before, John Trumbull had pointed out to the officers at Ticonderoga that Mount Defiance overlooked all their fortifications, and British guns on the mountain could drop plunging fire behind the lines of Ticonderoga and Mount Independence.

No one believed him. "I was ridiculed for advancing such an extravagant idea," Trumbull recalled, but through a series of tests he proved that a shot from Ticonderoga could reach the summit of Mount Defiance, which meant that a shot from Mount Defiance could easily reach Ticonderoga.

Still no one saw the threat. The mountain was deemed too steep and rugged for heavy guns to be hauled to its summit, but the Americans underestimated the logistical capacity of the British army. Burgoyne's second in command, Major General William Phillips, who was also chief of artillery, declared, "Where a goat can go, a man can go. And where a man can go, he can drag a gun."

On July 4, in brutal summer heat, the British began to cut a road to the top of the hill and drag up two 12-pounders. By noon the next day, the Americans manning the lines around Ticonderoga could see redcoats at the top of the hill, their guns in place. Mighty Fort Ticonderoga was suddenly laid at the feet of the British artillery.

That day, St. Clair called a council of general officers. He understood that abandoning Fort Ticonderoga would not play well in the Continental Congress, but he and the other generals understood as well that no other choice remained. The battery on Mount Defiance would soon open up on the American lines; Already British and Hessian troops were encircling Ticonderoga and Mount Independence. The line of retreat up Lake George had already been cut off, and soon the road from Mount Independence, the only remaining escape route, would be shut off as well. It was time to go.

That night the British batteries began pounding Ticonderoga and Mount Independence, and American batteries answered back, hoping to give the impression that nothing was afoot. In fact, the Americans were striking tents, packing gear, and preparing to march south. The sick, the supplies, and the women and children were loaded into boats and sent by water to Skenesborough. Just before dawn, the last of the garrison passed through Mount Independence and hurried along the miserable road that ran along the east side of the lake.

Retreating in the face of a superior enemy was a tricky maneuver, and St. Clair deserved credit for pulling it off well, but it was a retreat nonetheless. Just over two years after Benedict Arnold and Ethan Allen had taken Ticonderoga from the British, the fort was back in British hands.

CHAPTER *39* *Saratoga*

PHILIP SCHUYLER'S NORTHERN ARMY, the only force between Burgoyne and Albany, consisted of forty-five hundred effectives, around two-thirds of whom were Continental troops and the rest militia. Burgoyne's numbers were somewhat diminished by the men left behind to garrison Ticonderoga, but his army was still greatly superior. The only tactic open to Schuyler was to retreat in the face of the British and German troops and make their advance as slow and difficult as possible.

Burgoyne reached Skenesborough on July 6, sailing from Ticonderoga with the fleet. There he found the last remnants of Arnold's navy, abandoned by the fleeing Americans. The British took possession of the *Trumbull* and the *Liberty*, but the *Revenge, Gates,* and *Enterprise* had been set on fire by their crews and could not be saved. When fire reached their magazines, the *Gates* and the *Revenge* blew apart. The entire Lake Champlain fleet that the Americans had struggled so hard to create was gone.

Benedict Arnold arrived in Albany in mid-July, and Schuyler sent him forward with a mixed force of militia and Continental soldiers to harass and delay the enemy, cutting down trees in the path of their advance, burning bridges, and making Burgoyne's movements as difficult as possible.

At a glacial pace, Burgoyne pushed south. For several reasons, none of which quite seemed sufficient in retrospect, he decided not to backtrack from Skenesborough and move up Lake George, opting instead to cut his way along a barely passable route by Wood Creek. So far, everything had gone Burgoyne's way, and Digby could write, "As yet, the fickle Goddess Fortune had smiled upon our arms, and crowned our wishes with every kind of success."

Struggling in the oppressive July heat, cutting their way to Fort Edward, rebuilding bridges destroyed by the Americans and removing obstacles thrown across their path, Burgoyne's army made little more than a mile a day. Finally, near the end of July, the troops straggled into Fort Edward. It was there, while waiting for resupply, that word finally arrived from General William Howe, whom Burgoyne had expected would be pushing up the Hudson for a juncture of the two armies at Albany.

Howe, it turned out, had other plans. Rather than moving up the Hudson, he informed Burgoyne, he would be transporting his army by sea to the Chesapeake, from where he would march on Philadelphia. Burgoyne would be on his own.

The message from Howe was only the first in a series of indications that the fickle Goddess Fortune smiled no longer on the British invasion. Concerned about a shortage of supplies and a lack of horses for the Reidesel's Brunswick dragoons, Burgoyne on August 9 sent a column of soldiers—mostly Germans with some British regulars and Loyalists—on a march to the Hampshire Grants to capture American stores at Bennington. Accompanying them to provide local knowledge was Philip Skene. Unfortunately, as often happens to political exiles, Skene badly misjudged the temper of his former neighbors. Later recalling Skene's blundering, British artillery officer James Hadden would write, "with the best intentions in the world, he was a famous marplot . . . ," a nice archaic term for one who fouls up a plan through officious interference.

Ready to meet the Germans near Bennington was a New Hampshire brigade led by the crusty, generally uncooperative French and Indian War veteran General John Stark. Stark was joined by Seth Warner and remnants of his Green Mountain regiment, which had been badly mauled in battle at nearby Hubbardton shortly after Ticonderoga had been abandoned.

Stark, like Arnold, had distinguished himself early in the Revolution, only to be passed over for promotion. Unlike Arnold, Stark had resigned his commission and quit the army. Later, at the request of the

New Hampshire legislature, he had formed a purely New Hampshire brigade and was leading it under the condition that he answered to no one but the leaders of New Hampshire. He was the military equivalent of a privateer captain who would sometimes cooperate with federal authority, sometimes not, depending on his whim.

The British and German forces met the Americans on August 16, and when it was over, the Americans had won a decisive victory. Burgoyne's column lost about nine hundred men, most taken prisoner. The rest of the column, as well as a relief force sent out to help them, were driven back in a desperate nighttime retreat. The British loss at the Battle of Bennington was a major blow to Burgoyne. Not only would there be no supplies and horses, his column was now considerably weaker for the loss of the men.

Still, Burgoyne remained confident. For one thing, he had another card up his sleeve. As part of his plan for the conquest of the northern colonies, he had sent a second column of about fifteen hundred men, more than half of whom were Indians, under Lieutenant Colonel Barry St. Leger, on a sweeping march down the Mohawk River from Oswego, on Lake Ontario, to link up with his main army on the Hudson.

Burgoyne had received word that St. Leger was on his way and was laying siege to Fort Schuyler, on the Mohawk. What Burgoyne did not know was that Schuyler had sent Benedict Arnold to relieve the fort. Capturing a number of Loyalists en route to Fort Schuyler, Arnold convinced one of them, a man who apparently suffered from a mental disorder, to enter St. Leger's camp and report the advance of a superior American force. The trick worked. St. Leger's Indians abandoned him, and St. Leger was forced to turn back.

With each passing day, Burgoyne became more and more isolated.

Arnold and Gates

On August 19, Horatio Gates took command of the Northern Army. The loss of Ticonderoga had given Philip Schuyler's enemies in Congress the excuse they needed to replace him with the more politically favored Gates. (Schuyler would later demand a court-martial, be acquitted of any wrongdoing, and resign his commission.)

Gates was an unfortunate choice for Arnold. The two men had been mutually respectful, even friendly, the year before, but their relationship had since soured, with Gates discovering a bitter dislike for Arnold. Gates was jealous of Arnold's increasing fame and reputation. Both men were ambitious; Gates, in particular, was actively maneuvering to supersede Washington as commander in chief of the Continental army, and he knew that Washington and Arnold were friendly.

Perhaps worst of all in Gates's view was that Arnold was a friend of Schuyler's, and Gates loathed Schuyler. (It is ironic that Arnold, labeled by many historians as unpleasant and difficult, was resented by Gates in part because of the men with whom Arnold enjoyed relations of mutual respect and affection.) Arnold may have poisoned his relationship with Gates still further when he added two of Schuyler's former officers to his staff: Richard Varick, who had done excellent work the year before securing supplies for Arnold's fleet, and Henry Brockholst Livingston.

As August turned to September, Burgoyne's position grew increasingly perilous. Gates sent Major General Benjamin Lincoln north to threaten Burgoyne's ever lengthening supply line back to Skenesborough, and Stark's brigade continued to threaten the British from the east. Burgoyne wrote to Germain, complaining, "The Hampshire grants . . . abounds in the most active and most rebellious race of the continent and hangs like a gathering storm upon my left."

Unable to counter Burgoyne's advance with his own inferior force, Schuyler had fixed on a strategy of harassing the enemy and keeping just ahead of him. Now Burgoyne's forces were diminishing even as more and more American troops were sent to the northern front, swelling Gates's ranks. Gates judged the time right to stop running—to dig in and block Burgoyne's route to Albany.

On a ridge known as Bemis Heights, on the west bank of the Hudson, the Northern Army began entrenching, extending their lines west about three-quarters of a mile from the bluffs overlooking the river. If Burgoyne wanted to get to Albany now, he would have to fight his way through.

By August 30, Arnold was back from the Mohawk River. Schuyler had been in command when Arnold left; now Arnold reported to

Gates. At first the two men were courteous, each needing the other: Gates needed Arnold's fighting ability, and Arnold needed Gates to assure him a role in the coming fight. Gates gave Arnold command of the army's left wing.

For more than a month, Burgoyne remained near Fort Edward, gathering supplies. The Americans had grown proficient at stripping the countryside of anything the British could use, so supplies had to make their laborious way up Lake Champlain from Canada. To reach Albany, the British would have to cross the Hudson River, and once they did, there was a strong chance that their supply line from Skenesborough would be cut. Burgoyne wanted at least five weeks' worth of provisions before he took the risk of crossing the river.

By September 13 the British army was on the move again, crossing the Hudson on a floating bridge of the men's own making. A few days later the troops encamped just three miles north of Bemis Heights, and it was Gates's turn to tighten a noose. The now superior force entrenched in the British path made any further advance risky. Retreat was still possible but also risky, with Lincoln and Stark in the British army's rear.

But Burgoyne wasn't ready to consider retreating. He had finagled command of an army in order to win a stunning victory, and he still hoped to do just that. He, more than anyone, knew how badly Carleton's retreat had been greeted by Germain, and he did not wish to suffer the same fate. He decided to attack.

The First Battle of Freeman's Farm

On September 19, the British and German troops prepared to move out in three columns. Riedesel and his Germans marched along the road that bordered the river. The center column, with whom Burgoyne rode, was made up entirely of British regiments. On the right, sweeping around to hit the left side of the American lines, was an elite corps of grenadiers and light infantry led by Brigadier General Simon Fraser. Once the morning fog lifted, the three columns moved into position and waited for the signal cannon that would initiate the general advance.

At Gates's headquarters on Bemis Heights, word filtered in that the British were on the move. Horatio Gates, whose caution had earned him the nickname "Granny Gates," saw no reason to advance from his army's well-entrenched high ground. Let Burgoyne fling his men against the American earthworks.

Arnold, however, did not agree. He correctly surmised that Burgoyne's main thrust would be against the American left, his command, and if the British dragged heavy guns up to the high ground opposite Bemis Heights, they could batter the American lines. To Arnold, it seemed foolish to let Burgoyne set the conditions of engagement.

Finally Gates relented, but only so far as allowing Arnold to send out an infantry regiment and a corps of riflemen to watch the enemy's movements and harass them. The riflemen were led by big Daniel Morgan and the infantry by Henry Dearborn, both of whom had marched to Quebec with Arnold and been captured outside that city's walls.

A little after noon, Morgan's and Dearborn's men came upon startled British pickets at an open plot of land known as Freeman's Farm. The riflemen's murderously accurate fire took its toll, and the advance units of Fraser's wing were sent running.

They did not run long. Soon they regrouped and swept forward with the rest of the highly disciplined right and center wings of the British army. Fighting surged back and forth over rough, open ground as Arnold, riding furiously along the lines of fighting men, sent more and more troops into battle.

Here at last the Americans began to reap the benefits of the year's delay that their Lake Champlain navy had bought them. The men facing off against Burgoyne's veterans were no longer raw militia who had just left the plow to take up arms. These were trained soldiers, men who had now been fighting a year or more as part of a standing army.

The minutemen on Lexington Green had possessed courage enough, but not the discipline to stand in ranks and trade musket shots with professional soldiers. When they had tried, they broke and ran. Their fighting had been guerilla style, shooting from behind stone walls and trees at ordered ranks of marching redcoats, thus giving rise to the persistent legend that the entire American Revolution was fought that way.

It was not. The Americans who met Burgoyne's forces were the Continental Line, a trained and disciplined soldiery who could stand without wilting in the ordered rows of a European-style battlefield and trade volley for volley with an enemy. They were veterans such as Daniel Morgan and Henry Dearborn, who, the year before, had not yet been released from the terms of their parole as prisoners of war. Two years of warfare had shaped officers such as Benedict Arnold, a former apothecary, who could lead troops in the field with an energy and professionalism that even the British had to admire. General John Glover, commanding the American right wing, had been a ship captain just two years before, but now he was an officer who, while serving under Washington, had led men at Boston, at Long Island, across New Jersey, and at the Battles of Trenton and Princeton.

The army of late 1777 was a more formidable force than that of early 1776, and for that extra year of training, recruiting, and experience, the army owed much to Arnold's ragtag navy of 1776.

The fighting on the American left continued through the afternoon, with neither side winning a clear advantage, but Burgoyne eventually saw that his troops could not stand up to much more. He sent word to Riedesel, whose column had not engaged, to hurry reinforcements to his struggling middle and right columns.

Arnold, too, went looking for more men, having committed his entire left wing to the fight. He rode back to headquarters to plead with Gates, who had not left camp the entire day, to commit more troops. Gates was reluctant, but in the end he agreed to send part of a brigade to support Arnold's left wing.

Evening was descending when Riedesel's reinforcements reached Freeman's Farm. They included artillery captain Georg Pausch, who had commanded two gunboats during the Battle of Valcour Island and who now dragged with him two 6-pounder fieldpieces. Forming up on the Americans' flank, Pausch "fired twelve or fourteen shots in quick succession into the foe who were within good pistol shot distance."

The reinforcements, the artillery, and the coming darkness were enough for the Americans, who pulled back to Bemis Heights, leaving the field and a Pyrrhic victory to Burgoyne. British casualties had been substantially higher than those of the Americans, and each loss meant more to Burgoyne, who could not get reinforcements. "[T]he enemy gave ground on all sides and left us complete masters of the field of battle . . . ," Burgoyne wrote to Germain, and that much was true. But more to the point, Burgoyne had failed to improve his situation. In fact, he had made it worse.

"A Certain Pompous Little Fellow"

As the last of the fighting died out, Burgoyne pulled back his troops and began to entrench. The Americans expected him to resume the offensive the next day, but he did not.

Two days after the battle, Burgoyne received an offer from General Henry Clinton, commanding in New York, to send two thousand men up the Hudson—not to join Burgoyne but to create a diversion that might draw off some of Gates's troops. Burgoyne decided to sit tight and wait for Clinton's feint, and, soon after, he put his men on reduced rations.

Fighting of a different sort ensued in the American camp, chiefly between Arnold and Gates. Arnold had won the admiration of the officers and men of the army for his bold action at Freeman's Farm, whereas Gates, who had not wanted to attack at all and had not left headquarters once during the battle, came in for considerably less adulation. In a petty and vindictive gesture, Gates omitted from his report of the battle to Congress any mention of the officers involved, quite against the usual protocol of such reports. It was a slight aimed specifically at Arnold.

Gates then removed Morgan's riflemen from Arnold's command and took personal control of them, implying that Arnold had mishandled his troops. Through Gates's aide, James Wilkinson, a gossipy sycophant (as revealed through his ingratiating, backbiting correspondence) who had been with Arnold in Canada and had now attached himself to Gates, Gates spread rumors that Arnold had not participated in the battle at all.

Wilkinson wrote to St. Clair that "General Gates despises a certain pompous little fellow as much as you can."

Schuyler, who knew as well as anyone how Gates operated, concluded that Gates, now quite certain of victory, no longer needed Arnold and did not want to share any of the glory with him. He was probably right.

Arnold, naturally, was furious and made no effort to hide it. He stormed into Gates's headquarters and engaged his commander in a heated shouting match, with "high words and gross language," according to Wilkinson. Gates finally informed Arnold that he was no longer needed and that Lincoln would be taking command of the left wing and Arnold stormed out. Soon after, he requested a pass to leave camp and join Washington's army.

Colonel Enoch Poor, whose regiment was part of Arnold's left wing, had been one of the field-grade officers who had so antagonized Arnold during the court-martial of Moses Hazen the year before. At the time, Poor had called for Arnold's arrest, at which point Horatio Gates had argued that the army "must not be deprived of that excellent officer's service."

Now the situation reversed itself, and it was Poor who did not want to lose Arnold's services. He began an effort among the field officers to convince Arnold to stay, and they succeeded. But when Arnold decided to remain at Bemis Heights, Gates stripped him of his command, taking charge of the left wing himself. Arnold could stay, but he would have no troops to lead.

The Second Battle of Freeman's Farm

Through the first week of October, Burgoyne waited behind his entrenchments for some word from Clinton, but he heard nothing. Meanwhile his army was crumbling around him. Supplies were low, and sickness and desertion were increasing. The Americans kept up a constant harassment until the British and German troops were exhausted. Something had to be done.

On October 4, Burgoyne proposed flinging all but eight hundred of his men at the American left and rear in an attempt to break out, but his officers overwhelmingly objected, and he dropped the idea. A few days later he had another proposal; he would send out a "reconnaissance in force," about seventeen hundred men, to probe the American left and forage for food. If an all-out attack seemed feasible, they would launch it. If not, they would begin to retreat north.

The detached force, made up of the elite units of the army, formed up on the morning of October 7 and was under way at around one o'-clock in the afternoon. Once again Burgoyne divided his force into three columns and sent them marching around the American left, covering much of the same ground they had covered three weeks before.

When American scouts alerted Gates to the enemy's movement, he sent out James Wilkinson to observe them. Wilkinson returned with a report of a sizable British force on the march. "Well then," Gates said, "order on Morgan to begin the game."

Benedict Arnold, still in camp, requested permission from Gates to ride out and reconnoiter the enemy. Gates did not think he could trust Arnold to avoid a major and possibly unwanted engagement, but at length he relented, sending Lincoln along to keep Arnold in check.

Arnold and Lincoln soon returned and reported a significant enemy advance. Gates ordered Morgan's and Dearborn's troops to make a wide march around the enemy in hopes of flanking them, but Arnold deemed that insufficient. "That is nothing," he told Gates. "[Y]ou must send a strong force."

With that unsought and unwanted counsel, Arnold exhausted Gates's meager store of tolerance. Gates dismissed Arnold, telling him, "You have no business here," and Arnold stormed off to his head-quarters, where he could do no more than watch the smoke of battle rise over the tree line and listen to the distant sound of guns. Enforced inactivity was for him unbearable torment.

Morgan's and Dearborn's men hit Simon Fraser's column on the British right while a brigade under Brigadier General Ebenezer Learned moved against the center and Enoch Poor's brigade attacked the right. The British and Germans were soon overwhelmed by an American army greatly superior in size and every bit as capable as they were on the battlefield.

As the fighting reached its peak, Simon Fraser was mortally wounded and carried back to the British hospital. His wounding "helped to turn the fate of the day," Digby recorded. "When General Bourgogne saw him fall, he seemed then to feel in the highest degree our disagreeable situation." Both flanks of Burgoyne's attacking columns were in danger of being turned, and he faced an overwhelming force ahead, with more hurrying onto the field.

Into the middle of the fight rode Benedict Arnold. He would have found it intolerable to miss this, the culmination of all his battles and hardships on the northern front for more than two years, so he had downed a dipper full of rum, found a horse, and ridden toward the sound of the guns.

Approaching the lines, Arnold came across elements of militia from his home state of Connecticut. "My old Norwich and New London friends, God bless you!" he shouted, and the men cheered the sight of their fighting general in his blue-and-buff regimental coat. Men would note a certain madness in Arnold that day, a recklessness that bordered on suicidal—as if, perhaps, on some level, he hoped to end it all in one final blaze of glory.

Arnold raced on until he found Ebenezer Learned's division, which had been fighting most of the day and now was stalled in the face of stiff Hessian resistance. Arnold took command with no authority to do so, and Learned, outranked, graciously acquiesced. Waving his sword, Arnold led a charge against the Germans while American artillery blasted canister shot.

But the Germans were tough and would not give, and soon the Americans began to pull back. Just then, however, Morgan and Dearborn succeeded in sending the British troops on the German flanks running. Exposed on two sides, the Germans began to fall back. "Each man for himself, they made for the bushes," Pausch recalled.

Once their line was broken, the German and British retreat became a rout as panicked men fled before the superior American forces.

They raced back toward the two entrenchments that anchored the British right flank, named later for the officers who commanded them, the Breymann and Balcarres redoubts. Separated by an open field, the two earthworks were about half a mile apart, and in the middle of the field stood a couple of log cabins around which the British had built stockades to protect the gap between the works.

The sun was setting, and the enemy had been driven from the field. That probably would have been enough for most officers. Certainly Horatio Gates, who once again had remained in his headquarters all day, would have been satisfied. But Arnold was not. This was both the moment of glory he had pursued for two years and the moment of redemption to which his frustrated ambitions had pushed him.

Still on horseback, waving his sword, Arnold led an assault against the Balcarres redoubt, which was closest to his position. As more American troops hurried to the fight, Arnold rallied them and led them forward.

The defense, however, was too strong. The face of the redoubt was steep, and the retreating Germans and British who lined the walls of the earthworks blasted the Americans with lethal volleys of musket fire. The Americans fell back.

Realizing that a frontal assault was suicide, Arnold saw that the vulnerable spot in the British defense was the stockade in the open field between the two redoubts. Wheeling his horse, he charged off toward the head of the troops under Learned's direct command, riding through the gap between the American and British lines amidst a storm of musket fire.

Incredibly, he reached Learned's troops unscathed. Directing the men toward the stockade, he rallied other regiments who were coming into the fight, then charged forward, putting spurs to his horse, to lead his troops into the gap between the redoubts.

While Morgan's riflemen attacked the Breymann redoubt from the front, Arnold's troops poured through the gap and into the redoubt's rear. Panicked German soldiers flung away their weapons and fled. Breymann himself was killed, some said by his own men as he tried to stop them from running.

Just as Arnold was leading the final push into the redoubt, charging up the slope on which the earthworks stood, a platoon of Hessians delivered a volley at the Americans. A musket ball slammed into Arnold's left leg, the same leg that had been wounded during the attack on Quebec. His horse, shot as well, reared up and collapsed, falling on Arnold's wounded leg and shattering the bone.

Seeing Arnold fall, Henry Dearborn raced over and helped heave the dead animal off his old comrade's fractured and bloody leg. Dearborn asked Arnold if he was badly wounded. According to Dearborn, Arnold replied that he had been shot "in the same leg, and wished the ball had passed his heart."

End of the Line

The remainder of Burgoyne's army fell back into their strongest redoubts, hemmed in by the Americans and pounded by artillery. Two days after the battle, the British and German troops began a slow retreat northward, leaving behind their wounded in a field hospital.

Through a cold, hard rain, the exhausted, half-starved, thoroughly demoralized army slogged north to Saratoga. Prevented by American militia from crossing back over the Hudson, Burgoyne's army once again dug in, but soon they were surrounded by Gates's force, which had swelled to more than thirteen thousand men.

Burgoyne convened a council of his officers and proposed a number of options, including retreating, fighting, or surrendering. After a couple of days' discussion, it was concluded that the only option left was to seek an honorable capitulation.

Negotiations began on the morning of October 14. Burgoyne still harbored hopes of Clinton's coming to his aid, and stretched out the talks as long as he could, but after three days of quibbling and counteroffering he could stall no more. On October 17, John Burgoyne surrendered his army to Horatio Gates. It was the first time a British army had surrendered to an American force, and it would change everything.

Epilogue: *Turning Points*

THE BATTLE of Saratoga was a salutary turning point for America's fortunes, but it was a turning point of a very different sort in the life of Benedict Arnold.

The wounded general was carried from the field on a stretcher and eventually taken to Albany. His left leg, torn by the Hessian musket ball still lodged inside, had also suffered multiple fractures from the falling horse. The surgeons who examined him wanted to amputate, but Arnold would have none of it, fending off that suggestion repeatedly in the first few weeks of his slow and agonizing recovery. For five months he lay in bed, his leg secured in a fracture box, a hellish nightmare for so active a man.

Despair tortured Arnold more than his physical pain. Lying immobile in his hospital bed, he heard the news of Burgoyne's surrender and knew exactly how he would fare in Gates's report. He endured the adulation heaped on Gates, the gold medal awarded Gates by Congress, the talk of his brilliant victory.

True to form, Gates made little mention of Arnold's part, and Arnold, trapped in bed and too weak even to write, could do nothing to counter the impression that Gates alone had engineered the great victory. The men who had fought at Freeman's Farm and the officers with whom Arnold had served knew the part he had played, but the Continental Congress and the public at large did not.

In late November, Congress voted to restore Arnold to his former seniority. That might have done much to improve his bleak outlook had Congress admitted in doing so that they were righting a wrong and that Arnold deserved his seniority, but they did not. Rather, the promotion was handled more as a matter of paperwork, the correction of an oversight. Ever quick to perceive a slight, Arnold remained a peevish and irritable patient.

357

In the spring of 1778, he was finally well enough to travel to New Haven to be with his family, though his leg had by no means healed. He still had to be carried from place to place. At one point his wounds opened up again, and he required surgery to remove additional bone splinters. When at last his leg healed as much as it ever would, it was two inches shorter than the other.

In May, Arnold returned to active duty, but he was still unfit for the field command that Washington wished to give him. Instead, Washington made him military commander of Philadelphia, a post he assumed when the British pulled out of the city the following month.

Arnold was back in the service of his country, but that service was no longer foremost in his heart. His wound, his convalescence, and the lack of gratitude he perceived from his country had changed him. The glorious cause of liberty looked venal to him now, and his chief concern was looking out for Benedict Arnold. He had become the man whom his critics had accused him of being all along.

Once in command in Philadelphia, Arnold began a slide into treason. He lived in high style and entertained lavishly in America's largest city. He tangled with the municipal government. He met, fell in love with, and married eighteen-year-old Margaret Shippen, known as Peggy, the name of Arnold's first wife. The Shippen family had Loyalist tendencies, and, during the British occupation of Philadelphia, Peggy had become friends with a handsome young British officer named John André.

During one of Arnold's entanglements with local civilian authorities, he was accused of misusing his military office for personal gain. A court of inquiry found him guilty on two counts, and the Continental Congress ordered George Washington to reprimand him.

Reluctantly, Washington issued what was perhaps the kindest reprimand in history. Refusing to censure Arnold for any wrongdoing, he chastised him instead for "having forgotten that in proportion as you have rendered yourself formidable to our enemies, you should have been guarded and temperate in your deportment toward your fellow citizens." Washington ended the reprimand by saying, "I will myself furnish you, as far as it may be in my power, with opportunities of re-gaining the esteem of your country."

In a more temperate frame of mind, Arnold could probably have accepted those words in their intended spirit. Certainly he had been subjected to worse during his tempestuous career in the army of the United States. But Arnold was seeing ingratitude in every corner, and now he perceived that Washington, his patron, the man who had al-ways backed him, was turning on him as well. Benedict Arnold was a man ready to sell out his country.

In July 1779, true to his promise, Washington offered Arnold the command of the left wing of the army, the post of honor. No opportu-nity for redemption could have held more promise, but Arnold did not want it. He wanted command of the fort at West Point. He com-plained that his leg was still too injured for him to take the field, but that was not the real reason for his request. He had already agreed to turn West Point over to the British.

By August 1780, when Arnold's request was granted, he was in con-tact with Henry Clinton in New York, with John André acting as go-between. Possession of West Point would give Clinton control of the Hudson River and the possibility of unbroken movement and commu-nication between Canada and New York City—ironically, the very things that Arnold had fought so hard to prevent.

On September 22, Arnold and André finished negotiating the terms under which Arnold would facilitate the British capture of West Point. While proceeding overland back to New York, however, André was stopped by an American patrol, who found on him detailed draw-ings of West Point and a pass signed by Benedict Arnold.

On the morning of September 25, while at breakfast with fellow of-ficers, Arnold received a letter containing what for him was the most disastrous news possible. André was under arrest, and the papers found on him had been forwarded to Washington, whom Arnold was expecting any minute. The man who had sent the letter to Arnold clearly did not understand how the papers implicated the West Point commander, but Washington would.

Arnold excused himself from the table, found his wife, and explained what had happened. He called for a horse, then rode to the landing where his boat and crew were waiting. He ordered them to row down the Hudson to where a British ship, the *Vulture*, was riding at anchor. Then Arnold clambered up her boarding ladder and, in doing so, went over to the other side.

Franklin in France

Benjamin Franklin had thought his journey to Canada in the spring of 1776 would be the death of him, but he recovered, and less than five months later—after serving on the committee that drafted the Declaration of Independence—he embarked on an even more arduous and vastly more important mission. Taking passage aboard the Continental sloop-of-war *Reprisal*, under the able command of Captain Lambert Wickes, Franklin sailed for France.

At the time of Franklin's departure in the fall of 1776, American military affairs looked bleak. The Northern Army had been routed from Canada, and only Benedict Arnold's bold stand at Valcour Island had prevented Carleton from taking Ticonderoga and Mount Independence and perhaps pushing south to Albany. Few people, British or American, doubted that the invasion would be completed the following year.

Washington's army had been driven from New York and pushed clear across New Jersey. His bold attacks on Trenton and Princeton, which would do much to revive American spirits (though they were not, in fact, of great military significance), were still in the future when Franklin landed in the little French town of Auray on December 3, 1776.

Franklin was there to join American emissaries Silas Deane and Arthur Lee on a secret mission, negotiating a treaty with France. As distasteful as it was to many in Congress, it was also clear that the United States would not win the Revolution without foreign aid. The Americans were in Paris to convince the French monarch to enter an agreement of mutual friendship and trade.

Trade with the resource-rich, burgeoning markets in America had obvious appeal for France. Friendship was a more subtle thing, but either one carried the near certainty of another war with England. The French were eager to repay Great Britain for the humiliations their country had suffered at the end of the French and Indian War—including the loss of Quebec—but outright war with England would be a costly proposition.

Even before Franklin's arrival, France and Spain had secretly been providing funds and military supplies for the American war effort, much of it funneled through the enigmatic Pierre-Augustin Caron de Beaumarchais. That aid had been crucial to the survival of American arms thus far, but it was not enough to ensure an American victory. For that, the United States needed a real commitment, which meant a French army on American soil and a French fleet off the coast.

If anyone could convince the French to make that sort of commitment, it was Benjamin Franklin. The most famous man in America, he was famous in France as well, often placed on the same pedestal as Voltaire. Franklin's image was displayed everywhere. To the French he was the rustic philosopher, the scientist from the unspoiled New World, a quaint man of simple tastes, and the French found that charming in the extreme. Never mind that the sophisticated, crafty Franklin was none of those things. He understood his part and played it to perfection.

But for all of Franklin's clever manipulations, for all the esteem in which he and his fellow Americans were held, as well as the romance of their cause and the blow that the loss of the colonies would land on England, Louis XVI would not commit. For a year Franklin, Deane, and Lee played their diplomatic game, to no avail. France would give covert aid, but she would not sign a treaty.

Then, on December 4, 1777, a year and a day after Franklin arrived in France, everything changed. Jonathan Loring Austin, a messenger sent from Congress a month before, arrived at Franklin's residence outside Paris. Franklin, who had been fretting over William Howe's next move, had only one question for the messenger: "Sir, is Philadelphia taken?"

When Austin told him it had been, the aging Franklin turned and began to walk away. Here was yet another serious blow to the credibility and viability of the United States, a huge setback for his negotiations—

the loss of his adopted city. But as he walked away, Austin cried, "But, sir, I have greater news than that. General Burgoyne and his whole army are prisoners of war!"

The news was electrifying. It was, according to Franklin's grandson, William Temple Franklin, "received in France with as great demonstrations of joy, as if it had been a victory gained by their own arms." Given how infrequently the French had gained victory over the British with their own arms, they had to take joy where they could find it.

At the time of the announcement, the French cabinet had been wrestling, as they had for some time, with the question of what to do with regard to the United States. Franklin now suggested to the French ministry that "there was not a moment to be lost, if they wished to secure the fellowship of America, and detach her entirely from the mother country." The concern now for the French ministry was that the British loss at Saratoga would result in a peace treaty between England and the United States before France was able to capitalize on the conflict.

It was a valid fear. The British were putting out feelers in that direction, offering the Americans nearly anything they wanted short of outright independence.

On December 6, the French secretary to the Council of State met with the American commissioners at their hotel. He informed the Americans that "after a long and mature deliberation upon their propositions his majesty had determined to recognize the independence of, and enter into a treaty of commerce and alliance with, the United States of America." The "long and mature deliberation" had taken almost a year, but the king's decision had come just two days after the news of Saratoga reached France.

Negotiations followed. France had long linked its willingness to recognize the United States with Spain's willingness to join in, but when Spain balked, France decided to go it alone. Finally, on February 6, 1778, France and the United States signed a treaty of amity and commerce. The treaty stipulated, among other things, that both countries "engage not to lay down their arms, until the independence of the United States shall have been formally or tacitly assured." Two and a half years later, nine thousand French troops joined eleven thousand

Americans under Washington to surround Lord Charles Cornwallis's army at Yorktown, Virginia. French and American artillery bombarded the cornered army, while a French fleet anchored in the Chesapeake cut off any possibility of escape by sea. General Cornwallis's surrender finally ensured that independence.

The Echoes of Valcour Island

Burgoyne's surrender at Saratoga, the catalyst for France's formal entry into the war, was forged in the fall of 1776 when Carleton abandoned Lake Champlain and granted the United States an extra year of preparation, of organization, and of covert supply from France.

That series of events was one of several that would converge in America's improbable victory in the War for Independence. But it was a crucial part of that victory, and it was initiated by a minor but desperate naval battle almost exactly a year before Burgoyne's surrender, on a lake forty-five miles to the north.

It has been pointed out often enough that if Arnold had died at the Battle of Saratoga—as, perhaps, he hoped—he would have joined that pantheon of Revolutionary War heroes—George Washington, Henry Knox, Nathanael Greene, Daniel Morgan, John Paul Jones, even, deserving or not, Horatio Gates.

Benedict Arnold was responsible for the victory at Saratoga, as much as any one man could be. That honor is due him not just because of his leadership at the First Battle of Freeman's Farm or on that last, bold charge, but because he had set the stage for the battle itself. The defeat of John Burgoyne's army, the first great victory in the American Revolution, had its origin in the valiant, doomed stand made in a forgotten corner of a wilderness lake by Benedict Arnold's navy.

ACKNOWLEDGMENTS

THERE ARE, as always, many people to thank for their help with this effort. My thanks to Charley Seavey and Joe Donovick for their early help with research materials. John Townsend of the marvelous Town's End Books kindly provided a copy of his important document relating to the Battle of Valcour Island.

All of the folks at the Thompson-Pell Research Center at Fort Ticonderoga were very helpful, and I am particularly indebted to curator Chris Fox for his patient and invaluable assistance in researching this project. The fort itself is not to be missed by those with an interest in French and Indian War or Revolutionary War history.

My thanks also to Deborah Emmons-Andarawis at the Schuyler Mansion for her help, and all the great people at the Saratoga National Historical Park. Thanks also are due to Dale Henry at the Lake Champlain Maritime Museum for his insight into the practical aspects of gondola construction and seamanship. The Lake Champlain Maritime Museum may be a bit out of the way, but visiting it is well worth the effort.

Thanks are due to George Jepson of Tall Ships Books, the Rick Blaine of the maritime literary world. Thanks also to Ernie Haas for sharing with me his wonderful artwork which makes the Battle of Valcour Island that much easier to visualize. Thank you to Mark A. York, a descendant of Reuben Colburn, for information about the crucial role his ancestor played in Arnold's march to Quebec. The Colburn House in Pittston, Maine is on the National Register thanks to his efforts and is open to the public. Thanks to Phil Gorman and Andrew Sajor for their insights, from both a sailor's and a scientist's perspective, into the wind patterns on Lake Champlain. Stephanie Nelson and C. A. Finger both generously provided answers to nit-picky questions in their own areas of expertise.

Writing such a research-intensive work in the little coastal town of Harpswell, Maine, would be quite impossible if not for the excellent support I have received from the folks at the Curtis Memorial Library in Brunswick. They are Janet Fullerton, Linda Oliver, Sally Jeanne Kappler, Michael Arnold, Paul Dostie, Cheer Beth, and Paula Tefft. Thanks, folks, for not throwing up your hands in exasperation when you see yet another e-mail from me with the subject "ILL Request."

A special thanks is due to Charles "Pip" Pippenger for all of his help, expertise, and friendship during the making of this book. I count our fortuitous meeting at Fort Ticonderoga as one of the great benefits I have derived from this project.

My agent, Nat Sobel, is due more than the paltry thanks I can offer here, but I offer it anyway. And a very sincere thank you to all the folks at McGraw-Hill, including Ben McCanna, Molly Mulhern, Barbara Feller-Roth, Ann Pryor, and especially sailor/editor Jon Eaton for all of his effort on behalf of this book, and for preserving the memory of Benedict Arnold's navy.

Notes on Sources

Prologue

Chapelle, *American Sailing Navy;* Cronon, *Changes in the Land;* De Angelis, *Diary;* Frazer, *Letter,* BFTM, March 1961; NDAR: *Arnold to Schuyler,* 6:1275; *Waterbury to Gates,* 7:1295; *Arnold to Gates,* 6:1235; *Gates to Arnold,* 6:96; Wells, *Journal.*

Chapter 1

Arnold, *Arnold;* Bellesiles, *Revolutionary Outlaws;* Fischer, *Paul Revere's Ride;* Martin, *Arnold;* McCullough, *1776* and *John Adams;* Middlekauff, *Glorious Cause.*

Chapter 2

Bellico, *Sail and Steam;* Bellesiles, *Revolutionary Outlaws;* Bull, *Journal;* Jellison, *Ethan Allen;* Mackesy, *War for America;* Mott, *Journal, Mott to Massachusetts Congress;* NDAR: *Parsons to Trumbull;* Pell, *A Short History.*

Chapter 3

Arnold, *Arnold to the Gentlemen in the Southern Towns, Memorandum Book, Veritas;* Bellesiles, *Revolutionary Outlaws;* Bull, *Journal;* Feltham, *Report;* French, *Taking of Ticonderoga;* Martin, *Arnold;* Mott, *Journal, Mott to Massachusetts Congress;* NDAR.

Chapter 4

Arnold, *Memorandum Book, Veritas;* Bellesiles, *Revolutionary Outlaws;* Bull, *Journal;* DAR; Feltham, *Report;* French, *Taking of Ticonderoga;* Martin, *Arnold;* NDAR; Pell, *A Short History.*

Chapter 5

Arnold, *Arnold;* American Archives: Series 4, Vol. 2; Arnold, *Memorandum Book;* Bull, *Journal;* DAR; Feltham, *Report;* French, *Taking of Ticonderoga;* Martin, *Arnold;* NDAR: Oswald, *Journal;* Pell, *A Short History;* Phelps, *Letter.*

Chapter 6

American Archives: Series 4, Vol. 2; Arnold, *Memorandum Book;* Martin, *Arnold;* NDAR: Oswald, *Journal.*

Chapter 7

American Archives: *Arnold to Continental Congress,* 4, 2:976; *Account of Province Stores,* 4, 2:1009, 4, 2:987; *Report of the Crown Point Committee,* 4, 2:1596; *Arnold's Refusal to Serve,* 4, 2:1598–1599; *Spooner to Trumbull,* 4, 2:1540; Arnold, *Memorandum Book;* Martin, *Arnold;* NDAR: *Massachusetts Congress to Gentlemen Chosen to Repair to Ticonderoga.*

Chapter 8

American Archives: *Schuyler to Congress,* 4, 2:1645; *Hinman to Schuyler,* 4, 2:1605; *Reception of Schuyler at Albany,* 4, 2:1615; *Schuyler to Congress,* 4, 2:1702; *Schuyler to Congress,* 4, 2:1734; *Schuyler to Congress,* 4, 2:1760; *Schuyler to Washington,* 4, 3:50; *Smith to Schuyler,* 4, 3:14, *Schuyler to Washington,* 4, 2:1685; *Schuyler to Hancock,* 4, 3:13; *Duguid's Deposition,* 4, 3:12; Gerlach, *Schuyler;* Guernsey to Schuyler, *Schuyler Papers;* Tuckerman, *Life of Schuyler;* JCC: *124.*

Chapter 9

American Archives: *Massachusetts Congress to Gentlemen Chosen to Repair to Ticonderoga,* 4, 2:987; *Washington to Schuyler,* 4, 3:144; *Schuyler to Washington,* 4, 3:442; *Washington to Arnold,* 4, 3:765; *Arnold to Washington,* 4, 3:960, 1062; Ellis, *Washington;* PGW-RWS: *Washington to Arnold,* 3:198; Dearborn, *Journal;* Martin, *Arnold;* Roberts, *March to Quebec;* York, *NHL Colburn House Nomination.*

Chapter 10

Carleton

Carlton Letterbook; DAR: *Carleton to Dartmouth,* IX:157; Martin, *Arnold;* Mackesy, *War for America;* Smith, *Struggle.*

Schuyler and the Invasion of Canada

American Archives: *Report of Commission on Indian Affairs,* 4, 3:477; *Schuyler to Washington,* 4, 3:442; *Schuyler to Franklin,* 4, 3:242; *Schuyler to Hancock,* 4, 3:669; Brendenberg, *American Champlain Fleet* and *Royal Savage;* Livingston, *Journal;* Martin, *Arnold;* Roberts, *March to Quebec;* Trumbull, Benjamin, *Diary.*

Chapter 11

American Archives: *Arnold to Enos,* 4, 3:829; *Enos to Public,* 4, 3:1708; Dearborn, *Journal;* Martin, *Arnold;* Roberts, *March to Quebec.*

Chapter 12

American Archives: *Schuyler to Washington,* 4, 3:751; *Montgomery to Schuyler,* 4, 3:952, 1096; *Articles Proposed at Chambly,* 4, 3:1133; *Montgomery to Schuyler,* 4,

3:1392; *Preston to Montgomery*, 4, 3:1393; *Montgomery to Preston*, ibid.; *Articles Proposed at St. John's*, 4, 3:1394; *Bedel to New Hampshire Committee*, 4, 3:1208; *Schuyler to Congress*, 4, 3:1595; *Montgomery to Inhabitants of Montreal*, 4, 3:1596; Brendenberg, *American Champlain Fleet* and *Royal Savage;* Fassett, *Diary;* Jellison, *Ethan Allen;* Livingston, *Journal;* Martin, *Arnold;* Trumbull, Benjamin, *Diary.*

CHAPTER 13

Dearborn, *Journal;* Martin, *Arnold;* Roberts, *March to Quebec;* Ainslie, *Canada Preserved.*

CHAPTER 14

British

Carlton Letterbook; DAR: *Cramahé to Dartmouth*, XI:124; *Carleton to Dartmouth*, XI:173; *Cramahé to Dartmouth*, XI:173; *Carleton to Dartmouth*, XI:185.

American

Dearborn, *Journal;* Martin, *Arnold;* Roberts, *March to Quebec;* Ainslie, *Canada Preserved.*

CHAPTER 15

British

Ainslie, *Canada Preserved;* Bradley, *Lord Dorchester;* DAR: *Carleton to Dartmouth*, XI:185; Elting, *Military Uniforms.*

American

American Archives: *Montgomery to Schuyler*, 4, 4:188; *Montgomery to Livingston*, 4, 3:1638; *Montgomery to Schuyler*, 4, 4:464; Dearborn, *Journal;* Martin, *Arnold;* McCullough, *1776;* Roberts, *March to Quebec.*

CHAPTER 16

British

Ainslie, *Canada Preserved.*

American

American Archives: *Campbell to Wooster*, 4, 4:480; Dearborn, *Journal;* Martin, *Arnold;* Roberts, *March to Quebec;* Smith, *Struggle.*

Chapter 17

British

DAR: *Germain to Carleton*, XII:56; Enys, *Journals;* NDAR: *Germain to Admiralty,* 3:476; *Germain to Admiralty,* 3:523; *Douglas to Stephens,* 4:1451; Mackesy, *War for America.*

American, Boatbuilding

American Archives: *Schuyler to Hancock,* 4, 4:804; *Resolutions of Congress,* 4, 4:1662; *Schuyler to Congress,* 4, 4:805; *New York Provincial Congress,* 4, 4:889; *Hermanus Schuyler Letters;* Bratten, *Philadelphia;* Chapelle, *American Sailing Navy;* Fowler, *Rebels Under Sail;* NDAR: *Schuyler to Hancock,* 3:10; *Agreement to Build Bateaux,* 3:650.

American, Change of Command

NDAR: *Douglass to Hallett,* 4:421; *New York Provincial Congress to Schuyler,* 4:1252; *New York Committee of Safety to the Delegates,* 4:1309.

Chapter 18

American

American Archives: *Schuyler to Washington,* 4, 4:666; *Washington to Schuyler,* 4, 4:767; JCC: 4:39; *Schuyler to President of Congress,* 4, 5:91; Dearborn, *Journal;* Martin, *Arnold;* Roberts, *March to Quebec;* Wright, *Continental Army.*

British, The Early Fleet

Enys, *Journals;* NDAR: *Douglass to Stephens,* 4:1451; Mackesy, *War for America.*

Chapter 19

Martin, *Arnold;* Roberts, *March to Quebec;* American Archives: *Letter from Arnold,* 4, 5:512; *Arnold to Deane,* 4, 5:549; *Arnold to Schuyler,* 4, 5:1099.

Chapter 20

American, Commissioners

American Archives: *Letter from John Carroll,* 4, 5:1167; NDAR: 4:786; *Commissioners to President of Congress,* 4, 5:1166; *Hazen to Schuyler,* 4, 5:869; *Arnold to Schuyler,* 4, 5:1098; Carroll, *Journal;* Isaacson, *Benjamin Franklin: An American Life.*

American, Military

American Archives: *Thomas to Washington,* 4, 5:813; *Thomas to Washington,* 4, 5:1104; *Return of Forces Passing Ft. George,* 4, 5:1098; *Washington to Schuyler,* 4, 5:1124; *Schuyler to Washington,* 4, 5:1097; NDAR: 4:1405.

Chapter 21

British, Relief of Quebec

Ainslie, *Canada Preserved;* DAR: *Carleton to Germain,* XII:137; Enys, *Journals;* NDAR: *Douglas to Stephens,* 4:1451.

American, Quebec Retreat

American Archives: *Thomas to Washington,* 4, 6:453; *Arnold to Schuyler,* 4, 6:480; *Schuyler to Washington,* 4, 6:480; *Arnold to Chase,* 4, 6:580; *Commissioners to Hancock,* 4, 6:591; Martin, *Arnold;* Porter, *Journal;* Robbins, *Journal;* Wilkinson, *Memoir.*

Chapter 22

British, Relief of Quebec

Ainslie, *Canada Preserved; Carlton Letterbook;* DAR: *Carleton to Germain,* XII:137; Enys, *Journals;* Ketchum, *Saratoga;* Lamb, *British Soldier's Story;* Mackesy, *War for America;* NDAR: *Douglas to Stephens,* 4:1451.

Americans, Retreat

American Archives: *Hancock to Thomas,* 4, 6:558; *Hancock to Schuyler,* 4, 6:558; *Commissioners to Hancock,* 4, 6:589; Beebe, *Journal;* Baldwin, *Journal;* Carroll, *Journal;* Martin, *Arnold;* Porter, *Journal;* Robbins, *Journal.*

Chapter 23

American, Retreat

Beebe, *Journal;* Baldwin, *Journal;* Martin, *Arnold;* Porter, *Journal;* Robbins, *Journal.*

British, Second Embarkation

DAR: *Carleton to Germain,* X11:144; Digby, *Journal;* Lamb, *British Soldier's Story;* Pell, *Journal.*

Chapter 24

American

American Archives: *Schuyler to Washington,* 4, 6:1200; *Sullivan to Schuyler,* 5, 1:235; Fowler, *Rebels Under Sail;* Ketchum, *Saratoga;* Trumbull, *Autobiography;* PGW-RWS: 5, 584; NDAR: 5, 411; 5, 897.

British

Chapelle, *American Sailing Navy* and *History of American Sailing Ships;* Digby, *Journal;* Enys, *Journals;* Hadden, *Journal and Orderly Book;* NDAR: 5:523; *Carleton to Douglas,* 5:657; *Douglas to Stephens,* 5:762; *Carleton to Pownoll,*

5:845; *Carleton to Cramahé,* 5:845; *Douglas to Starke,* 5:957; *Letter from an Officer,* 5:1005; *Douglas to Stephens,* 5:1167; *Master's Log, Chanceaux,* 5:1266; Wasmus, *Eyewitness Account.*

CHAPTER 25

American Archives: *List of Artificers,* 5, 1:209; *Hartley to Arnold,* 5, 1:207; *Gates to Schuyler,* 5, 1:340; *Gates to Waterbury,* 5, 1:358; Baldwin, *Journal;* NDAR: *Gates to Arnold,* 5, 1057; *Gates to Hancock,* 5, 1099; *Trumbull to Father; Van Vechten Orderly Book.*

CHAPTER 26

British, Shipbuilding

Chapelle, *American Sailing Navy* and *History of American Sailing Ships;* Digby, *Journal;* Enys, *Journals;* Hadden, *Journal and Orderly Book;* NDAR: 5:523; *Carleton to Douglas,* 5:657; *Douglas to Stephens,* 5:762; *Carleton to Pownoll,* 5:845; *Carleton to Cramahé,* 5:845; *Douglas to Starke,* 5:957; *Letter from an Officer,* 5:1005; *Douglas to Stephens,* 5:1167; *Master's Log, Chanceaux,* 5:1266; Wasmus, *Eyewitness Account.*

American, Skenesborough

American Archives: *Gates to Schuyler,* 5, 1:340; *Gates to Waterbury,* 5, 1:358; Baldwin, *Journal;* NDAR: *Gates to Arnold,* 5, 1057; *Gates to Hancock,* 5, 1099; *Trumbull to Father; Trumbull's Orderly Book; Van Vechten Orderly Book; Wynkoop to Schuyler; Schuyler Papers.*

CHAPTER 27

American, Shipbuilding

American Archives:*Gates to Washington,* 5, 1:651; NDAR: *Gates to Hancock,* 5:1099; *Arnold to Gates,* 5:1210; *Arnold to Schuyler,* 5:1197; *Schuyler to Schuyler, Hermanus Schuyler Letters.*

American, Sailors and Marines

Allen, *Naval History;* American Archives: *Orders of Gates,* 5, 1:1187; NDAR: *Arnold to Schuyler,* 5:1197.

CHAPTER 28

American, Mortar

American Archives: *Arnold to Schuyler,* 5, 1:680; *Waterbury to Gates,* 5, 1:679; *Wynkoop to Gates,* 5, 1:680; Bratten, *Philadelphia.*

American, Fleet

American Archives: *Waterbury to Gates,* 5, 1:1114; NDAR: *Varick to Gansevoort,* 6:19; *Varick to Washington,* 6:33; *Varick to Schuyler,* 6:33; *Varick to Eddy,* 6:33; *Varick to Hughes,* 6:35; *Arnold to Gates,* 6:98; *Arnold to Schuyler,* 6:120; *Gates to Trumbull,* 6:145; *Hermanus Schuyler Letters;* Porter, *Journal.*

American, Trial

American Archives: *Gates to Hancock,* 5, 1:1268; *Minutes of the Court,* 5, 1:1273; Martin, *Arnold;* NDAR: *Gates to Arnold,* 5:1116; Porter, *Journal;* Wells, *Journal.*

Chapter 29

American, Arnold in Command

Bratten, *Philadelphia;* De Angelis, *Diary;* NDAR: *Gates to Arnold,* 6:95; *List of Armed Vessels* 6:224.

American, Arnold and Wynkoop

NDAR: *Wynkoop Memorial,* 6:320; *Arnold to Wynkoop,* 6:215; *Arnold to Gates,* 6:216; *Wynkoop to Gates,* 6, 216; *Gates to Arnold,* 6:223; *Gates to Schuyler,* 6:223.

American, Underway

NDAR: *Gates to Arnold,* 6:283; *Arnold to Wells,* 6:371; Wells, *Journal.*

Chapter 30

American, Line of Battle

American Archives: *Gilliland to Arnold,* 5, 2:112; NDAR: *Arnold to Wells,* 6:371; Wells, *Journal.*

American, Gondolas and Galleys

American Archives: *Waterbury to Gates,* 5, 2:185; *Gates to Trumbull,* 5, 2:127; *Gates to Schuyler,* 5, 2:185; *Gates to Waterbury,* 5, 2:127; *Gates to Schuyler,* 5, 2:294; *Hermanus Schuyler Letters.*

American, Attack and Salute

American Archives: *Gates to Schuyler,* 5, 2:185; *Letter from Mount Independence,* 5, 2:222; *Arnold to Gates,* 5, 2:265; NDAR: *Arnold to Gates,* 6:654; *Arnold to Gates,* 6:734; *Arnold to Gates,* 6:747; JCC: 6:765; Martin, *Arnold;* Wells, *Journal.*

British, South from St. John's

Digby, *Journal;* Enys, *Journals;* Hadden, *Journal and Orderly Book;* NDAR: *Douglas to Howe,* 6:45; *Douglas to Howe,* 6:135; *Douglas to Pownoll,* 6:951; *Douglas to Pownoll,* 6:1193; Pausch, *Journal;* Pell, *Journal;* Wasmus, *Eyewitness Account.*

CHAPTER 31

American, Defense

American Archives: *Arnold to Gates,* 5, 2:532; *Examination of Girard,* 5, 2:533; NDAR: *Gates to Arnold,* 6:791; *Arnold to Gates,* 6:837; *Arnold to Gates,* 6:925; Wells, *Journal.*

American, Gunboats

NDAR: *Arnold to Gates,* 6:837; *Arnold to Gates,* 6:925; Wells, *Journal.*

CHAPTER 32

American, Valcour Island

American Archives: *Arnold to Gates,* 5, 2:59; *Gates to Arnold,* 5, 2:555; NDAR: *Gates to Arnold,* 6:962; *Arnold to Gates,* 5, 2:834; *Gates to Arnold,* 6:1116; Wells, *Journal.*

British, Underway

Digby, *Journal;* Enys, *Journals;* Hadden, *Journal and Orderly Book;* NDAR: *Douglas to Howe,* 6:45; *Douglas to Howe,* 6:135; *Douglas to Pownoll,* 6:951; *Douglas to Pownoll,* 6:1193; Pausch, *Journal;* Pell, *Journal;* Wasmus, *Eyewitness Account.*

CHAPTER 33

American, Fleet

Chambers, *Atlas;* De Angelis, *Diary;* NDAR: *Arnold to Schuyler,* 6:1275; *Waterbury to Gates,* 7:1295; *Arnold to Gates,* 6:1235; *Return of the Fleet;* Stewart, *Most Unsettled Time;* Wells, *Journal.*

British, Fleet

Digby, *Journal;* Hadden, *Journal;* Knox, *Account of the Battle;* NDAR: *Douglas to Stephens,* 6:1344; Pausch, *Journal;* Pringle, *Letter;* Starke, et al., *Open Letter.*

CHAPTER 34

American, Fleet

Chambers, *Atlas;* De Angelis, *Diary;* NDAR: *Arnold to Schuyler,* 6:1275; *Waterbury to Gates,* 7:1295; *Arnold to Gates,* 6:1235; *Return of the Fleet;* Stewart, *Most Unsettled Time;* Wells, *Journal.*

British, Fleet

Digby, *Journal;* Hadden, *Journal;* Knox, *Account of the Battle;* NDAR: *Douglas to Stephens,* 6:1344; Osler, *Exmouth;* Pausch, *Journal;* Pringle, *Letter;* Starke, et al., *Open Letter.*

CHAPTER 35

American, Fleet

Chambers, *Atlas;* De Angelis, *Diary;* Markham, *Manuscript;* NDAR: *Arnold to Schuyler,* 6:1275; *Waterbury to Gates,* 7:1295; *Arnold to Gates,* 6:1235; *Return of the Fleet;* Stewart, *Most Unsettled Time;* Wells, *Journal.*

British, Fleet

Digby, *Journal;* Enys, *Journal;* Hadden, *Journal;* Knox, *Account of the Battle;* NDAR: *Douglas to Stephens,* 6:1344; Osler, *Exmouth;* Pausch, *Journal;* Pringle, *Letter;* Starke, et al., *Open Letter.*

CHAPTER 36

American

Baldwin, *Journal;* NDAR: *Arnold to Schuyler,* 6:1275; St. Clair, *Letter dated October 24;* Trumbull, *Autobiography;* Wayne, *Letter to Robinson.*

British

Carleton, *Papers;* Digby, *Journal;* Enys, *Journal;* Hadden, *Journal;* Knox, *Account of the Battle.*

CHAPTER 37

Arnold, *Arnold;* American Archives: *Schuyler to Congress,* 5,3:1062; *Gates to Hancock,* 5,3:874; *Washington to Arnold,* 5,3:1217; Martin, *Arnold;* McCullough, *1776;* Middlekauff, *Glorious Cause;* St. Clair Papers: *Wayne to Gates,* 386; *Wayne to Hancock,* 390.

CHAPTER 38

Arnold, *Arnold;* Carleton, *Papers;* Digby, *Journal;* A List of Officers . . . ; Ketchum, *Saratoga;* Mackesy, *War for America;* Martin, *Arnold;* Luzader, *Decision on the Hudson;* NDAR: *A British Officer's Account of the Danbury Raid,* 8:455; *Pownoll to Stephens,* 8:1036; *Pownoll to Sandwich,* 8:1037; *Officers Present at Fort George . . . ;* St. Clair Papers: *Council of General Officers . . . ,* 404.

CHAPTER 39

Arnold, *Arnold;* DAR: *Burgoyne to Germain,* XIV:164; *Burgoyne to Germain,* XIV:230; Digby, *Journal;* Ketchum, *Saratoga;* Martin, *Arnold;* Luzader, *Decision on the Hudson;* Pausch, *Journal;* St. Clair Papers.

EPILOGUE

Arnold, *Arnold;* Franklin, *Memoirs;* Martin, *Arnold;* Middlekauff, *Glorious Cause;* Schiff, *Great Improvisation.*

BIBLIOGRAPHY

ABBREVIATIONS

AA: American Archives
BFTM: Bulletin of the Fort Ticonderoga Museum
DAR: Documents of the American Revolution
FTM: Fort Ticonderoga Museum
JCC: Journal of the Continental Congress
NDAR: Naval Documents of the American Revolution
PGW-RWS: Papers of George Washington, Revolutionary War Series

PRIMARY SOURCES

Abbot, W. W., ed. *The Papers of George Washington, Revolutionary War Series*. Charlottesville: University Press of Virginia, 1993.

Ainslie, Thomas. *Canada Preserved: The Journal of Captain Thomas Ainslie*, Sheldon S. Cohen, ed. New York: New York University Press, 1968.

Anthony Wayne's Orderly Book. BFTM, Vol. III, No. 4.

Arnold, Benedict. *A Declaration of Principles*. BFTM, Vol. II, No. 3.

———. *Benedict Arnold to the Gentlemen in the Southern Towns*, May 8, 1775. Berkshire Atheneum, William Williams Collection.

———. *Benedict Arnold's Regimental Memorandum Book*. BFTM, Vol. XIV, No. 2. Winter 1982.

———. *Veritas Letter*. BFTM, Vol. V, No. 2. May 10, 1939.

Baldwin, Jeduthan. *The Revolutionary Journal of Col. Jeduthan Baldwin, 1775–1778*, Thomas William Baldwin, ed. Bangor, Maine: Printed for the De Burians, 1906.

Bull, Epaphras. *Journal of Epaphras Bull*. BFTM, Vol. VIII, No. 2. July 1948.

Campaign in Canada &c Under G. Carleton. BFTM, Vol. XI, No. 5. December 1964.

Carleton, Guy, et al. Letter from Guy Carleton to Lord George Germain, reprinted in The Town and Country Magazine. November 1776.

Carlton Letterbook, Library of Congress.

Carroll, Charles. Journal of Charles Carroll of Carrollton During His Visit to Canada in 1776, with a Memoir and Notes by Brantz Mayer. Baltimore: The Maryland Historical Society, 1876.

Chambers, Capt. William. *Atlas of Lake Champlain, 1779–1780.* Bennington, Vermont: Vermont Heritage Press, 1984.

Clark, William Bell, ed. *Naval Documents of the American Revolution,* Vol. 1–6. Washington: Naval Historical Center, 1968.

Davies, K. G., ed. *Documents of the American Revolution, 1770–1783.* Dublin: Irish University Press, 1975.

De Angelis, Pascal. *Diary of Pascal De Angelis,* manuscript. University of New York, Oswego.

Dearborn, Henry. *Narrative of the Saratoga Campaign.* BFTM, Vol. 1, No. 5. January 1929.

———. *Revolutionary War Journals of Henry Dearborn, 1775–1783,* Lloyd A. Brown and Howard H. Peckham, ed. New York: De Capo Press, 1971.

Digby, William. *The British Invasion of the North: the campaigns of Generals Carleton and Burgoyne, from Canada, 1776–1777, with the journal of Lieut. William Digby, of the 53rd, or Shropshire regiment of foot, illustrated with historical notes by James Phinney Baxter,* A.M. Albany, New York: J. Munsell's Sons, 1887.

Enys, John. *The American Journals of Lt. John Enys,* Elizabeth Cometti, ed. Syracuse, New York: The Adirondack Museum, Syracuse University Press, 1976.

Fassett, John. *The Diary of Capt. John Fassett, Jr.* in *The Follett-Dewey Fassett-Safford Ancestry,* by Harry Parker Ward. Columbus, Ohio: Press of Champlin Printing Co., 1896.

Feltham, Jocelyn, *Lt. Feltham's Report.* BFTM, Vol. V, No. 2. May 1939.

Franklin, Benjamin. *Memoirs of the Life and Writings of Benjamin Franklin,* William Temple Franklin, ed. Philadelphia: William Duane, 1818.

Frazer, Persifer. *Letters from Ticonderoga.* BFTM, Vol. X, No. 5 & 6. 1961.

Freiberg, Malcolm, ed. "The Reverend William Gordon's Autumn 1776 Tour of the Northwest." *The New England Quarterly,* Vol. LXV, No. 3. September 1992.

Hadden, Lt. James M., Royal Artillery. Hadden's Journal and Orderly Books: a Journal Kept in Canada and Upon Burgoyne's Campaign in 1776 and 1777, Horatio Rogers, ed. Boston: Gregg Press, 1972.

Hammond, Isaac W., ed. *Diary and Orderly Book of Sergeant Jonathan Burton of Wilton, N.H.* Concord, New Hampshire: Republican Press Association, 1885.

Kirkland, Frederic R., ed. *Journal of Lewis Beebe, a Physician on the Campaign Against Canada, 1776.* Philadelphia: The Historical Society of Pennsylvania, 1935.

Knox, Dr. Robert. Dr. Robert Knox's Account of the Battle of Valcour, October 11–13, 1776, J. Robert Maguire, ed. Vermont History, Vol. 46, No. 3. Summer 1978.

Lamb, Roger. *A British Soldier's Story: Roger Lamb's Narrative of the American Revolution*, Don N. Hagist, ed. Baraboo, Wisconsin: Ballindalloch Press, 2004.

A List of Officers promoted upon their arrival in England for their service in transporting the vessels into and destroying the Rebel Fleet on the Lake Champlain—1776 [partial transcript]. FTM manuscript.

Livingston, Henry. *Journal of Major Henry Livingston*. Philadelphia: The Pennsylvania Magazine of History and Biography, Vol. XXII, 1898.

Markham, Sally. *Manuscript written in 1846 in view of applying for a pension . . .* Copy at FTM.

Mott, Edward. *Journal of Capt. Edward Mott.* Hartford, Connecticut: Collections of the Connecticut Historical Society, I, 1860.

———. Edward Mott to the Massachusetts Congress, ibid.

Munro, Edmund. Letters from Edmund Munro to his Wife. FTM manuscript.

New York Convention and Committee of Safety, *Extracts from the Convention.* BFTM, Vol. IV, No. 7, July 1938.

Officers Present at Fort George for the Navy. FTM manuscript.

Oswald, Eleazer. Journal Kept by Eleazer Oswald on Lake Champlain. Reprinted in NDAR.

Parson, Col. Samuel. Samuel H. Parsons to Joseph Trumbull. Hartford, Connecticut: Collections of the Connecticut Historical Society, I, 1860.

Pausch, Captain George. *Journal of Captain Pausch,* William Stone, ed. and trans. New York: *The New York Times* and Arno Press, 1971 reprint.

Pell, Joshua. Diary of Joshua Pell, Junior, An Officer of the British Army in America, 1776–1777. BFTM, Vol. I, No. 6.

Phelps, Elisha. *Letter from Capt. Elisha Phelps, Commissary, to the General Assembly.* Hartford: Collections of the Connecticut Historical Society, Vol. I, 1860.

Porter, Elisha. Journal of Elisha Porter. Vol. X, No. 1, 1957.

Pringle, Thomas. Copy of a Letter from Captain Thomas Pringle, on board the Maria off Crown Point. London: The Town and Country Magazine, November 1776.

Report of the Congressional Committee, 1776. BFTM, Vol. III, No. 5.

Return of the fleet belonging to the United States of American on Lake Champlain . . . Photocopy of original document provided by John Townsend.

Robbins, Rev. Ammi R. Journal of the Rev. Ammi R. Robbins, a Chaplain in the American Army, in the Northern Campaign of 1776. New Haven: B. L. Hamlen, 1850.

Roberts, Kenneth, ed. *March to Quebec: Journals of the Members of Arnold's Expedition.* New York: Doubleday, Doran & Co. Inc., 1938.

St. Clair, Arthur. *The St. Clair Papers. The Life and Public Services of Arthur St. Clair,* William Henry Smith, ed. Cincinnati: Robert Clark & Co., 1882.

———. *Letter dated October 24th, 1776*, transcript at FTM.

Schuyler, Hermanus. *Letters of Hermanus Schuyler.* Adirondack Museum.

Schuyler Papers. Library of Congress.

Sewall, Henry. *The Diary of Henry Sewall.* BFTM, Vol. XI, No. 2, September 1963.

Snyder, Charles M. With Benedict Arnold at Valcour Island: The Diary of Pascal De Angelis. Vermont History XLII: 3, summer 1974.

Starke, John, John Schank, and Edward Longcroft. *An Open Letter to Captain Pringle.* BFTM, Vol. 1, No. 4.

Stewart, Jahiel. *A Most Unsettled Time on Lake Champlain: The October 1776 Journal of Jahiel Stewart,* Donald Wickman, ed. *Vermont History* 64, spring 1996, 89–98.

Supplies of the Washington Galley. BFTM, Vol. IV, No. 1, January 1936.

Terrot, Charles. *Terrot to Fott, Letter and Map.* FTM manuscript.

Trumbull, Benjamin. *The Diary of the Reverend Benjamin Trumbull,* Stephen H. P. Pell, ed. BFTM, Vol. XV, No. 2.

Trumbull, John. *The Autobiography of John Trumbull, Patriot-Artist,* Theodore Sizer, ed. New Haven: Yale University Press, 1953.

———. Colonel John Trumbull to His Father, Governor Jonathan Trumbull of Connecticut. BFTM, Vol. VI, No. 4, July 1942.

———. A Concise Journal or Minutes of the Principal Movements toward St. John's of the Siege and Surrender of the Forts There in 1775. Collections of the Connecticut Historical Society, Vol. 9, 1899.

———. *John Trumbull's Orderly Book.* BFTM, Vol. III, No. 1, 2, 3.

Van Vechten, Sam. *Samuel Van Vechten Orderly Book.* FTM manuscript.

Wasmus, J. F. *An Eyewitness Account of the American Revolution and New England Life: The Journal of J.F. Wasmus, German Company Surgeon, 1776–1783,* Helga Doblin, trans., Mary C. Lynn, ed. New York: Greenwood Press, 1990.

Wayne, Anthony. *Letter to Anthony Robinson.* Joseph Rubinfine American Historical Autographs List 114.

Who Took Fort Ticonderoga: The Documents in the Case. BFTM, Vol. IV, No. 3, January 1937.

Wigglesworth, Edward. *Colonel Wigglesworth's Diary Containing His Account of the Naval Battles on Lake Champlain, Oct. 11 and 13, 1776.* Philadelphia: Stan. V. Henkels, Jr., Literary and Art Auctioneer, Catalogue No. 1464, 1932.

Wilkinson, General James. *Memoir of My Own Time.* Vol. 1. Philadelphia: Abraham Small, 1816.

Wood, Colonel Joseph. Letter from Colonel Joseph Wood to Robert Morris. BFTM, Vol. I, No. 2.

SECONDARY SOURCES

Allen, Gardner. *A Naval History of the American Revolution.* Williamstown, Massachusetts: Corner House Publishers, 1970 (reprint of 1913 edition).

Arnold, Isaac. *The Life of Benedict Arnold, His Patriotism and His Treason.* Chicago: Jansen, McClurg & Company, 1880.

A List of Ships in the American and British Fleets in the Battle of Valcour Island. BFTM, Vol. I, No. 4.

Bellesiles, Michael A. *Revolutionary Outlaws: Ethan Allen and the Struggle for Independence on the Early American Frontier.* Charlottesville, Virginia: University of Virginia Press, 1993.

Bellico, Russell P. *Sail and Steam in the Mountains: A Maritime History of Lake George and Lake Champlain,* rev. ed. Fleischmanns, New York: Purple Mountain Press, 2001.

Bradley, A. G. *Lord Dorchester: The Makers of Canada.* Vol. V. Toronto: Morang & Co., Limited, 1910.

Bratten, John R. *The Gondola* Philadelphia *& the Battle of Lake Champlain.* College Station, Texas: Texas A&M University, 2002.

Brendenberg, Oscar E. *The American Champlain Fleet, 1775–77.* BFTM, Vol. XII, No. 4, September 1968.

———. *The Royal Savage.* BFTM, Vol. XII, No. 2, September 1966.

Caldwell, E. L. *Fort St. Jean on the Richelieu River.* BFTM, Vol. IV, No. 7, July 1938.

Chapelle, Howard I. *The History of the American Sailing Navy.* New York: W. W. Norton & Co., 1949.

———. *The History of American Sailing Ships.* New York: W. W. Norton & Co., 1935.

Cronon, William. *Changes in the Land: Indians, Colonists, and the Ecology of New England.* New York: Hill and Wang, 1983.

Ellis, Joseph J. *His Excellency, George Washington.* New York: Alfred A. Knopf, 2004.

Elting, John, ed. *Military Uniforms in America: The Era of the American Revolution, 1755–1795.* San Rafael, California: Presidio Press, 1974.

Esposito, Vincent J. *The West Point Atlas of American Wars.* Vol. 1. New York: Praeger Publishers, 1959.

Fischer, David Hackett. *Paul Revere's Ride.* New York: Oxford University Press, 1994.

Fowler, William M., Jr. *Rebels Under Sail: The American Navy During the Revolution.* New York: Charles Scribner's Sons, 1976.

French, Allen. *The Taking of Ticonderoga in 1775: the British Story.* Cambridge: Harvard University Press, 1928.

Furcron, Thomas B. *Mount Independence, 1776–1777.* BFTM, Vol. IX, No. 4, 1954.

Gerlach, Don R. *Philip Schuyler and the American Revolution in New York.* Lincoln, Nebraska: University of Nebraska Press, 1964.

Isaacson, Walter. *Benjamin Franklin: An American Life.* New York: Simon & Schuster, 2003.

Jackson, John. *The Pennsylvania Navy, 1775–1781: The Defense of the Delaware.* New Brunswick, New Jersey: Rutgers University Press, 1974.

Jellison, Charles A. *Ethan Allen, Frontier Rebel.* Syracuse, New York: Syracuse Press, 1969.

Ketchum, Richard M. *Saratoga: Turning Point of America's Revolutionary War.* New York: Henry Holt and Company, 1997.

Krueger, John W. Troop Life at the Champlain Valley Forts During the American Revolution. BFTM, Vol. XIV, No. 4, 5, 1984.

Lundeberg, Philip K. *The Gunboat* Philadelphia *and the Defense of Lake Champlain in 1776.* Basin Harbor, Vermont: Lake Champlain Maritime Museum, 1995.

Luzader, John. *Decision on the Hudson.* Fort Washington, Pennsylvania: Eastern National, 2002.

McCullough, David. *1776.* New York: Simon & Schuster, 2005.

———. *John Adams.* New York: Simon & Schuster, 2001.

Mackesy, Piers. *The War for America, 1775–1783.* Lincoln, Nebraska: The University of Nebraska Press, 1992.

Martin, James Kirby. *Benedict Arnold, Revolutionary War Hero: An American Warrior Reconsidered.* New York: New York University Press, 1997.

Middlekauff, Robert. *The Glorious Cause: The American Revolution, 1763–1789.* New York, Oxford: Oxford University Press, 1982.

Osler, Edward. *The Life and Times of Admiral Viscount Exmouth,* excerpted in BFTM, Vol. II, No. 5.

Pell, S. H. P. *Fort Ticonderoga: A Short History Compiled from Contemporary Sources.* Ticonderoga, New York: Fort Ticonderoga Museum, 1951.

Schiff, Stacy. *A Great Improvisation: Franklin, France and the Birth of America.* New York: Henry Holt and Company, 2005.

Smith, Justin H. *Our Struggle for the Fourteenth Colony: Canada and the American Revolution.* New York: G. P. Putnam's Sons, 1907.

Thomas, Clayton L., M.D., ed. *Taber's Cyclopedic Medical Dictionary.* Philadelphia: F. A. Davis Company, 1981.

Tuckerman, Bayard. *The Life of General Philip Schuyler.* New York: Dodd, Mead and Company, 1905.

Wright, Robert K. *The Continental Army.* Washington, D.C.: Center of Military History, United States Army, 1983.

York, Mark A., *Draft National Historic Landmark Nomination for Reuben Colburn House, Pittston, Maine 2002.* Copy on file at the Maine Historic Preservation Commission, Augusta, ME.

INDEX